THE SCHOOL OF HAWTHORNE

THE SCHOOL
OF HAWTHORNE

For Patti Ferreira,
with best wishes from
Dick Brodhead

Richard H. Brodhead

OXFORD UNIVERSITY PRESS

New York   Oxford

Oxford University Press

Oxford   New York   Toronto
Delhi   Bombay   Calcutta   Madras   Karachi
Petaling Jaya   Singapore   Hong Kong   Tokyo
Nairobi   Dar es Salaam   Cape Town
and associated companies in
Berlin   Ibadan

First published in 1986 by Oxford University Press, Inc.,
200 Madison Avenue, New York, New York 10016

First issued as an Oxford University Press paperback, 1989

Oxford is a registered trademark of Oxford University Press

Library of Congress Cataloging-in-Publication Data
· Brodhead, Richard H., 1947-
The school of Hawthorne.
Includes index.
1. American fiction—19th century—History and criticism.
2. Hawthorne, Nathaniel, 1804-1864—Criticism and interpretation.
3. Hawthorne, Nathaniel. 1804-1864—Influence.
4. James, Henry, 1843-1916—Criticism and interpretation.
4. Authorship—History.
5. Influence (Literary, artistic, etc.)   I. Title.
PS377.B68   1986   813'.3   85-28538
ISBN 0-19-504022-8
ISBN 0-19-506070-9 (PBK.)

2   4   6   8   10   9   7   5   3   1
Printed in the United States of America

For my Parents

PREFACE

The title of this book, *The School of Hawthorne,* is meant to carry several related senses. In part I use the phrase to suggest what it would in an art-historical context: a group of artists who work under a common influence, a group whose different manners are linked by their derivation from a common master. At the same time I want it to evoke not just the members of a shared tradition but also the schooling, literally the education, that their enrollment in such a tradition provides. In this sense the title connects Hawthorne to an organized process of instruction, the instruction by which beginning writers have been fitted for their careers. Out beyond that suggestion I intend the title to carry at least some hint of the more familiar and concrete sense of "school" as an actual edifice, a palpable institution—and so to call up, around a particular set of instructional relations, some sense of the institutional processes by which cultural knowledge is organized and transmitted.

The play among these meanings, no one of them alone, describes the project I undertake in the following pages. This book's task in part is to trace the artistic legacy of Hawthorne—what T. S. Eliot called the Hawthorne aspect—in later American fiction. In it I try to establish the centrality of Hawthorne to a line of writers virtually unbroken from his time into modernity, offering, in this regard, readings of some crucial American instances of inheritance and literary education. The nature of Hawthorne's impact on Melville is freshly argued here; his importance to Howells and Faulkner (so various are the writers Hawthorne touches) is explored at length; his intimate penetration not just of Henry James's work but of James's whole idea of authorship is followed from its earliest to its latest manifestations. But I understand the literary history of Hawthorne's tradition to be inseparable from the history of how literature itself has been organized as a cultural system in America. Accordingly, my readings of relations between writers and between texts keep moving in from, then leading back out toward, questions about the history of literary establishments; about how the literary past has been selected and enforced within such establishments; and about the changing organization, within such establishments, of the American authorial career.

The particular tradition I have chosen to study is, I know, a highly canonical one. Not only does it include the authors ranked greatest in modern estimates of American fiction: the relation of such writers to Hawthorne has itself become a virtually canonical topic, a constant subject of official study. In view of the weight that has been attached to it I hasten to add that my intention in returning to this group is not to try to reinstate the Hawthorne-Melville-James-Faulkner line as the Great Tradition in an exclusionary way. I do not believe that the American novel has (in Richard Chase's words) "its tradition." It has a wealth of competing and interpenetrating traditions; no one of these is more American than the others; and no author draws strength from one American vein alone.

Nevertheless, if I return to the high canonical American novelists it is out of the conviction that they exhibit forms of literary engagement whose possibilities we would not know of from the work of other writers, so that we can only forget them (as we once forgot their fellows) at the cost of loss of knowledge. If I return to them, it is also in the belief that we are now in a position to see these familiar authors under new lights. Renewed interest in writers formerly marked fit for forgetting has helped remind us that canons are selective and changing cultural constructions, not neutral registers of literary worth. This insight should lead us to extend the range of our literary attentions out beyond canonical boundaries. But it can also enable us to put a new question to canonical literature itself: to ask how its cultural status has been created and maintained, and with what consequences (canonicity as a historical fact inevitably *has* consequences) it has enjoyed the status it has. Similarly, non-canonical writing has brought back with it new knowledge of the social history of American authorship, an enriched sense of the social conditions that have both enabled and contained writers' assertions of themselves as writers. But the recovery of such knowledge from outside the canonical sphere can also raise a previously unasked question *about* the canonical sphere: lets us ask what conditions, of will surely but also of cultural placement and access to literary resources, enabled the profoundly *different* literary assertion of a Melville or a James, a difference of which their canonical status is in part a measure. Asking these new questions of well-known authors is my project in the chapters that follow.

This book is about *a* tradition, but it hopes to have something to say about tradition as such. One of its implications is that the pasts writers proceed from are much more variable than familiar theories of tradition formation allow. What sort of figures the operative past contains, what power they have invested in them, what bearing they have on present work, what will to continue or compete they inspire—these things differ profoundly from writer to writer (differ, even, at different moments of one writer's career). Accordingly, *what* pasts writers have at their backs and how a past of that heft came to be composed are central questions the study of tradition must investigate, not ones it can assume a constant answer to in advance. This book's other point is that traditions work on more levels than we are used to considering. Authors are the creators but not the sole creators of the literary past, as I read them here. Pasts are also composed by cultural institutions; authors (like the rest of us) learn to inhabit such institutions by memorizing and internalizing the versions of history they orchestrate; and if authors also manage to exceed or escape the merely institutional roles laid out for them, they do so in crucial part by making or claiming other pasts as their working tradition. My reading of the Hawthorne tradition hopes to show that tradition is always a literary transaction but never a literary transaction alone; that it also bears, in the most direct of fashions, on the way writers accept and remake literature's place in the human world at large.

This book has been a long time in the writing, and during its writing my understanding of its subject has altered in many ways. For this changed understanding—*my* schooling—I am indebted to a great many people, whom I can only very inadequately acknowledge here. My students deserve my first and most lasting thanks. Never unreceptive but never only receptive, they have helped me through the changes of mind that come to a temporary rest in this book. I do not acknowledge them singly because they are too many; but they will know, I trust, what they have meant to me, and will recognize themselves as my unnamed collaborators. I am indebted to several friends and colleagues in a more particular way. R. W. B. Lewis, who first introduced me to the Hawthorne tradition, and Robert Caserio have encouraged this book from its earliest stages. Amy Kaplan, David Leverenz, Christopher Wilson, Thomas Ferraro, Eric Sundquist, and Richard Millington have read chapters of my work in progress and made acute suggestions. Charles Hatten gave me valuable help in preparing the book's manuscript. Lawrence Buell read the finished book with a mixture of sympathy and discernment for which I will always be grateful. Cynthia Brodhead, Bryan Wolf, Jonathan Freedman, and William Stowe have not only read it but have listened to me thinking it out over many years. Their interest, intelligence, affection, and patience have been unfailing resources. Finally, I must thank Daniel Brodhead for his tolerance, companionship, and precocious interest in my work.

Two chapters of this book have appeared in print in earlier forms. An earlier version of Chapter Five, entitled "Hawthorne Among the Realists," was printed in *American Realism: New Essays,* edited by Eric

Sundquist and published by the Johns Hopkins University Press. An earlier version of Chapter Two appeared in A. Robert Lee's collection *Hawthorne: New Perspectives,* published by Vision Books and Barnes and Noble. I am grateful to the publishers for permission to reprint heavily revised versions of these pieces here.

New Haven   R.H.B
March 1986

CONTENTS

THE SCHOOL OF HAWTHORNE

HAWTHORNE AND TRADITION

WHAT IS OUR TRADITION? How did we become possessed of our tradition? What difference does it make for us to have a tradition—and to have the tradition we have, and not another? Asking these questions in the context of American literature puts them in an especially revealing light. Traditions, we know, begin when the past is purged of irrelevance. They come into existence when the full past, the sum of what has been, is allowed to fall from mind; then when a past worth remembering is selected and given memorable shape. This clarification has not failed to happen to American literature. American literature's significant past has been identified as decisively as one could wish. Its curiosity is that it has been identified equally finally in more than one way.

When future observers look back on the history of American literature in the middle of this century, they will find a clear answer to the question of what is central to American literature: the works of Melville, Emerson, Whitman, Thoreau, Dickinson, Poe, and Hawthorne, in its classical period, then of similarly selective groupings (Twain and James, Hemingway–Faulkner–Fitzgerald) in its later phases. Quite as striking as this answer itself will be the serenity with which it is given: it is produced confidently, with little sense that other answers are or ever could be equally possible. But this map of American literature, so widely accepted as to have the quality of self-evident truth from the late 1940s into the 1970s, was drawn no earlier than the 1920s. What came before it was another description of our national literary tradition—the object of at least as deep a consensus, probably much more widely disseminated as an article of cultural belief, and quite as long-lasting as the modern one has yet proved to be—that was all but completely different from the one we have known, placing Longfellow, not Dickinson, Whittier, not Whitman, Lowell, not Melville, and Holmes, not Poe, in the rank of our literary immortals. That canon, for sixty years the *truth* of our past, is now so long forgotten as to be scarcely remembered even as a historical curiosity. And it is no longer inconceivable that a revolution of the same order will happen again. Like our forgotten ancestors, we have *known* what our tradition was, known it even very recently. But no one can be sure that American literature will look as it once did twenty years from now, in face of current excavations of alternate versions of our past.

Among modern national literatures, American literature is probably unique in the amount of substitution it has tolerated in its apparently closed canon. (Not for nothing is this the official literature of the land of the replaceable.) But in its peculiar instability American literature helps illustrate a fact of all tradition: namely, that the past is not settled but in the process of becoming; that the past, which *is* a history, also *has* a history, has its own story of changes and creations. The past has the trick of appearing like the finished and fully realized state that comes before the openness of the present: in our eloquent common phrase, the past's nature is to seem over and done with. But in fact the past is always still in flux, in the midst of being pulled together in new configurations in response to the changing exigencies of later moments. We know from the histories of modern nations that every society that has consolidated itself into that new entity called the nation-state has had to fashion (if not invent) a new past to accomplish this process; and that with every great change in its forward development it has had to rewrite retroactively the story of where it came from. We know too that the past *par excellence* of the Western world has not been immune to change. The Greco-Roman tradition that, more convincingly than any other, has figured the immortality of great achievement in our civilization was reassembled and reasserted *as* a past as part of the cultural action we call the Renaissance; and even that powerful historical construction has not assured its perpetual cultural endurance.[1] In its combination of apparent fixedness and actual mutability American literature shares the life of such pasts and shows the condition of every past's life: that it lives in history, not outside or before it; and so that it lives in the element of change.

As it calls such change to our attention, American literature also gives a glimpse into the process by which pasts get recreated and publicly realized. American readers of a century ago no doubt regarded their time's map of American literature as faithfully reflecting what was great and enduring in their literature. Since no modern reader shares those superseded estimates, they now appear not as real recognitions but as individually accepted cultural constructs—constructs whose exact cultural origin we can reconstruct, should we so wish. With a little digging we can establish that the old version of our significant literary past arose alongside of, and spread itself in complicated interdependence with, the interlocking set of culture-directing agencies (the literary magazine, the public library, the reformed public school, and so on) that made their way into cultural authority in post-Civil War America, and that we still call by the historically dismissive term "genteel." These agencies drew that formation of literary tradition to themselves in their insurgent phases; and they established their very real authority in part by establishing the authority *of* that version of literary tradition.

The modernization of the American literary past—that purging, then refilling, by which American literature took on its familiar modern content in the early twentieth century—advertised itself as, and long continued to be accepted as, a triumphant release of our real literary heritage from the institutional constructions of official culture. But we are beginning to be far enough out from under the power of that new formulation to see that its revisions might really have delivered us not from a false to a true past but from an old to a new past-establishing system. Van Wyck Brooks's 1918 essay "On Creating a Usable Past"—the work that, as much as any other, started what Richard Ruland calls the rediscovery of American literature—reopened this field for fresh discovery and creation by exposing the received version of American literature as the invidious creation of "the professorial mind."[2] But the irony of Brooks's manifesto is that the past he pronounced vital gained broad acceptance by aligning itself with a newly emergent form of the very custodians Brooks thought he was rescuing it from. The rise of the rediscovered American literature of this century, we can now notice, exactly coincides with the rise of a new formation of the professoriate—a professoriate trained not so much in general humane learning as in field-specific expertise; and with the rise, interchangeably, of a cultural order giving new power to such a professoriate—the modern (only incipiently nineteenth-century) organization that vests authority in properly specialized experts, university professors among them.[3] Quite as directly as in that earlier historical chapter, the new, more specialized culture agents of the early twentieth century took the new formation of American literature to themselves. (They trained, as Brooks's older professoriate of course never had, in the new American literature as their discipline.) Quite as directly, this group too used its new authority to establish that map as the American literary past. (Modern readers learned what that literature was principally through college courses and their derivatives.) And we might at least speculate that their new version of the past also served, as the earlier one had its genteel sponsors, to underwrite their own new cultural authority. If there is anything the second or modern American canon is that the first or genteel canon was not, it is difficult. (The substitution of Dickinson for Longfellow is symptomatic.) *This* version of our literature requires the aid of expert assistance to bring it home to the common mind—and so helps support the value of expertise more generally.

To link a literary past to the groups and group interests that maintained it is to invite, I know, misunderstanding. Such linkages look all too much like the standard products of cheap conspiracy theories (the past as self-serving tool of a little band of power-hungry men), or else of the facile form of modern ahistoricism (history is a fiction too—like everything else).

But the point I see American literature's social history as making is a different one, one that really could be a commonplace: it is that no past lives without cultural mediation. The past, however worthy, does not survive by its own intrinsic power. The past is what passes: it shares in the slippage from living presence back into unreality that afflicts all mortal things. The past does not stay present *to* the present except through someone's preservation and public assertion of its memory—which only happens when someone takes an interest in it, or finds it (in any of several senses) in one's own interests.

Even then the past does not survive the transience of individual interest unless it can also objectify itself into a institution—a transpersonal or cultural structure that can carry it forward from its first rememberers and establish it in the understandings of others through time. Edward Shils writes, movingly but truly:

> The past . . . appear[s] in the present . . . against the obstacles of death and birth. Those who bore the things from the past within themselves die and the past things are left without anyone to possess them unless the newly born, who did not begin by possessing them, are induced to take them up.[4]

And it is by fashioning and empowering institutions that individuals induct their successors into their transmitted beliefs and cares. A past accordingly takes on centrality and living power to the extent that some institution or array of institutions gains the power to establish it as the past—which also means that a past lives or dies as the institutions that maintain it win, hold, or lose their sway over communal knowledge and concern. The classical tradition became the past again when the poets and scholars of the late Middle Ages first took an interest in it again, then fashioned the institutions—from substantial public ones like the school and the court to more purely formal ones like the convention of literary *imitatio*—that could make that tradition the foundation of a cultured humanity. And notoriously, the classical tradition has *been* the central past where and as the institutions enlisted to perpetuate it have held onto their power. Ours may prove to have been a moment when enduring new pasts were emerging to significance. Elaine Showalter gives an apt image for the multiple net-yet-canonical literatures that have pressed their way back into visibility in the last ten years when she writes:

> As the works of dozens of women writers have been rescued from what E. P. Thompson calls "the enormous condescension of posterity," and considered in relation to each other, the lost continent of the female tradition has risen like Atlantis from the sea of English literature.[5]

But one thing we can be sure of is that these new formation do not, as her image suggests, emerge of their own propulsion. They have not and will not surface except through the force of someone's or some group's interests. And whether they will stay above water on future maps of the literary continents is a question exactly *not* of their innate value (which never saved a past yet) but of whether those interests can successfully institutionalize themselves, can build new institutions and win old ones to the cause of *making* theirs be the past worth remembering.

We know something about the past, but we know much less about the social process of its creation. We know too little about what the past has been, at other presents than our own. We know still less about how the past interacts with the agencies that maintain it. (One thing an institution is not, we can presume, is a neutral medium, carrying the past forward without change or distortion.)

Just as important, we know too little about the difference it has made, not in theory but in lived reality, to have the past be instituted one way and not another. How the past is instituted makes an obvious difference for the past. How different parts of the past are taken up in the play of cultural institutions determines, we can guess but have not established, who they are made pasts for, what level of acculturation they are built into, what larger configuration of cultural elements they are made a part of, what kind of cultural value they will have attached to them. (Surely canonical American literature had a different kind of reality when it was incorporated into elementary-school education as a central part of citizenship training, as it was in the late nineteenth century.) And it is not only in their own inflated self-esteem that such institutions exert the power of life or death. What institutions refuse to incorporate into their organized public memory ceases to exist for those who rely on that memory—as Herman Melville, by being left out of accounts of American literature in the later nineteenth century, became a virtually nonexistent author, until his revival in the 1920s; as the women regionalist writers Paul Lauter has watched dropped from college anthologies after the 1920s passed, by that rejection, into what Van Wyck Brooks calls the "limbo of the non-elect."[6]

But if institutions make a difference for the past, that difference makes a difference in turn for present knowledge and creation. The past's conservators and revisers have always agreed that the past's availability has direct bearing on the life available to the present. Brooks's complaint on behalf of his contemporaries is that they have been impoverished of tradition's vital aid by the contemporary institutionalization of American literary history. In the figures of his essay a proper tradition is "a warm artery . . . lead[ing] from the present back into the past," and an unforeclosed past is "an inexhaustible storehouse of apt attitudes and adaptable ideals."[7] To construct a new version of tradition, in these terms, is to reconnect a writer to his life-supply, to restore to him the *store* of accumulated knowings and makings he can live and practice on. The notion that the past feeds or funds the present—the notion that it is or at least could be a later time's principle of enablement or strength—is more than a traditionalist's piety. It is established for us in concrete terms in a wealth of historical instances. Walt Whitman, courage-giver to so many great poets in this century, was not an inspiration for American poets in the nineteenth century, when the cultural institutions that structured the poetic realm refused to admit him to their organized past. (Then poets found their strength, such as it was, in another history: as Thomas Bailey Aldrich, a once-admired poet more forgotten now than even the word "limbo" can suggest, found his poetical vocation while reading Longfellow.)[8] Whitman became the great enabler he is (for instance) for Hart Crane's or William Carlos Williams's poetic assertions only after a change in those institutions brought him to the center of our poetic history: made him a past poets could possess and work out of. Similarly, the salvage operations now at work on various sunken literary continents will have as their justification, should they succeed, not that they gave equal literary representation to all (sufficiently clamorous) interest groups but that they enabled more fully realized forms of awareness and creation, by restoring the present's access to lost pasts.

The process by which pasts are formed and reformed is not separate from the process by which cultural institutions are made and remade. But this linkage is important because it is in turn not separate from what the inhabitants of those institutions can know and make. The question of what past is alive and on what terms it is available is the question too of how the present can fund its actions. It determines whether we can draw on the resources earlier makings have created, or whether we must live the narrower life of those doomed to be self-supporting.

Among American authors, Hawthorne has an especially intimate relation to the issue of tradition. Hawthorne is of course one of our great investigators of tradition. His chief subject is the way the past invisibly invests itself in the present, and the way the present alternately struggles against the past's weight and seeks to renew its embrace. More to the point here, this great historian *of* the past has had a special status *as* the past. Hawthorne was included in the nineteenth-century American canon from the beginning, and he eventually emerged as one of its two or three central figures. In the late nineteenth century he was the American author whose greatness seemed most incontestable, and who best displayed the literary virtues the then-prevailing canon constituted itself around. When that canon and its principles of selection fell from favor, as his original companions were sent into obscurity Hawthorne was found to have been misunderstood. The literary charms he was originally prized for were now found to be inessential to him, a kind of protective covering for an author of quite other tendencies: dividedness, subversiveness, darkness, demoralization— the very virtues around which the new American canon was largely grouped. Since he showed these tendencies so clearly, Hawthorne became central again to the new formation of American literature—just as central as he had been in the one it displaced.

As a result of this history, Hawthorne (along with Emerson, who underwent a somewhat different form of rehabilitation) is the only American author always to have been part of our significant past. And Hawthorne

has always had a special importance to the way that past has been composed. A marked peculiarity of Hawthorne's reception-history is that
people who have worked with him have always become, through that
process, specially attuned to the continuities of literary history. The Hawthorne chapters in F. O. Matthiessen's *American Renaissance* lead toward
the historical extension "From Hawthorne to James to Eliot." Paul Elmer
More's Shelburne essays on Hawthorne, the finest Hawthorne criticism of
the turn of the century, treat him similarly as a missing link, establishing
the continuity between such ancestors as Cotton Mather and such writers
of the present as Mary Wilkins Freeman.[9]

Within such studies Hawthorne functions supremely as the concatena-
tor, the author who pulls disparate writing into a coherent and continuous
line; this is the role he has played in the larger constructions of American
literature as well. D. H. Lawrence's *Studies in Classic American Literature*
(1923), a work of crucial importance in establishing the modern American canon, delivers an excitingly modern American literature out of the
body of old-fashioned classics by subjecting them to an operation of divi-
sion: an operation that splits them into a tame, mindlessly conventional
Victorian surface and a wild depth of passionate subversion. Lawrence's
revisionist tactic is to rewrite his own double evaluation of the old American classics as a duplicity practiced by the books themselves; and Hawthorne is the author Lawrence uses to effect this move. His double
Hawthorne—"that sugary, blue-eyed little darling of a Hawthorne" who
hides as behind a Shirley Temple mask "the impeccable truth of his art-
speech"[10]—is always his chief exhibit of the duplicitousness he claims is
typically American. And it is in his Hawthorne chapters that his case for
a characteristically American art of "subterfuge" is most powerfully argued. Richard Chase's *The American Novel and Its Tradition* is one of a
group of works articulating the distinctively American aspects of American literature that enabled that literature to assert itself as a separate
intellectual discipline in the 1950s. In Chase's work too Hawthorne figures
not just as an author in a tradition but as the agent of its constitution:
Chase establishes American fiction's difference around the antithesis of
novel and romance, a distinction taken directly from Hawthorne's prefaces.

The establisher of the coherence and continuity of American literature,
Hawthorne has functioned too as what might be called its entry guard,
the agent who admits new authors inside that line. Malcolm Cowley's
1946 *Portable Faulkner,* published when Faulkner's work had almost all
gone out of print and when he had virtually stopped writing fiction, played
a vital role in making Faulkner, so soon as 1950, an official American literary giant. Cowley begins this volume's influential introduction by linking
Faulkner to Hawthorne as an isolated experimenter, and ends it by likening him to Hawthorne as a regional mythographer; one might argue that
it was through the Hawthorne connection that Faulkner entered the American fictional line. Cowley's *Portable Hemingway,* similarly important historically for its effect of integrating the still-contemporary Hemingway into

the classical tradition (so soon do our contemporaries become our classics), does so, we might notice, by the same move: by taking Hemingway out of the line of London and Dreiser and inserting him (however implausibly) in the line of Hawthorne and Poe.[11]

Hawthorne's continuous presense in our literary past, together with his continuous role in the construction of that past, gives him special value for the study of the past's history. Hawthorne moves through our past like a kind of tracer-dye, baring the changing contours both of what it has included and of the terms and processes by which it has been built. His case is all the more valuable because it also enables us to establish, clearly and with thick detail, how the past so organized has come home to later moments. For reasons not altogether easy to explain, we have an extraordinarily dense sheaf of descriptions of the experience of reading Hawthorne, the experience not of "ideal readers" but of real men and women in historical time. Melville's excited account in the essay "Hawthorne and His Mosses" is the most famous of these. But we also have a record by Rebecca Harding Davis of how, perhaps ten years before Melville read Hawthorne's *Mosses,* she came across three "magic" stories in a "cheap book" she took up to her childhood's playhouse, stories she later found to be pirated from *Twice-Told Tales.* We have from Henry James a long account of his first adult reading of Hawthorne, but also of his much earlier childhood encounters first with a copy of *The Scarlet Letter* that "fixed his eyes as the book lay upon the table," then with a painting of Hester and Pearl that grew "vividly imprinted on my mind" and made him "vaguely frightened" and "uneasy." We have a long reminiscence of Hamlin Garland's discovering Hawthorne among the sets of "fine old classics" in a "ludicrously prescriptive" school library, on the newly settled Great Plains.[12] And the list could go on.

Because these accounts are so circumstantial, in Hawthorne's case we can establish not just what the American literary past has contained at various moments but also the paths of the past's transmission, the cultural mechanisms by which it has been made and kept present at later times. (A whole chapter of cultural history lies between Hawthorne the anonymous reprint and Hawthorne the prescribed classic.) Since they are so detailed, they also let us establish the way in which the past thus instituted and disseminated has come to present life, in the act of reception. The memoirs of Hawthorne-reading are monotonous in their tributes to his power. Over and over again readers describe themselves (as Hawthorne had described himself before the scarlet letter) as fascinated by his writings, fixed and held fast as in the suffering of a revelation. Such tributes give an extravagant demonstration of how what is taken up into the past can keep coming to life again with vital and halting force. But quite as valuable for the fullness of the record are the more guarded testimonies (for instance) of William Crary Brownell, editorial advisor to Scribner's and editor of Edith Wharton, for whom Hawthorne has only the ascribed power of a compulsory schoolroom text; or William Dean Howells, who recalls being "dominated" by Hawthorne's "potent spell" in his youth, but who wonders in his age whether Hawthorne might not now be an outworn taste.[13] Taken together these accounts help us chart the endlessly changing *life* of the past: the ceaseless fluctuation by which, as it passes through time, a past becomes now immediate, now remote or only historical in its reality; now a personal possession, now a merely institutional assertion; now dead, now again more alive than the living, in the varied experience of its receivers.

As it measures the pulse of the past, the history of Hawthorne's case also gives an instructive index of how tradition, through the process of transmission and reception, establishes a ground for later making. As early as 1850, or before Hawthorne had produced the bulk of his mature work, other writers began to incorporate him into their writing, and reformulate their projects on his plans. Melville overhauled the design of the work that became *Moby-Dick* after he read and met Hawthorne in 1850. (*Moby-Dick*'s first words are: "In Token of my admiration for his genius, This book is inscribed to NATHANIEL HAWTHORNE.") And *Moby-Dick* is only the first of a long line of American reworkings of Hawthorne—some of them indebted to him only superficially, but a surprising number, like Melville's, owing their literary ambitions to his work, and using it (as Laurence Holland says *The Portrait of a Lady* uses *The Scarlet Letter*) as "the very matrix of its fabulation."[14]

This line would include, in the generation after Melville, important and characteristic works by James and Howells, among others; in the naturalist generation, books like Stephen Crane's *The Red Badge of Courage,* which echoes Hawthorne distinctly if less centrally, and Harold Frederic's *The Damnation of Theron Ware,* signalled from its first page as a kind of mock-heroic retelling of *The Scarlet Letter.* Among American modernists it would include crucial works by Faulkner, who disclaimed knowledge of Hawthorne but wrote him (incongruously) into the central "Addie" and "Whitfield" chapters of *As I Lay Dying,* and whose extension of his range in *Light in August* and the books that follow it shows clear debt to the lessons of this master. Later still it would include Flannery O'Connor, the most recent reworker of Hawthorne's plots of compulsion and symbolic fixation, and the most recent author to say: "Hawthorne interests me considerably. I feel more of a kinship with him than with any other American."[15] Hawthorne is the only American fiction writer never to have lived in the limbo of the non-elect, but he is also the only such writer whose work has always incited and guided others' practice. If it shows how the past is amassed then, Hawthorne's history is also peculiarly revealing of tradition's productive aspect, and helps show the difference the past makes to what later makers can accomplish.

In the chapters that follow I set out to trace the passage by which Hawthorne was first organized *as* a literary past, then reactivated *from* the past in the work of other writers. I consider his relations to his followers to be important in themselves as chapters of literary history. (We do not have so many traditions that we can afford to be ignorant of them.) But I confess that my intent is also to use these relations as a kind of historical sample, a coherent set of concrete instances of which to ask the more general questions of how pasts get created and distributed, and what it means to live within or without the presence of such pasts. Hawthorne's tradition is used, here, to mount an inquiry into tradition itself. And since I end up taking a position on this subject (all writing on tradition is polemical), I may as well say now what it is.

The shortest way to name the point of view of the present work is to say that it does not see tradition as passing from author to author or from text to text, but as being mediated by an institutional context that is partly social in nature. Every work of writing is produced within a historically specific definition of such work's conditions of possibility. This definition is in part literary, comprising some particular definition of what literature is and is not (such definitions are not constant) as well as of the forms through writing is then available to be practiced. But while it is not reducible to it, this definition has an extraliterary dimension as well. No one writes except within a concrete cultural context that determines (among other things) what kind of value will attach to such writing; who it might have as its audience, and what kind of attention will be paid to it; what status in the world outside writing the author can win by doing such writing; and so on.[16]

What is worth insisting on here—though it awaits specific cases for its proving—is that tradition is not external to such literary-cultural definitions of the writer's work but passes down through them and realizes itself within them. The niches any period makes available for writers are established partly by the literary forms that are operative within that niche, and partly by the social place that niche is positioned in. But they are also established by the body of previous work or active precedent each such niche has written into it, as descriptive of the kind of work it intends. This body of texts defines the forms then in practice. And it is in the way they accept and resist such guides that writers *place* themselves in both their literary and their cultural positions. To be an Augustan poet is interchangeably to write in a delimited selection of genres (the epic translation, the Horatian verse-satire, the mock heroic); to write within a literary past—that of classical literature—that has been given a high degree of presence and normative power; and to write from a social position of newly intense competition with a popular culture then taking on aggressive new literary life. Remembering and recreating their appointed past is the way these poets realize their appointed forms. But displaying their allegiance to that past is also the way they mark their cultural difference from the not-so-traditioned lowlanders of Parnassus. To take an example from the other end of the cultural spectrum, to be a writer of what Nina Baym has termed "woman's fiction" in mid-nineteenth-century America is to write in another but equally selective set of formal and stylistic norms (the plain style, the female *bildungsroman*); for another but equally specified cultural ethos (the ethos of the new domesticity and female leisure); in another but equally definite specification of status (the status of independent professional producer, but *not* of the maker of works of art). *And* it is to write in another but equally coherent literary ecology: an ecology composed here primarily of other examples of the genre, among literary texts, but also and without distinction of such nonliterary works as hymnals, tracts, spiritual histories, and domestic advice manuals.[17] Here again it is by receiving and working on from this formation of past writing that such authors produced the literary difference of their work from other work. (Susan Warner's *The Wide, Wide World,* the book that found the mass audience *Moby-Dick* and *The Scarlet Letter* failed to find, differs from them in the form of its literariness—and differs because Warner is working out of a different definition *of* the literary.) And it is by working in that line of texts that they also reproduced the cultural difference of their work: made their work have the differentiated properties and priorities that let it be branded nonliterary, from a higher cultural stratum. (When women writers began to hang quotations from Flaubert over their writing desks—as Sarah Orne Jewett did in fact and as Kate Chopin must have done *in pectore*—we know that something has changed. But the change involves a change in the literariness of womens' writing *and* in the social structure of authorial roles *and* in the kind of tradition women now feel entitled to enroll in—the three realize themselves simultaneously.)

According to the view I am sketching here, literary tradition has a genuinely and distinctly intraliterary dimension to its actions. The way writings receive and exploit the presence of earlier writings is a drama in its own right, essential to the way they compose and assert themselves as human works. But this intraliterary drama never ceases to operate within the cultural dimension of literature's life. How texts come by their body of precedents remains a function of how literature is structured at their moment as a cultural category. And the way they realize their literary relations is inseparable from the *act* they make in the cultural situation that surrounds them, conceived in its broadest terms.

This understanding governs my procedures in the following chapters. My effort in them is to catch the full play between Hawthorne's and later writers' writings, to give full hearing to this level of interaction. But without minimizing its literary aspects I also try to think this interaction back onto its historical ground: to ask as part of what larger cultural structure Hawthorne came to his followers; and to ask how his example affects the act they make toward their particular historical world. My account of Melville, accordingly, considers not just his intense personal response to Hawthorne but also the literary situation of Melville's mid-career—especially the cultural occasions for the kind of oppositional writing Melville felt called on to undertake. And I look for Melville's use of Hawthorne not alone in the tropes and themes he borrows in his work, but in his whole attempt to formulate the literary form for such antagonistic expression—expression inevitably allied, in Melville's conception of it, with the act of literary prophecy. In the case of Howells and James the story of Hawthorne's influence becomes the story too of the stabilization of a differentiated sphere of serious literary writing after 1850 in America, a history in which Hawthorne plays an important part. But I then also try to read their rewritings of Hawthorne in terms of the moves they enable toward that sphere's changing historical situation: to see how Hawthorne helps Howells form his idea of literature's mission in a culture liberalized amiss, in the early 1880s; or how he helps James assert a new role for literature in the changing conditions of cultural literacy at the turn of the century.

Taken together, these cases make a statement about tradition in general that might be summarized this way. A tradition comes to an author with the organization of his work; and what tradition gives him is knowledge of how to *do* his work. But while I consider them representative in a genuine sense, I want to be wary of making these instances too representative. If there is anything students of tradition know it is that traditions are not interchangeable: each has its own cast, logic, and worldly career. Accordingly, this account of the paradigmatic quality of Hawthorne's tradition might best close by setting that notion aside and saying something instead about the particular deflection of his line.

Such an account might begin by noting that there is something odd about Hawthorne as the figure of the founder. We need make no judgment of comparative gifts in order to note that many authors are Hawthorne's superiors in their possession and realization of their powers. Dickens and Balzac, to name two contemporaries, are in an obvious way released by the writing of fiction, and their work is voluminous as a result. But Hawthorne was not comparably at home in his work: master of the short story, he experienced the short story as an insufficient form; when he extended himself in *The Scarlet Letter,* the result was to make him feel that he should have written another kind of book.[18] Because his work has such self-resistance built into it, surges of creative energy typically lead Hawthorne not to sustained productivity but to impasse and arrest: Hawthorne published forty short pieces between 1832 and 1839, but only one in 1840, and none in 1841; twenty more short works in 1843 and 1844, but then only three slight pieces in the five years that followed; three long romances between 1850 and 1852, but then only one more completed romance in the twelve more years he remained alive. ("A life of much smoulder and scanty fire,"[19] is Hawthorne's last summary of his career.)

A founder of a tradition is that tradition's image of achieved vocation. But a Hawthorne tradition must look back to a vocation in significant measure *un*achieved. Further, unlike the magnificent egotists who typically call traditions into being, Hawthorne shows virtually no will to direct the way of another. Unlike his neighbor Emerson, Hawthorne never recruited a disciple, and when others tried to cast themselves in that role he did not know what to do with them. A memorable passage from Mrs. Hawthorne's letters describes his response to Melville's approaches: "Nothing pleases me better than to sit & hear this growing man dash his tumultuous waves of thought up against Mr Hawthorne's great, genial, comprehending silences."[20] The young Howells could only say of his votive pilgrimage to the shrine of Hawthorne: "he was very shy and I was rather shy." (This is the comment that provoked the mortifying reply: "Oh, a couple of shysters!")[21] What Melville later termed Hawthorne's "non-cordialness" has an analogue in his work as well, which singularly refuses to organize itself for another's guidance. Emerson and Whitman, the only other American writers comparably prolific of tradition, speak to posterity and tell it how to continue their work, even when their message is the confusing: the way to follow me is not to follow me. By contrast, Hawthorne is uncommunicative of his work's intentions (the *dicta* of his prefaces are anything but directions). And the work itself, unaccompanied by such captions, gives little indication of what it is about or how it could be followed. Anthologists have had their way with him but Hawthorne himself gives no guide as to what his major work might be. (He chose the infantile "Snow Image" as the title story for the volume containing "Ethan Brand" and "My Kinsman, Major Molineux"; such moves help explain why until modern times his domestic and juvenile pieces were as authentic a part of his oeuvre as the darker tales we value now.) And to deduce from among his works the method or purpose *of* his work is to run into baffling problems. (What is romance, we ask with no ready answer, if *The Scarlet Letter, The House of the Seven Gables, The Blithedale Romance,* and *The Marble Faun* are all examples of it?)

The head of a tradition usually presents all too definite a project for his heirs to work on. But Hawthorne's tradition has an enigma for its source.[22] His indefiniteness does not prevent him from being followed. But it does mean that, to a significant extent, his successors have had to *make* the model they then could follow. Historically, it is striking to how late a date the authors working out of him fail to find a common program in his work—and on the other hand, how inventive they continue to be in determining his meaning as a possible source. Melville thought he found—but largely invented—"the grand truth about Nathaniel Hawthorne" that "He says NO! in thunder,"[23] as he thought he found—but largely invented—Hawthorne's program to be one of strenuous literary prophecy. But Harriet Beecher Stowe was no less inventive when, instructing housewives in how they might start careers as authors, she lit on Hawthorne's "The Old Apple Dealer" as a model they could use to write of the unthunderous eventlessness of everyday life.[24]

This necessary and continuing inventiveness has as its effect that the Hawthorne tradition, so far from being individuated as a body of work, can scarcely be identified by distinguishing marks. Hawthorne has been followed in many directions, including many opposite ones. There is a strong radical line in his tradition, a line of literary extremism and violent experimentation. (American literature's great formal revolutionaries have all been Hawthorne's students.) But there is also as thick and authentic a conservative line: Hawthorne's presence runs through American local-color fiction, formally the most traditionalist of its genres. A romance line comes out of Hawthorne (though none of its authors agree on what romance is, each having had to reinvent it). But a no less impressive realist line comes out of him too—one of American realism's native adaptations being that it adds Hawthorne to the ranks of its usual guides. There is what could be called a Protestant line in the Hawthorne tradition, continuing his study of post-Puritan self-absorption and moral torment. (I think for instance of Jewett's story "Poor Joanna," an "Ethan Brand" with its cultural sources made explicit.) But there is also a Catholic line: it leads to O'Connor, whose Hawthorne is mediated partly by the Dominican Congregation she stayed close to in Atlanta—an order founded, as it happens, by Hawthorne's daughter Rose.[25]

Because he gives so little guidance, Hawthorne's followers have been free to put him to any purpose they have required. The indefiniteness of his direction explains why his tradition, most unusually, has been compatible with every later project and resistant to none. But the very elusiveness that makes Hawthorne so adaptable as a model builds another trait into the legacy he offers. A strong head of tradition establishes a way for work to be done. But if he sets a way he also authorizes a way: by the weight of his example, he makes that the work worthy to be done. If Hawthorne does little to constrain his followers, he does little too to authorize the plans they take from him. They can put him in the service of what project they please, but he does not thereby validate that project. Instead he brings his enigmatic openness inside their work, unleashing his unconfirmingness on their own sense of mission.

Hawthorne's deserves study as a rich and various tradition. It offers in certain ways a paradigm of tradition. But part of its interest is as a variant on tradition—a variant, especially, on tradition's structure of authority. During the time his tradition-making power lasts, a founder stands for the realized form of a mode of creation. Hawthorne too has had this power for others: that is what they mean when they speak of his "potent spell." But what he has handed across, to those within this sway, has been in part an undoing of such founding authority. Invoking him in their later historical situations, writers have used him to help them know how their work could be done. But released in these new situations he has also taken on renewed life as a principle of literary self-questioning; he has remained a means by which authors can unthink their own convictions and cast their professions into what Howells calls "sorer doubt."[26]

❧ *Chapter Two* ❧

HAWTHORNE, MELVILLE, AND THE FICTION OF PROPHECY

AS AN INSTANCE OF TRADITION FORMATION, Melville's relation to Hawthorne is peculiar on at least two grounds. Figures of tradition stand as the great past for their successors. But Hawthorne was emphatically not past when Melville encountered him. Hawthorne was 46, or still in mid-life, when Melville (then 31) met him in August 1850; and Hawthorne was still very much in mid-career. In the summer of 1850 Hawthorne was the writer of the two collections *Twice-Told Tales* and *Mosses from an Old Manse,* and only just of *The Scarlet Letter:* three of the four long romances we think of as Hawthorne's major work were still unwritten when Melville discovered him. Hawthorne's most productive period came, in fact, just at this moment. *The Snow-Image and Other Tales* was assembled and *The House of the Seven Gables, A Wonder Book,* and *The Blithedale Romance* were all written between September 1850 and April 1852, or during the time of these writers' close involvement.

The Hawthorne–Melville connection presents the unusual spectacle of literary tradition being formed while the parent work is itself still in the forming. And Hawthorne's non-*pastness* also accounts for this relation's second oddity: that in this instance literary influence takes place without the usual removal from living, personal ground. When authors pass up into that sort of potent past that inspires tradition, they get objectified—or, as we say, immortalized—in the process. They become the authors of their work: their literary self, the self achieved and expressed through their writing, supplants the more transient self of living personality, as the one meant by their name. (Who is Shakespeare after 1623? The author of Shakespeare's plays.) Hawthorne was eventually to undergo this sort of abstraction in a virulent form, but since Melville came to him before this process set in, he still knew Hawthorne in his person. Every surviving source makes clear that it was the living, embodied Hawthorne—not just the Hawthorne of the page—that Melville found attractive. In the month after they met Hawthorne and Melville both read each other avidly, but they also exchanged visit after visit, as if seeking a pleasure only full personal presence could supply. (During this time Melville told Mrs. Hawthorne that "Mr Hawthorne was the first person whose physical being appeared to him wholly in harmony with the intellectual & spiritual.") Melville claimed to be fixed and fascinated by Hawthorne's tales in 1850, but even twenty years after their friendship was over he was still attributing Hawthorne's power to his personal aura. Vine, the Hawthorne portrait in Melville's *Clarel* (1876), is introduced as "A funeral man, yet richly fair— / Fair as the sabled violets be," whose "charm of subtle virtue shed / A personal influence coveted."[1]

In Hawthorne and Melville's case, a complex literary relation is superposed on and in part mediated by a complex relation between whole, not just literary, personalities. For this reason it does a central violence to this relation to read it as an interaction in the written realm merely. But the difficulty here is that while the Hawthorne–Melville relation does not function wholly in literary terms, it never functions wholly outside such terms either. Hawthorne deeply charmed Melville in their personal meetings. To bring this charming other into his own orbit Melville resorted to unparalleled feats of hospitality. ("I keep the word 'Welcome' all the time in my mouth,"[2] he says in his first suriving letter to Hawthorne.) His successes in winning Hawthorne's full communion touched off similarly unparalleled satisfactions—Melville's reply to Hawthorne's praise of *Moby-Dick* is outdone perhaps only by Whitman's *Calamus* poems, among nineteenth-century expressions of masculine social fulfillment. But the fact remains that it was the *author* Hawthorne whom Melville found personally magnetic. In 1850 and 1851 Melville (in his words) "regard[ed] Hawthorne (in his books) as evincing a quality of genius, immensely loftier, & more profound, too, than any other American has shown hitherto in the printed form."[3] And surely it was what he embodied in literary and cultural terms that made Hawthorne such a riveting person. No doubt Melville brought all kinds of personal needs to bear on Hawthorne. I have no trouble believing that he regarded Hawthorne, as Edwin Haviland Miller has suggested, in light of his needs for fatherly approval and male comradeship. But it is no less true that Melville connected Hawthorne, with special and overriding intensity, to his specifically authorial needs: put Hawthorne in the service of helping him conceive an urgently desired new *literary* identity.

What makes the Hawthorne–Melville relation a genuine case of tradition formation—rather than a chapter in the history of literary friendships only—is the fact that Melville seized Hawthorne as a figure of literary possibility. Melville used Hawthorne to reveal what literature in its most fully realized form could do, and so too to know what he, as a writer, could aspire to achieve. His construction of a new plan of authorship on the basis of Hawthorne's example is itself a literary event of the first importance. It is important because it led to the great phase of his own career: that burst of creativity and sustained exploration that reaches forward from *Moby-Dick* through *Pierre* to *The Piazza Tales* and beyond. But it is important in a more historical sense as well.

We are beginning to have a much more adequate understanding of the cultural organization of literature in America between 1840 and the Civil War. The older researches of William Charvat—still the cornerstone for the study of this subject—established this as a time when an expansion in the market for fiction began to make it more practicable for an American to take up a career solely as a writer, but also when cultural separations among different kinds of audiences and interests a writer might appeal to had not yet been well-established. Recent workers returning to Charvat's study of the history of literature's cultural ground have established the new social position American fiction moved into in the 1840s much more concretely. We can now see that the literary market expanded so rapidly after 1840 not out of an innate tendency to grow, but because of its conjunction, at this time, with a social development that provided new encouragement for reading: the new organization of work, family life, gender-roles, and moral structures of insurgent middle-class domesticity. As it removed women from the sphere of productive labor and made them custodians of nonmaterial values, the cult of domesticity created both a new domestic leisure reading could help fill and a new ethic to support that pastime. (As both a cultivating and a nonproductive labor reading became woman's work in a double sense, under nineteenth-century domesticity.) In consequence, after 1840 and critically so around 1850, fiction writing took on the power to reach very large audiences in America, on the condition that it align itself with the values the new domesticity was constituted around.[4]

These changes in fiction's cultural place entailed immediate consequences for writers and the roles they could claim. One form of these consequences is seen in the literary ladies' men Ann Douglas has described: the writers like N. P. Willis, George William Curtis, and Donald G. Mitchell ("Ik Marvel"), who found new power and prosperity open to them as managers of domestic culture's literary organs on the condition that they serve domestic interests and become, in literary terms, unassuming. Another consequence is seen in the (painfully named!) literary domestics Mary Kelley has recently studied: the writers like Susan Warner, Maria Cummins, Mrs. E. D. E. N. Southworth, and Sara Parton ("Fanny Fern") who inaugurated the bestseller as a cultural phenomenon in the 1850s. As Kelley shows, such writers took advantage of fiction's new conjunction with middle-class domesticity to pioneer a role for women in the public or extradomestic sphere. But the hidden cost of this linkage was that they remained constrained, even as public figures, within traditionally domestic definitions of their identities. They won access to literary expression, but only on terms that made literature a willing servant of domestic ideology. They realized the will to write, but without thereby becoming able to assert their right to such a will: they continued to claim that family needs, the sphere of woman's most traditionally approved concern, prompted their labors instead.[5]

Such study has greatly enriched our sense both of the kinds of writers who were active in pre-Civil War America and of the relation of all writing of that time to its social ground. But what is this study to do with a Melville—a writer who is the exact contemporary of Willis and Curtis and Warner and Parton; who worked in the same, *not* a different, literary and social milieu, but who stands not just in a different but in virtually the opposite relation to literature and its cultural accommodations? Myra Jehlen has hazarded that the difference between Melville and the domestic authors he emerged alongside of is a difference not only in their cultural politics but in "their relationship to writing as such." Melville (in Jehlen's phrases) "took himself seriously," he *"assumed* himself": he engaged in writing as the act an independent identity could be composed through. If he is not (like Kelley's domestics) "conceptually totally dependent," it is because writing, so seized, gave him a vantage point outside the affirmations of his culture: "his novel in the sentimental mode [*Pierre*] could take on sentimentalism because he had an alternative world on which to stand: himself."[6] These are important claims, but, if we accept them, they raise an anterior, historical question. Unless we are willing to grant that some writers simply transcend their historical occasion, they require us to ask: where, in his situation, did Melville find the means for his extremely different way of occupying that situation? How did Melville find, and how did Melville construct, the organizing *idea* of authorship that let him engage literature on such radically altered terms?

It is exactly here that Melville's relation to Hawthorne is so instructive. Hawthorne figured in the drama of self-conception that produced the fiercely self-*assuming* Melville of Melville's mid-career. In Melville's eyes, Hawthorne was what enabled him to conceive and assert himself as an author on altered terms. Hawthorne's influence on Melville takes the form first of a personal interaction, then of a literary relation. But both of these form part of a larger story too: the story of how (in Melville's term) an "other way" of authorship got established as an artistic possibility, in America in the 1850s.

We recognize Hawthorne's effect on Melville by the fact that, immediately upon encountering Hawthorne, Melville broke into new levels of expressive energy. Within days of reading Hawthorne, Melville, the author heretofore of a few short reviews, produced his critical masterpiece, the sustained rhapsody "Hawthorne and His Mosses." In Hawthorne's presence the man who told Sophia Hawthorne that he "was naturally so silent a man, that he was complained of a great deal on this account" became so voluble that she likened his talk to "tumultuous waves."[7] Melville's letters, never unexpressive, abruptly double, then triple their length, when he begins writing to this corespondent. Within this flow of talk, and as if animating it, Melville is aware that he is seizing on powers that are fundamentally new to him. Melville becomes truly confessional, for the one time in his correspondence, in his letters to Hawthorne, but it is not simply that he is sharing confidences. Instead (as in the famous meditation beginning "From my twenty-fifth year I date my life")[8] it is as if he is bringing himself *to* self-knowledge in the letters, grasping, in Hawthorne's imagined presence, the logic of his mental life. Similarly, Melville becomes boldly philosophical in his letters to Hawthorne, but it is not as if he is outlining positions already held. He seems to be coming *to* understanding as he writes, and gaining, through such writing, confidence that the great life mysteries are his to address.

The reason Hawthorne touched off this excited self-extension has something to do with Hawthorne, but it has much more to do with the point Melville had reached in his career when he met Hawthorne—a point I want to reconstruct with some care. Melville, we might begin by remembering, had become an author only five years before he met Hawthorne. In his debut Melville came to writing with considerable natural aptitude, but certainly with no special dedication to writing as a calling. Having had some experiences in exotic lands in his early manhood, Melville found that by writing them up in a form "a little touched up . . . but *true*" he could win an enthusiastic popular response for his work. After this venture he took on, as the organizing and sustaining idea of his work, the one he found in this reception. Having pleased a large, general public, Melville now adopted the aim so *to* please as the end of his writing: "calculated for popular reading, or for none at all," is his working motto in 1846. Having found a ready market for his adventures, Melville similarly accepted the idea of re-supplying that demand as his authorial identity: "South Sea Adventure" is, still in late 1847, "the feild where I garner."[9]

But this plan of authorship, newly constructed after the success of *Typee,* did not hold for long. This idea of literary self and purpose was sufficiently strong to govern the production of a second Polynesian novel and to start him on a third. But Melville then staged the first of those reorientations in midcourse that become a kind of signature of his career. As he told his publisher, while writing *Mardi* he had a "change in my determinations."[10] Having started another "narrative of *facts,*" without removing its initial traces he altered the book's plan to permit greater latitude, changing it first into an allegorical quest-romance, then into a travelling symposium, a free-floating feast of thought and talk. What Melville is searching for, in these revisions, is a format that will open his work more directly to the workings of his mind. Wrenching free from obligations either to rehearse real experience or to spin a continuous story, his effort in *Mardi* is to make each chapter an independent mental occasion: a chance for him to address whatever occurs to him as vigorously as he can, for the sake of finding out what he might have to say on that topic, without becoming bound to continue it or any other line.

Whitman once spoke of "a secret proclivity, American maybe, to dare and violate and make escapades."[11] This proclivity comes over Melvillean authorship with the writing of *Mardi,* and it takes the special form there of adventuresomeness *toward* the literary. What governs *Mardi,* after its early chapters, is the will, without knowing in advance where it will lead, to find out what else a writer can be than a garnerer in a fixed "feild." I might note in passing that, as he undertakes this exploratory self-extension, Melville already grasps how the reworking of literary tradition can help effect a reconstitution of authorial project and role. The first signs of *Mardi*'s eventual deviance from Melville's earlier way of writing are his early allusions to Burton's *Anatomy of Melancholy* and imitations of Sir Thomas Browne. These allusions—the first of many in this much more literature-conscious work—have behind them Melville's recently begun reading in Evert Duyckinck's "choice conservatory"[12] of older literatures. But they also display Melville's hereafter typical act of annexing the contents of libraries directly onto his own work in progress. In these instances, as later, Melville draws the most far-flung readings in around the project he is working on. Seizing their procedures, he at once converts them into voices *he* can try on. And it is through this quick apprehension, then assimilation of other writing into his own that Melville grasps new ideas of what writing can be and do.

This adventure of thinking through writing and of exploring writing's resources through imitation absorbed Melville for more than a year. The immediate yield of this project was the book *Mardi.* But in a more crucial and enduring sense its yield was the revolutionized idea of authorship that Melville became drawn to after this book. Several new strains enter Melville's thinking in *Mardi,* then move, in the year that follows (1849–50), to the center of his self-conception. For the first time in *Mardi,* then very strongly thereafter, Melville comes to identify writing with a wholly inward impulsion. You may think me unwise to have written this sort of book, Melville writes his new English publisher in June 1849, "but some of us scribblers . . . have a certain something unmanageable in us, that bids us do this or that, and be done it must—hit or miss."[13] Melville does not know this something's name, but he knows its forms and procedures. As he images it here and in other writings of this time, this "something" is a strong drive or will. It is imperious, simply not to be resisted: it bids us do things, and be done they must; in *Mardi*'s nautical image, it is a "blast resistless." And its action, when it cuts on, is to seize the work of writing and put that work in its own service: the "blast resistless" drives *Mardi*'s writer from his intended course; or in an even more violent image of the coercion of writing: "an iron-mailed hand clenches mine in a vice, and prints down every letter in my spite." The accession of this will produces a much more intense engagement of the writer in his work—composition as *Mardi* images it is a "seething" and "riveted" activity. But above all this will works to shift the ground of authorship within. Where before Melville thought of writing as produced for an audience's pleasure, now he speaks of it as produced by an inward urge: "My *instinct* is to out with the romance."[14] Where previously writing's proper form was dictated by market demand, now it answers its own demands: be done it must, hit or miss.

As it becomes associated with this other form of will, Melvillean authorship also becomes allied with a different mode of literary ambition. The literary ambition of *Typee*—if it can properly be said to have one—is to get published and, if possible, to get liked. The literary ambition of *Omoo* and at first of *Mardi* is to make *Typee*'s success a regular thing. But in *Mardi* and its wake Melville is reborn as a literary overreacher: a writer with grand notions of literary greatness, and with a strong will to realize himself on that scale through his work. "Permanent reputation" and "things immortal"[15] now become his obsession: the Melville of 1849–50 is more rawly hungry for literary immortality than any other nineteenth-century novelist I know of. Also at this time his reading—still voracious, heterogeneous, and actively appropriative—turns literature, much more than before, into a kingdom of greatness. Emerson, first heard in early 1849, is immediately greeted as an "uncommon man," "elevated above mediocrity." Shakespeare, first attentively read in this same season, becomes an incarnation of both literary genius and messianic spiritual power:

> Dolt & ass that I am I have lived more than 29 years, & until a few days ago, never made close acquaintance with the divine William. Ah, he's full of sermons-on-the-mount, and gentle, aye, almost as Jesus. I take such men to be inspired. . . . And if another Messiah ever comes twill be in Shakesper's person.[16]

Melville's generosity in passages like these is extraordinary, but it also shows the workings of his own giant will. For what he invests in great writers at this time is that enlarged personal power he hopes might be his in prospect.

As it links up with ambitions of this scope, writing also revises its sense of its cultural placement. The 1847 motto "calculated for popular reading, or for none at all" gives way, so soon as the "something unmanageable" letter of 1849, to the disdainful phrase "calculated merely to please the general reader."[17] What lies behind this change is not just the growth of Melvillean snobbery, but the fact that Melville has begun to rethink the cultural basis of literary value. The undifferentiated audience of general readers he had earlier aimed to please begins to be split, by his act of mind, into elite and popular audience zones, each supporting radically different levels of artistic activity. His writings of 1849–50 insist that there is one kind of writing for the many, another for the few, "those for whom it is intended"; that one aspires "simply for amusement," the other to be a "literary achievement"; that one audience's approval helps establish popularity, but the other's "permanent reputation." Wrapping himself in the conceit of "higher purposes,"[18] Melville mentally removes his work from the situation where general acceptance determines its value. In his new thinking writing becomes nonpopular, possibly even anti-popular, in aim: the proof that *Mardi* has "higher purposes," he tells his publisher Bentley, is the fact that it has *not* been generally accepted.

The last of these new developments—the hardest to name but the most important to grasp—is that after *Mardi* Melville comes to identify writing as the means to profundity of thought. Anyone who knows Melville between 1848 and 1851 knows that he is American literature's great victim of raptures of the deep; and the self-delighting activity he calls diving is intimately connected, for him, with his new, more driven kind of writing. In its seething *Mardi* already displays the movement we know best from his 1851 letters: a move in which Melville feels beckoned to address ultimate life mysteries; then, as he engages them, finds himself thrown churning forward from surmise to surmise, so that understandings entirely new to him seem to be being produced through the activity of articulation. The Melville of *Mardi,* as he becomes aware of a separate will to writing, also moves toward the concept that such writing is what *produces* the great writer's expanding "world of mind."[19] As he splits it into high and low, Melville now also divides writing into the kind that refuses and the kind that allows writing's potentially thought-*creating* powers.

Melville's state in the year after *Mardi* is that of a writer for whom writing has become, quite suddenly and unexpectedly, the focus of powerful new drives and ambitions. But to know his state in full we need to recognize that these ambitions, electrifying in the power they seemed to promise him, were also sources of intense new uncertainties and confusions. When he published *Mardi,* Melville discovered that readers and critics did not have much liking for work produced on that plan. He now learned in hard practice what he had airily accepted in theory: that if he was going to write in that self-delighting "other way," he would jeopardize the income his growing family depended on, and forfeit too the sort of public approval that had emboldened him to experiment in the first place. Quite as daunting as this lesson in the impracticality of his ambitions was the fact that these ambitions, so compelling to their bearer, were in crucial ways unable to validate the giant presumptions they touched off. Melville's idea of a literary culture of the happy few and higher purposes is plainly a validation device: an attempt to specify a ground other than that of popular approval on which the special merits of his project could be confirmed. But we need to remember, when we see this device in action, that this separate high literary culture was an imaginative invention of Melville's, not a historical reality. Prose fiction, Melville's genre, had never been given as a high cultural form in the England or America of Melville's time: its status at his moment was exactly as the form that merged high and low into a "universal" popular audience. (Witness the cases of two other authors Melville's English publisher also published: Cooper and Dickens.) In any case, there certainly was not, in Melville's America, such a thing as a formalized alternative audience a writer could appeal to against a popular one; this was not fully established until well after 1850, and was at best almost wholly incipient at *Mardi*'s time.[20] Since such an alternative audience did not exist in reality, Melville had to try to improvise it from the available materials (hence the appointment—not Melville's last—of Evert and George Duyckinck as *Mardi*'s "real" audience). More, since it did not exist in reality, the "assurance"[21] it could offer Melville's presumptions was at best a matter of anxious hope. So too with another ground of potential validation: the writing itself. It would be one thing to be seized with a sense of personal profundity and prospective immortality if one had just written, say, *The Divine Comedy*. But the author of *Mardi* quickly recognized that his work was grotesquely more impressive in its ambitions than in its displayed achievement. When he recognized its callowness, the work that should have established his right to such identifications threw them instead into deep doubt. The chapter of *Mardi* that bares Melville's presumption to immortality also shows him racked with anxiety that this presumption may be an insane delusion. He ends his reflections desperate for but at a perfect loss for evidence of his election:

> Ah, Oro! how may we know or not, we are what we would be? Hath genius any stamp and imprint, obvious to possessors? Hath it eyes to see itself; or is it blind? Or do we delude ourselves with being gods, and end in grubs?[22]

The Melville of 1849–50 then is inspired, we might even say afflicted, with a sense of literary calling in the highest degree elating. But he is almost completely uncertain, either that his ambitions can be made practicable or that he has any real warrant to hold such ambitions. His condition, accordingly, is one of anxiety-fraught suspension of purpose. He is sufficiently committed to his hoped-for future work to have disdain for work produced on his old plan of authorship. (He associates his two new "unmetaphysical" novels of this year with the degradation of mere manual labor: "they are two *jobs,* which I have done for money," he keeps telling everyone, "being forced to it, as other men are to sawing wood.") But he is not yet sure enough of the warrant for his hopes to convert them into a working authorial identity. It is still only his "earnest desire" "to write those sort of books which are said to 'fail.' "[23]

This highly charged state of vocational hope and confusion is the state Melville was in when he encountered Hawthorne in the summer of 1850. And if that encounter was a "shock" to him, it was because, in Hawthorne, he seemed to see his own most wildly imagined ambitions realized, and so purged of their attendant uncertainty. His encounter with Hawthorne is the supreme instance of the process by which, since the time of *Mardi,* Melville has gone out to other writers, magnified their praise, and thereby used them to help him grasp the idea of his own prospective career. Melville met Hawthorne on August 5, 1850; he read Hawthorne's *Mosses from an Old Manse* in the following days; and no more than a week later, he wrote his electrified recognition-piece "Hawthorne and His Mosses." In this essay we can watch him bringing forth, as if from Hawthorne's writing, an idea of incandescent importance to his writing life.

Melville begins this essay knowing only that Hawthorne is obscurely fascinating as a writer. To account for this fascination, he puts together as best he can a portrait of the author characterized by the *Mosses* pieces (in fact, this is also the Hawthorne of Hawthorne's early critical reputation): a genial author, too fine for broad popularity, associated with the rhythms of nature and the white melancholy of a "contemplative humor." (1156)[24] But Melville has what Henry James calls a *grasping* imagination, and so no sooner does he sketch this picture than he moves to get back behind it. His way of attempting this is to surmise that Hawthorne's manifest geniality must be the index to another, antithetical form of power. Hawthorne's visible soarings in the sun prove, Melville argues, that he must have a corresponding gift for penetrating depths, must have "a great, deep intellect, which drops down into the universe like a plummet." (1158) Melville now looks back to the tales for evidence of this so far purely surmised other Hawthorne, educing possible examples until, with a burst, he is able to say what that Hawthorne's power consists of. Having cited "Earth's Holocaust," Melville begins as if to take up two more relevant tales, but suddenly what he has been driving at is ready to be said:

> "The Christmas Banquet" and "The Bosom Serpent" would be fine subjects for a curious and elaborate analysis, touching the conjectural parts of the mind that produced them. For spite of all the Indian-summer sunlight on the hither side of Hawthorne's soul, the other side—like the dark half of the physical sphere—is shrouded in blackness, ten times black. (1158)

On the basis of this recognition, Melville can now completely revise his initial account. Hawthorne is *not* a nature author but the diviner, behind appearances, of the hidden guilt Calvinism called "Innate Depravity." Hawthorne is *not* a gentle author but the terrifying wielder of that "terrific thought." His light or bright side, so far from being even a complementary aspect, is there only in conjunction with that dark knowledge, to make that darkness visible: "You may be witched by his sunlight,—transported by the bright gildings in the skies he builds over you;—but there is the blackness of darkness beyond; and even his bright gildings but fringe, and play upon the edges of thunder-clouds." (1159)

This reading of Hawthorne is so famous that we need to remember to wonder at the authority and sheer mental speed with which Melville moves to this conception. (When he wrote this passage he had read one book by Hawthorne, and not even all of that.) In any case, having reached this point, Melville clearly exults in the sense that he has now *known* Hawthorne, and for the first time: "In one word, the world is mistaken in this Nathaniel Hawthorne," he crows; "he himself must often have smiled at its absurd misconception of him." (1159) But this very exultation fuels a further extension of Melville's inquiry, instead of bringing it to an end. What the knowledge of human depravity gives Hawthorne's fiction, Melville explains, is "the infinite obscure of his back-ground." Then, since this is itself obscure: "that back-ground, against which Shakespeare plays his grandest conceits." Then, since this requires amplification in turn (articulation now comes in wave on wave):

> it is those deep far-away things in him; those occasional flashings-forth of the intuitive Truth in him; those short, quick probings at the very axis of reality;—these are the things that make Shakespeare, Shakespeare. Through the mouths of the dark characters of Hamlet, Timon, Lear, and Iago, he craftily says, or sometimes insinuates the things, which we feel to be so terrifically true, that it were all but madness for any good man, in his own proper character, to utter, or even hint of them. Tormented into desperation, Lear the frantic King tears off the mask, and speaks the sane madness of vital truth. . . . And if I magnify Shakespeare, it is not so much for what he did do, as for what he did not do, or refrained from doing. For in this world of lies, Truth is forced to fly like a scared white doe in the woodlands; and only by cunning glimpses will she reveal herself, as in Shakespeare and other masters of the great Art of Telling the Truth,— even though it be covertly, and in snatches. (1159–60)

This passage is one of the great displays of Melville's powerfully synthetic habits of mind, and more particularly of his use of reading as a means to mental realization. His former reading stays livingly present to Melville, such that when he wants to grasp a new mental stimulus he instinctively moves to fuse it with other ones: Hawthorne is known, here, in conjunction with Shakespeare, but also with an array of uncited sources. (Carlyle's "The Hero as Prophet" is a palpable presence in this passage. So is Evert Duyckinck's 1845 essay on Hawthorne, where Melville would have found this passage: "No conventionalist art thou, or respecter of show and outside, but as keensighted a moralist as tempest-stricken Lear whose sagacity flashes forth from his exceedingly vexed soul like the lightning from the storm-driven clouds.")[25] At the same time that he amalgamates work with work, Melville also draws this amassing whole of his reading directly into the sphere of his own deepest preoccupations, such that the texts of his reading become at once saturated with those concerns and made an imagery in which those concerns can be thought through.

What Melville synthesizes through this process is a highly articulated notion of literature as a prophetical activity. In this passage's glowing conception great artists have the gift to pierce through what passes for reality and to know a more essential order people's ordinary sense of things excludes. Their power and their office, then, is to deliver knowledge of this alienated reality back to the world that would forget it. And the way they know, as the way they deliver knowledge, is through their special use of the word. Literature's special form of language, when its power is fully realized, becomes a flashing-forth or *speaking* of vital truth. The art created through such a language neither imitates the familiar world nor fabricates an aesthetic replacement for it but bears witness to what is—a great Art of Telling the Truth.

Literature seriously considered as a prophetical activity is a new idea to

Melville—more properly, is an idea we watch Melville in the act of conceiving—in "Hawthorne and His Mosses." And if this essay is almost uncontrollably euphoric, it is because the idea Melville forges here has such immediate and profound bearings on his own urgent obsessions. This notion of literary prophecy has the peculiar power to take the confused strains of Melville's post-*Mardi* idea of authorship up into itself and there fuse them into a coherent literary program. More, it has the power, in so doing, to supply those urges with the validation they had anxiously lacked. Within a conception like this, it becomes seriously *thinkable* that the will to writing Melville called "something unmanageable" might be no stray compulsion but a privileged inner prompting, the pressure of the Word one has been specially chosen to speak. In that case unleashing that urge to expression would represent no mere self-indulgence, as *Mardi* feared itself to be, but a high obedience to a specially appointed vocation. *What* that expression brings forth—the speculation *Mardi* loves but fears may be only pompous pseudoprofundity—could be seriously identified as new or neglected Truth: that grasp of ultimate things it is such speakers' privilege to deliver. And the problem of audience could be rethought too. In "Hawthorne and His Mosses" Melville is still obsessed with the difference between "circumscribed renown" (1159) and "mere mob renown" (1160). But as he works out this prophetical conception Melville transforms his old and quite vulnerable ideas of high and low into ones that require no actual, historical audience to confirm the writer's high purposes. The mere mob is unreceptive in Melville's new thinking not because it is lowbrow or culturally unenlightened but because, like ordinary humanity to the prophet's eyes, it *refuses the Truth*. Conversely, great art is great not because it is an artistic achievement but because it is possessed of the Truth. That it is not received, that it thrusts itself against the acceptances of its hearers, is the chief proof *of* its truth—the mark that it possesses that higher spiritual authority that sets the prophet apart.

In the idea of prophetical authorship, Melville's disruptive artistic impulses get *justified*. They get made into the central elements of another *kind* of writing, a kind carrying the most extreme form of privilege Melville can imagine. This is why, once Melville has fully seized this idea, his essay turns from a work of criticism into a virtual hymn of self-annunciation. The ostensible subject of "Hawthorne and His Mosses' " second half is America's coming cultural independence, but in reality Melville borrows the millennial rhetoric of 1840s American nationalism to announce the actual practicability, in the contemporary American world, of that spiritually potent authorship he has just dreamed. Baptist-like, Melville here proclaims that the "coming of the literary Shiloh of America" (1169) has already taken place, that our "American Shiloh, or 'master Genius' " (1169) is even now with us—in Hawthorne, as unrecognized in our midst as Christ was by the Jews he lived among (1154, 1162). And he manages his annunciation of Hawthorne in such a way as to make Hawthorne imply the advent of other writers of comparable power. "I commend to you, in the first place, Nathaniel Hawthorne" (1165), Melville proclaims—Hawthorne, that is, as he implies others coming behind him. He ends the essay prophesying, on the basis of Hawthorne, a plural incarnation of genius, a general infusion of literary-spiritual power that could live in him as well:

> May it not be, that this commanding mind has not been, is not, and never will be, individually developed in any one man? And would it, indeed, appear so unreasonable to suppose, that this great fullness and overflowing may be, or may be destined to be, shared by a plurality of men of genius? (1169)

The action of "Hawthorne and His Mosses" is of Melville first thinking a new idea of authorship, then, on the basis of that thought. emboldening himself to assert his own literary-prophetical vocation. And when we know this, we know Hawthorne's power for Melville. When they met in 1850, Hawthorne moved into the highly charged field of Melville's authorial anxieties and ambitions. Projecting these concerns out onto Hawthorne, Melville seemed to see *in* Hawthorne the kind of writer he aspired to be. And recognizing the "real" Hawthorne the world had mistaken enabled Melville to re-cognize his own potential literary identity: to attain to a new conception of literature's possible power, a conception that could legitimate the most extreme of his presumptions. To Melville Hawthorne hereafter stood as he who incarnated, and so showed the living, present possibility of, literary power prophetically imagined, and as he who licensed Melville's belief that such power might be his to claim.

The most telling evidence that the prophetical conception of authorship is what bound these two writers together, at least on Melville's side, is found in their so-called personal relationship. Melville, I have said, opened himself to Hawthorne in unprecedented ways. But it might be more helpful to say that he specialized a certain version of himself for presentation to Hawthorne. Among the other selves he can also be, the one Melville displays to Hawthorne always has certain sharply particularizing features: it is hyperenergized; it readily shifts into what might be called the gear of transcendence, an overdrive that thrusts beyond immediate occasions to cosmic or ontological topics; and it gets caught up in an endless forward movement of conception as it engages those topics. ("I can't stop yet" is the regular refrain of his letters.) This is the Melville we see in "Hawthorne and His Mosses." This is the Melville we find in every one of his letters to Hawthorne. And this is, by abundant testimony, the Melville Hawthorne always met in conversation. Already in February 1851 Melville is saying that the "pleasure" of a visit from Hawthorne is "getting him up in my snug room here, & discussing the Universe with a bottle of brandy & cigars." In May 1851 Sophia Hawthorne writes that "to Mr Hawthorne [Melville] speaks his innermost about GOD, the Devil & Life if so be he can get at the Truth," then adds: "Nothing pleases me better than to sit & hear this growing man dash his tumultuous waves of thought up against Mr Hawthorne's great, genial, comprehending silences." In August 1851, after Melville came over to spend his birthday with Hawthorne, Hawthorne records:

> After supper, I put Julian to bed; and Melville and I had a talk about time and eternity, things of this world and of the next, and publishers, and all possible and impossible matters, that lasted pretty deep into the night. . . .

Even five years later, when their close friendship had already been over for four years, the person who called on Hawthorne in Liverpool is still the same old Melville:

> We soon found ourselves on pretty much our former terms of sociability and confidence. . . . Melville, as he always does, began to reason of Providence and futurity, and of everything that lies beyond human ken, and informed me that he had "pretty much made up his mind to be annihilated"; but still he does not seem to rest in that anticipation; and, I think, will never rest until he gets hold of a definite belief.[26]

Melville obviously thought of Hawthorne as inviting or sponsoring a particular form of communication. And, very strikingly, the self Melville expressed toward Hawthorne is what we must call his prophetic self: the driven or compelled speaker, wildly unpopular in his conceptions, to whom God and Devil, "visable truth" and cosmic Powers are immediately present. The surviving letters, our chief record of the "ontological heroics"[27] Melville directed toward Hawthorne, are charged with this vein of speech, and return obsessively to the idea of the prophet's power and situation. The letter of 16 April 1851—written in response to Hawthorne's gift of *The House of the Seven Gables*—is a perfect piece of that overheated, heaven-aspiring, and forwardly driving style that is the Hawthorne style for Melville. ("What's the reason, Mr. Hawthorne, that in the last stages of metaphysics a fellow always falls to *swearing* so? I could rip an hour," it concludes.) It also puts forward (again identifying it as Hawthorne) a yet bolder version of the "Mosses" essay's heroic figure—a man who takes his stand on his own deep sense of things, over against both the mystifications of the cosmos and the deceived affirmations of ordinary thought: "There is the grand truth about Nathaniel Hawthorne. He says NO! in thunder; but the Devil himself cannot make him say *yes*. For all men who say *yes*, lie."[28] A letter eight weeks later links the writer even more directly to the prophet as persecuted bearer of alienated truth:

> Try to get a living by the Truth—and go to the Soup Societies. Heavens! Let any clergyman try to preach the Truth from its very stronghold, the pulpit, and they would ride him out of his church on his own pulpit bannister. It can hardly be doubted that all Reformers are bottomed upon the truth, more or less; and to the world at large are not reformers almost universally laughingstocks? Why so? Truth is ridiculous to men. . . . Though I wrote the Gospels in this century, I should die in the gutter.[29]

(By now Melville has worked his idea of the prophetic back to its radical Protestant sources. The accents here are those of Frank Lloyd Wright's militantly religious grandfather, whose motto was "TRUTH AGAINST THE WORLD"; or even of Milton, who calls Enoch in *Paradise Lost:*

> The only righteous in a World perverse,
> And therefore hated, therefore so beset
> With Foes for daring single to be just,
> And utter odious Truth.)[30]

Melville's relation to Hawthorne, I would be the last to deny, was played out on many levels, and in many moods. But the whole of that relation was framed within a dominant structure, on Melville's side at least. What structured this relation—and what Melville therefore had at stake on its success—was the concept of the real possibility of the prophetical artistic career. Hawthorne impressed Melville because he seemed to embody the writer gifted to know and speak hidden truths, if only covertly and by snatches. He drew Melville to him because he seemed seriously to allow what Melville was most ambitious to do. He seemed to license Melville to speak and write as he felt compelled to, in confident hope that such speaking might be of transcendent spiritual weight.

The reason we pay attention to Melville and Hawthorne's encounter is that just after this encounter, and in some crucial way in the wake of it, Melville undertook to write the book that became *Moby-Dick.* The facts of this matter are well known. In May 1850 Melville claimed to be half-done with a book that appears to have treated his whaling years on the same terms that *White-Jacket* had treated his naval experience. By late June Melville wrote to his English publisher that he would have a romance of the sperm whale fishery done by autumn. On August 7 (two days after the Hawthorne—Melville meeting) Evert Duyckinck, Melville's houseguest, reported that Melville had "a romantic, fanciful & literal & most enjoyable presentment of the Whale Fishery" "mostly done."[31] But then, for the second time in his career, Melville changed his determinations. He so massively reconceived the book he was writing that it took him another full year of driving labor to complete it (this, from the author who wrote *Redburn* in eight weeks); and, in its new form, the book that had been "most enjoyable" to Duyckinck the summer before had become annoying and disturbing to him instead.[32]

The reconceived *Moby-Dick* was written in Hawthorne's near neighborhood, during the time of Melville's close involvement with Hawthorne. And it is clear that Melville regarded it too as part of that special kind of communication Hawthorne seemed to sponsor. He entrusted Hawthorne with *Moby-Dick*'s "motto (the secret one)—Ego non baptiso te in nomine— but make out the rest yourself"; when the book was finished, he dedicated it to Hawthorne; and when Hawthorne read it understandingly, Melville announced that in its proper form it would have been written just to Hawthorne as its audience fit, though few:

> I should have a paper-mill established at one end of the house, and so have an endless riband of foolscap rolling in upon my desk; and upon that endless riband I should write a thousand—a million—billion thoughts, all under the form of a letter to you.[33]

Rarely has one writer's great book been so variously bound to another, contemporaneous author as *Moby-Dick* is to Hawthorne. But it is a further measure of the nature of this relation that, in each of these instances, Melville specifically ties *Moby-Dick* to Hawthorne by way of the concept of authorship born in "Hawthorne and His Mosses." The motto Melville shares is thus a "secret" one: part of that covert, deeply *un*public, ordinary-belief-inverting communication Melville there says great truth tellers exchange. His dedication is to Hawthorne "In Token of my admiration for his genius": that quasi-autonomous faculty, in his essay's thinking, whereby "spiritual truth" lodges "in" (1160) such authors. Most crucially, when Melville is gratified by Hawthorne's response to *Moby-Dick,* his pleasure takes the quite specific form of literary-prophetical confirmation. His letter of thanks casts Hawthorne as the audience specially empowered to confirm that his wildest authorial ambitions are warranted by his work. What Hawthorne saw to praise, as Melville imagines it, was less the book than the spirit that impelled it—a spirit he then links to classical figures of inspiration and divine possession:

> You did not care a penny for the book. But, now and then as you read, you understood the pervading thought that impelled the book—and that you praised. Was it not so? You were archangel enough to despise the imperfect body, and embrace the soul. Once you hugged the ugly Socrates because you saw the flame in his mouth, and heard the rushing of the demon,—the familiar,—and recognized the sound; for you have heard it in your own solitudes.

Since, in aspiring to such a privileged identity, Melville had run the risk of accepting a seriously insane self-identification, Hawthorne's recognition of the authenticity of his genius brings not gratified vanity but something much more intense: "unspeakable security." And since Hawthorne's own incarnation of genius has recognized a parallel incarnation in Melville, these two have become not fellow-artists merely but joint manifestations of the spirit:

> Whence come you, Hawthorne? By what right do you drink from my flagon of life? And when I put it to my lips—lo, they are yours and not mine. I feel that the Godhead is broken up like the bread at the Supper, and that we are the pieces. Hence this infinite fraternaty of feeling.[34]

I may seem to be waxing mystical when I say that, at the time of *Moby-Dick,* Melville made Hawthorne the guarantor of his literary-prophetical identity. But that is what Melville claims in this climactic letter to Hawthorne (the only non-family letter he ever signed "Herman"). And if we take this notion seriously, we get a much more adequate notion of how exactly Hawthorne affected the writing of *Moby-Dick*. The question what Hawthorne did for *Moby-Dick* has produced such answers as that he "fortified" Melville, that he made Melville "feel full of possibility," that he inspired Melville with "psychic energy and poise," "euphoria" and "confidence," and these things are all well said.[35] But what we can add here is that Hawthorne chiefly gave Melville these powers by enabling him to believe in the practicability, as an organizing idea for his work, of the prophetical model of literary authorship. There would have been no *Moby-Dick* without the accession, in Melville, of new levels of intellectual, imaginative, and rhetorical energy. And it was Melville's ability seriously to identify himself with this exhilarating concept, I would argue, that unleashed *Moby-Dick*'s new energies of thought and speech. Writing *Moby-Dick* did indeed take fortitude: it was an act of serious risk for Melville to divert a year's labor into a project of this sort, this time in full knowledge of the support he would thereby forgo. (We do not commonly remember that Melville contracted a $2050 loan at 9% interest while writing this book.)[36] And it was his ability to believe that his self-willed, publicly unsupported writing efforts had the exalted value this concept promised, I would claim, that gave him the courage to write "the other way." Hawthorne's gift to Melville was not so much that he outlined the book *Moby-Dick* as that he helped Melville think the terms on which he could become the writer of *Moby-Dick*. He helped Melville realize himself as a writer on an altered basis: if Melville (in Jehlen's words) assumed himself in his writing, took himself seriously, made himself a point to stand on outside and against his culture's affirmations, it was by embracing the prophetical conception of his art that he became able to do so.

The way Hawthorne acts on Melville's plan of authorship determines such influence as Hawthorne has inside this text. In approaching *Moby-Dick* it is important not to overstate Hawthorne's directing presence. The author of *Moby-Dick* is an author of very various gifts, few of which can find their likenesses in Hawthorne: Melville would look in vain, in Hawthorne's work, for models for *Moby-Dick*'s sort of inventive pedantry, or violent physical action, or racy cross-cultural comedy, or self-delighted rhetorical display. But one strand of this book does show Hawthorne's direct and decisive influence: Melville's figuring of his hero, and of the action he projects. All evidence suggests that Ahab and his quest were conceived into *Moby-Dick* after Melville rethought this work in late 1850. When Ahab is first invoked, he is imaged in the idiom of the heroic tradition at large. But when Melville reaches the point where he needs to specify the motives for Ahab's quest and the status it is to have as a statement about the world, he turns very directly to Hawthorne as an aid to conception.

As he looks to Hawthorne's fiction from the vantage of his new project, Melville's interests become much more tightly focussed than they were in

"Hawthorne and His Mosses." He now identifies Hawthorne with a handful of tales, and within them, with a single figure. The mark of this figure, as Melville reconstructs him, is that he has passed through a radical reorganization of selfhood, a process at once of extreme intensification and extreme reduction. In the chapters "Moby Dick" and "The Chart" Melville twice rehearses, in explicating Ahab's motive, a transformation repeatedly replayed in Hawthorne ("Ethan Brand" and the analysis of Chillingworth in Chapter 10 of *The Scarlet Letter* provide its classic versions)—a self-fracturing or self-fractioning whereby a faculty that has existed alongside others in an integrated personality suddenly separates itself off and assumes what Melville calls an "independent being of its own." (1007)[37] This now-independent faculty next extends its domination over the rest of the self, absorbing its collective powers into its one form of agency—as Ethan Brand's "intellect" absorbs the energies of "heart"; or as, in the "furious trope" of *Moby-Dick*, Ahabs "special lunacy stormed his general sanity, and carried it, and turned all its concentred cannon upon its own mad mark." (991) What results is a prodigious concentration of being, in which the desires available for the ordinary self's various projects get fixed and focussed on one object, and the energies available for the self's various moves get redirected into movement toward one end. What was once a person is now a project. Living becomes, for the hero thus transformed, a drive along the straight line toward a goal (so Ahab can say: "the path to my fixed purpose is laid with iron rails, whereon my soul is grooved to run." [972]) So consolidated are his being and his object that we name him fully in naming his goal: Ahab *is* he who hunts the White Whale, as Ethan Brand *is* he who searches for the Unpardonable Sin.

The figure (in a phrase Melville repeats from Hawthorne) mastered by one Idea, and compelled, by his Idea, to the unswerving execution of an inflexible program, is not, of course, Hawthorne's exclusive invention. The structure of selfhood I describe Melville as imitating from Hawthorne Angus Fletcher finds in all of allegory: Fletcher likens allegory's simplified agents to figures possessed by a daimon,* that form of intermediate deity whose effect as it descends on the human self is to narrow it to one function and direct it to one end.[38] The consolidation of the self that Hawthorne's fiction displays is also a standard feature of the gothic—I think of Godwin's Caleb Williams, who slips as easily from having ideas to being had by Ideas as Ethan Brand ("it was but a passing thought. And yet . . . the idea once having occurred to my mind, it was fixed there forever"); or I think of Frankenstein, like Ahab and Chillingworth both agent and victim of an idea that converts wholeness of being into a will for one thing ("one by one the various keys were touched that formed the mechanism of my being; chord after chord was sounded, and soon my mind filled with

---

* Melville, who knows this concept both from Goethe and from its classical roots, spells it "demon," as in his reference to "the rushing of [Socrates's] demon,—his familiar"; but I will continue to use spellings based on the alternate form "daimon," to make clear that the devil and the diabolical are not being referred to.

one thought, one conception, one purpose.")[39] But what Melville marks in Hawthorne is the fusion of monomania as a personality type with a peculiar mode of figuration. In Hawthorne the self recentered within a single faculty sees the world recentered in a parallel way. Its attention fixes on a single object, which it lifts out of the continuum of objects and makes into the sign of its obsession. Aylmer, the perfectionist bridegroom of "The Birthmark," isolates and resignifies Georgiana's facial blemish in this way, projecting his inward preoccupations upon it in such manifold and insistent ways (Hawthorne says that he connects it "with innumerable trains of thought, and modes of feeling")[40] as to convert it into a figure for the sum of his dreads, "the symbol of his wife's liability to sin, sorrow, decay, and death." He is in this the prototype for Hawthorne's idea-possessed men, who in the moment that they succumb to obsession also find an object—Reverend Hooper's black veil, Roderick Elliston's bosom serpent, Arthur Dimmesdale's scarlet letter—in which obsession lodges as an overdetermined meaning. Melville has clearly noticed the conjunction of monomania and figure-making in Hawthorne, because when he recreates Hawthorne's account of the daimonic consolidation of the self in *Moby-Dick,* he insists that its products are a pathology and a metaphor. According to Melville, Ahab's loss of his leg to Moby Dick generates a rage that activates and absorbs every other possible form of human rage until rage is so intense that it achieves a fusion of previously separate things, makes Ahab *"identify* with [the whale], not only all his bodily woes, but all his intellectual and spiritual exasperations." (989) As if still struggling to grasp this notion Melville runs through every way he can think of to say that Ahab's madness is a madness of metaphor: "the White Whale swam before him as the *monomaniac incarnation* of all those malicious agencies which some deep men feel eating in them"; or again: *"deleriously transferring* its idea to the abhorred white whale"; or again: "all evil, to *crazy* Ahab, was visibly *personified,* and made practically assailable in Moby Dick." (989; my italics)

The curious thing about emblem-makers in Hawthorne is that although it is clear, both to themselves and others, that the meanings they read into their chosen objects originate in an act of obsessive projection, once that projection is completed it takes on an oddly objective and authoritative status. Aylmer selects the birthmark as the symbol for a human condition that he cannot accept, but once he has done so neither Georgiana nor Hawthorne can work free of the notion that this is indeed the birthmark's meaning. Reverend Hooper converts a black veil into the symbol of that secret sin the knowledge of which torments him, but when he presents his neurotic emblem before others it takes on an "awful power"—the power to disclose them to themselves as the secret sinners Hooper claims them to be. Roderick Elliston, the chief case in Hawthorne of what might be called the symbolist as aggressor, thrusts his bosom serpent upon others as their meaning—he "mak[es] his own actual serpent . . . the type of each man's fatal error, or hoarded sin, or unquiet conscience." But the effect of this energetic self-projection is to bring forward the serpent that is them—"by obtruding his own bosom-serpent to the public gaze" he "drag[s] those of decent people from their lurking-places."[41]

Obsession in Hawthorne, this is to say, is associated not just with figuration but with figuration as a means to knowledge. The Hawthornesque obsessive deforms reality, subjects it to a perverse pressure that distorts and violates its familiar contours; but through this deformation he discovers another state of things that is instantly known to be more deeply real, and that is not to be known otherwise than through his obsessive deformations. Similarly, the Hawthornesque symbolist is a pure projectionist, writing out onto the world a condition that starts within himself; but through his projections he brings a real and general condition to expression, one that is not available except through his expressive projections.

The descent from here to Ahab is clear: for Ahab is above all a knower, and a knower on the same terms that Hawthorne's heroes are. Like Elliston or Hooper, he is a testifier: he embodies a statement of how things are in the world. Like them, his statement has no referent in the visible world. *He knows by his obsession:* he knows what he knows by his rage, as Hooper knows what he knows by his guilt. But the lack of objective external sanction for his frantic projection does not make it less authoritative. He is mad and therefore sees another world than the one we see—in Ahab's case, sees malign gods where we see only natural processes. But although it is known to be the product of insanity, this antithetical vision carries the power to make others recognize that they too know its truth. So it is that Ahab's insane symbolization can make the faithful Starbuck acknowledge life's "latent horror"; so it is that his insane quest can present itself to Ishmael as "mine." (973, 983)

Here it begins to come clear, I think, what Melville is finding in Hawthorne as he writes *Moby-Dick*. When Melville looks back to Hawthorne at this time, it is with a clarified will to practice a Hawthornesque mode of prophetical authorship—but also with a new curiosity, we might surmise, about how such authorship expresses itself inside a text. If the daimonized hero fixes and fascinates him now, it is because he seems to incarnate, in an imitable textual structure, such authorship's essential action: the process by which an ordinary self gets seized by an imperious will, becoming the witness, through this mastery, to a reality ordinary reality denies. Melville identifies the daimonic hero both with his prophetical ambitions and as the fictional structure that might express such ambitions. And this idea governs the way he transforms this figure as well.

With the Hawthornesque sources of Ahab as in "Hawthorne and His Mosses," Melville's way is to seize the operative idea of work that impresses him as quickly as he can, then to amalgamate it with many other sources, struggling, through the vigor or even violence of such conjunctions, to release the whole form of the concept each source partially expresses. At the same time that he recomposes this figure from Hawthorne, then, Melville freely assimilates it with every other form of strong selfhood he can call to mind: with Milton's Satan, Shakespeare's Lear and Macbeth, Tamburlaine, Prometheus, Goethe and Carlyle's myths of the hero, and so on.[42] (What other character in literature is *alluded* into being so much as Ahab is?) Through this process, Melville drives Hawthorne's hero-as-obsessive back into a full-scale heroic mode. Hawthorne's heroes are flattened by the daimons that seize them. But as Melville redraws this figure he makes it not two-dimensional but larger than life in the dimensions of its being. Reimagined on Melville's plan the obsessive hero becomes a character of authentic magnanimity, of greatly expanded powers of self-hood: great in its power of will, great in its power of reflection, great above all in its power of suffering. (Ahab never seems more outsized than when he lets out a "loud, animal sob, like that of a heart-stricken moose," or when, crushed by Moby Dick in his final pursuit, "far inland, nameless wails came from him, as desolate sounds from out ravines." [966, 1383])

As he magnifies Hawthorne's hero, Melville also drives back toward a deeper motive for this hero's unnatural selfhood. In Hawthorne daimonization is commonly a kind of fate, an irresistible process whose sources remain obscure. Aylmer's quest for mastery of nature is obviously rooted in some sort of elemental revulsion from our natural, mortal, embodied condition, but we learn nothing further about that revulsion: his inflection of character is simply *given*. But when Melville seizes on this sort of figure, he wants to know where its form of identity comes from; and in thinking this out he makes this character's extremely peculiar state be a response to our general condition, unmitigatedly faced. As Melville imagines him Ahab is against nature because he feels the full affront of the fact that nature is inhuman, is not structured as human things are, is not the world humans want and need—fully feels the fact (in Wallace Stevens's words) "that we live in a place / That is not our own and much more, not ourselves / And hard it is in spite of blazoned days." Ahab would assert his unconditional mastery over nature because he knows so unrelievedly that nature is our master: that it creates and uncreates (and mutilates) us without our will, that we are at best deposed heirs of the kingdom we feel we ought to rule.

Conjoining the obsessive hero with other heroic types, Melville restores him, we might say, to the great ground of his obsession. He restores him too to the tradition of great speech. Hawthorne's heroes express themselves largely symbolically. But by crossing this figure with the Miltonic and Shakespearean heroes of the great oration, Melville makes Ahab talk, as well, with real magniloquence. In particular he makes him, like Satan addressing the sun, or Lear on the heath, a great apostrophist: one who addresses the inanimate as if it were there to listen; and who makes that object be present as he speaks it, through the sheer power of his speech.

And it is through the raw lyricism of his addresses that Ahab speaks the world he knows. "Oh, thou dark Hindoo half of nature, who of drowned bones hast builded thy separate throne somewhere in the heart of these unverdured seas," Ahab prays in "The Dying Whale," "All thy unnamable imminglings float beneath me here; I am buoyed by breaths of once living things, exhaled as air, but water now." (1323) And as he speaks, the apparent world is supplanted by, then re-seen as the work of, a cosmic power Ahab alone knows: a power that is life-creating but not life-sustaining; seen as whose product inanimate nature is not matter merely, but the corpse of the life nature lets depart; so that we read, in every sight of inanimate nature, the promise of our own future extinction. In "The Candles," where the crew sees only the natural sublimity of St. Elmo's fire, Ahab sees another order: a god of pure force, nature ruled by a power perfectly omnipotent and perfectly impersonal. That god is present to Ahab—in the Carlylean phrase Melville superbly literalizes it glares or flares in upon Ahab[43]—but not to other men. But it gets *made* present to us, palpably and powerfully, through the power of Ahab's speech: the magnificent aria beginning "Oh! thou clear spirit of clear fire, . . . I own thy speechless, placeless power; but to the last gasp of my earthquake life will dispute it unconditional, unintegral mastery in me." (1333)

To a student of Hawthorne and Melville's relation, Ahab's profession of faith in unregenerating nature sounds like a more poetical version of Melville announcing that he had made up his mind to be annihilated. Ahab's address to Power in "The Candles" even more directly recalls Melville's "NO! in thunder" letter, with its vision of humanity as an assertion against the cosmic powers that would make it dependent. These resemblances are more than casual. For it is through Ahab, and more particularly through the heroic speech-function Melville devises for Ahab, that Melville's own prophetic strain finds expression in *Moby-Dick*. In building his monomaniac hero Melville traces a figure he finds outlined in Hawthorne. Vigorously expanding on it, he gives this figure powers it never had in Hawthorne's original. But it is exactly through this construction that he gives vent to what he thinks of as Hawthorne's sort of artistic assertion. This is how his own work unfolds a "background," makes an obscure further order seem directly present in the apparent world. This is how he speaks a world alien to common understanding, realized to us through his utterance. This is how he makes himself what Hawthorne let him dream: the writer who grasps and reveals an unseen world, through the special action of his speech.

Melville of course distances himself from his prophetic impulse by putting it in the character of Ahab. And if that impulse gets expressed in *Moby-Dick,* it is also powerfully contained. A Hawthornesque or prophetic reading of *Moby-Dick* always tends to understate the dominance, over the great mass of the book, of Ishmael: of a voice that knows that its dives cannot escape from the domain of thought and language into ultimate reality; and that therefore can exploit the impulses of prophecy not to reach at Truth but to fuel exploratory, self-delighting mental play. But in terms of Melville's career, his prophetic yearnings, not the containment mechanisms he devises for them in *Moby-Dick,* have the greater staying power. In his next book those yearnings show themselves much more nakedly, seize a more imperious control of the work at hand, and so bring Melville to a literary crisis *Moby-Dick* managed not to reach.

Pierre follows a Hawthornesque original even less strictly than *Moby-Dick* does, but it too organizes itself around the kind of action Melville links with Hawthorne above all. The plot Melville constructs here turns on a young man's discovery of his illegitimate sister and, through that, of the illicit sexual life of his idealized father. Melville tries hard to make this plot carry the burden of the sort of initiation he regards as Hawthornesque. (Isabel, Pierre's beckoner into new knowledge, lives, as Hawthorne did in 1851, in a red rural cottage, prominently adorned with two other Hawthorne emblems: mosses and gables.) Pierre's discovery of illicit parental sexuality, as Melville describes it, opens his eyes to a heretofore-hidden blackness of life in general, a "darker, though truer aspect of things." (84)[44] The revelation of this buried order immediately also shows Pierre that reality as he has known it has been a matter only of "hereditary forms and world-usages" (108), a cultural convention-system organized to keep this "truer aspect" out of sight. ("Men are jailers all; jailers of themselves" [110], Pierre cries, in profound echo of Hawthorne's vision of the social contract as a league of mutual repression.) And as it produces this revision of social reality Pierre's discovery also brings a transformation of self. As Pierre comes to know "the hidden things" (80) an "incipient offspring" begins 'foetally forming in him." (128) This new self wrests Pierre from the world of ordinary social engagements and remakes him as that trans-social or transcendent self who "know[s] what *is*." (80) As it does so it makes him too a man with a mission: against "the diving and ducking moralities of this earth" to "square myself by the inflexible rule of holy right" (129), and so to enact the true law of brotherhood in a world that refuses to know that law.

Melville works many new sources and conceptions into his retelling of the story of daimonization in *Pierre*.[45] But the most interesting difference in this book's treatment of this now-familiar process is that in *Pierre* daimonization is so much more undisguisedly linked with Melville's own artistic ambitions. Pierre like Ahab is a "profound willfulness" (393), but this time that willfulness is very intimately linked to the strain of personal messianism so marked in Melville's literary thinking after *Mardi*. Pierre's self-within-a-self is a "heaven-begotten Christ" (128) born within him, another version, that is, of the new Messiah Melville looked for in "Shakespers person" and the "literary Shiloh" whose coming haunts "Hawthorne and His Mosses." As it links up with Melville's strong christological urges (Melville was in his thirty-third year when he wrote *Pierre*), Pierre's special incarnation ties itself too to Melville's aspirations to literary genius. The "accession of the personal divine" in Pierre drives him in one way to lead a life of Christlike sacrifice, but in another to undertake a "deep book." (355) And the literary ambitions that propel this book are, transparently, those of Melville's own prophetical yearnings. Pierre's "burning desire" as a writer is "to deliver what he thought to be new, or at least

miserably neglected Truth to the world" (329), or as he even more exalt-
edly declares, "I will gospelize the world anew, and show them deeper
secrets than the Apocalypse!" (319) (Compare Melville to Hawthorne:
"Though I wrote the Gospels in this century, I should die in the gutter.")

That web of highly charged aspirations that entered Melvillean authorship with *Mardi,* then reached their crisis of self-acceptance when Melville
met Hawthorne, are directly implicated in the plot of *Pierre*'s career. And
as if because they surface here in such undisguised form, Melville finds
these ambitions considerably harder to control. *Pierre,* a book full of ideas
about how it might organize itself, has some quite brilliant notions of how
it might contain the will to prophecy this time around. It has obviously
occurred to Melville to try to read Pierre's prophetical impulses sociohis-
torically, as by-products of the new form of family life gaining ground in
his time. It has also occurred to him to study these impulses psychologi-
cally, in terms of the mind's self-disguise of its illicit desires. (In this phase
of his project Melville has *The Scarlet Letter* quite directly before him.)
But such plans get abrogated in *Pierre*—and abrogated, quite visibly, by
the resurgence of the prophetical will itself. Pierre, once treated in part as
a victim of domestic culture or of sexual self-deception, increasingly becomes a "noble soul" persecuted by the "dastardly world" (315) as the
book goes on. As this happens the book falls increasingly into Pierre's own
prophetical frame of vision—into a vision antagonistic, self-pitying, and
addicted to stark, transcendently abstract moral polarizations, as in: "The
wide world is banded against him; for lo you! he holds up the standard of
Right, and swears by the Eternal and True!" (315)

What *Pierre* charts—and harrowingly, because in full knowledge that its
own governing ambitions are its real subject—is the story of where the
prophetical impulse leads, when embraced so unrestrainedly. In this respect it is the story, for one thing, of the spiritual and even physical de-
structiveness of ambitions so defined. The accession of the personal divine
produces no new gospel in *Pierre,* but rather the drainage, from the bearer,
of the energies of ordinary life. "Gifted with loftiness" (393)—the phrase
can remind us of Ahab, "gifted with the high perception," but also of Melville's own assurance of "higher purposes"—Pierre suffers the diseases of
excessive elevation: the "superhuman" (361) is associated, in late *Pierre,*
with the bad transcendence of living women turned to "marble girl[s]"
(415) or of the amaranth flower, sterile and immortal. Pierre himself
shows the final yield of his election and elevation when, in a really fright-
ening passage, he becomes simply affectless, dead to stimuli of any sort—
"utterly without sympathy from any thing divine, human, brute, or vege-
table" (392); then, in an intensification even of this, devitalized in the
radical sense: "he did not have any ordinary life-feeling at all." (395).

As it wrecks its bearer's common life, the ambition *Pierre* studies and
is sick with wreaks a corresponding violence on its own transcendent goals.
The mark of Pierre's prophetical incarnation is that he organizes his life in
harsher and ever-more-abstracted polarities. But it is the nature of these

polarities that, when insisted on in such absolute form, they collapse in on themselves. "Henceforth I will know nothing but Truth" (80), Pierre declares at his prophetical awakening. Nothing is so inspiring to him as "to think of the Truth and the Lie!" (353) (Compare Melville: "For in this world of lies, Truth is forced to fly. . . .") But when he so relentlessly stakes himself on the existence of a Truth he never attains, the very notion of a deep or essential reality explodes itself—"Truth" shows its "everlasting elusiveness" (393)—and the antithesis True/False annihilates itself as a form of significant opposition. "To follow Virtue to her uttermost vista, where common souls never go" (318), in a parallel discovery, is to reach not the place of the Right but the place where Virtue and Vice collapse into indistinguishable "trash," then into empty "nothing." (319) In literary terms, to insist strongly enough on the opposition between the "deep book" and "some shallow nothing of a novel" (355) produces not a realized Art of Truth but a collapse of the deeps into the shallows and of all writing into "coiner's book[s]." (414) Promising to lead to a perfect authenticity of life, knowing, and speaking, prophecy's animating conceit leads instead to an explosion of its own organizing concepts, abolishing, in the process, the mental equipment whereby any kind of significant direction or opposition could be thought. Its end is the "neuter" (418) condition, a white world of perfect undifferentiability:

> it is not for man to follow the trail of truth too far, since by so doing he entirely loses the directing compass of his mind; for arrived at the Pole, to whose barrenness only it points, there, the needle indifferently respects all points of the horizon alike. (196)

What *Pierre* demonstrates—in full knowledge that it does not thereby escape from this predicament—is the inherent tendency of a prophetical conception of authorship to collapse its own ground. And this lesson has a larger application than to Melville's case alone. After all, Melville is not the only author of his time to organize his work around a prophetical literary conception. This conception is equally central to such exact contemporaries of Melville's as Whitman, or Thoreau, or Jones Very (who intermittently believed he was the Second Coming.)[46] Historically, this is *the* other literary self-conception, besides the domestic one, operative in American writing of the 1850s. It is the other idea writers there could find ready access to, to motivate their work. And it is the idea that released what, along with the new popular literature of domesticity, is the other authentic literary product of the American 1850s: that massively individuated, morally as well as formally innovative writing, unpurchased by the public but undaunted by its lack of public support, of which *Moby-Dick, Leaves of Grass,* and *Walden* are the three great examples. (Harriet Beecher Stowe, who spent some time in later life trying to plot out a tradition of female prophecy, authorizes the assertion of *Uncle Tom's Cabin* through this conception too, and so shows that the prophetic and domestic strains of 1850s authorship could be combined.) Melville's case demon-

strates what it is about this authorial conception that lets it activate a literature of these features. His case shows how this conception excites and
energizes the writer, defends him against the public's wishes, and warrants
him to believe that his most eccentric impulses are the ones he is most
bound to pursue. But his case also dramatizes the fact that the same features that equip this conception to unleash such unconventional imaginative energies also make it unsustaining, as a program of authorship. *Pierre*
shows that the conception of prophecy, promising to release him from the
world of lies or fictions, tempts its bearer to embrace it as an actual identity, not a temporarily assumed role, but that it is a psychic and artistic
disaster when so embraced. (Jones Very and Hawthorne's demented de-
votee Delia Bacon—witness to the truth that the *real* Shakespeare was not
Shakespeare—show the real-life consequences of taking prophetical appointment too literally.) *Pierre* also suggests that it is the nature of the
prophetical conception, when persisted in, to demand of the author more
than he can create—and so to stymie the labor it first inspired. We might
read, in this, the reason why the American careers founded on this conception take the form of short bursts of dazzling creativity followed by increasingly impaired efforts to renew that level of achievement—Whitman's
and Thoreau's pattern as it is Melville's. (This pattern persists for the
more modern writers who have been drawn to the prophetical literary conception—James Agee, James Baldwin, and Flannery O'Connor are three
very various examples.)

Since Melville entered into the idea of prophetical vocation by way of
Hawthorne, it might occur to us to ask, at this point, how Hawthorne
avoided the extremities Melville reaches in *Pierre*. And might not the
answer just be that Hawthorne stayed clear of the whole prophetic syndrome? As a personality structure and as a way of mobilizing personal belief and its expressions, prophetical selfhood is a powerful form in America in the 1850s. We need only read evangelical sermons or reformist
speeches of this time, or remember Henry Adams's claim that antislavery
threw Massachusetts back onto Puritan holy warfare,[47] to learn that what
we see in Melville, or Whitman, or Thoreau is only the more purely literary expression of a much more widespread cultural phenomenon. But
Hawthorne displays the prophetical personality about as little as anyone
one could name from his time. The evidence is that this is the one human
type he could least abide: I remember here Coverdale's ennui at Hollingsworth's "prolonged fiddling upon one string," or Hawthorne's remark on
John Brown, the great political avatar of the prophetic type in the 1850s,
that "nobody was ever more justly hanged."[48] Writing inspired by the idea
of prophecy is known at once by its air of intense conviction, and America
produced as much self-convicted writing in this decade as anyone would
ever care to read. But Hawthorne's writing is known by its feints and in-
directions, not its professions of its beliefs; in fact Hawthorne may be the
literary writer of his time whose writing is freest from such strains.

As the orientation point for his own prophetical program, this would imply, Melville lighted on the one major author of his time who was seriously immune to such authorship's attractions. And this would lead to a further conclusion that students of the Melville–Hawthorne relation must, at some point, face: namely, that Melville was just totally wrong about Hawthorne as an authorial model—so wrong, we might say, that it would take a genius to *be* so wrong. But another reading is possible as well. It would be easy to produce, from inside Hawthorne's writings, a massive censure and repudiation of prophetical ambitions. (What could Melville have thought when he read this, in *The House of the Seven Gables?* "Persons who have wandered, or been expelled, out of the common track of things, even were it for a better system, desire nothing so much as to be led back.")[49] But, as Melville noticed, Hawthorne shows a recurring fascination with art's possibly reality-disclosing power (as when Holgrave, in that same book, literally uncovers the "secret character" beneath the "merest surface" of his sitters' presented selves through his act of portraiture). And at times something very close to what Melville understands as prophecy seems to be taking place in Hawthorne's books. In the forest scene of *The Scarlet Letter,* for example, Hester (and the book she now seizes control of) is mastered by a powerful will; that will makes her strong in speech; and what that speaking does is first to disclaim the truth of merely social designations of obligation or value, then (on the authority of its own convictions) to *speak* a drastically revised moral covenant: "what we did had a consecration of its own."[50]

It is easy to see how Melville might read such a scene as literature, however covertly, gospelizing the world anew. But if we concede that energies like those of prophecy are at work in Hawthorne's writing, the crucial question then becomes on what terms those energies are entertained. Obviously, in *The Scarlet Letter* these energies are fiercely contained—contained first by Dimmesdale, who uses the vigor Hester inspires in him to re-deliver their love to the authority of the old law; then by Hester, who chooses to re-subject herself to the badge of censure she had removed in this scene; and throughout by the book itself, which, on every re-reading, always releases Hester's assertion as a living possibility, then always forbids it to become an achieved reality. Readers of Melvillean persuasions usually dislike this movement of limitation, taking it as sign of a failure of courage. But the logic of lost nerve is not really the logic of *The Scarlet Letter*'s return. After all, what generated Hester's powers of moral reimagination is the action of the law that condemned her. Before her punishment, Hester's illicit desires are strong enough to have led her into adultery. But it is her experience of legal condemnation, her constant, painful coercion into the category of the transgressive, that turns her vitalities "from passion and feeling, to thought,"[51] and so generates in her the much more powerfully transgressive free-*thinking* she achieves in the forest scene. But since her passionate counter-perception is itself the product of the orthodoxy it inverts, it cannot, as it tells itself in the forest scene, stand wholly apart from that scheme. Hester's imaginativeness is not a power by itself but one half of a larger structure the other part of which is the law that constrains her: the two forces, conceptually opposite, are grasped as interdependent and even mutually generative in the powerful thinking of *The Scarlet Letter*. When Hester resumes her letter, it is in no simple surrender to the authority of worldly law. It is in recognition of the inextricableness (imaged *in* her letter) of subversion from the authority that calls forth subversion, of freedom from the law whose breaking creates freedom's possibility, of imaginative creation from the restricting conventions that allow such creation to be.

Hawthorne's difference from his more overtly prophetical contemporaries, such an account would let us say, is not that his work is closed to prophetical energies, but that it eludes the conceptual commitments such energies bring along. Prophecy is the mode of fierce either/ors—of the Truth against the Lie, the Right against the Wrong—but Hawthorne exploits the energies of prophecy without accepting its schemes of mutually exclusive opposition. His work realizes the prophetical impulse neither as the Truth nor as a violation of the natural order but as part of a system whose elements imply and affirm their opposites: in which conventionality breeds anticonventional aggressions, imaginative assertion helps validate the shared conventional world, and so on.

Read in this way, Melville did not just get Hawthorne wrong: he got him right and wrong at the same time. By approaching Hawthorne in a prophetical mood, Melville was able to discover the authentically prophetic strains of Hawthorne's imagination. (Who else had even seen these before Melville?) But his own prophetical interests made Melville read this as the only true Hawthorne, so that in the act of grasping this aspect Melville also failed to grasp its allegiance to its apparent opposites. Melville got the full benefit of this mistaking. By reading Hawthorne as he did, Melville won crucial backing for his own, altogether more adventurous imaginative ambitions—backing to which we owe the realization of *Moby-Dick*. But this mistaking was not without its cost. In *Pierre* Melville reaches the point where prophecy's cherished idea of Truth manages first to delegitimate any kind of existing conventional structure as a Lie, then to explode the idea of Truth as a basis for work or thought. Melville's work might have averted this self-abolition if it had learned a different lesson in Hawthorne's school: that prophecy is most productive as an artistic program when it does not quite believe it knows the whole, grand truth.

I said before that Melville experienced Hawthorne as confirming his prophetical aspirations when he read and praised *Moby-Dick*. There is evidence that he experienced the later abortion of his prophetical career through Hawthorne's eyes as well.

One of the most powerful fantasies to emerge toward the end of *Pierre* is the cool, philosophical face of Plotinus Plinlimmon, leering at Pierre as he attempts to write. Virtually every detail of this portrait ties Plinlimmon to Melville's Hawthorne. Pierre has found Plinlimmon's work unmemorable, as Melville had found Hawthorne's, before he meets him in person. In his person, Plinlimmon has Hawthorne's blue eyes and famous detachment of manner. He has a "face of repose" (339), a standard word for Hawthorne's manner around 1850; his face is systematically voided of affect or expression, as Melville later remembered Hawthorne's to be (he writes in *Clarel:* "not responsive was Vine's cheer, / Discharged of every meaning sign"); his clothes, like his face, "seemed to disguise this man" (338) (compare Hawthorne on his publicly visible self in the newly written preface to *The Snow Image:* "these things hide the man, instead of displaying him.")[52] Plinlimmon's disengagement from his own feelings is haunting because it speaks a disengagement too from the life issues that might inspire strong feeling. Plinlimmon is honored as a profound thinker, but he himself prefers not to engage in philosophical speculation (as Hawthorne returned silence to Melville's energetic divings; Plinlimmon, possibly like Hawthorne, prefers his followers' champagne to their ontological heroics.) His only known philosophical position, expressed in his pamphlet "EI" or "Chronometricals and Horologicals," is that the ethical norms that prevail in the world are just communal conventions, radically disjoined from "Heaven's own Truth." But he affirms that both of these systems are valid in their own way, and that "by their very contradictions they are made to correspond." (249)

The power not to get vexed by the mysteries of life—the power not even to want to go into them—is what the ardently speculative Melville must have found incomprehensible in Hawthorne as their relation went on. And Plinlimmon's thought has just the feature Melville's must have found exasperating in Hawthorne's: the ability to affirm the simultaneous validity of apparently exclusive opposites, and specifically to affirm the value of the conventional in full knowledge that it is merely conventional. Plinlimmon, we might say, is Hawthorne reseen as something very different from a prophet; and this is what gives him his new, eerie power. Plinlimmon appears just after Pierre undertakes to write his truth-delivering deep book, and he appears as a nightmare-projection of such authorship's deep self-doubts: Pierre comes to believe that "by some magical means or other the face had got hold of his secret" (342), and sees Plinlimmon as silently mocking him for his presumptions. This, we can suppose, is how Hawthorne must have looked to Melville as he pressed on through *Pierre:* as a figure after all not engaged in his same project; but as the man who was in on the secret of his project; and so as one who knew him for an egotistical fool.

If my reading is right, it reminds us of how the personal side of Hawthorne and Melville's relation fed into and amplified its literary aspect. Hawthorne's reserve commonly made others feel that he was looking for them to initiate a relation. But then, when he failed to join in the exchange he seemed to invite, he made others feel embarrassed at their own sociability. (When Hawthorne died, Emerson lamented his lifelong failure to "conquer a friendship" with him: "It was easy to talk with him,—there were no barriers,—only, he said so little, that I talked too much, and stopped only because, as he gave no indications, I feared to exceed.")[53] Melville obviously went through this same cycle of feeling specially "drawn out" by Hawthorne's "sociable silences," then feeling reproached, by those same silences, for talking as he did.[54] But since he invested his authorial ambitions in his personal relation with Hawthorne, he set the end-points of this cycle at much greater extremes. Having projected his risky ambitions onto Hawthorne, Melville gave him the power, whenever he seemed responsive, to seem to be confirming his right to such aspirations: when Hawthorne liked *Moby-Dick,* Melville felt "unspeakable security." By the same token, whenever Hawthorne's silence seemed less than fully sociable, Melville felt his reserve as reservation about his artistic project—reservation truly devastating since it came from the figure chosen to underwrite that project's validity.

When Melville's authorship reaches the crisis it reaches in *Pierre,* and when Hawthorne becomes mixed up with such punishing self-criticisms in Melville's mind, we might assume that their relation is at its end. But Melville continued to look to Hawthorne in 1852 and 1853, as he struggled to find a way for his authorship to go on. The first writing project Melville undertook after *Pierre* was a work he outlined at length in a letter to Hawthorne and tried to get Hawthorne to write: the story of the patient fidelity of a Nantucket woman whose sailor-husband deserted her, then came back long after he was thought dead. The "Agatha" letters of 1852 show Melville again trying to plant an idea of authorship on Hawthorne, then to receive it back *from* Hawthorne as a project Hawthorne had invited him to. The letters show too how Melville felt after his great attempt at such a supporting exchange had failed: abandonment is the content of the Hawthorne relationship as the "Agatha" letters image it.

But in a sense the most interesting thing about the "Agatha" letters is that they show Melville paying attention to a new part of Hawthorne's work: to what Melville calls "your *London husband,*"[55] or the early tale "Wakefield." "Wakefield" is an intriguing tale for Melville to be thinking about because it renders the same Hawthornesque figure who had always fascinated Melville in a somewhat different way. Like Hooper, or Brand, or Ahab, or Pierre, Wakefield is a man found out by a fate, by an idea that descends on him, wrests him from the world of ordinary habits and relations, and compels him to unwavering adherence to a peculiar personal program. This is the familiar process of daimonization; but in "Wakefield" daimonization is a process almost perfectly opaque. Wakefield's personal program—to live one block away from home for twenty years while never going home—has no motivation even suggested for it. His program leads to no symbolic counter-expression: Wakefield is the hero as literally uncommunicative man. If his special fate makes Wakefield seem like a "figure" for some unknown truth of our condition, that truth remains almost perfectly elusive. Hawthorne hazards the moral that, by stepping out of our social places even for a moment, "a man exposes himself to a fearful risk of losing his place forever."[56] But Wakefield remains a fascinating freak, impressive because so little susceptible to explication.

"Wakefield" presents Hawthorne's daimonic agent acting in a reversed role—as a figure not of assertive will but of withdrawal and passivity, and as the bearer not of revelation but of mystery itself. The lesson is not lost on Melville. In "Bartleby the Scrivener," the first work he published after *Pierre,* Melville creates his own version of this passive, unimpassioned, unexplained, and inexpressive character. And in "Bartleby" Melville also catches—from "Wakefield," we can surmise—a new idea for his work. In "Bartleby" Melville's fiction becomes, for the first time, *short:* curtailed in its expression, no longer aiming at what Melville had called "full articulations." His fiction now emulates the detachment it had found so distressing in *Pierre:* it sets itself apart from its author, no longer offering to speak or develop his personal mind. Above all, his fiction does not try to penetrate the depths of a more essential reality. Like "Wakefield" it builds power through the secrets it keeps, not those it tries to tell.

In the more secretive stories of *The Piazza Tales,* then in *The Confidence-Man,* which finds fiction's analogy not in the gospels but in the apocrypha or scripture without a warrant, Melville goes on to explore the new ways fiction can be conceived that open up when a prophetical conception gets pressed to its limits. Hawthorne does not preside over this new work quite as much as he once did,[57] but I think it instructive that Melville should find his way to this work in part by rethinking Hawthorne's example. It is a mark of Hawthorne's persisting power to help other writers see their work, as it is of Melville's persisting creativity as a reader of Hawthorne's aims, that Melville can still take guidance from Hawthorne even in learning how to move away from him—can use him to help frame a post-prophetical plan of authorship, as he used him to frame a prophetical one before.

Chapter Three

MANUFACTURING YOU
INTO A PERSONAGE
Hawthorne, the Canon, and the
Institutionalization of American Literature

IT IS A LITTLE OF A WONDER how many things Melville managed to get wrong about Hawthorne during the time of their close connection. Melville was wrong, to start with, about Hawthorne's social disposition. The writer he made out as a solitary traveller, available for the alternative intimacies of fellow outsiders—"Ah! it's a long stage, with no inn in sight, and night coming, and the body cold. But with you for a passenger, I am content and can be happy"[1]—was in fact the most perfectly domestic of all American writers, the one most devoted to the family as the scene of fulfilling relation (Hawthorne's famous reserve, it could be argued, is a sign not of a general social disability but of his reserving of full intimacy for the home); and Hawthorne was never more intensely or contentedly absorbed in family life than he was in his Berkshire years. Melville was wrong too about the social attitude of Hawthorne's work. He constructed his image of Hawthorne the heroic nonparticipant—the man with no baggage, the affirmer of no social affirmations—at the very time when Hawthorne's writing was at its most ingratiating. It is typical of Melville's timing that he invented Hawthorne the titanic thunderer while Hawthorne was producing *The House of the Seven Gables,* with its novel "pleasantness of running interest"; or that he moaned that his own books would go down to children with their gingerbread just when Hawthorne was actively courting the juvenile market, with *A Wonder-Book for Girls and Boys.*

But in certain respects the most glaring of Melville's misreadings was of the cultural standing of Hawthorne's works. Melville erected Hawthorne as the patron for a fiercely oppositional school of writing exactly at the moment when Hawthorne was winning official acceptance as America's greatest novelist. Having followed Hawthorne's apparent lead into the deepest depths of unpopularity and critical proscription, Melville had the unnerving experience of seeing his master given the most cordial of public receptions. Two months after the publication of *Pierre,* with the fiasco of its reception still unfolding around him, Melville writes to Hawthorne, with evident surprise:

> My Dear Hawthorne:—This name of *"Hawthorne"* seems to be ubiqui-
> tous. I have been on something of a tour lately, and it has saluted me
> vocally and typographically in all sorts of places & in all sorts of ways.—I
> was at the solitary Crusoeish island of Naushon (one of the Elisabeth
> group) and there, on a stately piazza, I saw it gilded on the back of a
> very new book, and in the hands of a clergyman.—I went to visit a gentle-
> man in Brooklyne, and as we were sitting at our wine, in came the lady of
> the house, holding a beaming volume in her hand, from the city—"My
> Dear," to her husband, "I have brought you *Hawthorne's* new book." I
> entered the cars at Boston for this place. In came a lively boy *"Haw-
> thorne's* new book!"—In good time I arrived home. Said my lady-wife
> "there is Mr *Hawthorne's* new book, come by mail"[2]

Indeed from the point of view of literary history, the real irony of the Melville–Hawthorne relationship is that Melville was *not* wrong in his es-timation of Hawthorne. Melville was mistaken in thinking that the world was mistaken in Hawthorne: beginning in 1850, and persisting with little variation for at least the next sixty years, American literary culture con-tinued to assign Hawthorne exactly the kind of preeminence that Melville had given him. In consequence, the turn toward Hawthorne as inspiration and guide that Melville thought his own peculiar achievement became, for writers emerging not long after Melville, a standard, even a compulsory literary relation. The captivity scene so strikingly recorded in "Hawthorne and His Mosses"—the discovery of the enthralling power of Hawthorne's texts, which operates simultaneously as a discovery of literary power it-self—becomes something like a stock episode in late nineteenth-century American literary biography. Melville's recognition scene of 1850 replays itself ten years later, for William Dean Howells:

> I read the *Marble Faun* first, and then the *Scarlet Letter,* and then the
> *House of Seven Gables,* and then the *Blithedale Romance.* . . . They all
> moved me with a sort of effect such as I had not felt before. They were so
> far from time and place that, although most of them related to our coun-
> try and epoch, I could not imagine anything approximate from them; and
> Hawthorne himself seemed a remote and impalpable agency, rather than
> a person whom one might actually meet, as not long afterward happened
> with me. I did not hold the sort of fancied converse with him that I held
> with other authors, and I cannot pretend that I had the affection for him
> that attracted me to them. But he held me by his potent spell, and for a
> time he dominated me as completely as any author I have read. More
> truly than any other American author he has been a passion with me.[3]

It repeats itself again for Henry James, in Newport in 1863:

> I fondly felt it in those days invaluable that I had during certain last and
> otherwise rather blank months at Newport taken in for the first time and

at one straight draught the full sweet sense of our one fine romancer's work—for sweet it then above all seemed to me; and I remember well how, while the process day after day drew itself admirably out, I found the actual exquisite taste of it, the strain of the revelation, justify up to the notch whatever had been weak in my delay. This prolonged hanging off from true knowledge had been the more odd, so that I couldn't have explained it, I felt, through the fact that The Wonder-Book and Twice-Told Tales had helped to enchant our childhood; the consequence at any rate seemed happy, since without it, very measurably, the sudden sense of recognition would have been less uplifting a wave. The joy of the recognition was to know at the time no lapse—was in fact through the years never to know one. . . .[4]

It repeats itself again for Hamlin Garland, in a country schoolhouse in Iowa sometime around 1878:

Our school library at that time was pitifully small and ludicrously prescriptive, but its shelves held a few of the fine old classics, Scott, Dickens, and Thackeray—the kind of books which can always be had in sets at very low prices—and in nosing about among these I fell, one day, upon two small red volumes called *Mosses from an Old Manse*. Of course I had read of the author, for these books were listed in my *History of American Literature,* but I had never, up to this moment, dared to open one of them. I was a discoverer.

I turned a page or two, and instantly my mental horizon widened. When I had finished the *Artist of the Beautiful,* the great Puritan romancer had laid his spell upon me everlastingly. Even as I walked homeward to my lunch, I read. I ate with the book beside my plate. I neglected my classes that afternoon, and as soon as I had absorbed this volume I secured the other and devoted myself to it with almost equal intensity. The stately diction, the rich and glowing imagery, the mystical radiance, and the aloofness of the author's personality all united to create in me a worshipful admiration which made all other interests pale and faint. It was my first profound literary passion and I was dazzled by the glory of it.[5]

The proof that such early fascinations did endure is found throughout American fiction of the post-Civil War decades. The whole cohort of new writers who emerged after the war—James, most famously, but equally Howells, deForest, Jewett, Cable, Garland, Mary Wilkins Freeman, Harold Frederic, Edward Bellamy—partake of what James calls "the whole rich interpenetration"[6] of authorship and Hawthorne. Hawthorne's fiction appears as an organizing presence throughout their writing—in their lesser, frankly derivative works, to be sure; but even more forcefully in their strongest works, the ones (in many of their cases, the one) by which they have been remembered: works like Cable's Creoleization of *The House of the Seven Gables, The Grandissimes;* or Frederic's witty updating of *The Scarlet Letter, The Damnation of Theron Ware;* or Jewett's beautiful fusion of Hawthorne's fictions of New England as backwater and his fables of monomania, *The Country of the Pointed Firs.*

I will be trying to describe the exact nature of Hawthorne's influence on this generation of his successors later on. But what needs to be stressed at this point is this influences's scope and force. It is scarcely too much to say that—with some exceptions that are partly significant *as* exceptions—Hawthorne presides over the writing of prose fiction in America in the later half of the nineteenth century. When the writers of this generation look back to an American literary past, it is above all Hawthorne that they look to.[7] From decade to decade they seem more and more oblivious to Hawthorne's contemporaries (Cooper, Irving, Poe, Melville), or at least oblivious to them as possible models; but during this time Hawthorne's presence to their minds only grows. The late-nineteenth-century enfranchisement of new foreign literary models—first English, then French and Russian—that might have been expected to dislodge Hawthorne from his place in fact worked the other way. With each discovery of some impressive new power that fiction might possess Hawthorne was discovered to have had that power too, such that the many renovations of fiction's projects during this time tended to renew, not diminish, his relevance to later writing.[8] For American authors of the post-Civil War generation Hawthorne is not a model or an influence among others. They look to him as something more like a founder: he who established the work they now seek to continue. His precedent is, for them, almost synonymous with literature itself: to undertake the writer's work at this time is to join in an activity that Hawthorne is incorporated in the idea of, and so inevitably to enter into an intercourse with him.

Hawthorne had a kind of hold over the whole literary enterprise of the generation that followed him that no other figure in the history of American fiction has exerted, before or since, and it might well be asked how he attained it. The first thing to be said by way of an answer is that the single and greatly enlarged eminence that Hawthorne possesses inside the writing of this time exactly reproduces his stature in American culture at large. The only major American author never to have been underestimated, Hawthorne enjoyed an even more extraordinary prestige in the late nineteenth century than he ever has since. Melville's elated discovery of him exactly coincided with a consolidation of critical opinion in which Hawthorne, already admired as an author among others, got separated off from his previously comparable contemporaries, and elevated to the rank of a national classic. Evert Duyckinck, the patron with no taste for Melville's major works, announced on the appearance of *The Scarlet Letter* that "our literature has given to the world no truer product of the American soil . . . than Nathaniel Hawthorne"; a year later Edwin P. Whipple, Hawthorne's favorite critic, pronounced *The House of the Seven Gables* "the deepest work of imagination ever produced on the American continent," and Rufus Griswold, the spoiler of Poe's fame, proclaimed it "the purest piece of imagination in our prose literature"; and these estimates quickly hardened into official opinion.[9] Hawthorne's exquisiteness as an artist and his preeminence among American fiction writers get asserted with monotonous regularity in the critical literature of the next sixty years. Repeated a thousand times, these views were not once, to my knowledge, publicly challenged during this time: it is a measure of their consensual force that writers otherwise so unlike as James and Twain, Harriet Beecher Stowe and Matthew Arnold, all subscribed to them.[10] Even better evidence of the consensus behind them is the fact that, increasingly as this period progresses, these estimates get asserted without further comment—as if Hawthorne's absolute preeminence were simply the truth, a fact it would occur to no one to have to justify or establish.

The estimation of Hawthorne that was virtually unanimous in the critical world in the nineteenth century was by no means confined to that world. Readers asked to rank great authors regularly put Hawthorne at the top of the list of American fiction writers, and in the top rank of all writers; in a poll conducted by *The Critic* in 1893 to identify the ten greatest American books, for instance, *The Scarlet Letter* came in second, a hair behind Emerson's *Essays,* and Hawthorne came in first in votes received overall. Such schemes were given more visible and durable cultural expression at the same moment. In a wonderful literalization of the notion that great writers preside over the domain of letters, when the Library of Congress was rebuilt in the 1890s, Hawthorne's monumental bust was installed, along with Emerson's and Irving's, on the portico—and again, with no explanation or justification of the selection. When the Hall of Fame was established at New York University in 1900, Hawthorne was again in the company (with Emerson, Irving, and Longfellow) of those installed, by the vote of America's great living men, in the ranks of its national immortals. Here too the monumentalization of Hawthorne and his peers—cut in the eternity of marble, and ranged in the same pantheon as America's founding fathers and public heroes—reflects a remarkable consensus. They got the same share of votes from university presidents and supreme court justices as from living authors; and the general public, polled by newspapers in Brooklyn and Minneapolis, made the same choices as the electors.[11]

The extraordinary cultural status that Hawthorne was accorded in the Gilded Age might seem like a merely appropriate recognition of his extraordinary powers. But as Henry James writes *a propos* of the classicization of Hawthorne in his time, while an author is unlikely to attain to the cultural status of classic greatness without having uncommon qualities in his work, "it is not to that only, to being in himself exquisite and right, that any man was ever so fortunate as to owe the supreme distinction." A classic, James reflects in his letter for the centennial celebration of Hawthorne's birth, is not something a work *is* but something it becomes, through an "interesting process." And that process is not merely one of accurate recognition of properties within a work. It involves the setting in action, on the work's behalf, of what James calls "better machinery than their authors could have set in motion"[12]—the play of the various agencies that organize and administer the literary sphere, that establish its shape and its place in general culture. Hawthorne's own case bears James out: for if Hawthorne owes something of his later illustriousness to his own rare powers, he owes everything to the way in which literature was institutionalized in nineteenth-century America. As this chapter tries to show, Hawthorne was established as a literary eminence by an interlocking system of literary institutions that were themselves newly emerging at the same time as his writings—institutions that undertook the promotion of Hawthorne as one of their chief projects, and that in turn recruited authority to themselves through their association with a figure of his greatness.

Critics and biographers who pay attention to the interaction between Hawthorne's writing and the institutions that produced and disseminated it tend to focus on his early association with the giftbook *The Token,* and, following his own lead in the preface to *Twice-Told Tales,* to brood on the ways in which the necessity of appearing in such an unsophisticated format may have damaged him as a writer. The injuries this mode of publication did him are clear. Its short-selection format might be said to have miniaturized his writing, requiring him to break down the larger compositional structures—the framings and interrelatings of tales—that he had earlier devised for his work. Its practice of keeping authors anonymous made him unable to make a name for himself in the 1830s, unable, by means of his published writing, to establish and confirm a public identity. Its low level of pay (*The Token* is notorious for having paid Hawthorne $108 for eight tales in 1837)[13] forced him to take on other work to support himself, work that brought his literary productivity to a halt. But another version of this story could be told, one that would emphasize how quickly, after this beginning, Hawthorne hooked up with the new publishing institutions that superseded the giftbooks, and how surely he continued to attach himself to just those institutions that could establish the greatest degree of prestige for his work.

The first chapter of this story takes place in the 1840s. Hawthorne became prolific again when he found a new outlet for his work, the newly established *United States Magazine and Democratic Review.* This magazine was edited by the arch-celebrant of Manifest Destiny, John Louis O'Sullivan, but apparently largely managed, in its literary affairs, by O'Sullivan's fellow Democrat, Evert Duyckinck.[14] Duyckinck is now known principally as the patron who failed to recognize *Moby-Dick* as a masterpiece, and secondarily as a great advocate of American literary nationalism in the 1840s. But his place in literary history would be better understood if he were recognized not just as a cultural nationalist but specifically as the proponent of an indigenous American *high* culture. Duyckinck sought to establish a national literature by building various kinds of institutional support for such a literature: by bringing American authors into regular association with one another; by convincing Wiley and Putnam to publish native works in a library of American literature, to be brought out in parallel fashion with another library of well-established English classics; by helping found and manage a new kind of literary periodical, one that would be comparable in its literary standards to the established reviews of the Old World. (The one he eventually edited, the *Literary World,* might be considered one of America's first high-cultural journals, combining as is did literary reviews of high quality with general coverage of the contemporary fine arts.) The Hawthorne of the 1840s was one of the most direct beneficiaries of Duyckinck's cultural labors. Duyckinck brought out Hawthorne's new pieces, collected in *Mosses from an Old Manse,* in Wiley and Putnam's American library. Or to put the matter more strongly: the first Hawthorne volume not to require a subvention, and the first to reach even a moderately sized audience, was produced through a format of Duyckinck's devising. In his capacity as literary reviewer Duyckinck also wrote, between 1841 and 1851, four of the articles that most durably established Hawthorne's claims to fame. (An 1845 letter from O'Sullivan to Hawthorne shows how much Duyckinck's reviews were part of a concerted effort to promote Hawthorne, as well as the patronage-politics strategy that underlay this campaign: "For the purpose of presenting you more advantageously, I have got Duyckinck to write an article about you in the April Democratic; and what is more, I want you to consent to sit for a daguerreotype, that I may take your head off in it . . . By manufacturing you thus into a Personage, I want to raise your mark higher in Polk's appreciation.") [15]

But the crucial chapter in the story of the cultural production of Hawthorne begins in 1850. This is of course when Hawthorne published *The Scarlet Letter;* just as important, it is also when he was taken on by a new publisher, James T. Fields. Fields, as much as anyone, is the figure who brought Duyckinck's cultural projects to fruition. Duyckinck's literary publishing scheme was soon discontinued; but Fields became, and continued to be, the great publisher-patron of American authors: by 1850 he had added first Whittier, then Holmes and Longfellow, then Hawthorne, to a publishing list that also included, by 1860, Emerson, Lowell, Thoreau, and Stowe. Not only did Fields build a stronger list than Duyckinck: the real difference between them is in the strength of the institutional backing that they built for their authors. In the 1840s and 1850s Fields turned the firm of Ticknor and Fields into a strong publishing house, specializing in and strongly committed (as Wiley and Putnam was not) to the publication of fine literature. Fields was able to make his house strong because, at exactly the same time that he was acquiring his stable of American authors, he was also inventing new ways of marketing their works. Fields in these years in effect pioneered the art of book promotion. He began the practice of advertising beyond local markets, thereafter making advertising into a central part of book production. (Fields's firm spent $140 for a year's advertising in 1844, but $1847 for nine months' worth in 1854, and $4693 for sixteen months in 1855–56.) [16] He pioneered in the creation of a kind of factitious "news" about writing, keeping his authors fresh before the market by planting continuous rumors and tidbits about them in local papers. He converted reviewing into a form of advertising too, using his friendly relations with editors he advertised with to get them to give favorable notice to books he published—or even to print reviews he himself had had written.[17]

Fields was one of the great geniuses of American literary merchandising—"your brilliant advertising and arrangements," Emerson wrote him, "have made me so popular"[18]—and one way to define Fields's place in American letters is to say that he recreated literature as a *form* of merchandise: a commodity aimed at a market, a market the producer undertakes to create. (By advertising the Ticknor and Fields list prominently inside the books he published, Fields even turned the book from marketed object to marketing act.)[19] But in a sense Fields's real accomplishment is less that he saw how to market literature than that he established "literature" as a market category. At a time when the paying audience for imaginative writing was expanding (the 1850s is the decade of the new blockbuster bestseller),[20] Fields found a way to identify a certain portion of that writing as distinguished—as of elevated quality, as of premium cultural value; then to build a market for that writing on the basis of that distinction. Fields solidified this differentiated category of the literary not only by printing the contemporary works that *were* the most distinguished, or that *were* the most highly literary (though his eye for such works is impressive); he established it too by devising ways to identify and confirm the literary *as* a difference before the market. His inventions in this regard include the production features he found to stamp on his books, features that both mark them off as separate from other books and confer on them an air of distinction—features like the Ticknor and Fields format of conspicuously good paper and handsome brown boards, promising that what is inside is serious and well-made; or like the Ticknor and Fields imprint itself, which came, through its association with "quality" authors, to create the presumption of quality in the books it adorned.[21] (Fields sent, as a wedding gift to Harriet Beecher Stowe's daughter, a complete set of Hawthorne, bound in white leather—proof both that Fields cannot touch a work without dreaming up new ways to distribute it, and that he cannot distribute a work without inventing new features to announce its elevated, here even sanctified, character.)[22] His difference-supporting inventions include as well the range of paraliterary institutions Fields erected around the literature he published, to reconfirm and endlessly to advertise its cultural specialness—institutions like the salon he established in his famous house on Charles Street, a scene where he could both produce his authors as a kind of sacred cultural elite and win new recruits to the spreading of their fame;[23] or like the *Atlantic Monthly,* which Fields took over in 1859 and made into what Duyckinck had always dreamed of: a literary periodical of recognized cultural authority, devoted both to printing that special kind of writing called literature and to ruling on what writing possesses that quality. (One function of Fields's *Atlantic,* not surprisingly, was to print his authors and keep pronouncing them unparalleled.)

In fact the canon of American literature as the nineteenth century knew it—the canon that was assembled in the 1850s, quickly superseded the weaker one (of Cooper, Irving, and Bryant) that had preceded it, and then reigned with unchallenged and ever-strengthening force until the 1920s—can be said to have been largely Fields's creation.[24] It is his creation in the sense that he located and grouped together the authors who composed that canon—principally, Longfellow, Emerson, Hawthorne, Holmes, Lowell, and Whittier. But it is his creation even more centrally in the sense that he helped establish and gave massive institutional reinforcement to the distinction that made that canon thinkable—the distinction whereby certain writers who were still contemporaries could be marked off as uniquely gifted, as the producers of work of enormously and absolutely different value from that of other contemporary writers. Fields the canon-former and institution-builder is the agent, in the literary domain, of a general social process—its results are everywhere in the late nineteenth century, but he reminds us that it began in mid-century—through which American culture was reorganized on a more steeply hierarchical plan, featuring sharp gradations of levels of cultural value.[25] (Fields, one might say, represents this process in its fullness, Duyckinck at a transitional phase, which already values a culture it thinks of as high but does not yet insist on the hierarchical differentiations such a culture would require. Fields's American library is emphatically discriminating, Duyckinck's still a very mixed affair; unlike Fields's it includes both men and women [Margaret Fuller], both established writers and newcomers [the Melville of *Typee*], both literature and nonfiction [J. Ross Browne's *Etchings of a Whaling Cruise*]. Duyckinck's great *Cyclopaedia of American Literature* (1855) includes a little of everybody who ever wrote in America; Fields's *Yesterdays with Authors* [1872] has room for giants only.) As Fields and the cultural process he served performed their functions, they began to make it possible to be a writer in America in quite a different way from anything that had been possible heretofore. On the one hand, they made it possible to write for, and to find support in, a differentiated realm of literary writing. On the other, they made it possible that such writing could establish, for its creator, a previously unimaginable level of cultural prestige.[26]

Hawthorne, as we have already seen, consolidated his reputation as a classic author in the early 1850s. To this it can now be added that when he was thus classicized, Hawthorne attained to a form of public status that was itself being newly described and legitimated. And his case gives stunning evidence of the relation of nineteenth-century canonization to Fields's institutional ministrations. Hawthorne wrote Fields in 1862, "my literary success, whatever it has been or may be, is the result of my connection with you,"[27] and this is no exaggeration. It was Fields, in 1850, who produced the book that clinched Hawthorne's fame: in his own lurid account, Fields, Chillingworth-fashion, forcibly dragged to light the half-completed manuscript that Hawthorne was keeping secret; and it was on his advice that Hawthorne made *The Scarlet Letter* a separate book, *not* entitled *Old-Time Legends: Together with Sketches, Experimental and Ideal*.[28] It was

Fields who helped create the climate for the work that followed. Hawthorne became truly prolific, really for the first and last time in his career, in the two years after *The Scarlet Letter*—this is when he wrote *The House of the Seven Gables, The Blithedale Romance, A Wonder Book, Tanglewood Tales,* and his life of Franklin Pierce; and he himself attributed his productivity to the new demand Fields had created for his writings.[29] By also republishing *Twice-Told Tales* (in 1851) and *Mosses from an Old Manse* (in 1854), and causing Hawthorne to gather his last uncollected writings in *The Snow-Image and Other Tales* (1851), Fields made Hawthorne seem even more prolific than he was. Through this strategy Fields brought to Hawthorne's new audience the writings that had earlier failed to find an audience. He also converted Hawthorne's work into an *oeuvre:* the volumes Hawthorne produced in straggling fashion Fields pulled together into a visible body, the body of work establishing the identity "Hawthorne."

The beauty of Fields's publishing contrivances was that he could arrange for Hawthorne's reception at the same time that he arranged for his publication. Hawthorne was the beneficiary of a full-fledged Fieldsian advertising campaign (the *Literary World* ran an extract from "The Custom House" as a pre-publication "selection"). Fields no doubt also helped produce Hawthorne's reviews. It is a striking fact—and suggestive, as well, of how little Hawthorne's recognition was an unmediated process—that the critics who proclaimed Hawthorne a classic were, almost to a man, insiders in Fields's network of friends of the house: Griswold, who found *The House of the Seven Gables* so purely imaginative, wrote Fields, on another occasion: "I puff your books without any regard to their quality"; Whipple, who found that novel the deepest work yet produced in America, was a boyhood friend of Fields's, and a lifelong collusionist.[30] When Hawthorne again stopped producing in 1852, Fields's ever more intricate institutional machinery continued to manufacture him into a personage. His firm's secondary publications kept touting the genius of Nathaniel Hawthorne: the Hawthorne chapter in Henry Giles's *Illustrations of Genius in Relation to Culture and Society* (Ticknor and Fields, 1854), for instance, begins by affirming him America's most distinctive author. When reviews of Hawthorne slowed, Fields arranged for the critics to get access to "new" material, the basis for new articles—the *National Magazine* of 1853 carries a long article by Richard Henry Stoddard, another of Fields's friendly reviewers, whom Fields had introduced to Hawthorne and for whom he got Hawthorne to write an autobiographical reminiscence.[31] When Hawthorne returned to America in 1860 (on the same boat as Fields), Fields arranged a well-publicized banquet for the national novelist. Fields's new *Atlantic* ran Hawthorne's English reminiscences, then issued by Ticknor and Fields as *Our Old Home.* Hawthorne died with a serial unfinished in the *Atlantic;* Fields orchestrated the chorus of his obituaries; and Fields spent his own last days reminiscing about Hawthorne in print.

Hawthorne offers, as I have said, a striking instance of how American writers' cultural identities were created and sustained by an interlocking network of literary agencies in the nineteenth century, agencies that were themselves being fashioned at the same time as those authors' writings. He shows as well how the positions of author and institution reinforce each other in such an arrangement: if Fields's publishing machinery helped make Hawthorne's reputation, it is no less true that Hawthorne's highly visible and exclusive association with Fields helped confer luster on Fields's firm, his magazine, and his salon—prestige those institutions could then distribute onto other authors, in turn. After the phase of direct collaboration between Hawthorne and Fields, Hawthorne's reputation continued to benefit from—and not doubt to benefit—later versions of the institutions Fields helped elaborate. Hawthorne continued to be the focus of public literary "events" that might be thought of as sequels to Fields's banquets: events like the reading, before the Harvard chapter of Phi Beta Kappa in 1879, of an ode to Hawthorne by the laureate of the late nineteenth century, Edmund Clarence Stedman, with Longfellow, Whittier, Holmes, Lowell, and Emerson—a canon displayed as a canon—in conspicuous attendance; or the Hawthorne Centennial Celebration of 1904, which gave another generation of official literary eminences the chance to display themselves as eminences.[32] The new literary magazines that emerged alongside the *Atlantic*—and that shared with it a virtual monopoly on literary publishing through the 1880s—similarly continued to enforce Hawthorne's significance. *Harper's,* for example, ran another long piece by Stoddard on Hawthorne in 1872. Richard Watson Gilder's *Century,* the first literary periodical to build something like a mass circulation, printed four full-length essays on Hawthorne and two frontispiece portraits of him between 1884 and 1887 alone—the very years when it was also publishing *Huckleberry Finn, The Rise of Silas Lapham,* and *The Bostonians.*

But Field's efforts were continued most directly by the firms that succeeded Ticknor and Fields—James R. Osgood and Co., then, after Henry Houghton bought out the failing Osgood, Houghton Mifflin. These firms always had as a central part of their institutional identity their association with the American classics, and they saw to it that Hawthorne, Emerson, Longfellow, and the rest were regularly reissued, in formats that announced their classic status. Hawthorne had already appeared in a Ticknor and Fields Blue and Gold edition and an Osgood Little Classics edition when Houghton negotiated the takeover of the New England canon. (This took place at the Whittier birthday dinner where Mark Twain made his famous failed joke about canonical authorship.)[33] After this takeover, the large annuities Fields and Osgood had contracted to pay these authors and their heirs and the large indebtedness he inherited from Osgood were incentives to Houghton to market his classics yet more vigorously. The result, as Ellen Ballou shows in her history of the early years of Houghton Mifflin, was a new effort, beginning about 1880, to repackage these books for every level of the market. Hawthorne the classic got spread much more widely through literary culture by this process. He reappeared as a poten- tially popular author, in a cheap paperback edition; also as a collecter's item, in the new *de luxe* edition he was the second author (after Long- fellow) to receive; also as a staple for the new middle-class home library of this time, in the format Houghton Mifflin perfected to identify the standard authors, the Riverside Edition of the Complete Works. (Haw- thorne's appeared in 1883.)[34]

But Houghton Mifflin's greatest innovation—the most crucial, after Fields's, in the whole history of the production of Hawthorne—was the recreation of the New England classics as texts for schools. The hero of this story is Houghton's lifelong editor, Horace Scudder. Scudder is one of those nineteenth-century figures who seem to have belonged simulta- neously to the managment of every literary and cultural institution, and who integrated their workings in practical terms; as Houghton Mifflin's chief editor, he was also a manager of childrens' magazines, an eventual editor of the *Atlantic,* and a longtime member of the Massachusetts Board of Education. Motivated on the one hand by a deeply Arnoldian belief in the spiritual value of literary classics and their supreme social significance in a democracy, and on the other by his firms's concern to capture a share of the rapidly expanding textbook market, Scudder caused Houghton Mif- flin to reissue its list of American classics as inexpensive school texts, in the Riverside Literature Series. Scudder, a recognized theorist of education as well as a partisan of a late-nineteenth-century pedagogical revolution against rote learning from old-style graded readers, meant for the River- side Literature Series to embody a new kind of textbook, vehicle for a new form of education. And it was by creating the rationale for this new kind of text, as much as by producing the texts themselves, that Scudder made his educational mark.[35] In an address to the National Teachers Association in San Francisco in 1888 and in a series of articles in the *Atlantic,* Scudder popularized an argument for the privileged status of American classics as school texts that runs like this. The function of America's public schools (this is a nineteenth-century truism) is to make good citizens: strongly to acculturate the young, to incorporate them deep within the American ethos. That ethos—what Scudder calls "the deposit of nationality"—is present in every American institution, but it is most pow- erfully expressed "through art, and mainly through the art of letters." "It is literature, therefore, that holds in precipitation the genius of the coun- try." And if this is so, then (here Scudder covertly merges the assumption of canonical hierarchy with that of national spirit) "the higher the form of literature, the more consummate the expression of that spirit." For the institution of public education to discharge its socializing function, then (and Scudder assumes a general anxiety that America's cultural coherence is in danger of dilution or radical disruption: he is writing during the Hay- market anarchist trial), nothing could be more valuable than "steady, un- remitting attention to American classics":

The sentiment of patriotism must be kept fresh and living in the hearts of the young through quick and immediate contact with the sources of that sentiment; and the most helpful means are those spiritual deposits of patriotism which we find in noble poetry and lofty prose, as communicated by men who have lived patriotic lives and been fed with coals from the altar.[36]

Behind these essays we can observe a refiguring, not just of educational curricula, but of the whole status of literature in American social life. Duyckinck, Fields, and the friends of literature in the mid-century generation thought of literature as one element *of* high culture, one of the fine arts that adorn a people's life. But Scudder's later reasoning gives literature a much more crucial position in culture's very ground. Literature becomes the embodiment of what Americans share, the chief incarnation of the ethos that gives them existence as a people. More, it becomes the central agency of acculturation: the channel through which that ethos is disseminated, and above all the means by which outsiders are brought inside it. (American literature as Scudder presents it is literally that which Americanizes.) This thinking is characteristic of a movement, among figures of Scudder's background in the 1880s and 1890s, to promote a New England culture just then slipping into the past as a source of future national stability amidst wrenching social changes, and Scudder shows all the contradictions this movement typically contains. His cultural program is, first off, both deeply democratic and deeply antidemocratic. He wants to make culture available to every American girl and boy; but the culture he has in mind is conceived quite exclusively, on a model in which only certain "high" sorts of expression register as culture at all. (We might compare him in this to the late-nineteenth-century librarians Dee Garrison has studied, who looked to the new public library both to open the world of letters to all and to enforce antipopular standards of cultural taste.) And his program, again characteristically, promotes the appreciation of the rare qualities of classical art while also transparently using that art as a means of social engineering: as a way to perpetuate general social allegiance to a traditional elite culture, and to eradicate cultural differences that might disrupt its sway.[37] (The literary canon of course is especially well suited to these ends, giving as it does a monopoly on classical status to native-born authors with Anglo-Saxon names, and imparting, in the very idea of the classic, habits of hierarchical and self-subordinating thinking.)

Scudder's success in the late-nineteenth-century project of trying to maximize participation in an elite version of culture was really extraordinary: his and Houghton Mifflin's successful promotion of the American classics as school texts gave the American literary canon a wholly new order of cultural presence and force. Scudder's labors finally created, among schoolchildren, the mass audience that this literature (except in Longfellow's case) had never enjoyed before (the Riverside Literature Series, already selling in the hundreds of thousands in the 1880s, was still moving a million copies a year in 1917);[38] or to put it another way, Scudder finally succeeded in making Hawthorne and his fellow literati *popular* authors, popular, exactly, *as* classics. In addition to expanding the scale on which they were disseminated, Scudder and the educational movements he worked with also helped give the American canon a wholly new degree of cultural legitimation. The logic that he formulated and that thousands of teachers passed on turned this body of texts into classics in the fullest sense. It gave them the status of that which deserves to be studied, that which constitutes a national heritage and bears a national culture, and it incorporated the assumption of this worth into the most elementary levels of national literacy.[39]

We get a sense of the new kinds of enforcements of canonical values that these developments produced when we look into the educational literature of the late nineteenth century. Brander Matthews's *Introduction to American Literature,* which sold at least a quarter of a million copies after it was published in 1896, clearly signals the canon's entry into the realm of administered knowledge, requiring the student-reader to give correct answers to such questions as: "What qualities combined to make Hawthorne the greatest American writer of fiction that has yet appeared?"[40] (The right answers are provided in the text; "he wasn't" is not one of them.) Mary E. Burt, a Chicago teacher who enthusiastically championed Scudder's program from the teacher's side, suggests that the picture might have had brighter spots. To doubters she writes, in her spirited 1889 book *Literary Landmarks:*

> Many teachers have proved to their own satisfaction that young children prefer great classics to weak reading. I have seen a hundred young people in fifth and sixth grades spontaneously applaud, with no prompting from any teacher, the finest and subtlest thought in analyses of Hawthorne's Great Stone Face and The Christmas Banquet, where I had expected a very funny essay to win all the enthusiasm.[41]

It might be added that the kind of pedagogization we get a glimpse of here is only one phase in a more general incorporation of literature into education in the late nineteenth century. American literature was first taken up into the universities (themselves largely new creations of this time) at almost exactly the same time that it was entering the public school curriculum. Yale offered "Hawthorne's Imagination" as a subject for the Junior essay in 1884,[42] signalling his emergence as part of that learning called the higher. (Harvard's hosting of Stedman's Hawthorne ode in 1879 is more evidence of his arrival in this new institutional setting.) It is also at this time that American literature first emerges as an academic expertise, and that university professors begin to make their names by writing books on this field—books like the two-volume *American Literature* (1887–89) of Charles Francis Richardson, after 1882 professor (for some years the only professor) of English at Dartmouth; or *Initial Studies in American Literature* (1892), by Professor Henry Augustus Beers of Yale (this volume was widely distributed as a Chatauqua self-education text); or *A Literary History of America* (1900), by Harvard's Barrett Wendell.

What we are really seeing, in the appearance of the academic history of American literature, is a literary and social development we are deeply familiar with: the rise of the academic as the recognized authority on literature, and of the university as the place where literature is discriminated and transmitted.[43] One thing that the kind of history I have been writing here might remind us is that both of these givens of our own cultural order are fairly recent historical developments (they are still very much nascent in 1900). It might remind us too that as it emerged in America, the university as literary authority was a late development in a general exfoliation of institutions—including new publishing houses, new styles of magazines, the new cadre of cultural custodians that managed those agencies, the reformed public education system, and so on—that grew up around literature in the nineteenth century and that took over its cultural administration. (The lines of transmission from the existing to the emerging establishment are easy to trace: Richardson, for instance, professor of English at Dartmouth, also wrote a *Primer of American Literature* for Houghton Mifflin to use as a school text; in his youth he was noted for having memorized the price list of Ticknor and Fields.[44] Howells, Field's assistant, then himself editor of the *Atlantic,* was offered the first professorship of English at the new model university of the 1880s, Johns Hopkins.)

By now there is no need to repeat that classic American literature, as the nineteenth century knew it, was largely these institutions' creation. They were the means by which it was selected, integrated into a cultural unity, disseminated to readers in a culture, and underwritten as of supreme cultural value. (The late-century academic histories, which retrace the official form of the canon with no variations, only represent, one might say, a new way of making it official.) But what might still bear insisting is the extent to which all of the nineteenth-century institutions that established themselves as authorities on literature were committed to a vision of literature as a special (and specially elevated) form of expression.[45] To say that they were committed to this vision puts it mildly. Their operation *as* institutions, one might better say, was exactly *to institute this vision of literature as a cultural reality*—as the new literary journals, the *Atlantic* and its followers, made there *be* a difference, in the realm of print, between literary writing and writing that isn't "literature"; as the new pedagogy of Scudder and Mary Burt *drove* new divisions between true literature and other things children might read, then instructed children in how to make this differentiation for themselves;[46] as the new academic literary history of Richardson and Wendell made American literary history *be* the history of the immortals, not, as it was in Griswold's, Duyckinck's, and Charles Cleveland's older collections, the history of writing by Americans in general.[47] When these institutions formed and transmitted an American canon, they did so by assimilating American literature to this conception of the literary. They canonized certain writers (and not others) because they *were* literary in a certain way; then they made these writers *represent* the idea and value of literature thus defined to their culture.

Hawthorne was always a special favorite of the figures and institutions I have been describing. From Duyckinck and Fields through Stedman and Gilder and Scudder to Richardson (who calls Hawthorne "the only")[48] and Wendell (whose *History* moves straight from "Hawthorne" to "The Decline"), the builders of an American national literature in the nineteenth century were always especially attracted to Hawthorne, and went to special lengths to hymn his glory. When Hawthorne was thus raised into the highest heaven of nineteenth-century culture, he too was assimilated to the concept of the literary I have been describing. And it was his peculiar distinction to be identified especially intimately *with* the literary. He became, in the nineteenth century's favorite word for him, the *exquisite* author; Wendell gives the other New England giants certain powers as artists, but equates Hawthorne with the thing itself—Emerson is the prophet, Lowell the humanist, "Nathaniel Hawthorne, above and beyond the others an artist."[49] The writer who could once fairly call himself "the obscurest man of letters in America" became, during the nineteenth century, one of the two or three most eminent. But he did so on the condition that he become something else as well: the incarnation and exemplary case of literature in the nineteenth century's sense of the word.

I am far from thinking that nineteenth-century writers—any more than anyone else—could only have seen the Hawthorne that their institutional setting presented them with. But as inevitably as any readers of any author, they surely saw their Hawthorne within the context that their literary institutions created. And it is to the action of those institutions that we must look to understand the terms on which they encountered Hawthorne.

Those terms can now be defined more precisely. I said before that Hawthorne presides over the writing of fiction in post-Civil War America. To this it can now be added that his status, for the writers of that time, is specifically that of the classic. Hawthorne has something like the place in their work that Homer or Virgil or Horace have in Augustan literature, or that Milton (earlier versions of the classic that American writers of this period show little interest in) has in Romantic poetry: that of a past that is constantly remembered in the act of writing, as the authoritative version of what the later work attempts.[50] It will be clear by now why Hawthorne (and not some other writer) emerged as American fiction's classical past: one of the curiosities of the nineteenth-century canon is that Hawthorne is the only prose-fiction writer included in it. It will also be clear, I hope, how he became part of a past of *that* stature. One thing that America's new literary institutions did in the nineteenth century was to give the past itself a new shape and force: to recast it into a select group of eminent figures, then to build those figures a kind of cultural centrality authors had not had before—including a new exemplary dominion over both literacy in general and the domain of later writing. Hawthorne's power over his successors in the Gilded Age—a power of an order quite different from what any earlier novelist exerts over his own work, or from what earlier novelists exert over later ones at this period in Europe—is the product of a redistribution of literary power itself in post-Civil War America, in which writing gets placed under new kinds and degrees of authority and control.

What Hawthorne represents to his nineteenth-century successors, the history of his institutionalization also equips us to see, is, really, literature—literature as the institutions of that time define it. These authors experience Hawthorne as the canon represents him: as if he were somehow interchangeable with literature itself. James's sublime recognition of Hawthorne, we can notice retroactively, is also a recognition of that indefinable quality that makes some writing special and supremely valuable: what he recognizes is

> that his work was all charged with a *tone,* a full and rare tone of prose, and . . . this made for it an extraordinary value in an air in which absolutely nobody's else was or has shown since any aptitude for being.[51]

Garland too records his falling under Hawthorne's spell as an awakening to literature itself: a discovery of the difference between a privileged and a lower order of writing, a discovery that commits him to observe a whole system of parallel discriminations:

> Eager to know more of this necromancer I searched the town for others of his books, but found only *American Notes* [sic] and *The Scarlet Letter.*
> Gradually I returned to something like my normal interests in baseball and my classmates, but never again did I fall to the low level of *Jack Harkaway.* I now possessed a literary touchstone with which I tested the quality of other books and other minds, and my intellectual arrogance, I fear, sometimes made me an unpleasant companion. The fact that Ethel did not "like" Hawthorne, sank her to a lower level in my estimation.[52]

What Hawthorne represents to the generation that followed him, these and a hundred similar examples show, is literature itself, as the prestigious institutions of their generation articulate it. It can be added that the way the authors of this time come into relation with Hawthorne is by seeking to enter the literary field that these same institutions establish. The same institutions that in one of their operations erected an authoritative national literary past also opened up, in the mid-nineteenth century, a specialized literary domain for writers to appear in. And the writers who chose this—this set of publishing institutions, and this set of literary values—as their domain were the ones who felt Hawthorne's precedent most strongly. Howells, Fields's assistant, then successor, at the *Atlantic,* who as a young man (as he recalls) "had his being . . . wholly in literature,"[53] is an example of such a writer; so is James, whose early work was an *Atlantic* staple, and who like Howells had the "deeply reserved but quite unabashed design of becoming as 'literary' as might be";[54] so is Jewett, the most literary of the regionalists, and an early discovery of Howells's who was long edited by Scudder and who lived with Fields's widow in his Charles Street house. We can map Hawthorne's nineteenth-century influence with perfect accuracy if we say that writers feel the strength of his literary authority in proportion as they identify with literature as their high-cultural institutions organize it. James, the writer who makes this identification most strongly, has the longest and most intricate relation with Hawthorne; writers who position themselves away from such institutions have him much less on their minds. Hawthorne does not preside over story-paper fiction, or dime novels, or womens' romances: unlike Cooper or Poe, he has, so far as I know, no influence on popular fiction of the late nineteenth century. He does not preside in regions that held out against the cultural hegemony of the Northeast, as the South did until the 1880s. (But when writers from the South try to break into the Northern literary domain they have Hawthorne held up to them quickly enough; Gilder, as editor of *Scribner's* in the 1870s, instructed the uninitiated George Washington Cable to read Hawthorne and Turgenev, to see how real artists handled ideas in fiction.)[55] He is a lesser influence on writers who take a stand against the newly institutionalized literary domain—the great example here is Mark Twain, who was of course featured in periodicals like the *Atlantic* and the *Century,* but who had a deep aversion to the high-cultural organization of the literary, and to Hawthorne along with it;[56] but I might also mention Garland, the proponent of regionalism and loud-mouthed denouncer, in *Crumbling Idols* (1894), of literary centers and canonical masters, who implies in his autobiography that he turned *to* regionalism exactly to get out from under the excessive authority of Hawthorne's example.[57]

When postwar authors enter into imaginative relation with Hawthorne, this is to imply, they are never simply confronting a fascinating earlier text. Willy nilly they are also always confronting the institutional establishment that appropriated Hawthorne's texts and pressed their claims *and* the idea of literature that that establishment maintains. This is a far cry from Melville's situation of not many years before, when Hawthorne was still available as a personal enthusiasm, whose significance could be privately, even wildly, invented. But the situations, though very different, are not quite as different as they appear. It remains to be said that the institutional processes that did so much to monumentalize Hawthorne and to present him as exemplary did little to make clear how his example worked. Nineteenth-century readers were told a thousand times that Hawthorne is our most exquisite artist, but if they asked what his exquisiteness consisted of, they were only told to go read more Hawthorne. (Harriet Beecher Stowe's self-help essays for housewives aspiring to be authors, in the 1869 issues of *Hearth and Home,* tell them to read Hawthorne's *American Notebooks* to watch "the process by which the greatest American writer formed that inimitable style"; but since she offers no hints to that style's secret, she leaves him as inimitable as she found him.)[58] A central feature of the nineteenth-century canonization of Hawthorne is its extraordinary, sometimes even celebratory, vagueness as to what the exact grounds for his canonization are. The result is to recreate in a new historical setting what I take to be the recurrent situation of Hawthorne in American literature: he again becomes the locus of terribly great authority as an artistic model, *and* of just as great uncertainty about what his significance as a model might be.

If we ask how Hawthorne's example in fact worked in the later nineteenth century, the answer the fiction suggests is that writers put him to every use they needed. Hawthorne serves as a central model for the realists' experiments in psychological representation: the brilliant representations of reverie in books like *A Modern Instance* and *The Damnation of Theron Ware,* for instance, look back quite directly to Hawthorne's work in *The Scarlet Letter.* He also serves as one of the chief prototypes for the dominant mode of American fiction from the 1870s through the 1890s, regional writing. The unbendable, supercharged monomaniacs that fill the pages of Jewett and Freeman descend quite as directly from Hawthorne as from New England life; and *The House of the Seven Gables* becomes, for these writers and others, a standard reference on the treatment of the social psychology of the cultural backwater. But we get these authors' achievements wrong if we think of them as following Hawthorne in these ways. What they are really doing is making new Hawthornes for their purposes: inventing, from within their own writing projects, new versions of what his meaning as a model might consist of. And the fact that they put Hawthorne to these uses does not limit his potentiality. While the realists are rewriting Hawthorne as exemplary realist, Edward Bellamy can also rediscover him as a model for parabolic romance, in *Doctor Heidenhof's Process;* while the regionalists are claiming Hawthorne as provincial, James can also use him to model his novel of the metropolis, *The Princess Casamassima.*

For James, Bellamy, Howells, Jewett, Frederic, Freeman, and their contemporaries, Hawthorne has a different kind of reality than he had for Melville. Melville knew (or thought he knew) Hawthorne as a person; they know him only as a personage. Melville could happen upon Hawthorne's work and discover its greatness for himself; they meet him already included in an official culture, with the largest possible estimate of his greatness already an institutionalized fact. But in certain respects their relation with him is not changed. Hawthorne is still, for them as he was for Melville, the most powerful and immediate figure of the great writer that they know. They too look to his work as the place where the most exciting potentialities of their own art are gathered. But they too find that his work keeps the secrets of its and their art—or yields them only to those who actively invent them.

LATE HAWTHORNE, OR THE WOES OF THE IMMORTALS

Scribbled romance poorly.
                    Hawthorne's notebook, 1858

I hardly know what takes away his strength.
                    Mrs. Hawthorne, 1864

DIFFERENT LITERARY FORMS have been associated, at different moments of literary history, with different sorts of career trajectories and patterns of normal production. The pattern for the novel in the nineteenth century is easy to name: this is the time of what Henry James calls "the great army of constant producers."[1] The authors who dominated this genre— Scott, Balzac, Dickens, Thackeray, Trollope, Daudet, Zola, and the rest— wrote not just novels but shelves of them. The form of authorship they define is strongly associated with the production of new works at regular intervals, continued over a long span of years.

Many American authors fit this normative pattern—Cooper does; James and Howells do; even Melville does, for a stretch of seven books—but Hawthorne is not one of them. His show of long works—four completed romances—is small by any nineteenth-century standard (even that of Flaubert, who pioneered a new pattern of constipated authorship). And the productivity he does exhibit is curiously unsustained. Hawthorne was not incapable of working in the regular way. In mid-career he converted to the system of annual production, publishing *The Scarlet Letter, The House of the Seven Gables,* and *The Blithedale Romance* in successive years from 1850 to 1852. But the interest of Hawthorne's case is that, having managed successfully to establish himself within this production system, he then abruptly fell out of it. After three years of bumper crops, Hawthorne wrote nothing literary for the next five years; in the remaining twelve years of his life after 1852 he produced a total of one more published work of fiction.

This falling off is not explained by Hawthorne's having resigned from the novel's form of work, as, in different ways, such constant producers as Melville, Hardy, and Tolstoy did in their late careers. Hawthorne wrote nothing between 1853 and 1857 because he was United States Consul at

Liverpool at this time, a post, as he thought, that left no room for literary labors.[2] But when he left this post, he turned back to fiction-writing as his natural and chosen work; and between 1858 and 1864 he worked away steadily at new fiction projects—worked at them, if anything, even harder than he had in his earlier productive phase. The matter with late Hawthorne is not that he has repudiated or lost interest in his career, but that the work he used to produce with relative ease has now become, in some fundamental sense, unwriteable. Everyone can think of authors whose late works fall below, even dismally below, the level of their earlier performance. (Faulkner is a glaring American example.) But Hawthorne's late projects, published in the Centenary Edition as *The American Claimant Manuscripts* and *The Elixir of Life Manuscripts,* show something different and altogether graver: these are the novels of a writer whose powers of novel making have dysfunctioned, a writer grown incompetent at the most elementary procedures of novelistic composition. Hawthorne is as fixated on an originating idea in these manuscripts as he was in *The Scarlet Letter,* but now he literally does not know what to make of his ideas: does not know what story they might throw forward, or what they might be made to signify. He writes and writes (length is always proportionate to loss of direction in Hawthorne after 1850) as if, by sheer prolix verbalization, he might happen onto the story he is meaning to write. But the more he writes, the more he is aware that the point of his work still eludes him: "still there is something wanting to make an action for the story," he interjects in his manuscript; and again: "there is still a want of something, which I can by no means get at, nor describe what it is."[3] He starts these stories over, and over, and over, as if a fresh attempt might get him past his former blind spots. But each new draft quickly comes to mirror the old ones, and brings him right back to the point where the work breaks down: "Oh, Heavens! I have not the least notion how to get on. I never was in such a sad predicament before."[4]

Hawthorne's uncompleted romances are the works of an author whose works have become inconceivable to him. *The Marble Faun,* the one fiction Hawthorne did publish after 1852, is in every sense more finished than these romances, but it very obviously shares in the problems they display. *The Marble Faun* is another book in which writing has become troublesome. Unlike any of Hawthorne's earlier works, once drafted, it had to be completely redrafted, and the book repeatedly suggests that its composition has been a tedious chore. (When he introduces the Faun of Praxiteles, Hawthorne writes, as if with dismayed surprise: "But we must do more than merely refer to this exquisite work of art; it must be described.)"[5] It also shows the difficulty Hawthorne has in making his late works coherent—and his reliance, in distress, on compositional shortcuts that aggravate the problem of integration. It is well known that Hawthorne imported bulky scenic descriptions and art-historical reflections into *The Marble Faun* from his notebooks (late Hawthorne always seems to hope that he might find a way to make his works other than by actually composing them). But this dependency produces a work made of chunks of prose that have nothing to do with each other—with a little action here, a little scenery there, each oblivious to the other's existence. Above all, *The Marble Faun* shows the decay of Hawthorne's powers of imaginative resolution already well advanced. *The Marble Faun* recreates Hawthornesque ambiguity as sheer vagueness. Hester's transgressive past is sharply registered, if unnarrated; by contrast, Miriam's is all a fog. The plot intrigue in *Blithedale* is obscure to Coverdale; that in *The Marble Faun* is simply unimagined. We may like or not like what John Lothrop Motley called "the misty way in which the story is indicated rather than revealed";[6] but there is no denying that *The Marble Faun*'s way is a misty one. This is the work of an author for whom fiction's ground of motivation and transformative action has become inaccessible, unsusceptible to imaginative production or definition.

I am not interested in condemning Hawthorne's late writings. But it seems to me that to understand late Hawthorne at all we need to start from the fact that writing has become, for him, a severely disabled activity. Not all writing: Hawthorne found it easy to turn out ruminative prose essays in his late years, and some of these efforts—particularly "Chiefly About War Matters" and the introduction to *Our Old Home,* "Consular Experiences"—deserve ranking with the best of his work. It is specifically fiction writing, or what Hawthorne calls scribbling romance—the creation of story, and of what a well-told story can express—for which he became, in Fields's appropriate word, "incapacitated."[7] Hawthorne would share the view that the central fact about his so-called last phase is that, as a writer of fiction, he virtually failed to have one. The real question about his late career is not what he wrote then but what went wrong with writing.

The few critics who have thought about Hawthorne's authorial collapse have largely agreed on the causes for it. One often cited is the Civil War. The bloodshed and war fever that most of his fellow writers found exhilarating Hawthorne found simply depressing; he himself, in *Our Old Home* and elsewhere, sees this public convulsion as what shut down the project of romance.[8] And no account of Hawthorne's last years fails to mention his rapid descent into age and death. Literary biography has few more ghastly tales than that of Hawthorne's enfeeblement, his abject and unreversing loss of physical and mental force in his last years, and it seems natural to view his loss of power as a writer as one phase in a more general failure of force for life. But explanations like these, while helpful in part, are not entirely satisfying. Hawthorne's disability really preceded the events that are its purported causes: he was already far gone in incapacitated authorship when the war and his aging began. And we might at least wonder whether the causation is not the other way around: whether the lassitude, depression, and longing for non-being that dominated Hawthorne's old age were not themselves largely products of his failure as a writer, of his tormenting consciousness of himself (in his phrase) as a "broken-down author."

I want to suggest another kind of reason for Hawthorne's authorial collapse. I want to argue that the impairment of his authorial powers has less to do with political or physiological changes than with the change he experienced in the cultural status of the writer's work. The last chapter charted a general reorganization, in America in the mid-nineteenth century, both of the shape of the category of the literary and of literature's place in culture. As we have seen, this reorganization involved a number of interrelated developments. It involved the founding and empowering of a new set of institutions—publishing houses, magazines, and so on—to administer the literary sphere. These institutions worked, as part of their action, to divide the field of writing with new sharpness, to split writing into separate categories of literary and popular, hierarchically related as high and low. In the same process they also refashioned the social status of authorship—creating a new, inferior status for the popular writer, but also building for certain literary writers a greatly augmented stature, as transcendent achievers and national treasures. And at the same time that they constructed this canonical or classical rank they also recreated literary writing as a field *with* a canon, an activity presided over by certain luminous and authoritative exemplars. These developments, which taken together comprise one of the great redefinitions of literature's nature and stature in American cultural history, established their new order as a real social fact during the 1850s. The separation between high and low fiction was still fairly weakly maintained in America in 1850, but it was strongly established by 1860. There is still difference of opinion, especially outside Boston, about who the great American authors are, in 1850; by 1860 the nineteenth-century canon was fully in place and accepted as far afield as New York, the border states, and the midwest.[9]

What this meant for Hawthorne is that when he resumed his writing after his years off as consul, the work of writing had been redefined. While he was not producing any, his writing was being placed in a newly designated category of elevated and valuable expression; while he was not being an author, he was himself becoming a new kind of author, one of America's immortals and literature's patron saints. The burden such changes put on him is clear. Hawthorne was the first author to have to contend with the canonical stature of Hawthorne (this is why I include him among his own successors). He was the first to face the challenge his precedent set for later writers: that of having to produce their work within a new institutional organization of the literary. The changes that took place inside his writing result at least in part from changes imposed on it from outside, from its need to adjust itself to the new position built for it from without.

In the last chapter I traced the process by which, during his own lifetime, America's new literary institutions appropriated Hawthorne and recreated him as a cultural eminence. Here we can ask, how did Hawthorne respond to this remaking of his public identity? Biographical evidence gives a complicated answer. It is clear, first of all, that Hawthorne was not hostile to the cultural agencies that took him over and in no way resisted the role they fashioned for him. When he became famous in the 1850s, Hawthorne learned to play the part of author-as-celebrity, even, apparently, to enjoy it. The Hawthorne who was lionized at English banquets and Italian artistic gatherings became poised and outgoing—Hawthorne the reticent became socially adept, if he ever did, *through* the role of celebrity; when he came back to America Hawthorne continued to answer requests for autographs even after his literary authorship had definitively broken down.[10] And, really, Hawthorne was more than compliant with his fame; he appears at many points to have been actively complicit in the campaigns to promote him to celebrity status. Likenesses of authors in the nineteenth century are *ipso facto* acts of promotion, spreading the fact of an author's personal existence and confirming him as a person of note. Melville refused to be daguerreotyped for Duyckinck; but Hawthorne was an indefatigable poser, sitting, in his last years alone, for photographs by J. J. E. Mayall, W. H. Getchell, James Wallace Black, and Matthew Brady (this one of imperial size); for a marble bust by Louisa Landor and a marble bas-relief by Edward Kuntze; and for a portrait in oils by Emanuel Leutze, decorator of the Capitol and painter of "Washington Crossing the Delaware."[11] Hawthorne helped write the material Richard Henry Stoddard used in his 1853 essay on him, including the paragraph that helped found the biographical myth of his unworldliness—so that the aloof Hawthorne of popular conception is in fact an image an engaged Hawthorne helped to contrive.[12]

But another body of evidence suggests that if Hawthorne played the part of legendary author and living classic, he did so without much ease or conviction. Howells's reminiscence of his first visit to New England in 1860 in *Literary Friends and Acquaintance* gives the richest record we have of the moment when the mid-century reinstitution of the literary order had just become established: the moment when the nineteenth-century American canon had just assumed its full authority and come to domineer over new entrants to the literary field. Howells recalls that when "the passionate pilgrim from the West approached his holy land at Boston,"[13] he found the new New England luminaries all too willing to play the part of gods—except for Hawthorne, who alone did not inwardly accept or exact tributes to his outwardly designated status. Howells remembers a Hawthorne available to celebrity-hunters but embarrassed by the status they thrust upon him—"he was as much abashed by our encounter as I was,"[14] Howells writes; and this picture is confirmed, with variations, from other sources. Rebecca Harding Davis, then a new authoress from Wheeling (not yet West) Virginia, was inducted into Boston's literary sanctum by its custodian and creator, James T. Fields, in 1862—a time Davis, like Howells, registers as the hegemonic moment of the new American literature:

We were in the first flush of our triumph in the beginnings of a national literature. We talked much of it. Irving, Prescott, and Longfellow had been English, we said, but these new men—Holmes and Lowell and Hawthorne—were our own, the indigenous growth of the soil.[15]

Davis too found Hawthorne "in the Boston fraternity but not of it": willing to pose before her with his fellow immortals, but full of irony toward the importance they all too gladly accepted as their real worth. Her reminiscence *Bits of Gossip* leaves a racy account of Hawthorne sitting by, "his laughing, sagacious eyes watching us, full of mockery," while Emerson and Alcott pontificated about the War she alone had actually seen, then puncturing their vatic self-inflations with: "We cannot see that thing at so long a range. Let us go to dinner."[16] To these pictures of Hawthorne the embarrassed or self-mocking lion Henry James Sr. adds a portrait of the celebrity as near-aggressor and panic-stricken fraud. In an 1860 letter to Emerson he records Hawthorne's appearance at the Saturday Club, dutifully turned out for the social rites of literary celebrity, but looking there like "a rogue who suddenly finds himself in a company of detectives"; then staring fixedly at his plate throughout dinner so as to avoid having to return the conversation of Charles Eliot Norton, high priest of the religion of high culture.[17]

The biographical record gives glimpses of Hawthorne as by turns acquiescent in, actively committed to, amused, or made nervous, or even reduced to silence by the new cultural position defined for him as an author. But the best place to see how that position looked to him is in his writing—particularly *The Marble Faun*. Published in the hour of its triumph, *The Marble Faun* is written in full awareness of the contemporary reorganization of the literary sphere. This awareness is evident in Hawthorne's prefatory elegy for the gentle reader of his earlier books, with its clear recognition that the conditions for literary communication have undergone historical change; or again in his many asides, in the book, about marble statuary and the modern reproduction of contemporaries as immortals. But the awareness is by no means confined to such over allusions: it is present in the very composition of the novel's world. *The Marble Faun*'s most striking difference from Hawthorne's earlier romances is of course that it is set in Europe. But what this means in practice is that it is set in a museum-world: a world furnished with and organized around works of art. Not the sort of works we have seen before in Hawthorne—the letter Hester embroiders, or the photograph Holgrave develops, or the charade Zenobia performs. Art in *The Marble Faun* exists primarily as completed artifact, something already made and already designated as of classic value. These artifacts loom over the book's present, indeed possess such authority that the present can only refigure what is prefigured in them—as Donatello repeats the Faun of Praxiteles, or as Hilda and Miriam reincarnate the Beatrice of Guido Reni. The sculptures are classical, and the paintings Italian Renaissance, but the world they constitute is really that of mid-nineteenth-century American culture.* *The Marble Faun*'s fictive world mirrors quite precisely the real world Howells arrived in the year *The Marble Faun* was published: a world in which art has been strongly reidentified not with the work of making but with a canon of masters and masterpieces; a world where certain figures have become so prestigious that later workers must make constant reference to their preestablished precedent.

The altered shape of experience within *The Marble Faun,* I am trying to suggest, reflects the altered shape of the world that surrounds it—of the cultural configuration that, upon publication, this novel would be taken up into. *The Marble Faun* also includes, as one of its most striking new inventions, a representation of the forces that erect and sustain such a configuration. Hilda was criticized, when *The Marble Faun* appeared, as yet another Hawthornesque pale maiden; but Hawthorne was right to defend himself against the charge of self-repetition. What makes Hilda different from Phoebe or Priscilla is that in this incarnation, the pale maiden is centrally associated with a will toward a specific sort of cultural organization. Hilda is the bearer of a militant high-cultural spirit. She is the exponent of the canonical attitude, the attitude that identifies art with an exclusive group of transcendent makers. Miriam and Kenyon paint and sculpt. They are artists, and they know each other as artists. But for Hilda only the Old Masters are artists, and the only artists are the Masters. (This is of course the attitude Hawthorne himself became the beneficiary of in the later nineteenth century: for Horace Scudder in 1888 as for Howells in 1860, American literature *is* six great authors, and one of them is Hawthorne.) Hilda not only adores the canon: she incarnates the kind of conceptual and cultural agency that gives art a canonical shape. Hilda lives "at a height" (52), she dwells in "loftiness" (53) (we can again remember Scudder on "noble poetry and lofty prose"); or, to put it another way, Hilda embodies the force that establishes the existence of such a thing as a distinct "high" level of being and expression. The world becomes verticalized in her presence: things that can exist on the same plane elsewhere in the novel become, in her neighborhood, rigidly separated into that which is "above our vanities and passions" and that which shares in "our moral dust and mud." (53) In this Hilda figures the sort of forces that, in *The Marble Faun*'s own decade, worked to stratify a previously unified field of literary expression into separated literary and popular categories. Miriam, an "amateur" (20) artist undisciplined by trained study

---

* Whenever they were painted, in any case, as objects of mass veneration the Old Masters are really a phenomenon of the second half of the nineteenth century, in America at least, products in the fine arts of that move to fix the rank of authoritative practitioners that also produced, in the department of literature, the American literary canon. The functional interchangeability of the Old Masters and the nineteenth-century literary canon—evidenced, for instance, by the fact that *Century* had its frontispiece of Hawthorne engraved by the artist who also did its Old Masters reproductions (a real-life Hilda)—deserves fuller exploration.

of the Masters, is the painter indiscriminately of sublime theological subjects and homely domestic sketches. As such she represents what is, by
1860, an older artistic order—the kind of order in which Hawthorne's fiction was published alongside Catharine Sedgwick's, as it was in the 1830s;
or in which Hawthorne himself produced both terrific tales and homey
sketches, as he did throughout the 1840s. Hilda embodies the new scheme
that made such mixings unthinkable. When it enters her field, some forms
of expression get marked as inestimably "better and loftier," and the others
become consequently debased and debasing—they "lower the standard of
art to the comprehension of the spectator." (60) The novel itself makes
clear how this distinction corresponds to the one newly established between
Hawthorne's kind of work and that of his popular competitors:

> The handmaid of Raphael, whom she loved with a virgin's love! Would
> it have been worth Hilda's while to relinquish this office for the sake of
> giving the world a picture or two which it would call original; pretty
> fancies of snow and moonlight; the counterpart in picture, of so many
> feminine achievements in literature! (61)

Hawthorne figures, in Hilda, the remaking of the category of the truly
artistic that was taking place in his novel's time. He figures too a parallel
remaking of the attitude of art's observer. Hilda images, in extraordinarily
precise detail, the mid-nineteenth-century development in which the freshly
segregated sphere of secular high art became sacralized, made a new locus
for the sacred as it departed from its customary haunts. Hilda is deeply
religious, but art is what she worships: she at least would have had no
trouble talking with Charles Eliot Norton, whose art-religion hers closely
mirrors.[18] (It was Norton, we can remember, who presided over Henry
James Jr.'s "positive consecration to letters" four years after he rendered
Hawthorne speechless.) The Masters are quite literally sacred—are *the*
sacred—to Hilda. To view their work is to be "in their awful presence"
(57)—just as Howells, visiting America's new old masters in the year of
Hilda's appearance, sought out "the presence of a famous man," was
"abashed when [he] first came into [Lowell's] presence," found himself in
Hawthorne's "presence," made a "confused retreat from Emerson's presence."[19] As a "worshipper" of "genius" who views art works "reverently,
not to say religiously" (58, 57), Hilda belongs to a historical transformation of art into an object *of* reverence (compare Howells's will "to venerate
those New England luminaries"); an object whose use is to reinforce the
attitude of deference in general (so J. G. Holland, editor of *Scribner's,*
thanked the canonical American authors for staying alive, and so "help-
[ing] to save the American nation from the total wreck and destruction of
the sentiment of reverence.")[20] In the best fashion of the late-nineteenth-
century apostles of culture, Hilda worships art in a twofold manner. First
she subjects it to "appreciation" (56)—focuses and savors the inestimable
"excellence" (56) stored in the work of art. Then she copies it and makes
it commonly available—

From the dark, chill corner of a gallery—from some curtained chapel in a church, where the light came seldom and aslant—from the prince's carefully guarded cabinet, where not one eye in thousands was permitted to behold it—she brought the wondrous picture into daylight, and gave all its magic splendor for the enjoyment of the world (60):

prefiguring, here, the bringing of elite culture to all through mass reproduction that was the late nineteenth century's dream, and that saw Hawthorne himself installed in millions of schools and homes.[21]

The Marble Faun's new cultural order—the socially remade definition of literature's nature and place that it was produced within—is, all of this implies, not something external to the novel: an objective situation it enters after it is made. Rather, the novel takes its externally given position up inside itself; it stages the situation that awaits it within its imaginative action. *The Marble Faun* reproduces the cultural forms and forces that define its place, we might add, to the end of exploring what they mean. This novel is Hawthorne's attempt, through the creation of a fiction, to read the new "real" world built around his art, and to find out what it does to artistic expression.

Hawthorne's restaging of the coming of high culture in *The Marble Faun* understands this configuration by associating it, in the person of Hilda, with a series of other ones. Hilda is characterized by a certain sort of cultural will, but equally by a certain sort of erotic organization, the one nineteenth-century womens' historians call "passionlessness."[22] Hilda lives at a height above erotic passions among others—her flower is no "blossom of fervid hue and spicy fragrance" (374) but the alpine "snowdrop," flower of frigid elevations. Her depassionalization makes her, as she makes art, the object of the hierarchizing and self-denying emotion of reverence. (In a scene borrowed directly from *Pierre,* Kenyon freezes in "reverent pause" (404) before Hilda's snow-white single bed.) Hilda is equally strongly associated with an ethical vision that sees the human world as governed by inviolable and immitigable laws. Miriam, pre-professional artist and still-eroticized woman, always responds to others as a person to a person—whatever she did, Beatrice Cenci is "still a woman, . . . still a sister" to Miriam, so much so that her technical moral state becomes unimportant: "be her sin or sorrow what they might!" (68) But for Hilda the law comes first, and men and women must be what the law proclaims them—her verdict on Beatrice is: "Her doom is just!" (66)[23] Through this characterization, Hilda's worship of the Masters is revealed as part of a larger project for erecting subordination-demanding institutions. Through her Hawthorne reads the advent of a canonical model of art as one phase of a more general objectification of authority in his culture, the artistic yield of a process whose products also include the intensification of the superego's abstracting legalism and the compulsory etherealization of erotic life.

At the same time that it gives Hilda's version of culture this wider range of reference, Hawthorne's fictive invention in *The Marble Faun* also works to track the operation of this version of culture, or literally to plot its action. Hilda's role in the action of *The Marble Faun* is mostly to disso-ciate herself from it. Accidental witness to Donatello's crime, Hilda under-goes initiation vicariously, by witnessing the initiation of another. But her response to even this highly mediated form of "fallen" experience is to re-fuse to participate in it. The first thing Hilda does after seeing Donatello's crime is to refuse Miriam's plea for sympathy and contact, a refusal that is dramatically rendered as the drawing of an inviolable boundary across previously continuous space:

> Hilda was standing in the middle of the room. When her friend made a step or two from the door, she put forth her hands with an involuntary repellent gesture, so expressive, that Miriam at once felt a great chasm opening itself between them two. They might gaze at one another from the opposite side, but without the possibility of ever meeting more; or, at least, since the chasm could never be bridged over, they must tread the whole round of Eternity to meet on the other side. (207)

As *The Marble Faun* sees it, one essential action of what Hilda repre-sents is to institute separations, to recast the world into rigidly separated zones of experience and expression. Another—really it is *the* other, so lim-ited is Hilda's range of functions in the novel—is to police the district she has marked off as unpolluted. She is a tireless monitor of cultural re-sponses: when Kenyon makes a joke about St. Peter's, she is quick to re-join: "I revere this glorious church for itself and its purposes" (369); when Miriam speaks irreverently about Guido Reni, Hilda is there to en-force the right canonical attitude:

> "Miriam!" exclaimed her friend reproachfully. "You grieve me, and you know it, by pretending to speak contemptuously of the most beautiful and divinest figure that mortal painter ever drew." (139)

By the same token, Hilda is a tireless suppresser of expression that might contaminate her cultural project. Hilda's chief work is as a silencer: "Hush, naughty one!" (8); "let us never speak of it again!" (383) She obviously hopes that in stamping out dissident speech, she might also eradicate the thought that inspired it: "Hush! Do not even utter her name! Try not to think of it!" (383) is her motto's full form.

It would be possible to make a long list of things Hilda will not allow to be said: she has the genius for multiplying subversion of a totalitarian re-gime, which she resembles in other ways as well. But what Hilda is most deeply committed to silencing in *The Marble Faun* is the author's apparent message. This novel announces itself as a retelling of "the story of the Fall of Man" (434). (For all its apparent universality, this theme also engages the cultural-historical issue of its moment: the fall story as this novel puts it poses the question above all of the origin and significance of a separate, "higher" level of human faculty.) The novel's reading of the fall, reiterated a dozen times in its late chapters, is that the same transgression through which innocence and untrammeled instinctual spontaneity are lost is also the way into the vale of soul making, the place of suffering and knowledge where we attain to the distinctively human qualities of conscience, reflection, and moral intelligence.* I risk irreverence to say that this reading of the fall may be profound, but it is certainly not novel: already well established long before Milton, it was a humanistic truism in the nineteenth century. But the curiosity of *The Marble Faun* is that Hilda finds the doctrine of the *felix culpa* new and inexpressibly shocking. Indeed Hilda's real role in the novel is to lie in wait for this doctrine's emergence, so she can slap it down: "Never!," she tells Kenyon, when he first asks her to entertain the idea that a fall might be fortunate; when he tries again at the novel's close, she is firmer yet:

> "Oh, hush!" cried Hilda, shrinking from him with an expression of horror which wounded the poor, speculative sculptor to the soul. "This is terrible; and I could weep for you, if you indeed believe it." (460)

What are we to make of a novel that so prominently hushes the speech it seems designed to express? And why is Hilda shocked by what is, to all appearances, so platitudinous a message? The answer, I think, has less to do with the content of the *felix culpa* doctrine than with the form of expression it embodies in the novel. This doctrine has the status, in the novel, of something guessed, risked, discovered in peril: "I tremble at my own thoughts," says Miriam as she voices it, "yet must needs probe them to their depths." (434) Above all, it has the status of something *made*—and, explicitly, made by means of an artist's expressive act. Miriam pieces out this doctrine, but only after she and Donatello have pieced together the statue of Venus they find in fragments in the campagna. Kenyon, the novel's practitioner of fortunate-fall therapy before he recants his creed, does not have this wisdom in advance: he comes to know it when he sculpts Donatello's bust, and comes to know it *by means of* his sculptor's work—that free play with his expressive medium by which he first recaptures Donatello's look at the moment of his crime, than transforms Donatello the transgressor into Donatello the mature man.

The idea of the fortunate fall is not already available in *The Marble*

---

* It might be argued, though, that this is only what the novel *thinks* it thinks about the fall of man. For all the times that he is said to do so, we do not see Donatello become more richly human as the novel progresses. What he becomes is a double of Hilda: a creature of repressive elevation. After his fall, he moves up in a tower, just like Hilda. There he learns the art of repression, the art of "thrusting [his emotions] down into the prison-cells where he usually kept them confined" (250)—the mental art of Hilda, who, we are told, excels at "voluntary forgetfulness." (382) Apparently with Hilda's contrivance, Donatello himself, earlier representative of unrenounced instinctual gratifications, ends up renouncing his desires and entering a "prison" (467)—repressing himself in service to abstract law. By this account, Hilda objects to the story of the fall because it is really the secret story of her own real origins— the story of the "high's" emergence as a repressive construction produced *by* the transgression it punishes and denies.

Faun. It is a creation: it is brought to existence, as a moral possibility, through a human expressive act. The specific form of that act—and the reason why it can create new possibilities for thought and experience—is that it remakes the structure of the field of knowledge. The *work* of art, as Miriam and Kenyon practice it, is to remold conceptual opposites: to express as coexisting and interdependent what has previously seemed mutually exclusive. Kenyon's bust makes it conceivable that Donatello is both innocent and guilty, and his crime both destructive and constructive. Miriam's reconstructed Venus recovers the possibility that women might be simultaneously erotic and chaste, and indistinguishably earthy and divine. The *felix culpa* notion is the product *par excellence* of such creation, establishing the convertibility of terms like "crime" and "blessing" (434), "fall" and "rise" (460), and rendering man's fallen nature not the bad opposite but the very source of his so-called "higher" self.

The expressive acts that produce the idea of *felix culpa* here and the view of expression that these acts embody are deeply familiar to readers of earlier Hawthorne. Kenyon's magic sculpture strongly recalls Holgrave's magic photography in *The House of the Seven Gables,* that other art that rendered not surface features but the "likeness of [the] inner man" (271), and so disclosed the identity of apparently different things. The production of the *felix culpa* reminds one even more strongly of Hester's needlework in *The Scarlet Letter* and the passionate application of artistic force by which she expressed as identical what she received as opposed: made a badge of shame be also a badge of pride, sign of the identity of transgressive desire and constructive energy; or, in her dressing of Pearl, "wrought out the similitude . . . between the object of her affection and the emblem of her guilt and torture."[24]

The weight the doctrine of the fortunate fall really carries in *The Marble Faun,* such likenesses suggest, is that of a reassertion of the enabling faith of Hawthorne's high romantic moment: the faith that art can be not a likeness of already familiar things but a genuine new making; and that *what* art can bring to existence are those moral and cognitive possibilities that "reality's" structures of thought close down. This is exactly what Hilda finds repulsive in the doctrine. She cannot stand to have established dualisms collapsed and remolded:

> "There is, I believe, only one right and one wrong; and I do not understand (and may God keep me from ever understanding) how two things so totally unlike can be mistaken for one another; nor how two mortal foes—as Right and Wrong surely are—can work together in the same deed." (384)

She will not allow that moral knowledge might be or need to be new-*made,* at all:

> "Do you not perceive what a mockery your creed makes, not only of all religious sentiments, but of moral law, and how it annuls and obliterates whatever precepts of Heaven are written deepest within us?" (460)

What Hilda wants to silence, in *The Marble Faun,* is expression itself, as romance once defined it. As the novel plots it, her version of the world sustains itself by suppressing art in one of its forms, as a meaning-constructing action.

When we say Hilda, *The Marble Faun* teaches us, we really mean the mid-nineteenth-century organization of the cultural sphere; and this novel shows how Hawthorne stands toward that development. The novel is not, finally, critical of Hilda—quite the reverse. For all its constructive labors, *The Marble Faun* never does generate an alternative that can discredit and supplant Hilda's vision. Her view overpowers all others, hers is the book's last work (hush!): in her presence the maker of the countervision of the fortunate fall denies that he ever believed that at all. Her ascendancy in the book mirrors Hawthorne's own cultural adjustment. Hawthorne was *not* a dissident in the new American order of culture. Other writers were, in varying degrees. Between 1850 and 1860 Melville tried to assert an oppositional alternative to the artistic culture then establishing itself as official, withdrawing his work from the public sphere after he failed. In this time Stowe, more cagily, found a way to grab some of the prestige of the newly founded high literary culture without losing her authority as a popular writer. But Hawthorne accepted the role of high-cultural author in its full official form, Saturday Club lunches, literary pilgrims, and all—and accepted it, apparently, without it having occurred to him that he could refuse it or modify its terms.

But if Hawthorne did not resist the definition this new cultural organization imposed on his art, he did cast up this order's cost to him—by writing *The Marble Faun. The Marble Faun* recognizes that when art gets taken up into a high-cultural structure like the new American one, its function becomes not to dissolve and redraw cultural categories but exactly to emblematize preestablished oppositions: to stand for the high as opposed to the low, the sacred as opposed to the profane, and so on. But when it becomes art's public mission to reinforce the way things are already known, *The Marble Faun* suggests, the result is to make it a bore. Hilda worships art on terms that link it inextricably to boredom. The striking chapter "The Emptiness of the Picture Galleries" shows her stilling of art's conceptual play as leaving nothing going on in the paintings she visits: they become "a crust of paint over an emptiness." (341) Arranged as Hilda prefers it, publicly displayed in canonical form, art becomes at once the source of "reverence" and "torpor" (335), the inspirer of "that icy Demon of Weariness, who haunts great picture galleries." (336) Hawthorne here prophesies the fate of his own works, which went on to be honored in unparalleled ways, but on terms that neutralized what might have been innovative or disruptive in them[25]—terms that made his works great bores to countless readers by century's end. As Hawthorne acceded to the role of canonical author he himself began to find his work a bore. His dominant passions in the years of his greatest fame were apathy, lassitude, and ennui. And already in *The Marble Faun* he sees writing as the source of ennui:

this book's author looks enviously at sculptors, who can ship their ideas off to the carver and so be spared what Hawthorne calls "the drudgery of actual performance." (115)

The Marble Faun's other recognition is that when art is taken into a high-cultural structure it gets defined as different from other expression, such that as it gets exalted it is simultaneously removed from the category of general human doing and making. Hilda's career as a copyist shows the consequence of this. Her veneration elevates the Masters to a height from which her own painting looks poor and low, so that as a necessary corollary to her idolization of artists she renounces her own powers of "original achievement":

> It has probably happened in many other instances, as it did in Hilda's case, that she ceased to aim at original achievement in consequence of the very gifts, which so exquisitely fitted her to profit by familiarity with the works of the mighty Old Masters. Reverencing these wonderful men so deeply, she was too grateful for all they bestowed upon her—too loyal— too humble, in their awful presence—to think of enrolling herself in their society. . . . So Hilda became a copyist. (57)

This is another prophecy of Hawthorne's own artistic future: for the more he accepted his place as classic author, the harder he found it to make his own work. When Hawthorne returned to America in 1860 he built a tower onto his house with a writing-room on its top floor. But after he got himself (in Fields's words) "fitly shrined"[26] at this Hilda-like elevation, nothing came out. "I spend two or three hours a day in my sky-parlor, and duly spread a quire of paper on my desk," he wrote Ticknor in early 1861, "but no very important result has followed, thus far."[27] From this point on Hawthorne alternately sat in the pose of literary celebrity and worked in vain at his romances—activities that are not unconnected, *The Marble Faun* leads us to think. In his hour of final fame he himself became, at last, a copyist: drafting and redrafting works that never did get made, because he could no longer stand toward them as their maker.

Hawthorne accepted the designation that the mid-century reorganization of American culture placed on him and his work. But he did so with a strong sense that those designations were deeply disabling to his kind of creation. We can understand, in this light, why he spent his last years trying to write about an elixir that confers immortality, but brings unforeseen miseries in the process. It seems fitting in more ways than were intended that when Hawthorne died in 1864, at his funeral, conducted with full literary honors and America's other immortals all in attendance ("ideal pall-bearers,"[28] Mrs. Hawthorne called them), the manuscript of his unachievable work was displayed with pomp upon his coffin.

Chapter Five

HOWELLS
Literary History and the Realist Vocation

> I read the *Marble Faun* first, and then the *Scarlet Letter,* and then the
> *House of Seven Gables,* and then the *Blithedale Romance.* . . . They all
> moved me with a sort of effect such as I had not felt before. They were
> so far from time and place that, although most of them related to our
> country and epoch, I could not imagine anything approximate from them;
> and Hawthorne himself seemed a remote and impalpable agency, rather
> than a person whom one might actually meet, as not long afterward hap-
> pened to me. I did not hold the sort of fancied converse with him that I
> held with other authors, and I cannot pretend that I had the affection for
> him that attracted me to them. But he held me by his potent spell, and for
> a time he dominated me as completely as any author I have read. More
> truly than any other American author he has been a passion with me.
>
> HOWELLS, *My Literary Passions*

IF WE WERE LOOKING for a figure to stand for the opposite of Hawthorne's
kind of author, William Dean Howells would make an obvious choice.
Hawthorne was nineteenth-century American culture's embodiment of the
private literary person: its figure of the artist as one who dwells apart in a
private imaginative region, a region he gives the public access to in his
work, without himself becoming available through that process. By contrast, Howells was the nineteenth century's great figure of the artist as public man. A prolific writer, greatly more so than Hawthorne ever was, Howells was also almost constantly engaged, throughout his long career, in
performing the public offices that establish literature's public life. As assistant editor, then editor, of the *Atlantic* from 1866 to 1881, Howells
managed America's most prestigious literary magazine at the time when
literary magazines were becoming prominent instruments of American middle-class culture. A tireless columnist, first for the *Atlantic,* then for the
more widely circulated *Harper's Monthly,* then for such new mass-market
organs of the 1890s as *Cosmopolitan* and *Ladies Home Journal,* Howells
set his taste-instructing views on literary and cultural questions before the
ever-expanding audiences these magazines assembled, with monthly regularity. By these means, themselves most unHawthornesque, Howells succeeded in the yet more unHawthornesque task of making himself known to
the public of his time. He won massive recognition for himself as a kind

of personal embodiment of the institution of letters, a status he held in the public mind from the 1880s well into this century.[1] And he won recognition for *himself:* he communicated to the literary public, over and beyond his works, dense knowledge of that set of commitments and preferences that made up his personal position.

To the public they both addressed, Howells seemed as available as Hawthorne was elusive, as forthcoming as Hawthorne was self-withholding. And the difference in the kind of public identity they achieved reflects an equally significant difference in the way Hawthorne and Howells conceive of the literary writer's cultural function. Hawthorne's perennial challenge as a writer is that of trying to define a suitably marginal form for his work's social position. The place of artistic power in his fiction is always literally a marginal one: Hester makes new letters in her cottage on the edge of town; Holgrave develops new pictures in his room in a retired house's back gable; Coverdale guesses new social relations in his hermitage, a treehouse just in peeping-distance of Blithedale. Hawthorne's own difficult task, we might say, is that of making available for himself the kind of textual space he images in these physical places—a position where his work will still be in contact with the forms and processes of "real" social life, but will be sufficiently removed from their sway to allow it freely to re-figure them. But Howells's urge is exactly to close down the distance Hawthorne wants to open up. Howells wants to collapse the literary sphere back into the sphere of social reality, and so to identify the writer's making power with a broader exercise of civic authority. The Howells who broadcast his views on the state of American civilization in his monthly columns is animated by a conviction completely foreign to Hawthorne: the conviction that to be a maker of fiction is to be both privileged and obliged to participate in the primary production of social reality. Hawthorne's fragilely maintained idea of literature as a "theater removed" is at best disturbing, at worst repulsive to Howells. Literature commands his full loyalty only when it can make itself out to be not literary only, but a central agency of communal life.

The fiction Howells looked to to discharge fiction's civic obligations is the brand known as realism, and Howells's championing of literary realism sets him in strong opposition as well to Hawthorne's preferred literary mode. Hawthorne was nineteenth-century America's most articulate advocate of romance, a form that, as he defines it, realizes the dream of ideal marginality. In Hawthorne's idea of it romance is less a literary form than a cultural condition: romance exists when literature can establish a covenant suspending the control over it of the codes of social normality (the expectation of verisimilitude), and chartering it to produce reality, within its "fairy precinct," "under circumstances . . . of the writer's own choosing or creation." One of Howells's great aims as a literary polemicist (though he claimed to exempt Hawthorne from his strictures) was to revoke the public license Hawthorne had pleaded for. Romance becomes, in Howells's vigorous redescription of it, the literary equivalent of narcissism, and the producer, as a staple form of entertainment, of a culture ill able to maintain a common reality other than the sum of its members' egoistic self-inflations.[2] Howells's parallel mission was to win public adherence to the antithetical kind of fiction that Hawthorne had described but not yet had a name for: a fiction that severely renounces fiction's power of fabrication and countercreation, and subjects itself to the discipline of "a very minute fidelity, not merely to the possible, but to the probable and ordinary course of man's experience."

These oppositions—of public role, cultural attitude, and formal preference—are striking and central ones. They represent not minor or merely apparent divergences, but fundamental differences in the way these authors form the idea of their work and assert its place in the world. But Howells's very stand as the major American opponent to Hawthorne's conception of the literary makes it all the more interesting that he should have had a deep and continuing involvement with Hawthorne. Howells, whose sympathetic knowledge of earlier American writers was probably unsurpassed in his generation, nevertheless says of Hawthorne in the autobiography of his reading: "More truly than any other American author he has been a passion with me." His own work bears this out: for all of Howells's command of earlier literature, and for all his closeness to many of its celebrated figures, Hawthorne and Hawthorne alone, among possible American precedents, is strongly present to Howells in the making of his novels. As I want to show here, Hawthorne was in fact never more alive to Howells than at the moment when he was forming his notion of realism. And part of Howells's understanding of realism comes from his facing of what Hawthorne represented, both as model and as challenge to this work.

I present Howells as an unexpected (and also largely unrecognized) member in the tradition of Hawthorne. He stands here too as a figure for what might be called the unforeseeableness *of* tradition: part of the point Howells makes, as a figure in the school of Hawthorne, is that there is no saying in advance what writers an earlier writer will or will not touch, what writers will or will not enlist him as their guide. But I confess that my interest in Howells, in this context, is less in the terms of his membership in Hawthorne's tradition than in what he shows about how tradition itself gets forged. I have said that tradition has to do with the past's funding of the present—with the way acts of making and knowing, once performed, become available again to someone else's performing, through the transmission of their memory in a work. I have also been maintaining that works do not transmit themselves. They rely on a partly extraliterary process (there is not one of these: the process is not invariant), the play of a larger set of institutional forces, to keep them present as the past, and to establish their relevance to present makings. But here it can be added that the cultural mechanics of literary perpetuation, while they may be a precondition for tradition formation, do not of themselves create tradition. The making of tradition also requires another—a complementary but essentially antithetical—process whereby the transmitted past gets, so to speak, decoded as a guide for practice. For a work to become a source of tradition a later worker must locate it as a significant model; must find—by which we really mean invent or construct—what its significance as a model might consist of (we forget that the exemplary nature of past works is not necessarily obvious, when a tradition is still forming); then must devise a way to imitate what he has isolated, or to reactivate its powers in his own making. Howells, one of the first authors to receive Hawthorne specifically as a *past,* shows especially revealingly how the American literary past was organized and communicated between generations in the nineteenth century. He shows even better that other process, equally invisible to us, by which the past thus transmitted got reconstructed into a usable past. I offer him here as an object lesson in the process by which American writers of the later nineteenth century struggled to convert a heavily institutionalized literary history into an image of their own beings and becomings—a process indistinguishable from their achievement of their own full power.

The paths of transmission by which Hawthorne came down to Howells are, at first sight at least, unusually easy to trace. Howells has left an eloquent record, in *My Literary Passions,* of his entrancing first reading of Hawthorne, in Columbus in the winter of 1859–60. And in *Literary Friends and Acquaintance* Howells gives a poignant reminiscence of his meeting with Hawthorne in Concord the following spring. Howells here recalls the rather stiff conversation between the shy Hawthorne and his equally shy votary, conversation that reached its satisfactory conclusion when Hawthorne wrote, on a card of introduction to Emerson: "I find this young man worthy."[3] Both of these accounts register Hawthorne as a figure with whom Howells felt an instant, strong, and unparalleled relation. In *My Literary Passions* Howells meets Hawthorne's fiction as a "potent spell," a literary force so powerful that Howells (for once) cannot think of it as coming from a human agent, and so strong that he can only relate to it as the submissive object of its dominating sway. In *Literary Friends and Acquaintance,* by contrast, Howells singles Hawthorne out for his literary humanity. Hawthorne alone among the giants of New England letters whom Howells called on in 1860 did not strike him as acting the giant and coaxing tributes to his greatness; and Howells remembers how he accordingly identified Hawthorne as his possible protector in the world of literary intimidation, the figure he could run back to for comfort, for instance, from the self-aggrandizements of Emerson.[4]

This first reading and early meeting formed, no doubt, the ground for Howells's subsequent relationship with Hawthorne. But we get only a very partial understanding of what Hawthorne was to Howells—even in these first encounters—if we think of their relation as taking place only between a person and a person or a reader and a text. Howells's reception of this figure at this time needs to be understood, for one thing, within the history of his own artistic biography. The year Howells met and read Hawthorne was always most significant to Howells as the year of his full emergence into literature, an emergence marked, for him, by the printing of his poems in the *Atlantic*. This development in turn needs to be understood in conjunction with another, exactly coincidental, development in American literature's own institutional history. In *Literary Friends and Acquaintance* Howells strongly emphasizes that his debut in literature intersected with a major remaking of the forms through which literature was ordered and arrayed in America. The moment of his accession was also, he underlines, the moment when what he calls the "great New England group"[5]—he lists them as Lowell, Longfellow, Emerson, Hawthorne, Holmes, Whittier, and Stowe—rose to new heights in the literary heavens. The hour of these writers' greatest power, it was also, and indistinguishably, the moment when certain forms of authorship were becoming newly prestigious or "great" in public terms—and when figures not in this rank were being placed, accordingly, at a new hierarchical remove from them. (The vocabulary of Howells the literary pilgrim is the vocabulary of insistent differentials of status: he is the venerator, the New England authors his "luminaries"; he is the "prentice," they are the "masters"; he is the "obscure subaltern," they are "his general.")[6] Reflecting and enforcing this development, it was the time too of the successful establishment of a new kind of publishing institution, designed to publish and distinguish an especially select grade of literary writing. Howells identifies these as "the Atlantic Monthly, which had lately adventured in the fine air of high literature"; and "Ticknor and Fields, who were literary publishers in a sense such as the business world has known nowhere else before or since."[7]

Howells's debut *in* literature coincided with a reorganization of the cultural sphere *of* literature—with that demarcation and institutional reinforcement of a separate, prestigious sphere of high or literary writing, in the 1850s and 1860s, that we have been considering, from different angles, in the last two chapters. As Howells's memoirs make clear, the consequence for him of coming into the literary field as it acquired this altered public shape was that his literary aspirations became powerfully identified with literature's new public configurations. The fact that Howells came to authorship just when it took on this impressive new institutional form inevitably made him look toward those institutions as the place where authorship could be fully achieved; more, it made him internalize their newly asserted design of the literary sphere as his personal definition of what literature meant. We read the marks of this fateful conjunction of ambition and institutional setting all through Howells's early career. Howells first wanted to make his name as a poet. But after 1859, being a poet for Howells becomes all but synonymous with being published in the *Atlantic:* to write poetry is to aim it *toward* that publication; and being accepted *in* that publication is what certifies the writing to be poetry.[8] When Howells turned from poetry to descriptive writing, he persisted in identifying the will to write with the will to be produced by certain writerly institutions. In an 1865 letter he writes Ticknor and Fields in the obvious hope that if he does not ask them to publish his newly written *Venetian Life,* he might get them to agree to be its distributing agent—then, baring his real wish by extending the favor he begs, he asks what he would have to do to get his book published, say, in Ticknor and Fields's trademark binding.[9] Howells's movement onto the editorial staff of the *Atlantic* in 1866 was the consummation of his historically conditioned literary dream. Lionel Trilling's famous slap at Howells the writer-editor—"he devoted himself to a literary career not so much out of disinterested love for literature as out of a sense that literature was an institutional activity by which he might make something of himself in the worldly way"[10]—gets the psychological and cultural-historical meaning of Howells's early career exactly wrong. To edit the *Atlantic* is not, for Howells, to buy into a secondary form of literary life. To manage this institution is to occupy what he knows as literature's central place of power: it is to realize himself *in* the literary in the most compelling way he is able to imagine it.

When Howells took up the *Atlantic* position early in 1866 he moved, we might notice, into the identical cultural space that Hawthorne had inhabited as recently as two years before. Hawthorne's patron and public creator, James T. Fields, became Howells's boss. Hawthorne's periodical outlet, the *Atlantic,* became Howells's as well. Howells wrote, therefore, for the same readership that had been amassed to read Hawthorne. And when he succeeded with that audience, Howells won his way into Hawthorne's old places of honor. (Howells was elected to the Saturday Club, after having been blackballed once, in 1874.) Seeing Howells move into Hawthorne's place should remind us how illusory the separation is that we erect between pre-Civil War and postwar American authors. The logic they learned from their contemporary culture of letters compelled the writers starting out in the 1860s and 1870s to try to establish themselves in exactly the same institutional structures that such figures as Hawthorne and Emerson had occupied (however ambivalently) before them. But Howells's and Hawthorne's institutional connection, while it helps expose this now largely buried continuity in American literary history, can also serve to remind us that the older writers' experience of those structures is only half of their story. The canonical position that Hawthorne had fashioned for him was only one of many new kinds of authorial roles that this new set of literary arrangements brought into being: the same reorganization that produced this culturally monumental senior position also opened up new kinds of positions for younger authors, in the 1860s.* And if Hawthorne is right that this reorganization of cultural position was damaging to the work of canonized authors, its effects on the work-lives of younger writers were by no means only disabling.

---

* The establishment of a high-literary zone produced, of course, not just these positions but a redefinition of *all* authorial positions in America. With the advent of the *Atlantic* as a place of status, other publications became redefined as sub-*Atlantic,* and writing for them got experienced as producing a secondary or impaired status. Rebecca Harding Davis felt impaired in this way when she began writing for *Peterson's,* after the *Atlantic* dropped her in the mid-1860; so (I would guess) did a writer Howells was always sending off to journals he implied were inferior to his own, his sister Aurelia.

Howells's early career shows especially clearly the new terms on which it became possible to realize oneself as an author in America, when authorship got transferred onto this new institutional ground. Having access to the newly created high-literary organs of mid-century brought about a very dramatic change, his case shows, in the economics of authorship. Hawthorne found literary writing all but untenable as a source of support for most of his writing life. Writing for the low rates paid by *The Token* and *The Democratic Review,* and subject to their irregular schemes of payment, Hawthorne was only able to support himself (very marginally) as a writer for short periods before 1850, and that by working in a hacklike fashion. (In the year he wrote *The Scarlet Letter,* we do not often remember, Hawthorne was reduced to accepting a charitable fund got together by his friends.) The accessibility of a new journal like the *Atlantic* turned literary writing into a potentially lucrative activity. By joining the staff of the *Atlantic* Howells earned first $3500, then $5000 a year—a figure sufficient not only to make authorship practicable as a specialized career (Howells worked in no Customs House after 1865), but even to let him live in a handsome display of style. (The regularity and security of the *Atlantic's* payment, it might be added, made Howells into America's first literary author addicted to salary wages—an economic dependency he explores very acutely in *A Hazard of New Fortunes.*) [11]

Being able to realize oneself on the terms Howells had available to him produced an equally striking change in the writer's public status. Hawthorne's real complaint about the literary-institutional circumstances he began in was not that they did not pay enough, but that they did not bring him adequately before the public. Working in the absence of well-developed means to publication, "The Devil in Manuscript" laments, makes the writer a literal nonentity: a figure who does not exist for others, who has not been made real to others through the communication of his work. In sharp contrast with early Hawthorne, "for a good many years, the obscurest man of letters in America," Howells became a somebody right away, from the start of his *Atlantic* appointment. As the selector of contributions and the regular reviewer for the established journal of literary record, Howells became well recognized as an authority in the literary sphere. (The *Atlantic* editorship is the first institutional base for that more public kind of authorship I have said that Howells achieved.) Known to readers and writers by virtue of his position, Howells also enjoyed full standing in all the adjacent spheres where literary prestige was reciprocally recognized. The new professionalizing universities of the 1870s and early 1880s looked to Howells as the obvious candidate for their literary professorships. [12] And they did so, quite obviously, because of his institutional position: surely it was Howells's long and distinguished editorship, much more than his authorship of *A Modern Instance* or *A Woman's Reason,* that Daniel Coit Gilman found convertible into a professorial credential, when he tried to win Howells for Johns Hopkins.

Becoming an author in America's new mid-century organization of the literary sphere made authorship into a new kind of economic relation. It gave a new and more general character to the author's public standing. It also entailed, by the same process, a new relation to literary history. The *Atlantic* was always identified in Howells's eyes with Holmes, Lowell, and the "great New England group." He thought of the *Atlantic* as the place where these writers published; and he saw their association with it as the source of the *Atlantic*'s public authority.[13] This meant that to become an author on Howells's terms—terms that linked authorship both to writing and to administration of this journal—*as* it gave him a secure salary, and *as* it gave him a solid social position, also put him at the service of New England's literary giants. Being the editor of their periodical made America's then newly canonical figures constantly present to Howells. And it made it an integral part of his work to perpetuate those authors and maintain their canonical form.

Part of Howells's work, as editor, was to seek out new contributions from these older writers (his first act as editor was to seek out a sequel to *The Autocrat at the Breakfast Table* from Holmes), then to stop the presses when such pieces came to hand, so that they could be prominently displayed. Part of Howells's work was to organize literary banquets, banquets that had as one of their chief purposes the display of the *Atlantic*'s new writers in the same company as its giants.[14] It was an essential part of Howells's labor as a man of letters to be a conservator of America's official literary past, and a public joiner of its past with its future. What needs to be emphasized about this arrangement is that it did not derive only from personal needs or desires. Howells sought out, and spent considerable time well into middle age maintaining, close personal relations with many of the classical authors of his time: he was Holmes's neighbor, Longfellow's regular dinner guest (and finally literary executor), James Russell Lowell's surrogate son.[15] But these relations, played out day after day between person and person, never ceased to be grounded in and mediated by a determinate literary-institutional context. It was by their participation in a certain organization of literary culture that these figures took on the size they had for Howells. Their special status for him as the "greater great,"[16] embodiments of an authority no one can ever hope to dispossess them of, was the product not of their innate power, and not only of Howells's father-seeking psyche, but of the cultural weight that had attached to them, in the mid-nineteenth century's institutions of letters. Conversely, it was by Howells's enrollment *in* a historically specific culture of letters that he became, in his own understanding, these figures' appointed conservator. This kind of filialism (Trilling calls it the *pius Aeneas* side of Howells)[17] is *not* especially evident where we might expect it to appear by nature—in Howells's artistic adolescence, in his Columbus years. Rather it enters Howells's sense of purpose as *he* enters the mid-century literary ethos—Boston as literary center, the world of the *Atlantic,* and the system of understandings they maintained.[18]

What I am suggesting is that the literary past Howells found present and significant to him was the product neither of that past itself nor of his personal receptivities, but rather of a cultural process through which both his moment's past and his relation to it were given. And this holds for Howells's relation to Hawthorne as well. Howells claims to have been imaginatively subjugated by Hawthorne's texts, and reverent of his person—but in both of these responses we can read a personal realization of a culturally conditioned form of experience. Howells's responses to Hawthorne are exactly the responses mandated, on the reader's side, by the cultural enshrinement of a national canon that was being so vigorously performed at that moment: Howells's is the prescribed attitude toward the American classics as figures incalculably great, figures not of one's own mortal kind, objects fit for veneration, and even more for sheer self-abasing submission. Hawthorne did continue to be closely present to Howells's imagination—but this too was due as much to the cultural structure of Howells's authorial position as to Hawthorne's inherent magic. Hawthorne was kept present to Howells by his daily working environment: his superior at the *Atlantic* was famous as Hawthorne's publisher and friend; when he became editor, Howells's assistant (Howells's Howells) was George P. Lathrop, Hawthorne's son-in-law, biographer, and editor. Howells printed Hawthorne's unfinished *Septimius Felton* in the first issue of the *Atlantic* that he edited (in his own more occult idiom: "as if from the grave, Hawthorne rose in the first number I made up, with "Septimius Felton" in his wizard hand"):[19] bringing Hawthorne before the public became part, in other words, of Howells's official task. And keeping Hawthorne freshly honored (on appropriately unqualified terms) became one of Howells's institutional responsibilities: in his *Atlantic* notices he reviews a new edition of *The Scarlet Letter* in 1877, apparently only to have the pleasure of calling that book part of America's "best and highest literature"; two years later his reviews take Henry James to task for belittling (in his *Hawthorne*) our unbelittleable national classic.[20]

Did Hawthorne exert no "potent spell" on Howells? Who could deny that he did? But it helps, not hurts, our sense of this transaction to know that the power Hawthorne exerted and the terms on which Howells was receptive to that power were set not by themselves alone, but also by the cultural context in which they came together.

In the third chapter of this book I tried to reconstruct the cultural mechanisms by which Hawthorne took on extended life in the later nineteenth century. If my argument here holds, it completes the case proposed there: shows that Hawthorne became present to later nineteenth-century writers by no vague process, but as they entered the institutions through which Hawthorne was culturally disseminated. But if I now turn to ask how Hawthorne—or for that matter, any of the literary past thus assembled—actually worked on these later writers' writing, Howells's case gives (at first) an odd reply. An honest answer to the question how Howells's culturally appointed significant past influences the fiction he wrote in his *Atlantic* years is that it hardly does. Howells's early novels—*Their Wedding Journey* (1871), *A Chance Acquaintance* (1873), *A Foregone Conclusion* (1875), and *The Lady of the Aroostook* (1879)—are in significant measure novel: fresh of formula, convention-forming more than convention-repeating.[21] If they seem literarily derived, it is in a very general way, and from foreign, and in American terms recent, authors (Turgenev is often justly mentioned as the inspirer of *A Foregone Conclusion*). They are not visibly indebted to the New England literary canon. Indeed, they show no real awareness that that literature exists.

What might be called the nonderivativeness of Howells's early fiction is, coming from a writer personally and professionally so strongly allied with his age's version of an American tradition, a fact that calls for explaining. We can take it, if we choose, as proof of Howells's real imaginative independence in the midst of the many institutional dependencies he appeared to incur. But we might also wonder whether it does not bespeak something peculiar in the way this literary conservator entertains his tradition. From Howells's work in the 1870s we might judge that he lived in a perfectly bifurcated world. One part of his world contains the sainted body of canonical literature; but this world has no ingress or egress to his other world, that of his own writing. It is as if Howells honors past writing in a way that deprives it of bearing on his own work—so that his writing carries on by its own light, unilluminated by the past it claims to find inspiring.

When a privileged literary corpus was selected and institutionalized in the nineteenth century, as *The Marble Faun* already foresaw, it was organized on severely objectifying terms. This corpus was presented as the work of unique and inimitable masters, such that it tended to be severed, by the very terms on which it was valued, from effective relation to later writing. The nonintercourse between Howells's chosen exempla and his own actual writing shows a personal artistic consequence of this cultural formation of tradition, the location of the prestigious past outside and over against, rather than as the source of, later authors' work. (This phenomenon extends out beyond Howells. Already in the 1880s—while the classic American canon was still being legitimated and actively promoted—students of American literature began to notice that this great tradition was strangely unprogenitive, barren of issue in contemporary art.)[22]

The nonderivativeness that results, I would argue, from this arrangement is always conjoined with another feature in Howells's early work—its persistent (and eventually self-conscious) slightness. As Howells continued to turn out novels through the 1870s, sympathetic readers who at first admired his work began to find it somehow self-curtailed, more minor, in aim and achievement, than the ability it displayed would seem to warrant. (Here is Henry James to Howells, *apropos* of *The Lady of the Aroostook*: "I sometimes wish in this manner for something a little larger. . . . You are sure of your manner now; you have brought it to a capital point and you have only to apply it. But apply it largely and freely—attack the great field of American life on as many sides as you can.")[23] Howells's own letters become obsessed, after 1875 or so, with the issue of his work's scale. If I do not try "a larger canvass with many peop's in it," he writes to one of the critics of his diminutiveness in that year, I have principled reasons for not doing so: "isn't the real dramatic encounter always between two persons only?"[24] (But note how his continuation links small size to anxiety of fiction's possible generic illegitimacy: "Besides, I can only forgive myself for writing novels at all on the ground that the poor girl urged in extenuation of her unlegalized addition to the census: it was such a very *little* baby!") But Howells himself, even as he invents better and better justifications for the short work (in 1877: Shakespeare's plays aren't long!), also becomes increasingly aware that the issue his work's smallness raises is less than of proper formal dimension than that of the size of his artistic will—the scale on which he aims to realize himself, as an artistic power. "I still don't agree with you that a novel need be long in order to be great," he writes in 1877. "But perhaps I'm really without desire for the sort of success you believe in for me."[25]

It might occur to us to wonder if Howells's nonderivativeness and his self-conscious minority might not be connected. The Howells of the 1870s, strongly affected by the canonical attitude, regularly locates the New England classics in the category of the unapproachable and unmatchable, or what Howells calls the "greater great." But since, by this thinking, Howells always concedes the position of greatness to the possession of others, it is not surprising that his own work appears to him deficient in greatness. My suspicion is that, as his anxiety over his persisting littleness increased, Howells realized the connection between these two features of his work and saw that connection's implication: that if he was to become a major author himself, he would need to work out a new relation to his appointed masters—would need to challenge them for their position, and convert the power he saw in them into power he himself could exert.

My evidence for this surmise is found in Howells's fifth novel, *The Undiscovered Country* (1880). Both Howells and his critics read *The Undiscovered Country* as an act of self-extension, an attempt to enlarge the scale both of his books and of his own achieved powers.[26] And it is in this first of his consciously self-augmenting works that Howells also first turns back to his classical literary past and offers to recreate it. *The Undiscovered Country* is about spiritualism, and the past work Howells enfranchises as his model in it is Hawthorne's *The Blithedale Romance*. Howells's heroine Egeira Boynton, like Hawthorne's Priscilla, is a phenomenon in the mesmeric line, a possibly clairvoyant maiden coerced into a career of exhibitionism by her spiritual master (in Howells's case, her father). And Howells uses the striking figure of the medium and her control, in the manner of Hawthorne, to explore the relation of love and control. Howells follows Hawthorne in presenting the spiritualist relation as one of perfect asymmetry of power: in this relation, by virtue of the "magnetism" or "attraction" between them, one party becomes the "control," the other the "passive instrument" of his resolute "will" (53).[27] ("It is you who do it,"

Egeira tells her father; "I see, or seem to see, whatever you tell me." [68])
The questions Howells raises as he dramatizes this relation were all Hawthorne's before him: how much the logic of domination and submission
figured in this bizarre pairing might be characteristic of all attractions;
what kind of injury is done and received, by such domination and submission; and whether another kind of attraction is imaginable that could purge
love of its menacing element of force.

The Undiscovered Country is interesting in the history of American tradition formation because it represents an attempt to revise the nature *of*
tradition: to make the honored past cease to be a self-enclosed prior achievement, and to convert it into a stimulus and guide for later making. This
book certainly also shows the labor of later invention that was required, in
the nineteenth century American case at least, to turn the past into the present's possible source. For Howells's accomplishment in *The Undiscovered
Country* is to *make* Hawthorne *into* his precedent. Throughout the nineteenth century *Blithedale* was the least-read and least remarked-on of
Hawthorne's romances. It was not already available for Howells's purposes: Howells had to find it, to invent it *as* a model, as he wrote his book.
Similarly, the nineteenth-century dissemination of Hawthorne nowhere
comments, as far as I know, on Hawthorne's impressive thematics of emotional power. It was Howells, in *The Undiscovered Country,* who located
that phase of Hawthorne's work, and who appointed it as Hawthorne's
legacy.[28]

That said, it must be added that Howells's revival of Hawthorne here is
pretty tame. In Howells's benign version of Hawthorne's fable the mesmeric control is a kind of spiritualist Quixote, innocent, even childlike, in
his delusions—purged, in other words, of the erotic vindictiveness Matthew
Maule visits on Alice Pyncheon in her trance, or the crass manipulation
to which Westervelt subjects Priscilla. And the medium herself—girlishly
healthy, not devitalized like Priscilla—is, in Howells's telling, not harmed,
indeed not really even touched, by the domination she endures. Unlike
Alice Pyncheon, Egeira is not deeply and shamefully violated by her master's exercise of potency; unlike Priscilla, she is not stunted by her passivity, or made into a seeker of new dominators. The web of power is, in any
case, easily dispelled in Howells. As *The Undiscovered Country* sees it,
Egeira's clairvoyant powers get "terminated by the lapse of time" (291)—
expire naturally, and without a struggle, as she grows up. And when she
emerges from her emotional dependency, the novel is at pains to insist, she
need not fear that adult love will renew her childhood's enthrallments. Her
suitor Ford loves her so (or love here is so unpossessive) "that I couldn't
have taken your love itself against your will." (410) If "something makes"
(411) Egeira love him, she finally recognizes, it is not the force of his will
but the force of her own desires.

We might think of *The Undiscovered Country* as a benevolent revision
of *Blithedale,* a correction of Hawthorne's dark underestimations of the
freeing powers of nature and volition. But it would be quite as fair to say

of these revisions that Howells is simply missing Hawthorne's point. What Howells at first seems to grasp is the way, for Hawthorne, the extremely peculiar bond of medium and control could be seen to image the play of power inherent in ordinary life's most normal relations. The bond of spiritualism, at the book's opening, is perversely indistinguishable from the bond of family itself: Boynton's power over Egeira is that he is her father; she submits to him because she loves him as a daughter. But the effect of Howells's softenings is to dispel this implication—to make this reciprocity of domination and submission the strange opposite of, not a figure for, love's natural workings. If Hawthorne gets reduced in this process, so, much more crucially, does Howells. For the effect of his revisions is to puncture the significance of his chosen dramatic situation. Stripped of its figural power, its power to offer a revealing model for relations other than itself, the relation of Boynton and Egeira becomes simply a freak—a non-recurring bond, having nothing to do with anything but itself.

If we say that Howells locates Hawthorne as a model in *The Undiscovered Country,* we need to add that he only half-grasps, here, what that model could teach him. And the drift of his adopted plot from general psychological implication to this sort of unmeaning idiosyncrasy suggests too that in limiting Hawthorne's potential for significance, Howells also limits the help Hawthorne could give him in augmenting the dimensions of his work. To give another example of this process: *Blithedale* makes the Veiled Lady an index to a larger cultural situation. She is the emblem there of a culture addicted to spectacle, and so trapped in a split of cultural life into roles of spectacular display and roles of passive spectatorship. She images as well the self-subverting effects of a secularized culture's spiritual nostalgia. Such nostalgia (her case suggests) makes the public look for the spiritual in the realm of spectacular entertainment; but this only furthers the spirit's degradation, converting it into a commercially managed theatrical property. The Howells of *The Undiscovered Country* grasps Hawthorne's spiritual maiden, but not the web of cultural implication Hawthorne weaves around her. The result is that his book simply fails to articulate a social dimension for its significance. The spiritualist plot as Howells realizes it is culturally unmeaning, a sign of nothing beyond itself—as the Shakers who protect Egeira in her country sojourn become no more revealing of contemporary spiritual history than the shepherds of pastoral, or Snow White's seven dwarves.

Howells does not overcome the problem of being a minor author in *The Undiscovered Country.* In certain ways the thinnest of his early works, this book shows how he remains minor—how he keeps himself from activating the larger forms of implication that his works might have subtended. But the self-extension that Howells tries and fails to achieve in this book does take place in Howells's career, just afterward. The year after he wrote *The Undiscovered Country* Howells brought his work through a crisis of conception, a deliberate and thoroughgoing reformulation of the ordering of his writing project. He resigned as editor of the *Atlantic* in January

1881—an act carrying the force of a self-weaning, a forcible self-separation from the institutional structures that nurtured his early authorship. His plan now becomes "to devote myself to authorship":[29] to become a full-time, not half-time writer, and just as important, to win his status hereafter through his writings, not through his institutional position. In another set of terms his plan now is "to throw myself upon the market":[30] to support himself directly through the sale of his writing, rather than by working for an institutionally paid salary. In keeping with these movements to terminate dependencies and to incorporate power back into his work, Howells sets out at this same moment aggressively to expand his work's achieved scale. In a letter of February 1881 outlining the proposed *A Modern Instance* for the editors of *Century*—a letter that should be taken as forming one completed action with his earlier letter of resignation—Howells exultantly appoints this new work as the book in which he will take on big subjects and so show himself a major author: "I feel that I have a theme only less intense and pathetic than slavery," he writes here; "the story is on no mean scale geographically"; and again: "I believe that I have got a *great* motive."[31]

The position Howells brilliantly invents for himself, when he sets out to inaugurate his major phase in 1881, is that of the fictional historian of the family and of the state of modern domestic life. Howells is no doubt right that his new "motive" is itself more resonant and important than the subjects of his earlier work. (In addressing the problem of spiritualism in *The Undiscovered Country,* after all, Howells was tackling one of the great nonissues of American social life in 1880.) But the difference of achievement in *A Modern Instance* is the result not alone of its subject, but of the new ways Howells finds to realize his subject's potential significance. In *A Modern Instance* Howells represents marriage (as the realists say) typically. Without in any sense generalizing the marriage of Bartley Hubbard and Marcia Gaylord, Howells nevertheless sees this union in such a way as to grasp how it takes its individual shape from more generally pertaining cultural conditions. Bartley and Marcia become engaged without their families' prior consent, marry out of their families' presence, and set up their household at a distance from their families—and these facts are seen as resultant from, and expressive of, a general decline, in contemporary society, of parents' control over their children's erotic and marital lives. Bartley and Marcia arrange their own (civil) marriage ceremony, and set up a home without social affiliations except through Bartley's job—individual experiences found expressive, again, of the modern family's new isolation from older communal institutions like neighborhood and church. *A Modern Instance* shows the modern marital family become, by a general reorganization of cultural authority, self-creating, self-sanctioning, and self-supporting. And Howells's powerful vision in this book is that when the family comes to depend for its institutional sustenance on the wills and affections of its members, it comes to be at the mercy *of* those wills and affections. The family comes to be at the mercy of the indifference, or dwindling of sentiment, that marriage itself produces (as in Bartley). And it comes to be at the mercy, as in Marcia's case, of the violence intrinsic to affection itself.

In *A Modern Instance* the married family unit has become, for historical reasons, a largely self-disciplining cultural agency. But it is also part of Howells's point that the same historical processes that have made this unit self-regulating have also sapped it of its powers of self-regulation. The logic of *A Modern Instance* is that as it becomes shorn of relation to strong sources of external authority (parent, church, community), the family begins to produce deficiencies of internal authority in the characters it forms.[32] Deprived of strongly instituted authorities around them, the characters of *A Modern Instance* have nothing to internalize as authority within them. They become by this means weak in their powers of self-control, poorly able to uphold a binding collective order outside the order of their wills. As the family becomes culturally self-supporting, it produces two mutually entailing entities in *A Modern Instance*. One is marriage as a transitory and self-collapsing union ("we were incompatible," Bartley Hubbard is the first character in American fiction to say). The other is a modern kind of self—a self loose-hanging, weakly acculturated, poor in internal means to build or uphold a world shared with others.

In making this kind of analysis of the modern family, Howells seizes and develops exactly the sort of social and psychological implications that had remained undiscovered in *The Undiscovered Country*. And one of the means that enables Howells to realize his subject in this larger way is a new and profounder grasp of Hawthorne. Howells's project in *A Modern Instance* requires from him a close notation of what he considers a new kind of personality—a character in which internalized cultural authority is strong enough still to impinge on self-esteem, but no longer strong enough to regulate thought or behavior. Howells's very brilliant representations (in Bartley) of what is in his terms a modern sort of selfhood derive quite directly from Hawthorne's ancient precedents. *The Scarlet Letter* becomes Howells's guide to the workings of the half-conscientious mind, the mind that demands of itself that it square itself before what it knows as the law, but that knows a hundred psychic subterfuges by which to evade its own requirements.

In finding this guidance in *A Modern Instance,* Howells finds or constructs for himself a much more compelling version of Hawthorne's example. Hereafter the Hawthorne who fascinates Howells is always the Hawthorne of bad conscience, located here. And this book makes clear how Howells's larger grasping of his model's power permits a larger empowering of his own work. By remembering Hawthorne as he does in *A Modern Instance,* Howells in effect recovers for fiction a lost or dormant power; he recreates, in a modern instance, what he calls "the fine, important analysis of Hawthorne,"[33] the fiction of psychological exploration that Hawthorne had pioneered.

But part of the interest of *A Modern Instance* is that having given Howells this kind of guidance all along, Hawthorne's influence suddenly becomes much more overt and domineering in the novel's later chapters. Ben Halleck, a minor figure heretofore, becomes a principal character of *A Modern Instance* after the Hubbard marriage collapses in Chapter 31; as he does so he becomes a compilation of Hawthornesque topoi of guilt. Halleck resembles Dimmesdale in that he harbors an adulterous passion within a nature that is morbidly conscientious, such that the experience of his desire makes him feel ever more abominably loathesome and sinful. Like Dimmesdale he becomes a "remorseful hypocrite," the prisoner of a reputation for virtue that makes his efforts at oblique confession unavailing. "I wish I could convince somebody of my wickedness," he tells the lawyer Atherton in Chapter 33,

> "But it seems to be useless to try. I say things that ought to raise the roof, both to you here and to Olive at home, and you tell me you don't believe me, and she tells me that Mrs. Hubbard thinks me a saint." (287)[34]

Like Hawthorne's guilt-hoarders—Reverend Hooper, for example—Halleck's obsession with his own secret sin enables him to intuit the sins of others. In a reversal of aggression with close precedents in "The Minister's Black Veil" and "Egotism; or the Bosom Serpent," Halleck now leaves off torturing himself and begins denouncing the collective hypocrisy by which others keep their similar inward conditions from showing:

> "Such is the effect of character! And yet out of the fulness of the heart, the mouth speaketh. Out of the heart proceed all those unpleasant things enumerated in Scripture; but if you bottle them up there, and keep your label fresh, it's all that's required of you, by your fellow-beings, at least. What an amusing thing morality would be if it were not—otherwise." (287)

Next Halleck falls into a Dimmesdalean fit of eschatological longing, a fantasy of the pleasures attendant on the final exposure of earthly secrets. Now paraphrasing the tenth chapter of *The Scarlet Letter,* he continues:

> "Christ being imagined, can't you see what a comfort, what a rapture, it must have been to all these poor souls to come into such a presence and be looked through and through? The relief, the rest, the complete exposure of Judgment day—" (287–88)

Then in another reversal Halleck turns from fantasies of divine exposure to fantasies of communal exposure, of a ritual uncovering of the mass of foul sin that hides itself behind the community's virtuous exteriors (his source is now "Young Goodman Brown"):

> "Every day is Judgment Day," said Atherton.
> "Yes, I know your doctrine. But I mean the Last Day. We ought to have something in anticipation of it, here, in our social system. Character is a superstition, a wretched fetish. Once a year wouldn't be too often to seize upon sinners whose blameless life has placed them above suspicion, and turn them inside out before the community, so as to show people

how the smoke of the Pit had been quietly blackening their interior. That would destroy character as a cult." (288)

Hereafter the whole career of Halleck becomes perfectly Dimmesdalean, especially his move from guilty desire through draining self-torment to a renewal of the desire he still experiences as guilty. (Halleck's abrupt conversion into an orthodox minister in the last chapter might be said to complete his transformation into Dimmesdale.) And as he collapses back into his Hawthornesque prototypes, other elements in the novel begin to behave in similar fashion. Marcia's daughter Flavia, for example, previously a dormant character, now begins to play the part of Hester's little Pearl, asking preternaturally intelligent questions about her ambiguous family structure ("What *is* Mr. Halleck, mamma? . . . Is he my uncle, or my cousin, or what?" [341]) between bouts of impish merriment.

This portion of *A Modern Instance* shows how extremely definite the memory of Hawthorne is in the minds of his late-nineteenth-century successors. And it gives a stunning example of Hawthorne's continuing hold over their imaginings—of his power, once invoked, to exceed his commission and wrest later works toward unforeseen ends. To say what Hawthorne's vigorous intrusions do to Howells's designs in *A Modern Instance* it is necessary to describe the role of Halleck in the novel's final section. The most salient fact about Halleck is that he travels through the novel in partnership with Atherton, appearing principally in debating scenes with him, and functioning principally as a counter to his voice. Atherton, the portfolio manager and all-purpose sage, is himself newly prominent after Chapter 32, and like Halleck at this point he changes his role. Previously, Atherton has functioned as the voice that called Halleck's neurotically moralistic judgments into question. In his principal prior appearance he has tried to argue Ben out of his melodramatic vision of Marcia's marriage—to convince him that Marcia does not see herself (as Ben does) as the innocent victim of her husband's base nature; that even if she does feel victimized, she will know how to convert her injury into marital revenges in the future; in other words, that marriage is a state of mutual forbearances and mutual victimizations, such that a moral judgment of either of its partners in isolation is impossible. But from the thirty-third chapter on, Atherton functions exactly as what he was not before: the agent of judgment, the voice of the law. From now on his job in the novel is to determine and name the moral status of others' wishes and acts—"I tell you that you are suffering guiltily" (292), he tells Halleck—and then to repeat his verdict over and over, in case anyone missed it the first time: "you know he wasn't right, Clara" (332); "Don't you see that his being in love with her when she was another man's wife is what he feels it to be,—an indelible stain?" (362)

Atherton's new office is to compel those human situations he had previously found enigmatic to range themselves under the headings right and wrong, innocent or guilty. This form of determination is not only new for him. It has also been conspicuously missing from the novel as a whole in its first thirty-one chapters.[35] The goods and evils Atherton now sees as polarized Howells had earlier shown as inseparably mixed: before he becomes (in the book's eyes) simply a scoundrel Bartley Hubbard had been both shifty and oddly winning, both self-indulgent and occasionally thoughtful; before it becomes (in the book's eyes) a sacred institution to be maintained at any cost marriage had been recognized as a scene of shared help and shared cruelty, a structure of support that also breeds within it the energies of its own destruction.

But, above all, judgment has been rendered difficult in this novel by the very movements of its prose. The narrative voice of *A Modern Instance,* for all that it withholds overt comment, it by no means morally neutral. This voice registers intense moral anxiety about the forms of conduct and relationship it has to speak about. It cannot allude to an attribute of Bartley Hubbard without becoming disturbed, without enshrouding it in an atmosphere of suspicion—Bartley's carriage, out for a ride on the Sabbath, is already on the second page of the novel an "ill-timed vehicle" (2); that Bartley does not consider the editorship of the Equity *Free Press* a lifelong commitment raises grave questions about his sincerity and steadfastness of purpose. But typically, once the narrative has evoked an attitude of judgment, it then renders questionable the position from which judgment was arrived at. It notes the apparently telling fact that Bartley's college letters of recommendation praise his intelligence but fail to comment on his "moral characteristics" (16)—but then goes on to reflect that moral characteristics may not, after all, be pertinent qualifications for the job in question. It mentions the flirtatious correspondences Bartley has kept up with a number of young women—surely, further proof of the egotism by which he arranges to enjoy the affection he inspires in others without committing himself to reciprocate it; but the narrative then reflects that such correspondences are perfectly commonplace in America, a custom permitted and encouraged by "the laxness of our social life" (19). It dwells on the fact that Bartley shops around at various houses of worship—confirming, again, his essential opportunism, the casualness with which he invests himself in relationships that require deep commitment; but then it notes that the code from which this judgment would proceed is itself in abeyance—that Equity has reached the stage of religious liberalization where attendance at a single church is not only not required, but not even preferred.

A Modern Instance describes a culture moving into a phase of "relaxation and uncertainty" (18). It describes a culture whose previously rigid communal codes—domestic, ethical, religious, professional—have recently lost the force of their social authority.[36] Howells analyzes this cultural moment quite brilliantly; but the interesting thing about *A Modern Instance* is that the novel itself more or less consciously participates in the process it describes. In Howells's narrative as in his Equity or Boston, the moral instincts associated with an older, stricter social order survive—

the "modern" consistently strikes this novel as lax, degenerate, demoralized. But every time Howells tries to implement old-fashioned principles, he ends up exposing their lack of authority at the modern moment. *A Modern Instance* is morally open-ended not because its author knows that experience is complex and hard to judge, and not because its author is too good an artist to render judgment overtly. It is morally open-ended because it lacks the means by which to make itself closed: because it knows that the cultural standards it would invoke to render judgment are in abeyance, deprived of cultural force. It moves forward in a rhythm of invoked and suspended judgment, recoiling from ethical "relaxation" into a posture of renewed rigidity, then lapsing from rigidity into renewed uncertainty.

It is well known that somewhere around the thirty-first chapter the writing of *A Modern Instance* became too much for Howells. He suffered a nervous collapse that left him bedridden for nearly two months, and he completed the novel while still in a state of convalescence.[37] Kenneth Lynn has plausibly argued that Howells collapsed under the strain of dealing so intimately with the unruly impulses in himself and his own marriage.[38] But surely the major strain Howells was under in the first thirty-one chapters of *A Modern Instance* was that of persisting in the state of moral anxiety I have been describing—in the anxiety generated by his repeated exposure that judgments he deeply wished to make were without real foundation. When, resuming the novel after his collapse, Howells moves Atherton to the fore and recasts him as the arbiter of morals, he is attempting a fictional solution to the crisis of authority that has led him and his novel to break down. Using the privileges of fictive invention, he constructs a character who still has that clarity and certainty of vision that Howells has not been able to locate within the contemporary social world. And exploiting the rhetorical power of authorial eloquence, he lets that figure voice his vision in such accents that it once again sounds authoritative and unassailable. Atherton might be described as the means by which a lapsing social code rhetorically reconstitutes itself as a binding moral law, objectively sanctioned and universally enforceable. This is the action performed by all his major speeches:

> "Have you really come back here to give your father's honest name, and the example of a man of your own blameless life, in support of conditions that tempt people to marry with a mental reservation, and that weaken every marriage bond with the guilty hope of escape whenever a fickle mind, or secret lust, or wicked will may dictate? Have you come to join yourself to those miserable specters who go shrinking through the world, afraid of their own past, and anxious to hide it from those they hold dear; or do you propose to defy the world, to help form within it the community of outcasts with whom shame is not shame, nor dishonor, dishonor?"
> (317–318)

> "No one sins or suffers to himself in a civilized state,—or religious state; it's the same thing. Every link in the chain feels the effect of the violence,

more or less intimately. We rise or fall together in Christian society. It's strange that it should be so hard to realize a thing that every experience of life teaches. We keep thinking of offenses against the common good as if they were abstractions!" (334)

What Ben Halleck embodies in *A Modern Instance* is resistance to the thrust of this coercive moralization. Halleck's office is to hold out against the dominations of Atherton's rhetorical process, both by opposing it with another kind of voice, and by exposing the factitious nature of its authority. This is where Hawthorne comes in: for the Hawthornisms of *A Modern Instance* are exactly the means by which Halleck (and the novel) unmask Atherton's neoorthodoxy. The ironic vision of Hawthorne's secret sinners gives Halleck and Howells the means to reveal that Atherton's apparently objective codes of value are really only conventional labelling systems, systems that bear no relation to the true naure of inward experience:

> "Out of the heart proceed all those unpleasant things enumerated in Scripture; but if you bottle them up there, and keep your label fresh, it's all that's required of you, by your fellow-beings, at least." (287)

The same Hawthornesque vision gives Halleck and Howells the terms to say that Atherton's apparently objective moral scheme is really only a communal fabrication, a fabrication that bears no relation to that community's own real nature:

> "Character is a superstition, a wretched fetish. Once a year wouldn't be too often to seize upon sinners whose blameless life has placed them above suspicion, and turn them inside out before the community, so as to show people how the smoke of the Pit had been quietly blackening their interior. That would destroy character as a cult." (287–288)

When Hawthorne rematerializes within Howell's consciousness in *A Modern Instance,* he is evoked there by an imaginative crisis, a crisis in the determination of ethical significance. And the part he plays in this crisis is to fend off another force it has evoked—the narrow-minded and ill-grounded moralism with which Howells responds to the uncertainties of modern instances. This crisis and Hawthorne's role in it become the more important when we recognize that what is being played out, in the conclusion of *A Modern Instance,* is Howells's emerging definition of realism itself. *A Modern Instance* is the book where Howells's mature realism is really born, and this book should remind us that his realism is born *out* of a sense of weakness in the fabric of contemporary reality: out of a sense that the agencies that have traditionally sustained his culture's system of personal and communal reality—the family, the church, and their internalizations in conscience—are becoming disempowered in the later nineteenth century. The lapse of the authority of these interinvolved cultural agencies gives Howells's realism, quite directly in *A Modern Instance,* its first great subject. But that lapse also gives it its evolving sense of mission.

As Howells reads it, the artistic meaning of this general cultural erosion is that the cultural power previously vested in institutions like family and church is devolving, at his moment, upon the institution of literature, and particularly on its great popular form, prose ficition. Bromfield Corey tells his son in *The Rise of Silas Lapham:*

> "All civilization comes through literature now, especially in our country. Once we were softened, if not polished, by religion; but I suspect that the pulpit counts for much less now in civilizing."

For Howells the result of the contemporary dislocation of cultural authority is that as a staple of public mental recreation, the novel, which in some other historical situation might have the place of a culturally marginal entertainment form, has become, in his world, a central agency of acculturation and reality production: like the family and the church before it, the cultural force most powerfully authorized to form and maintain, in individual minds, a collective definition of the permitted and the proscribed, the normal and the aberrant, the serious and the unserious. This historical analysis of literature's cultural position in late-nineteenth-century America—which we need not dismiss as fantastic: cultural historians now look to *A Modern Instance's* decade as the time when the new mass-entertainment media like magazines (in which fiction like Howells's was printed) were taking on power as dominant acculturating agencies in American life[39]—is what motivates Howells's embrace of realism as a form and creed. Fiction for Howells does not only imitate reality. It produces reality—establishes and sustains the sense of the world on which its audience lives and acts. For this reason, fiction cannot be permitted to fabricate idly—lest real men and women be misinformed in the knowledge that they live by. From this deeply felt sense of fiction's powers and obligations it is an easy step to an embrace of realism as something like a moral reconstruction program. Realism thus conceived easily comes to believe that being truthful means being morally instructive: the novelist would be no better than "the attendant who fills [the] pipe" of "the habitué of an opium-joint," Howells says in an important essay, if he did not "distinguish so clearly that no reader of his may be misled, between what is right and what is wrong, what is noble and what is base, what is health and what is perdition, in the actions and characters he portrays."[40] For realism thus conceived sees its essential function as a moral one: that of strengthening the public's enfeebled mechanisms of moral judgment, of shoring up and clarifying the structures of moral perception that Howells fears contemporary experience is blurring and eroding.

With this for his mission, it is no wonder if doing the realist's work makes Howells feel privileged, even righteous. (Alan Trachtenberg correctly calls realism Howells's "conviction of rectitude.")[41] But his way of forming the definition of realism has a hidden consequence. For in Howells's historiography the novel emerges as the new base for the ethical system on the condition of that system becoming inoperable, in the extraliterary world: fiction comes to cultural authority, in Howells's map, when authority in its traditional cultural forms gets exposed as fictitious. This buries a crucial contradiction inside the realist's practice. Its consequence is that when the Howellsian realist performs his proud office of telling the truth in fiction, he is always actually engaging, by his own covert admission, in an act of fabrication: a use of fiction's power to *make* real what it cannot *find* real, outside itself. (What is *The Rise of Silas Lapham,* that centerpiece of Howellsian realism, in whose America families are strong, values are intact, and the inward hold of principle is if anything too tight, not too loose? An imitation of objective social actuality? Or a use of fiction's verisimilar powers to make something seem to be the case that Howells had known to be radically unreal in *A Modern Instance?*)

The contradiction between the competing understandings built into Howells's definition of realism is what gets exposed in the conclusion of *A Modern Instance.* The ending of this novel gives a powerful early example of how Howells's sense of ungroundedness makes him vulnerable to the lures of realism as moralizing mission. Writing in the doubt-inducing manner of this book's first half touches off a kind of ethical backlash in Howells,[42] so that he flees from his own ironies into a fiction of strident moral positivism, loudly (in the voice of Atherton) instructing his reader in the rightness of the right, and the wrongness of the wrong. But as he falls into this role, another voice in his fiction—a voice spoken by Halleck, but scripted by Hawthorne—speaks up to proclaim such writing's self-deceits. Against the powerful convictions Howells's moral realism generates of its own righteousness and truth, this voice brands such realism as fabrication—a fictive making and enforcing of the thing it claims is real.

In their encounter at the end of *A Modern Instance,* Howells finds what will remain, for him, the central Hawthorne—not the plotter of psychic enthrallments, and not even the historian of the guilty mind, but Hawthorne the unsettler of moral sense. "None of Hawthorne's fables," Howells says as his last word on Hawthorne in *My Literary Passions,*

> are without a profound and distant reach into the recesses of nature and of being. He came back from his researches with no solution of the question, with no message, indeed, but the awful warning, "Be true, be true," which is the burden of the *Scarlet Letter;* yet in all his books there is the hue of thoughts we think only in the presence of the mysteries of life and death. It is not his fault that this is not intelligence, that it knots the brow in sorer doubt rather than shapes the lips to utterance of the things that can never be said.[43]

In writing *A Modern Instance* Howells releases once more the Hawthorne that every literary institutionalization tends to contain: Hawthorne the doubt bearer, dissolver of the ground on which value of any sort could be determined. What Howells wins from this encounter is, within *A Modern Instance,* help in resisting his urge to make things certain: "I don't know! I don't know!" (362), this book's debate about the immorality of remarriage manages to conclude, in obvious echo of Hester Prynne's terminal "I know not! I know not!" But what he wins in a more enduring way is understanding of his just-forming literary and social project. Through the next decade Howells carries on with the task of trying to formulate a contemporary social ethic and to enforce its reign within his culture. But even as he does so he never loses a certain skepticism toward his own project. This skepticism is Hawthorn's legacy to Howells. For what Hawthorne helps Howells to understand in *A Modern Instance* is that the writer is never in such danger of perpetrating a new communal fiction as when he is most assured that what he is saying is really right.

◆ Chapter Six ◆

HENRY JAMES
Tradition and the Work of Writing

[Sargent] is various and experimental; if I am not mistaken, he sees each work that he produces in a light of its own, not turning off successive portraits according to some well-tried receipt which has proved useful in the case of their predecessors; nevertheless there is one idea that pervades them all, in a different degree, and gives them a family resemblance—the idea that it would be inspiring to know just how Velasquez would have treated the theme.   HENRY JAMES, "John S. Sargent"

HENRY JAMES's relation to Hawthorne has been a subject for discussion as long as there has been a James to discuss. The book that more than any other fixed the contours of nineteenth-century American literature for twentieth-century readers—F. O. Matthiessen's *American Renaissance*—incorporated James into its Hawthorne chapters, and so gave James and Hawthorne to modern study as figures in a line. But this move was already well established when Matthiessen made it: T. S. Eliot had proclaimed the centrality of a "Hawthorne aspect" in James when James's work first stood as a completed corpus, in his epitaphic 1919 essay of that name. In fact Eliot's aspect had been detected earlier still, when James first emerged as a figure of potentially major significance. Writing in the wake of the publication of *The Portrait of a Lady,* Howells had announced in 1882 that James was inaugurating a new era for the novel, and transforming prose fiction into a finer art; and one way he described that art was by saying that it derived from Hawthorne and George Eliot, not Dickens and Thackeray. Nor was the recognition new even then. Already in 1870, when Henry James was still eleven years from being the author of *The Portrait of a Lady,* when he was not yet even the author of the paltry early *Watch and Ward,* William James had spotted his famous resemblance, and used it to posit an American fictional line: "it . . . tickled my national feeling not a little to note the resemblance of Hawthorne's style to yours and Howells's, even as I had earlier noted the converse. That you and Howells with all the models of English literature to follow, should needs involuntarily have imitated (as it were) this American, seems to point to the existence of some real American mental quality."[1]

As these examples suggest, the idea of a Hawthorne tradition is not only

104

itself thoroughly traditional, in the context of James studies: this idea has been historically central to the way James has been grasped and known. From an early moment one of the regular ways in which readers have tried to understand what James was doing in his work was by reading it on the analogy of Hawthorne's. And placing James in Hawthorne's line has continued to be one of our chief means for determining his place in American literature.

If we ask why it is that James is so insistently seen in this of all possible relations, his writings give a ready answer: for James's fiction displays its descent from Hawthorne in peculiarly persistent and obtrusive ways. The pervasion by Hawthorne that I find widespread in later American writing is of a wholly different order in James's case. However intensely Melville and Howells feel the authority of Hawthorne's art, it is of the essence of both relations that they are transient. At a crisis in their careers, these writers suddenly find Hawthorne much more important to their work. They work through their crises of self-conception (in part) by working through the meaning of his example. But when they have done so, he recedes from the field of their concern. Other literary models, and other influences than literary ones, preside over the works they go on to write: developments obvious enough if we look forward from *Moby-Dick* and *Pierre* to *The Confidence Man,* or from *The Undiscovered Country* and *A Modern Instance* to *The Rise of Silas Lapham* and *A Hazard of New Fortunes.*

But the striking fact about James's involvement with Hawthorne is that it is exactly not a *passing* thing. Henry James presents the great instance in American literature of the achieved artistic career: he embodies a unique instance of productivity extended without decline over the whole course of a long life. But although James's writing life is fifty years in length, there is no time in it so early that Hawthorne is not already a part of it, as there is no time so late that we can confidently say that Hawthorne's influence has been outgrown. "The Beast in the Jungle," a tale of 1903, descends from Hawthorne precedents quite as directly as an 1868 tale like "The Story of a Masterpiece"; James's very late additions to the unfinished *The Sense of the Past* display some of the most overt obtrusions of Hawthorne in his whole oeuvre. Similarly, James's is of all nineteenth-century literary careers the one richest in self-renovation; so given is James to the reformulation of his work that we discuss his career as we do national traditions, in terms of periods of style and artistic project. But James's renovations of the nature *of* his work do not dislodge Hawthorne's presence *to* his work. He is there, strongly but not unexpectedly, in James's apprentice pieces and early international novels. But he is there again, as or more powerfully, in the realist-political writing that James appointed as his new form of work in the 1880s. And he is if anything more pervasive in late James, as one of the chief constituents of the famous late style.

One of James's differences from Hawthorne's other successors is that he never stops succeeding Hawthorne. James stands toward Hawthorne as toward something like an enabling condition, a relation it makes no sense to think of entering into or departing from. The depth of this bond explains what I take to be his other great difference from his fellow heirs: the fact that his work is more deeply informed by Hawthorne, that Hawthorne operates on his writing so to speak from further back. An example will show what I mean. James's notebook records that in 1887 he heard from a half-brother of Vernon Lee

> a curious thing of Capt. Silsbee—the Boston art-critic and Shelley-worshipper; that is of a curious adventure of his. Miss Claremont, Byron's *ci-devant* mistress, (the mother of Allegra) was living, until lately, here in Florence, at a great age, 80 or thereabouts, and with her lived her niece, a younger Miss Claremont—of about 50. Silsbee knew that they had interesting papers—letters of Shelley's and Byron's—he had known it for a long time and cherished the idea of getting hold of them. To this end he laid the plan of going to lodge with the Misses Claremont—hoping that the old lady in view of her great age and failing condition would die while he was there, so that he might then put his hand upon the documents, which she hugged close in life. He carried out this scheme—and things *se passèrent* as he had expected. The old woman *did* die—and then he approached the younger one—the old maid of 50—on the subject of his desires. Her answer was—"I will give you all the letters if you marry me!" He says that Silsbee *court encore*.[2]

The play of gossip, the buzz of social storytelling, brings James here a wonderful plot, the outline for one of his great novellas. The story he hears is quite complete. But for James to turn this well-formed anecdote into "The Aspern Papers" he of course needs to reinvent the whole thing: to reconceive and re-express the story in the forms of written literary narrative. What I find striking is that when James subjects his source to this process of reconception, the elements of the story begin to behave not as they did in the anecdote, but as elements do in Hawthorne's fiction. A man who pretends to lodge with an old woman when he really has designs on her family secrets reminds James, we must suppose, of Holgrave in *The House of the Seven Gables*—for in the novella the old woman's house features an attached garden, as Hepzibah Pyncheon's did and as Claire Clairmont's most likely did not, in which the lodger putters and courts the old woman's niece. An enclosed garden in Italy appears to have recalled Rappaccini's garden, for the younger woman in James's tale quite incongruously assumes a set of traits that belonged to Hawthorne's Beatrice: she has spent her life in a state of protective enclosure; she is artless, defenseless, and sexually unenlightened; meeting a man in her garden, she falls in love without understanding what she is feeling; offering herself to him uncalculatingly, she is unable to understand the simultaneous repulsion and attraction that her undisguised desire excites in him. Once Tina becomes assimilated to the figure of Beatrice, the parent-figure takes on features of Dr. Rappaccini: Juliana becomes fiercely manipulative of others' desires; she keeps her garden under surveillance; her eyes are endowed with occult powers of visual penetration. The structure of a prying observer who becomes the object of the gaze he would subject others to obviously recalls *The Blithedale Romance* too for James. As James recreates him Captain Silsbee takes on every property of Miles Coverdale, from his voyeuristic obsessions to his elegantly self-mocking tone of voice. All of the incidental imagery associated with privacy and its violation in *Blithedale* also appears to adorn Silsbee's tale—most stunningly, when James's publishing scoundrel imagines behind Juliana's green eyeshade the "ghastly death's head" or "grinning skull" that Theodore dreaded to meet if he lifted the Veiled Lady's veil.

I do not pretend to be able to reconstruct the sequence of steps by which James reimagined "The Aspern Papers." But I do find this example revealing of how Hawthorne acts in James's imaginings. It would be quite inadequate to say that James turns to *The House of the Seven Gables* or "Rappaccini's Daughter" or *The Blithedale Romance* as models. These works are in no sense separate from him: the author of "The Aspern Papers" has perfectly internalized them. And internalized them, specifically, as part of his own equipment of narrative invention: such that to begin to compose a tale is to activate a process that Hawthorne is already part of.

This form of incorporation is the ground, I think, for the persistent resemblance of James to Hawthorne, so striking at every level of his work. James is—to give him one last accolade—one of the great distinct identities in the history of prose fiction. We know his work as his infallibly, and by a hundred tokens: it is always highly individuated, in imagination and expression. But the peculiarity of James's case is that the more some aspect of his work strikes us as quintessentially Jamesian, the more likely it is also to remind us of Hawthorne. (Witness the adventure of vicariousness in "The Aspern Papers"—the Jamesian adventure *par excellence,* but one that we see him recreate here, turn by turn, out of Hawthorne.) The reason for this is not just that Hawthorne happened to anticipate James's chief concerns. It is that James has built Hawthorne into the generative processes of his art. To conceive, in James's case, is to conceive with Hawthorne's aid: to imagine a narrative world is to have recourse to Hawthorne's imaginings; to *know* his subjects is to grasp them in Hawthorne's light. Hawthorne always seems to have come before James because James is always projecting him backward as his predecessor, stationing him as the earlier worker who enables his later work to get done.

Once the Hawthorne–James relation is established, it is customary to turn to their books and watch how they interact. But to make this move is to skip a stage of inquiry. This implication of Hawthorne in James—this relation (unparalleled in my knowledge) in which a powerful and otherwise independent novelist composes and sustains himself by means of a continued dependence upon a single precursor—is a fact more curious than any instance of influence it covers. It embodies, really, a historical aberration; it marks a difference, not alone in the way later fiction bears Hawthorne's influence, but in the way fiction has borne literary influence at all. Seen in these terms, this relation might tempt us to ask questions of a different order. It makes us ask not what James's debt is to Hawthorne, but what has happened to the novel, in James's hands, to make it take on this odd structure of indebtedness; not what James carries forward from Hawthorne, but why in his version of it the novel is so emphatically derived, from sources of this sort.

These questions could be answered in a variety of ways. But my own strong sense is that the difference in the way James's novel bears influence (a difference of which the influence of Hawthorne is both a symptom and the prime example) is not explicable in terms of influence alone. This altered form of literary traditionality is one of a whole set of related transformations that James's practice performs on the nature of the novel. These transformations in turn reflect James's inauguration of not just a different way of writing but a different way of thinking about the kind of work that writing it. The historical drama of James's career, as I read it, lies in his reconstruction, eventually of the practice, but first and more crucially of the idea, of the novelist's work. His reorganization of influence, mysterious in its own terms, makes good sense when read as part of this larger action, which I must now describe.

When I assert that James remade the idea of his work I risk making him sound self-generating, as if he had created both his writing itself and the conditions of its possibility. Of course this is not the case. James's work, as much as any other writer's, implies the prior existence of an institutional context—a concrete set of cultural structures and understandings that establish literature (a form defined in a certain way) as something one can write, and the writer (a role positioned in a certain way) as something one can be. If we ask what the institutional setting is that James's writing presumes, the answer is that it is much the same as Howells's. James started publishing at almost exactly the same time as Howells, and through exactly the same organs. His first literary essays, like Howells's "turning point" essay on Italian comedy, were published in Charles Eliot Norton's and James Russell Lowell's revitalized *North American Review*. (Norton administered the admission to literary candidacy to James that Lowell administered to Howells.) His early journalistic writing was sought by the new organ of liberal intelligence *The Nation,* Howells's first place of literary employ. And his fiction went, like Howells's, to the new literary magazine of his time, *The Atlantic*.

The story of Howells's relation to *The Atlantic* is always told. James's comparable story is less well known, though his ties to this channel of publication are no less strong. *The Atlantic* early on adopted James not just as an author it would publish, but as an author peculiarly expressive of the institutional character it wished to maintain. Howells said in 1867 that *The Atlantic* would take as many stories as it could get from James, although it was already clear that James was less than popular with *The Atlantic*'s readership; when Horace Scudder took over as editor twenty years later, he wrote to renew James's attachment to *The Atlantic,* explaining that he aimed to identify this journal with "the permanent elements in American literature."[3] Throughout the nineteenth century *The Atlantic* remained James's principal place of production and one of his principal sources of support. It serialized almost all his early novels: *Watch and Ward, Roderick Hudson, The American, The Europeans, The Portrait of a Lady.* When James's next novel, *The Bostonians,* bombed in *The Century*—when James failed to get in on the broadening of the public and the commercial base for literary writing that *The Century* pioneered in the 1880s and that gave Howells's realism its social base—he went back to *The Atlantic,* which ran *The Princess Casamassima,* then "The Aspern Papers." When James then lost the English market outlets he had established in the late 1870s (he broke with Macmillan in 1889, when Macmillan proposed to cut his advance after the dismal reception of *The Bostonians* and *The Princess Casamassima*), *The Atlantic* faithfully ran *The Tragic Muse,* through all its endless installments.[4]

I dwell on these institutional connections partly because they are little known, partly in order to insist that James's writing *had* a historically specific institutional setting. But seeing James too as an *Atlantic* writer can remind us of another point worth making: namely, that if no writer can become a writer except within some public organization of the literary sphere, writers can organize their authorship within the same organization of literature in extremely different ways. James, we might say, occupies the same literary situation as Howells, but he realizes that situation in quite another way. James has, to name an obvious difference, little involvement with the public and social dimensions of his institutional setting that are so important for Howells. Howells worked as an editor of *The Atlantic,* occupied the chief public position and exercised the public power of this institution, as part of his program of authorship. James refused comparable positions on *The Nation* and the *North American Review* as incompatible with the authorship he aspired to. (James preceded Lionel Trilling in reading Howells's acceptance of such posts as proof that he was, in literary terms, second rate.)[5] Howells socialized in *Atlantic* circles, worked *at* the socializing that held a circle together around that journal. In expatriating, James made himself an absentee contributor and sought other literary company than the Bostonian type.

But to say that James does not embrace his institutional context in its public aspects is not to say that James does not fully participate in this context. What do we mean by an institution of literature, anyway? In part we mean a set of social structures that build literature its public and give it its economic ground. (Publishing institutions like magazines are the chief instances of such structures in the case of nineteenth-century prose fiction.) But we also mean a set of conceptual structures: the definitions

of literature's nature and cultural position that those more tangible structures coalesce around and then help enforce. The conceptual scheme of
any particular institution of literature is likely to be at best half-articu-
lated, and composed of various strains. The one expressed in *The Atlantic*
in the later nineteenth century holds at least the following elements in
solution: an idea of literary discrimination, the sense that writing is and
should be differentiated into mediocre and distinguished classes; an idea
of the moral or civic function of letters, the sense that the dissemination
of distinguished writing can improve the tone of a culture and raise the
level of its intelligence; an idea of entertainment, the sense that literature
also has as a legitimate goal to interest and please a family-style audience.
(When Fields took over *The Atlantic* he complained that Lowell had
made it insufficiently entertaining.)[6]

Since it contained such a mixed program, writers entering this institution could build, from within it, very different definitions of their appointed work. Howells, I think it is fair to say, identified with all of these
strains, and his theory of realism as a high-class family entertainment that
serves to upgrade collective mental life can be read as his reinvention, as a
personal artistic program, of the mixed aspirations of his early institutional
setting. Faced with the same array of potential definitions of his work,
James remained indifferent to most of them. *James identified instead almost exclusively with the idea of literary discrimination.* What he read in
his surrounding was above all the message that literature could be *distinguished;* what he took inside as his self-definition was the goal of doing
distinguished work.

I say this because everything about James's early artistic program turns
on the idea of the potential *highness* of writing. The reviews James began
publishing in 1864 are excruciatingly condescending to the popular lady
novelists they often treat,[7] and this not just because James is snobbish.
The writer of these reviews has seen that prose fiction can be distinguished
as high or low (the distinction James's periodicals were invented to make);
when he joins in the public world of literature, it is by offering to enforce
this distinction in a rigorous way. James's scorn of Howells's editorial labors is scorn, specifically, for an idea of authorship insufficiently high: "he
has passed into the stage which I suppose is the eventual fate of all secondary and tertiary talents," James writes Grace Norton in 1870, with his
usual insistence on gradation, "worked off his slender Primitive [capital],
found a place and a routine and an income"; and to Charles Eliot Norton
on the same occasion: "It's rather sad, I think, to see Americans of the
younger sort so unconscious and unambitious of the commission to do the
best."[8] James's early projections of his own future work define it never in
terms of content or mission, but always in terms of the differentiated
quality it is to possess. He writes in 1868: "I write little and only tales,
which I think it likely I shall continue to manufacture in a hackish manner, for that which is bread. They *cannot* of necessity be very good; but
they *shall not* be very bad." And in 1871: "To write a series of good little

tales I deem ample work for a lifetime. I dream that my lifetime shall have done it." And in 1873: "To produce some little exemplary works of art is my narrow and lowly dream. They are to have less 'brain' than *Middlemarch;* but (I boldly proclaim it) they are to have more *form*."⁹

Examples like these begin to show the features of James's peculiar but completely characteristic way of accommodating himself to the social organization of his work. It is not that James's work is not surrounded by such organization. But, typically, as James enters into that controlling form he also subjects it to a powerful personal distortion, such that some of its elements become much more prominent than they were originally, while other elements recede from view. Just as typical as this perceptual restructuring is the fierce internalization of external controls that follows it. James finds, established outside of him, a difference between kinds and grades of literary work. But he then appropriates this differentiation so intensely as to appear to reverse the direction of compulsion. (*I require the best of myself,* even if no one else does, James's early writing says.) Indeed he takes it inside so intensely as to produce new realms of difference itself: next to the distinction I require of myself, his letters on Howells imply, the discriminations of merely institutional discriminators are a lower order of thing.

It is just as characteristic that when James internalizes a defining external structure in this way, he also subjects it to a prodigious personalizing elaboration, superposing it on and fusing it with other structures not related except *by* his conceptualizing act.¹⁰ We can feel in his conversion of the republic of letters into a strenuous meritocracy how the practice of selectivity he finds institutionalized around him has been conjoined, in his thinking, with the high-culture sentiment of the 1860s and 1870s. Much more than Howells, and more than any other American author I know, James shares in the kind of cultural belief-system that finds its champion in Matthew Arnold and, closer to home, in Charles Eliot Norton. James joins such figures in looking to the great works of human art as a repository of pure value: we hear this sentiment when he speaks of "the comparatively small library of books that we rank as the most precious things in our heritage," or when he writes in *The Princess Casamassima* (as through Hyacinth's eyes) that "the monuments and treasures of art, the great palaces and properties, the conquests of learning and taste" are "inestimably precious and beautiful," well worth the social injustices that helped produce them.¹¹ He joins them too in the corollary belief that cultural works of this order are known *through* discriminations of value and serve to teach us how to *make* discriminations of value. "Nothing counts, of course, in art, but the excellent; nothing exists, however briefly, for estimation, for appreciation, but the superlative," James writes in "The Lesson of Balzac"; words that accord with Arnold's thought in "The Study of Poetry": "if [the poet] is a real classic, if his work belongs to the class of the very best (for this is the true and right meaning of the word *classic, classical*), then the great thing for us is to feel and enjoy his work as deeply as ever we can, and to appreciate the wide difference between it and all work which has not the same high character."[12] By bringing this structure of sentiment into his institutional context, James makes its working distinction between the literary and the subliterary seem to involve this much more value-fraught distinction between the supremely excellent and the forgettable rest. His own strong sense of the "commission to do one's *best*" as a writer implies this special valuation of "the class of the very best," and becomes immediately translatable into personal devotion to the cultural ideal. The letter to Norton that coins this phrase continues: "For myself, the love of art and letters grows steadily with my growth."[13]

At the same time that James is reconceiving his literary situation in terms of the categories of the religion of culture, he is also infusing it with his own version of what Burton Bledstein calls the culture of professionalism. Bledstein and other historians have recently pointed to the 1870s and 1880s (the decades of James's early career) as the time of the birth of the professions and professionalism in their modern forms. Beginning at this time many forms of work—public health, library work, medicine, the academic professions, among others—that had earlier been more diffusely defined reorganized themselves into narrow specializations, the special domain of those with access to specialized training and lore. In a parallel transformation, work-lives in these professions, hitherto more loosely determined, got remade in such a way as to take on the taut boundaries and tight internal coherence that mark the professional form of career.[14] Henry James has no visible involvement in the public struggles over professional reincorporation that characterize the history of work in his time, but he displays the new ethos of the professionalizing movement in classic form. James's "commission to do one's *best*" bespeaks not just strong personal ambition but James's erection, within the world of writing, of a new structure of ambition: one in which high achievement within one's chosen field stands as an unqualified imperative and a good in itself. (My work will be *good,* James asserts, ignoring the more traditional questions what it will be good *for,* or who it will be good *to.*) Howells looks to the position of literary author opened up in his and James's time as a place to win status and do service. James, more professionalistically, sees it as meeting his need for *career:* "To write a series of good little tales I deem ample work for a life-time. . . . It's at least a relief to have arranged one's life-time!"[15]

We can speak of James's participation in late-nineteenth-century professionalism, or in the nineteenth-century religion of secular culture, but James peculiarly refuses to be reduced to such outward developments. We are seeing, here, the reason: for James's way of occupying such structures is not just to be structured *by* them but at the same time to rework them—to combine them, to conflate them, to subject them to eccentric imaginative fusions. James's way of entering into the religion of culture, thus, produces forms of it unknown outside his practice. In overlaying this structure of thought on the literary situation that surrounds him, James confers the premium of aesthetic height on a category that had never been thought high, that had always been marked as the reverse of high, before: prose fiction. In making this fusion James also converts the excellent into *something one could write*—moves high culture into the sphere of possible production, not only of contemplation of past glories. (James's great difference from other American proponents of high culture in his time, besides the fact that he does not use this idea to cloak a social program of elite control, is that he makes the worship of art an incitement to creation, not an alternative to doing the *work* of art.)[16] James inhabits the structures of professionalism, similarly, in such a way as to give them in a new form. The imperative to constantly renewed achievement becomes, in his self-erected *profession à un,* an imperative for once to *aesthetic* accomplishment; and disciplined careerism becomes the path less to professional success than to artistic glory.

Recognizing this process of transformation is crucial to any attempt to understand James's place in the social history of literary production. Especially next to an author like Howells, whose work is so sensitive to every change in the organization of its social position, James's work seems much less in touch with such external developments, much more attuned to its own internal program. The explanation for this difference is not that James was somehow immune to the social definition of literary work. It is that James refigured such definitions as he entered them—with the result that they exerted their real organizing power over his writing less in the form in which he found them in the world than in the form in which he recomposed them. By means of the internalizations and interfusions I have been describing, James constructed, out of the materials of his historical situation, something like a personal form for the institution of literature. Through these elaborations he built, if not new public agencies of literature, a new structure of literary conception—a new set of ideas of literature's nature and position from which his work could take direction and against which it could be measured.

James's personal reinstitution of literature involves, for one thing, the remaking of the idea of the kind of labor writing is. Fiction has always been written with different degrees of skill, but the writing of fiction was never defined as a particularly skilled form of labor, certainly not in a way that would restrict access to its ranks. Throughout the nineteenth century in both England and America, writing novels remained something one could always turn to, whenever whim or domestic distress required; and the history of the novel is full of stories of smash successes produced at the first or second try. But James subjects the Anglo-American institution of fiction writing to a fantasy of vocational upgrading. The novel becomes, in James's thinking, an arena of mastery—work susceptible to a special high grade of performance, that derives not from happy knack but from disciplined training in a special skill. Note how this early letter defines writing as something one must *learn,* by a protracted and laborious process: "It is something to have learned how to write, and when I look round me and see how few people (doing my sort of work) know how (to my sense), I don't regret my step by step evolution."[17]

At the same time that it upgrades his skill level, James's reinstitution of the novel also elaborates a new plan for the work-life of the novel's maker. Before James prose fiction was associated with no presumption of specialization. In fact this form had always thrived on the mixing of works: besides being a novelist Fielding had been a magistrate, Sterne a clergyman, Hawthorne a customs inspector and consul, Stowe a homemaker and domestic advisor, Trollope a post office bureaucrat, Howells an editor, and so on. But James gives the idea of the work-life appropriate to the novelist an altogether different shape. For one thing—and his professionalizing urges show strongly here—James makes writing seem to bear the requirement of exclusive dedication and total investment of self. Balzac is James's early work-hero because he makes his whole self available to his work— this author is, in James's admiring phrase, "identical with [his] productive faculty."[18] When James sees his own late work stretch out before him, it gives him the joy of feeling that he may now be able to give himself to his work yet more fully: "One has prayed and hoped and waited, in a word, to be able to work *more*. And now, toward the end, it seems, within its limits, to have come."[19] As he gives it this sort of specializing cast, James also situates the writer's work in a new form of work-biography. As James defines it, writing like the other new specialized professions of the late nineteenth century becomes much more intensely identified as a *life*'s work—identified with the idea of a lifelong program of appointed labors, all of which must be completed in series to make up the successful career.[20] There is no better place to see James's free elaboration of the ordering forms of his work than in his invention of a myth of the ideal authorial career. Borrowed from the cultural mythology of the fine arts (principally painting), then cobbled together into a quasi-professional career narrative, James's ideas of the novelists's apprenticeship, masterpiece-moment, years of mastery, and late phase are parts of a gorgeous private vocational fantasy—but an invention (such are his powers of pretense) that James always experiences as an autonomous authority, a structure he must make himself comply with.

James projects, as one of the ideas that govern his practice, a new conception of the novelist's work, one that links him to high-level workers both in and outside of the artistic sphere. As he does so he also produces a new governing conception of the novel *as* a work. Here is an early but characteristic Jamesian meditation on what a novel is or can be (I take it from his 1873 review of *Middlemarch*):

> We can well remember how keenly we wondered, while its earlier chapters unfolded themselves, what turn in the way of form the story would take—that of an organized, moulded, balanced composition, gratifying the reader with a sense of design and construction, or a mere chain of episodes, broken into accidental lengths and unconscious of the influence of a plan.[21]

This passage is useful in my context because it shows so clearly the aesthetic consequences of James's realignment of the novelist's status. Locating the novel as a high form of work, James looks for his peers not in the realm of novelists but in the ranks of those arts already designated as fine arts, like painting. As he does so, James quite naturally begins to import into his own sphere an aesthetic language that had been generated by that other art, as part of what marked it *fine*. The effect of this repatriation of painterly language into discussion of the novel is, really, to produce a new system of properties for the novel. James here articulates, *in* the novel and *as* the novel, a set of features that no doubt novels had always possessed, but that had never been part of the novel's idea of itself: its achieved internal form, the inward disposition of formal arrangements by which it composes and expresses its subject. Once James produces this new system of attributes in the novel, as this example already shows, it provides a new way to position the novel as a category of expression. Works now become, on the basis of whether they possess or fail to possess the quality of "composition," members of the class of truly artistic writing, or else of the lower class of the usual thing. Produced by the distinction James introduces among grades of workers, this distinction of aesthetic quality then helps confirm that distinction: the existence (newly instituted by James) of a separable grade of really *composed* fiction is what proves that some novelists are *fine* artists after all.

In reconceiving of the novel as composition, James redraws the novel's place in the category of literature—establishes, in the already differentiated realm of literary writing, a class of novel that is literary in a more exalted and restrictive sense. In doing so he simultaneously readjusts the place the novel claims in the world. To the extent that it has a conscious idea of itself, the nineteenth-century Anglo-American novel is governed by a loose notion of the novel's continuity with the community of its readers' experience. Readers and writers largely saw the novel as taking its world in from the world of life; and they saw it as appealing *out* to the general sphere of shared belief, custom, and experience to validate its expression.[22] James's assertion of the novel's composedness implicitly downgrades its relational sides. That the novel can be highly worked means, for James, that it takes value *from* that work. "The pains of labor regulate and consecrate my progeny,"[23] James characteristically declares. The novel (in my idea of it) is belabored, born through pains of labor. That labor expresses itself on the work as composition or the making of form—the pains of labor *regulate* the work. And that laborious creation of form is indistinguishably what produces the work's value—as it regulates it also *consecrates* my progeny. Since what gives the work value, in this definition, is not the life it registers but the way it subjects that life to the meaning-producing pressures of formal activity, James's self-erected institution of fiction moves the ground of validation inside the novel, into the internal achievedness of its form. The novel becomes in this way a separate sphere, ruled by its own form of skill and evaluable only in terms of the practice of its art. (Again the new nineteenth-century professions, which exempted themselves from external regulation by reelaborating their internal disciplines, come to mind as an extraliterary analogy.) The realm of uncomposed experience—now called mere "life"—gets made correspondingly external to the novel, neither its source nor its court of appeal: "questions of art are questions (in the widest sense) of execution; questions of morality are quite another affair."[24]

James reimagines the novelist's vocational stature; he redefines the nature of his work; he also, and no less centrally, reconceives the novel's history and its relation to its history. One of the differences between prose fiction and other art forms that ranked higher in the nineteenth-century ordering of the arts is that it did not have a strongly formalized history of generic accomplishment. Like other uncanonical art forms—Joseph Kerman reminds us that this was true of music until the early nineteenth century[25]— and very much unlike, say, poetry, the Anglo-American novel before James tends to be most absorbed with fairly recent work, and to let older work drop from mind as it goes forward in time. When this novel does revive older models it does so at will and in idiosyncratic combinations: its past is not set in a fixed or persistent form. James's own literary consciousness is, in this respect, the normal one of his genre. James shows no active consciousness of classical ancient or English literature. (He shows less such consciousness, perhaps, than any other writer of comparable status.[26]) Even within his special form James's historical awareness is highly selective: he occasionally mentions Richardson and Fielding and Scott, but he shows no detailed interest in them; he knows Dickens and Thackeray, the great authors of his youth, but he treats their sort of work from an early date as *passé*. The writers who are strongly present to him are his near-contemporaries: Turgenev, Eliot, Flaubert, Zola, but also Cherbuliez, Howells, Bourget, Stevenson, and so on. James's peculiarity is that he gives this not-remarkable literary horizon the form, in his thinking, of a canonical history. In an invention as eccentric as any we have seen, he converts the recent authors he most admires into so many Masters (the idea is as new with James as the term, in the history of prose fiction).[27] The novel becomes, in a parallel process, what might be called a master-ridden form: a genre presided over by a fixed row of great achievers, who are seen as having established the possibilities of the form.

James's constructions both of a fictional canon and of fiction as a canon-governed form are most fully displayed in the series of late essays—"Gustave Flaubert" (1902), "Émile Zola" (1903), the letter to the Hawthorne centenary (1904), "The Lesson of Balzac" (1905)—in which he makes memorial visits to the "seated statue[s][28] of his great precursors. But these constructions are just as strongly felt in his fiction. For one of the peculiarities of James's fiction is its strong and persistent orientation toward the works of other writers. His work differs from his masters' in the degree to which it organizes itself as *from* a master. No Balzac novel that I know points to a prior author as systematically as *Washington Square* points to Balzac; no Eliot novel is so full of an identifiable earlier book as *The Portrait of a Lady* is of *Middlemarch* and *Daniel Deronda;* no Hawthorne novel is so pointedly sourced elsewhere as *The Bostonians* is sourced in Hawthorne; no Turgenev novel is so much a tale from another as *The Princess Casamassima* is a tale from Turgenev. The novel becomes, in James's hands, a form written in continual awareness of a fixed set of literary precedents. Literary influences (selectively made) influence it more deeply; equally important, it specializes its sources much more tightly to the literary portion of its surrounding. What Harry Levin once called the novel's "impenitent intercourse with the outer world"[29]—its customary perviousness not just to other books but to contemporary cultural expression in all its forms—becomes, in James, contained and restructured. His intercourse is first and foremost with other masters of his form; nonliterary influences act on him more remotely, through the mediation of literary relations.[30] Contemporary agitation over the question of woman's place puts its mark quite directly on *The Blithedale Romance;* James's *The Bostonians* knows this agitation less as a social movement than as a theme from Hawthorne. When Turgenev takes up the subject of revolutionary violence in *Virgin Soil* he is dealing with a new fact of Russian political history. When James revives this subject in *The Princess Casamassima* he is responding much more to the figure of Turgenev.

Such changes within James's fiction indicate a prior change, I would argue, in the way James draws the shape of the novel's sphere of influence. James makes the novel's organizing history be its literary history: he breaks its literary antecedents off from other portions of its context and gives them new primacy as the forces it must engage. Another way to put this is to say that James institutes for the novel a structure of influence like that of the traditional high arts. Against its custom, he loads it with the memory of its masters and their achievements, such that to be at work in this form is to be always working out one's relation to one's giant forebears—and to have other forms of relation become, correspondingly, less important.[31]

This reconstitution of the novel's sphere of influence—a genuine Jamesian novelty—is in turn an essential phase in the more general reconstruction of the novel as a literary and social category that James effects; a move, I would insist, that comes out of a specific literary-historical situation. What we have seen of the careers of Howells and James suggests that the notion of the literary novel, stabilized and successfully institutionalized in America in the 1850s and 1860s, came open for redefinition again in the later nineteenth century, such that the writers who were intimately connected with that form faced the challenge, in their mature careers, not only of producing new novels but of reworking the governing idea of their form. Howells's gospel of realism—less a theory of representation than an attempt to reenvision the whole operation of prose fiction in American culture—is one response to this challenge. Seen as radical in its time, the realist program reveals itself, in the terms I am using here, as a kind of neotraditionalism: in his effort to maximize the novel's derivation from and service to extraliterary experience, Howells attempts to revive and reassert the novel's customary broad connection with contemporary communal life. Faced with the same challenge, James's action is to unthink the novel from its customary connections and obligations and to give its idea in a new form: one that makes its literariness—its possession of the properties that distinguish literary from other expression—its defining feature; and that thus bounds it off as a separate sphere of creation requiring consideration and appreciation in its own special terms.

The way James effects this separation of the novel's sphere is by subjecting this form to new schemes of internal authority. James's vocational designs, for example, place the novelist in a structure of greatly intensified demand, raising as they do the level at which he is requried to perform and spreading a schedule of required performance over the whole course of his writing life. But fashioning such new self-requirements is one way James mends the status of his art—relocates it among those prestigious (and self-controlling) human labors known as *disciplines*. James's ideal of premeditated formal design erects the same sort of structure around the work of fiction that his career ideal erects around the worker: an abstracted and totalizing plan which each particular of the work is required to conform with. And as we have seen, his fabrication of this idea of form is one way James endows the novel with the properties of an internal system, and so separates it from systems other than itself.

James's new plan of fictional tradition—in which earlier writers are made into exemplary figures later workers must confront—is one more of the new schemes of authority James invents to subject the novel to. And this increased traditionalization of the novel works quite as directly as the new ideals of form and career to put the novel in a new position. By giving the novel its own row of past masters James improves prose fiction's claim to the rights and dignities of a high art, and lends historical color to the notion of the present novel writer as possible master. More, situating the novel within this new idea of influence helps bring about a change in its real relations. Produced within a context that features literary texts as the body of relevant precedent, the novel actually *becomes* literary in a new way: a work that points to literary works (not others) as its chief antecedents and that groups itself with literary works (not others) as its real companions. So far from being a separate or merely marginal project, James's traditioning of the novel reveals itself here as a central aspect of his central labor: the conversion of the novel into—in a more exclusive and differentiated sense of the word—a *literary* form.

I have travelled a long way around, it might appear, to get back to the subject of James and Hawthorne. My excuse is that it is only in terms of James's general reorganization of literary influence—itself a part of his more general reorganization of the novel's idea of itself—that this particular relationship makes full sense. One way that James increases the literary autonomy of the novel is by increasing the authority, over it, of literary tradition. His cult of mastery makes him highly responsive to the work of every author he regards as masterful—James is, early and late, a great student of his contemporaries and fellows. But it makes him especially sensitive to a certain kind of figure from the literary past.

As "The Lesson of Balzac" makes clear, in its fully realized form the Jamesian plan of authorship implies the recognition and continuing centrality of an exemplary founder. This founder is in a sense synonymous with the genre prose fiction. The full possibility of that form is realized and recorded in his work: "when I think, either with envy or with terror, of the nature and the effort of the Novelist, I think of something that reaches its highest expression in him." Therefore later writers can best possess and extend that form by possessing themselves of his example: "I may at once intimate that the family [of novelists] strikes me as likely to recover its wasted heritage, and pull itself together for another chance, on condition only of shutting itself up, for an hour of wholesome heart-searching, with the image of its founder."[32]

Many writers, in theory, might occupy the niche that James describes here. But for an American starting out in authorship in the mid-nineteenth century, the choice would have been nearly inevitable. James began his career just when Hawthorne was being recognized and promoted, by processes I have already described, as the great American writer of literary fiction, and he quickly found Hawthorne as the sort of founding father he required. As he recalls in *Notes of a Son and Brother,* James discovered Hawthorne in his twentieth year, at exactly the time when his own literary ambitions were being formed:

> I fondly felt it in those days invaluable that I had during certain last and otherwise rather blank months at Newport taken in for the first time and at one straight draught the full sweet sense of our one fine romancer's work—for sweet it then above all seemed to me; and I remember well how, while the process day after day drew itself admirably out, I found the actual exquisite taste of it, the strain of the revelation, justify up to the notch whatever had been weak in my delay.

Coming to Hawthorne just when he was hatching "my deeply reserved but quite unabashed design of becoming as 'literary' as might be," James found Hawthorne's work a revelation of what literary writing might be:

> And the tone had been, in its beauty—for me at least—ever so appreciably American; which proved to what a use American matter could be put by an American hand: a consummation involving, it appeared, the happiest moral. For the moral was that an American could be an artist, one of the finest, without "going outside" about it, as I liked to say; quite in fact as if Hawthorne had become one just by being American *enough,* by the felicity of how the artist in him missed nothing, suspected nothing, that the ambient air didn't affect him as containing.[33]

The terms on which James first encountered Hawthorne explain, I think, the peculiar place Hawthorne continues to hold in his work. James is never as frank in his acknowledgment either of Hawthorne's achievements or of his derivation from Hawthorne as he is, say, of Balzac, the writer he delights to call "the father of us all."[34] But Hawthorne's, much more than Balzac's, is the fiction his own fiction most palpably remembers; as Hawthorne's is the example he returns to study whenever he is in search of new direction. The reason is not just that Hawthorne is a rich quarry (though James shows that he is), or that Hawthorne in fact prefigures James's chief concerns (though James's continuous imitation makes this too seem to be the case). It is that James identifies authorship itself as something Hawthorne helped establish, such that to work *as* a writer is to work *in* Hawthorne's line. For the author who built the figure of the exemplary founder into the idea of the novelist's work, Hawthorne always occupied the place of founder. We read a description of what Hawthorne is to James, through the long course of his writing, in his final encomium to the master of his form:

> We do not, at any rate, get away from him; he is behind us, at the worst, when he is not before, and I feel that any course about the country we explore is ever best held by keeping him, through the trees of the forest, in sight. So far as we do move, we move round him; every road comes back to him; he sits there, in spite of us, so massively, for orientation.[35]

◄§ *Chapter Seven* §►

JAMES IN THE BEGINNING

> If I were to recommend method in any part of the study of a Painter, it would be in regard to invention; that young Students should not presume to think themselves qualified to invent, till they were acquainted with those stores of invention the world already possesses, and had by that means accumulated sufficient materials for the mind to work with. It would certainly be no improper method of forming the mind of a young Artist, to begin with such exercises as the Italians call a *Pasticcio* composition of the different excellencies which are dispersed in all other works of the same kind. It is not supposed that he is to stop here, but that he is to acquire by this means the art of selecting, first what is truly excellent in Art, and then what is still more excellent in Nature; a task, which, without this previous study, he will be but ill qualified to perform.
>
> SIR JOSHUA REYNOLDS, *Discourses on Art*

> "How do you study sculptures, anyhow?"
> "By looking at models and imitating them."
> HENRY JAMES, *Roderick Hudson*

JAMES gives special weight to the death of Hawthorne in his autobiography. He remembers it with intense emotion, recollecting in moving detail how he heard the news while sitting "half-dressed, late of a summer morning" in his darkened bedroom, and how it provoked a "pang that made me positively and loyally cry." And he places this event so as to increase its importance. He groups it with a series of crises that took place after his family moved from Newport to Ashburton Place in Boston, and that made his years there "packed with drama of a finer consistency than any I had yet tasted." On one side he links it with the events marking the end of the Civil War, introducing it in the same sentence with the assassination of Abraham Lincoln—and thereby suggesting an equivalence between the "assault" of Hawthorne's death on "my private consciousness" and the assault of Lincoln's death on the nation's. On the other side he links it to the acceptance for publication in 1864 of "my first fond attempt at literary criticism" and Charles Eliot Norton's resultant invitation to him to contribute regularly to the *North American Review*. In retrospect, James comes to regard his half hour in Norton's library at Shady Hill as embodying "a positive consecration to letters," "the beginning of so many intentions"; he converts it into the moment of initiation in the narrative of his calling to a literary career, the moment when anxious desire ripens into "assurance" of his election to an artistic vocation. In *Notes of a Son and Brother* James welds his visit to Shady Hill and his reception of the news of Hawthorne's death—events without other relation to one another than their chronological coincidence—into a coherent narrative unit. The result is that the death of Hawthorne figures in it not as an isolated experience of bereavement but as an episode in James's early drama of vocation, in the forging of what he calls "my quite unabashed design of becoming as 'literary' as might be."[1]

The reflections on Hawthorne in *Notes of a Son and Brother* are important because they show James at the end of his career willing to recognize and confess the depth of his attachment to Hawthorne as he never had before. But their real interest lies in James's suggestion that Hawthorne has a special connection to his early manhood and, specifically, to the early phases in the establishment of his career. What form the connection takes he does not explain. At times he speaks of Hawthorne as of a precedent or role model. The pang of his grief was intense, James writes, because in the previous months he had found in Hawthorne's writing "work . . . all charged with a *tone* . . . in an air in which absolutely no one else's was"; his discovery of Hawthorne, he implies, was the discovery that writing could be beautiful and that an American could produce such writing, "that an American could be an artist, one of the finest, without 'going outside' about it."[2] But the passage as a whole hints more darkly that James does not so much follow Hawthorne as replace him, implying as it does a link between James's metaphorical birth as an artist and Hawthorne's literal death. As James tells it, he is greeted into the rank of men of letters exactly as Hawthorne is ushered out; the room in which he hears of Hawthorne's death is also, he emphasizes, "my cherished chamber of application," the scene of his first efforts as a writer. (His emphasis of these coincidences make one suspect that James was aware, though he does not mention it, of the curious fact that Hawthorne died within six weeks of James's attainment of his majority.) What kind of a connection in fact exists between his beginning and Hawthorne's end can only be clarified by turning back to James's earliest writings and following their evolution. But James's last words on this subject provide a clue as to where to look for this connection. They suggest that his indebtedness to Hawthorne and his discovery of his vocation are two aspects of the same thing; put another way, they urge us to recognize that his relation to Hawthorne operates first off at the level of the organization of his career.

Any study of the beginning of James's writing life must immediately confront two apparently contradictory facts. The first is that few other novelists have had so strong and so early a sense of calling to authorship as James had. The twenty-one-year-old recalled in *Notes of a Son and Brother* already has an "unabashed design"; looking back to his Ashburton Place years in an 1881 reminiscence James again remembers his youthful eagerness and writes: "What strikes me is the definiteness, the unerringness of those longings."[3] What strikes him in his earlier self, in other words, is not just the intensity but the directedness of his desires, his early disposition toward one activity, not another as his life's work. The phrase "consecration to letters," while it is a late description of an early experience, also reminds us that authorship never had the status merely of a secular profession for James, but instead of a vocation in the religious sense: a life-structuring task through which one both performs one's work in the world and discharges one's obligations to the source of one's being. James has a feeling that is common among the poets but rare among the novelists in the Anglo-American tradition, the feeling that his role has been chosen for him by some power larger than himself, that he is (in Wordsworth's words) "a renovated spirit singled out, / Such hope was mine, for holy services."

The second great fact about James's early writing life is that if few authors have had so strong a sense of calling, no novelist of equal eminence has had such trouble getting started in his vocation, no novelist has taken so long between when he dedicated himself to writing and when he began to produce work that would justify his dedication. Reading through his first ten years' literary output—the twenty-one stories published between 1864 and 1873 and the novel *Watch and Ward*—one marvels at how long James went on writing without finding his own actual direction as a writer. Hawthorne worked in obscurity for a much longer period than James; but his suppressed first novel *Fanshawe,* if premature, already organizes its material in the oppositions that will govern his later writing, and the idiosyncratic patterns of verbal and imaginative style that we call "Hawthorne" are brought to mature expression in some of his earliest published tales. This is what James's early work fails to do. Though some (but by no means all) of the stories are accomplished enough as pieces of writing, they have curiously little to do with one another, let alone with James's later work. Not having tapped into the source of imaginative power that compels an author's work to take on an individuated shape, James veers aimlessly from manner to manner, producing (to take one sequence) now a gothic romance in "DeGrey," now a charade of social misprision in "Osborne's Revenge," now a highly colored historical costume drama in "Gabrielle de Bergerac," and so on. As he reflects in the later tale "The Middle Years," as a beginning author James "was so clumsily constituted that he had to teach himself by mistakes."[4] In an 1875 essay he looks with admiration on the careers of Scott, Thackeray, George Eliot, and George Sand, who waited until they were past thirty, and then "without prelude, or with brief prelude, produced a novel that was a masterpiece"; but he recognizes his own strange career reflected in the mirror of Balzac's, the author who "learned his trade so largely by experiment and so little by divination that in order to discover what he could do he . . . had to make specific trial of each of the things he could not do."[5]

In his first ten or twelve years as a writer, as James later expressed it, "his development had been abnormally slow, almost grotesquely gradual."[6] During this time he seems to have become increasingly aware of the distance between his aspirations and his achievements. His letters reveal a Miltonic preoccupation with unripeness and delayed maturation. "I grow more slowly than it must seem in Cambridge, that I ought," he writes in one letter to William James; "but that I do grow, I hope continually to prove." And in another: "Mysterious and incontrollable (even to one's self) is the growth of one's mind. Little by little, I trust, my abilities will catch up with my ambitions."[7] While the moment cannot be established with any degree of certainty, it is clear that at some point during these years James evolved a working understanding of his youthful writing as forming a definite period in a career. In one of the first of his characteristic institutional inventions, he imported into his work a classical notion of apprenticeship: a formalized first phase in the projected plot of a creative biography, during which the young artist sets himself to learn the skills that will enable him to become a master later on. Although the origin of a conscious plan of apprenticeship cannot be documented, it is already present as an intention within the work in James's tales of 1868, and the idea grows in clarity and regulatory power as James proceeds. Toward the end of his self-appointed apprenticeship, thus, James can speak of it as a conscious and fully articulated program. In an 1878 letter responding to William's strictures on *The Europeans* he writes:

> I think you are altogether right in returning always to the importance of subject. I hold to this, strongly; and if I don't as yet seem to proceed upon it more, it is because, being "very artistic," I have a constant impulse to try experiments of form, in which I wish to not run the risk of wasting or gratuitously using big situations. But to these I am coming now. It is something to have learned to write, and when I look round me and see how few people (doing my sort of work) know how (to my sense), I don't regret my step by step evolution.[8]

William's mistake is that he has failed to read *The Europeans* in the context of Henry's evolution; he judges as if Henry were attempting a full-grown work, rather than preparing through lesser pieces for the greater ones to come. James himself now visualizes his career in terms of a detailed developmental timetable, a progressive series of phases each of which has a different kind of work appropriate to it, the function of which is to equip one for the greater challenges of the next. In this letter as nowhere else it is clear what needs the concept of apprenticeship meets for James. On the one hand, it gives him a way of understanding and accepting the peculiar rhythms of his own development—of acknowledging his slow maturation and his need to learn by mistakes, and converting them into purposeful parts of his artistic evolution. (Not least of the services the concept of apprenticeship rendered James was to keep his hopes up, to give him grounds to believe that his inferior productions were nevertheless preliminary stages of a superior work yet to be produced.)[9] On the other hand, the concept also enables him to take practical steps to further his development: it prescribes a regimen of exercises by which he can build up the skills in which he is deficient.

One of the apprentice exercises he undertakes in his early tales is what he calls "learning to write": the acquisition of stylistic fluency and facility through systematic practice. Another is the development of the faculty of invention by means of imitation. The idea of apprenticeship that James constructs for himself is derived less from literary precedents than from the fine arts, and one of the things it entails is a fairly explicit prescription of the use the young artist should make of the Old Masters. Reviewing James's tales between 1864 and 1873 one is struck by the fact that at a certain point they become not less but more derivative. And conspicuously derivative: alluding to their originals as if to announce themselves as in the manner of this master, or based on a motif by that—as "The Madonna of the Future" and "The Sweetheart of M. Briseux" point to their origin in Balzac's "Le Chef d'oeuvre inconnu," or as "The Last of the Valerii" refers to its source in Mérimée's "La Venus d'Ille."[10] At an early moment in his career James seems to have recognized that in order to increase his own imaginative strength he needed to acquire the strengths of those who had practiced his craft before him. Thereafter he sets about constituting the storytellers of the previous generation as his models, relinquishing his own power of invention in order to imitate theirs.

This is where Hawthorne comes in. Hawthorne is not a noticeable presence in James's earliest tales. He enters James's work at the point when James undertakes to serve an apprenticeship, as a master James proposes to sit to. In his writings of 1868, by far the most prolific of his early years, and the year in which he is most evidently determined to add to his repertoire of styles, James begins more or less systematically returning to Hawthorne and taking off from his example.[11] Two tales of this year have as their apparent motive the wish to write in the manner of Hawthorne; these are "The Romance of Certain Old Clothes," a costume drama set in colonial Massachusetts, in which a battle of wills between two sisters is rendered through the occult mechanism of a fatal curse, and the feeble "A Problem," which like Hawthorne's "The Threefold Destiny" presents a homely drama of domestic relations presided over by an apparently supernatural fate, a weird prophecy that comes to be fulfilled in an unexpected way by perfectly ordinary occurrences. More ambitious as apprentice pieces are two other stories in which James takes over the central elements of a Hawthornesque plot, using them to organize a work of his own. In "The Story of a Masterpiece," a middle-aged man finds his suspicions of the heartlessness of the woman he is about to marry confirmed by the expression she wears in the portrait he has commissioned of her. This is the first of a long series of tales in which James reworks the conceit of Hawthorne's "The Prophetic Pictures," his characters' chic art-historical patter not concealing the fact that here as in Hawthorne portraiture is an occult art of visionary penetration. "It seemed to Lennox," James writes, "that some strangely potent agency had won from his mistress the confession of her inmost soul, and had written it there upon the canvas in firm yet passionate lines." (1:285) The agency is not strange, however, to readers of Hawthorne, who have already been informed that "it is [the artist's] gift . . . to see the inmost soul, and by a power indefinable even to himself, to make it glow or darken upon the canvas."[12]

James is even more scrupulously derivative in "De Grey: A Romance," published five months after "The Story of a Masterpiece." This tale concerns a family whose male heirs are cursed to have their love be fatal to the woman who is its first object, the curse continuing to operate in generation after generation (in a delightful burst of extravagance James traces it back to the time of the Crusades) until the story's present, when Margaret Aldis, the fiancée of Paul De Grey, musters the energy of her love and wills that the curse be undone; but by her "prodigious act of volition" (1:416) the curse is not revoked but only reversed, so that while she is spared, Paul dies in her place. (This is one of many James stories governed by a strict law of conservation of erotic energy, such that Margaret's passionate force increases at the cost of draining Paul of his.) James's principal purpose in writing "De Grey: A Romance" seems to be to see how many Hawthornesque *topoi* he can reproduce in the same work. In addition to its hereditary curse, "De Grey" borrows the sets of *The House of the Seven Gables,* locating its action in an "excellent old mansion" built in the style of an earlier period, with an adjoining garden and summer house in which the scions of ancient families can court fresh young maidens brought into the family from outside. It carefully reproduces the special-effects devices of that book—James opens the tale, for instance, by introducing the De Greys in a state of apparent tranquility and prosperity, but then surrounding them with a chorus of gossiping women whose superstitious intuitions obscure them in an atmosphere of ambiguity and horror. Margaret Aldis herself is a composite of the heroines of Hawthorne. Like Sylph Etherege, she is seduced by a picture of her beloved. Like Faith Egerton in "The Threefold Destiny," she is the prize that her lover, after "roaming about Europe, in a vague, restless search for his future," finds "quietly awaiting him at his own deserted hearth-stone." (1:409) Like Priscilla in *The Blithedale Romance,* whose skill at needlepoint she inherits, the harshness of her early life has given her "a certain tenuity and fragility of aspects, a lightness of tread, a softness of voice, a faintness of coloring"; like Priscilla she moves like a spirit commanded in a trance— "like one whose soul had detached itself and was wandering through space, she rose, on Mrs Dr Grey's at last giving her an order, and moved forward as if in compliance; and then, suddenly rushing forward toward the old woman, she fell on her knees, and buried her head in her lap and burst into a paroxysm of sobs." (1:396) (Her behavior here particularly recalls Priscilla's compulsive kneeling to Zenobia.) When aroused by Paul's love, this frail blossom undergoes a strange transformation, a kind of hideously compressed puberty—and an even stranger transformation from Priscilla into Hawthorne's Beatrice:

> He had bent to pluck this pallid flower of sunless household growth; he had dipped its slender stem in the living waters of his love, and lo! it had lifted its head, and spread its petals, and brightened into splendid purple and green. This glowing potency of loveliness filled him with a tremor which was almost a foreboding. (1:418)

"De Grey: A Romance" is important for the study of James's relation to Hawthorne not because it bears so many specific debts to Hawthorne but because it shows the terms on which James contracted to go into Hawthorne's debt. "De Grey" is literally an exercise in pastiche, an attempt to reproduce in one work the varied excellencies dispersed through Hawthorne's fiction. As such it represents a serious artistic effort—but James is serious not about making the story significant in its own right, but about using it as an occasion to master a Master's range of motion. James begins his formal career by consciously submitting himself to Hawthorne's tutelage, for the sake of expanding his own resources of expression.

"De Grey" also shows exceptionally clearly what the early James sees in Hawthorne, what he first construes as an object of imitation. Two aspects of Hawthorne in particular attract him at this stage of his career. One is Hawthorne's treatment of magical foreknowledge—foreknowledge as it is embodied in fatal curses, fortune tellings, prophetic works of art, and so on. What interests James, and Hawthorne before him, is not the supernatural origin of prophetic knowledge but rather the structure it unfolds in a story, a structure in which two rival determinations of experience vie with one another: one in which actions are known in advance as inevitable steps in a fixed pattern, the other in which characters shape an uncertain future by acts of will and choice in the present. Operating at this level, James's characters fight off the constrictions of a preordained design: Margaret Aldis curses the curse; Perdita in "Certain Old Clothes" appropriates the wardrobe in defiance of the sister's curse; the married couple in "A Problem" struggle to defeat the prophecy that each of them will marry twice. But their actions end up not thwarting the design but only completing it in unforeseen ways: Margaret's revocation makes the curse light on Paul; the couple in "A Problem" realize their fate by separating and remarrying one another. The play between two orders of determinism in these tales exactly mirrors that in "The Prophetic Pictures," for instance, where Walter and Elinor's marriage exists simultaneously as an immutable prophecy contained in a fixed set of images and as a mutable daily relationship, the prophecy both foredooming their lived relation to take its form and depending on actual evolutions in their relation for its fulfillment; or in "The Threefold Destiny," where Ralph Cranfield's specially appointed fate first leads to estrangement from, then finds its completion in, the happenings of ordinary life. James is the only author I know of to have located this minor but genuine vein of Hawthorne, the part of his writing that plays with the apparent opposition but final coincidence of designs projected in advance and experience unfolding from within.

The other thing that James returns to repeatedly in this early group of tales is Hawthorne's treatment of sexual ambivalence, especially of the emotional tensions aroused by the occasion of marriage. The real similarity between "The Story of a Masterpiece" and "The Prophetic Pictures" lies in their use of the stock device of the magical portrait to uncover the secret desires and dreads a man and a woman feel when they contemplate one another as a prospective husband or wife. (John Lennox in James's story inherits both Elinor's fear of her fiancé and Walter's streak of sadistic aggression, drawing a knife to slash Marian Everett's portrait as Walter draws a knife to stab Elinor.) "De Grey" follows "Rappaccini's Daughter" not just in its descriptions of a heroine supercharged with exotic, sensual vitality but in its focus on the attraction and repulsion this vitality inspires in a prospective lover. Paul De Grey, like Hawthorne's Giovanni, feels a "dreadful delight" as he contemplates his beloved's "glowing potency": it makes him "long to possess" her (1:418), but it also makes him fear that she will infect him with a "noxious influence" or "drain" him of his own vital spirits, so that he ends up recoiling from her as from something "distasteful, loathesome," "enchanted, baleful, fatal." (1:425–27) (In effect, the conclusion of "De Grey" takes Giovanni's point of view on women as *belles empoisonneuses,* releasing it from the irony Hawthorne subjected it to in "Rappaccini's Daughter.") This group of tales is full of prematurely womanly maidens who make their fiancés shudder. Since Hawthorne's fiction contains what must be the densest population of shuddering bridgrooms in the history of fiction, it is not surprising that James should turn to him for literary prototypes through which to represent this obsessively recurrent emotional situation.

Considered in another way, this early group of tales is almost more interesting as a demonstration of what James fails to see in Hawthorne—or at least fails to be able to express—than of what he does see. The Hawthorne tales that serve as their models remained among James's favorites, but we need only think ahead to his later reworkings of them—his reworking of "The Prophetic Pictures" in "The Liar" (1888), for instance, or of "Rappaccini's Daughter" in "The Aspern Papers" (1888), or of "The Threefold Destiny" in "The Beast in the Jungle" (1903)—to see what a limited range of Hawthorne's thematic resonance he is able to reproduce at this stage, and also how restricted is his ability to expand on Hawthornesque conceits. But as we move forward in James's work this situation begins to change. After this initial round of apprentice pieces James continues to return to Hawthorne as a source of ideas, but he begins to handle more freely the motifs he imports.

The difference is already evident in "The Passionate Pilgrim," written in 1871. As Peter Buitenhuis has noted, this story takes its basic plot from the chapter "Consular Experiences" in Hawthorne's *Our Old Home,* in which Hawthorne tells of the visits to his Liverpool consular office of a dignified American who is convinced that he is the rightful heir to a noble English title and estate, and who has found confirmation for his theory of his lineage in "a portrait bearing a striking resemblance to himself" in the picture-gallery of the family's country seat[13]—as James's Clement Searle finds himself doubled in the Reynolds portrait of an earlier Clement Searle hanging in his would-be family estate. Though James is still telling tales from Hawthorne in "The Passionate Pilgrim," he takes a noticeably more active stance toward his model than he did, for example, in "De Grey." Here instead of retracing a pattern already completed in Hawthorne he takes over a suggestion which it is for him to work up into a tale. (There is no better proof of the affinity of imagination between these two writers than the fact that James develops Hawthorne's donnée in this story much as Hawthorne himself did in an unfinished work that James could not have known in 1871, *The Ancestral Footstep*.) Also, while James depends on Hawthorne's anecdote to supply the outline of his action, he rather assertively fills it in with material that is certifiably of his own making. To see him laying into the narrative of "The Passionate Pilgrim" bulky descriptive paragraphs taken from the letters home and the travel sketches he wrote during visits to London, Oxford, and Worcestershire is to see him beginning to displace Hawthorne's invention with invention of his own—though as this story shows, he only begins to be able to include his own experience in his fiction by first adopting, then elaborating on schemas borrowed from previous authors.

His more assertive handling of models is evident again in "The Last of the Valerii," written in 1873 and published in 1874. Putting this story over against "The Passionate Pilgrim" provides a measure of the spurts of growth James undergoes as his writing career continues. This tale has a technical proficiency conspicuously lacking in the earlier one. In it James manages to rationalize the role of a narrator who both observes and provokes the action, a phenomenon strangely unexplained in "Pilgrim"; the Old World setting is now an integral and continuous presence in the tale, not confined to discrete chunks of choice descriptive prose; the style of the tale is marvellously fluent and poised, not marred by the violations of register so common in the earlier work ("Do you feel it? Do you tingle? Are you hot? Are you cold?" [2:287]). James continues to import his plots from the workshops of the Masters, but now he moves easily to modify and recombine them. The archaeological fantasy of "The Last of the Valerii" is derived from Mérimée's "La Venus d'Ille," in which a newly excavated statue of a pagan goddess becomes a rival to a newly solemnized marriage. This tale is apparently associated in James's mind with the forty-sixth chapter of *The Marble Faun*, in which Miriam and Donatello excavate a pagan Venus (who is again represented as the antithesis of modern marriage: Kenyon must in effect choose between Venus and Hilda); and as Marius Bewley was the first to remark, in retelling Mérimée's tale James endows it with thematic content that is specifically Hawthornesque.[14] Count

Valerio, the Italian nobleman of ancient family who marries a wealthy American girl at the start of the story, inherits the healthy physicality of Mérimée's Alphonse de Peyrehourade, but James reads this trait as Hawthorne reads it in Donatello: as a sign of atavism, of reversion to a primitive—preintellectual and premoral—state of development. (James's narrator underlines: "He's the natural man!" [3:95]) Similarly, excavation in this tale carries the kind of weight it does throughout Hawthorne's work. James's story is fraught with a Hawthornesque sense of historical animism, a sense that other orders of time are instinct with strange, menacing life. The archaic past, thus, is not superseded: it is "stirring there beneath" (3:100), still alive under the accretions of historical experience that cover it, and to dig it up, to bring it to light, is to unleash its power as a tyranny over the present. When the goddess worshipped by his forebears is unearthed thus the Count falls under the domination of his "urgent ancestry" (3:107), involuntarily returning to their pagan practices. What James recaptures here is Hawthorne's sense that to recover lost origins is to be victimized by them, delivered over to a compulsion to repeat. The moral to be drawn from an American's attempt to recover his English past, Hawthorne writes in his notes for *The Ancestral Footstep,* is:

> Let the past alone; do not seek to renew it; press on to higher and better things—at all events to other things; and be assured that the right way can never be that which leads you back to the identical shapes that you long ago left behind. Onward, onward, onward![15]

So in "The Last of the Valerii" an initial movement to unearth or recover the past is followed by a movement to reinter it, to push it back behind or beneath. James's American-born Countess restores her husband to their marriage by reburying the statue she had caused to be dug up, acting on the Hawthornesque understanding that in order to make room for one's own time, a present that is not the past endlessly repeated, one has first to raise the past to consciousness but then to thrust it back out of the present by an act of will.

Leon Edel notes in his biography of Henry James that "The Last of the Valerii," with its implied message "that the past contains a fund of evil dangerous to love and to life," marks James's "first clear statement of one of his major themes: the corruption to be found in Europe by an American still innocent." He goes on to assign the emergence of this theme in James's fiction to causes in James's buried psyche: on one level it reflects the "buried fear of evil" that originated in his childhood memories; on another it suggests "his intuitive understanding that he would have to bury his personal past, the past of Quincy Street, and make his way in a disengaged present."[16] But it is more illuminating, to my mind, to think of this theme's emergence into James's writing as the result not of the proddings of the unconscious but of a conscious act of literary imitation. "The Last of the Valerii" may be thematically richer than "De Grey: A Romance," but it generates thematic content in exactly the same manner: by casting earlier literary works as models, and reproducing their images in such a way as to reconstruct the web of association that we call their "vision." I do not mean to imply that themes are merely literary properties to early James, without significant relation to the pressures of his mind. But I would stress that *if* the idea of the past's persistence as a destructive force corresponds to an urgent fantasy in James's psyche, he does not learn to release this fantasy into his fiction *until* he has first found the means for its literary expression, which he does by imitating its expression in Hawthorne.

Expressing his own most powerful patterns of consciousness in fiction, if I am reading him correctly, is precisely what James does not do in his earliest writing; instead it is what he comes to be able to do, as the result of a practical program of literary apprenticeship. To see this is to see what the real function of apprenticeship is for James. Its aim is by no means confined to acquiring a repertoire of executive skills: its real aim is the formulation of James's artistic identity, which he accomplishes by first re-creating the identity of others. "The Last of the Valerii" shows his program of self-creation or self-derivation through imitation beginning to produce its desired effects. We note immediately how, as a result of his previous attempts, James is now able to reproduce not merely local features of Hawthorne's fiction but his whole sense of the past. And exactly as he comes to have this sort of command of Hawthorne, he also begins to produce something that we recognize as distinctively and essentially his own. "The Last of the Valerii" is another tale of marital anxiety and adjustment. In his reversion to pagan worship the Count abstracts himself from his marriage, and—like John Lennox and Paul De Grey in James's earlier tales, and like the abstracted votarists in Hawthorne (for instance Aylmer, in "The Birthmark")—he comes to "shudder" (3:117) at his wife's touch. But this story works through to a resolution unprecedented in its predecessors, in which the Countess makes a prodigious act of volition not to drain her husband but to recover him as a husband, to redeem him from a regressive form of love that he himself knows he needs to be rescued from. She is one of the clearest prototypes in James's fiction of Maggie Verver, and it is the measure of James's growth that "The Last of the Valerii" finally impresses one less as a late reworking of *The Marble Faun* than as an early draft of *The Golden Bowl*.

By the time of "The Last of the Valerii," James has had the benefit of apprenticeship, and is ready to bring this phase of his career to a close. The fiction he writes in 1873–74 shows an author anxious to move on to another stage. "The Madonna of the Future" (1873), one of a series of works about failed vocational transitions that span James's career and mark its significant divisions, is a fantasy about becoming stalled in the phase of apprenticeship. The painter Theobald is stuck in a ritual of self-preparation that has the effect of indefinitely postponing the act of artistic production: "I never began!," he laments; "I waited and waited to be worthier to begin, and wasted my life in preparation." (3:47) *Roderick Hud-*

son, started in 1874, emphatically expresses the artist's will "to begin," to "go in for big things," to make masterpieces of one's own instead of languishing in "passive enjoyment" of a precursor's "grandeur."[17] Outside of his fiction James's will to be at the end of apprenticeship is evident in his feverish planning of a program of writing that will constitute a literary debut. When he learns in 1873 that his father has made efforts to arrange for the publication of a volume of his stories, James lets him know that he has different plans.

> Briefly, I don't care to do it, just now. I value none of my early tales enough to bring them forth again, and if I did, should absolutely need to give them an amount of verbal retouching which it would be very difficult out here to effect. What I desire is this: to make a volume, a short time hence, of tales on the theme of American adventurers in Europe, leading off with the *Passionate Pilgrim.* I have three or four more to write: one I have lately sent to Howells and have half finished another. They will all have been the work of the last three years and be much better and maturer than their predecessors.[18]

His desire is for a volume that will not be a mere collection of work completed but a celebration of a developmental stage; at this point James begins to segregate his early tales into the category of juvenilia and sets to work completing the tales that will be tokens of his newly attained maturity. It is clear from the essay on Balzac in *French Poets and Novelists* that in the mid-1870s James is giving considerable attention to the ages at which previous authors began writing novels (the appropriate time for the first novel, he decides, is at age thirty or just afterward; James turned thirty in 1873), and when he contracts to write *Roderick Hudson* in 1874 he sees his attempt at a greater form as meeting a developmental need: "Let me say finally," he writes home in March, 1874, "that father when he gets answers from *Scribner* and the *Atlantic* had better accept 1000$ rather than let the thing fall. The writing and publishing of a novel is almost as desirable a thing for me as the getting a large sum for it."[19] The publication in 1875 of James's first three books—*A Passionate Pilgrim and Other Tales, Roderick Hudson,* and the collection of travel pieces *Transatlantic Sketches*—represents a carefully staged act of appearance, announcing the end of James's learning period and his emergence as an author in his own right.

One of the ways in which James announces his artistic emergence is by signalling a change in his relation to his predecessor. James's tales of 1868 present their author as a student of the Master's works; his 1875 volumes present him as something more like the master's successor. The relations of *Roderick Hudson* and *The Marble Faun* have often been commented on; what has not been noted is that *Roderick Hudson* resembles Hawthorne's romance much more closely at its beginning than it does elsewhere. In the first chapters set in Rome James takes over Hawthorne's earlier dramatization of the studio and social lives of American artists in Italy, but he does not continue this thread of the action in his later chapters. He is careful to associate Roderick with the human faun Donatello ("Looking at him as he lay stretched in the shade, Rowland vaguely likened him to some beautiful, supple, restless, bright-eyed animal" [187], he writes); but he does not pursue this aspect of Roderick's character beyond a certain point, choosing to develop him not as a natural man fallen into corruption but as a natural artist seized with a massive block. James follows Hawthorne most obviously in the scenes in which Roderick's art works are set up as emblems or externalizations of his moral and psychological condition, but after establishing an allegorical progression from Thirsty Youth to Adam to A Lady Listening, a more worldly sculpture that betrays the intrusion of "fundamental vices" (263) into Roderick's art and character, James introduces further statues rather randomly, then discontinues the series entirely. The author of *Roderick Hudson* wants to be seen to take over elements of Hawthorne's work—his borrowings from *The Marble Faun* constitute virtual allusions to it—but then to give them a treatment of his own. He invokes the earlier presence of Hawthorne to emphasize both his continuation and his independence from him—to declare, in effect, that he takes up where Hawthorne left off.

Such a reading of *Roderick Hudson* might be dubious if it were not reinforced by the volume of tales James selected for publication in 1875. In view of everything he had written by this time, his choice of "The Passionate Pilgrim" to stand as the first story in his first collection of stories was by no means inevitable. It is not the best written of the stories he included (many would consider it the worst); it is not the first written ("The Romance of Certain Old Clothes" is three years older); it is not, as it is often said to be, James's first treatment of the International Theme (the unadopted "Travelling Companions" preceded it); nor is it the tale in the volume that best represents his mature handling of this theme ("The Last of the Valerii," "Madame de Mauves," and "Eugene Pickering" could all be argued to do so better). But the piece James appointed to be the beginning of his tales is the one that most distinctly repeats the message of *Roderick Hudson*. It again asserts a conspicuous relation to Hawthorne—and specifically to late Hawthorne (*Our Old Home* is Hawthorne's last completed volume, as *The Marble Faun* is his last completed romance), as if to announce that its author begins where Hawthorne ends. And James again chooses to lead off with a work in which he visibly goes on beyond where Hawthorne stopped: in "The Passionate Pilgrim" he tells the story Hawthorne left untold, brings to completed form what Hawthorne had only dimly suggested. The complex relation James establishes in which he simultaneously receives materials from Hawthorne, continues and completes what he began, and departs from him to move in directions of his own is exactly that of heir, and it is appropriate that the tale in which James expresses this relation is about what it means to establish oneself as an inheritor. Clement Searle's laying claim to an Old World title images not just James's imaginative appropriation of Europe but also his appropriation of Hawthorne. Now that I have retold it, he implies, the story that was Hawthorne's has become mine. I am the heir of Hawthorne, James declares in his debt; his literary estate is now my rightful possession.

The developmental logic of James's early relation to Hawthorne should now be clear. After an initial period of disorganization, James begins to compose an identity in his writing by identifying with Hawthorne as a model. As he becomes increasingly proficient at imitation, he achieves a deepening understanding of the intentions of the figure he imitates; at the same time he grows more and more able to give distinctive twists to the movements he repeats. Finally he is ready to emerge from the submissiveness of imitation, to assert himself as an independent identity and to claim his model's powers as his own. The volumes of 1875 mark the end of the process by which James works through literary precedents to find his own beginning. Thereafter he is eager to be done with Hawthorne, to establish his autonomy and relegate Hawthorne to the past.

This new attitude helps to explain his rather exaggerated display of reluctance to undertake the critical biography of Hawthorne that he was asked to contribute to the English Men of Letters Series in the late 1870s.[20] It also helps to explain why the volume he finally did write in 1879 is so cold and aloof. In considering his *Hawthorne* it is well to remember that as a critic James despised mere appreciation. From his earliest reviews to his final critical essays his favorite exercise as a critic is locating the point at which an author's characteristic strengths begin to produce his characteristic weaknesses, or describing the shape of the field of blindness to which an author's field of vision commits him. And James feels especially obliged to be critical on this occasion: he is writing in the wake of George Parsons Lathrop's widely received *A Study of Hawthorne* (1876), a virtual sacralization of Hawthorne's life and works whose indiscriminate homage James saw as typifying the failure of intelligence in Anglo-American literary culture.[21] But for all his professions of disinterested desire to restore a fit sense of proportion to the discussion of Hawthorne, there is an obvious element of personal aggression in James's critical act in this book. His *Hawthorne* is an attempt, in both the positive and the negative sense of the phrase, to put his predecessor in his place.

From the first page, this book presents the spectacle of an author eager to establish his distance from his subject, an author horrified lest we think that he values his subject too highly—or even very highly at all. Hawthorne's life is well worth writing about, James begins—even if nothing interesting happened in it—because he is the most eminent figure in a national literature. Of course there is not much *of* that literature; and of course being most eminent is not so difficult when there is no competition; but modest nosegay that American literature is, Hawthorne is surely its sweetest flower. Then he starts over. Hawthorne savors of his region, he notes. Whether it is worthwhile learning about New England just to appreciate Hawthorne, "I need not pronounce"; but at least he does reflect that region more vividly than anyone else. Not *very* vividly, mind you—his descriptions are not very concretely particularized; "but none the less. . . ." (319–21)[22] These opening paragraphs, in which Hawthorne's claims to fame are projected toward the vanishing point, begin the process of systematic reduction that operates throughout the book. James thus emphasizes the small scale of Hawthorne's tales in such a way as to make him appear not a master of the short story but a kind of miniaturist, the author of "little tales," "little attempts, little sketches, a little world." (361) His approach makes Hawthorne's writing seem as slight in significance as it is in size. He noticeably avoids Hawthorne's strongest work, consistently focussing on him where he is weakest—thus having named "Roger Malvin's Burial," "Rappaccini's Daughter," and "Young Goodman Brown" as "little masterpieces" (again this "little"!), he says nothing further about them, but instead discusses at some length "Night Sketches," a work that generates the conclusion only that much of Hawthorne is "so light, so slight, so tenderly trivial" (348) that it would do it harm to give it serious critical attention. (James does write at greater length on Hawthorne's four romances, but with some exceptions to be noted in later chapters, he prefers to discuss what they are not to what they are; half of his consideration of *The Scarlet Letter* is devoted to demonstrating that it is not Lockhart's *Adam Blair*.) Over and over again James denies that Hawthorne's works have a substantial vision behind them, the merits of which might be discussed in their own right as a statement about life. What they have instead (the word becomes a kind of traitor's kiss in this volume) is "charm"— that exquisite, impalpable grace to be found in perfection in works that have no other claim to importance.

James's evacuation of substantial content from Hawthorne's fiction is evident even in what I take to be his most provocatively original contribution, his reading of Hawthorne's blackness. James is saying nothing new in nineteenth-century Hawthorne criticism when he describes his outlook as permeated with Puritanism, such that "to him as to them, the consciousness of *sin* was the most importunate fact of life." (326) His novelty lies in his specification of the terms on which Hawthorne entertains this vision. He holds it, James says, as a Puritan would, except *"minus* the conviction"*: he regards innate depravity "from the poetic and aesthetic point of view" (365), accepts it not as transcendentally grounded truth but as material for imaginative play.

> He played with it and used it as a pigment; he treated it, as the metaphysicians say, objectively. He was not discomposed, disturbed, haunted by it, in the manner of its usual and regular victims, who had not the little postern door of fancy to slip through, to the other side of the wall. (363)

This account has a simple kind of descriptive accuracy to it: it reminds us that as an artist Hawthorne uses the materials of a religious vision for the purposes of *literary* creation. And James's picturing of Hawthorne as a kind of gamesman of the moral world—"always at play, always entertaining itself, always engaged in a game of hide and seek in the region in which it seemed to him that the game could best be played—among the shadows and substructions, the dark-based pilllars and supports, of our moral nature" (340)—is part of a worthy critical design, that of redirecting appreciation from the content of Hawthorne's moral affirmations to his imaginative consideration of moral questions. But, inevitably, the language through which James introduces the morally playful Hawthorne has the effect of trivializing him. In place of the Melvillean Titan who said NO! in thunder, James's Hawthorne is a child sporting amid his "toys." (363) Melville cannot altogether tell whether Hawthorne uses "mystical blackness" merely "as a means to . . . wondrous effects" "or whether there really lurks in him, perhaps unknown to himself, a touch of Puritanic gloom." But James can: his Hawthorne is not disturbed or haunted by innate depravity; black is merely his favorite pigment. Here as elsewhere the principal effect of James's approach is to deny that Hawthorne's writing is informed by a deeply felt and seriously entertained vision of human life. Hawthorne is again confined to the realm of graceful aesthetic effects, it being the mark of his genius for James that it makes heavy moral burdens "evaporate in the light and charming fumes of artistic production." (363)

What makes James's *Hawthorne* interesting is that after systematically depriving Hawthorne of weight, size, and thickness, he goes on to interpret the resulting lacks as symptoms of a cultural condition. James's Hawthorne is a man of disembodied fancy: "there is in all of [his writings] something cold and light and thin, something belonging to the imagination alone" (339); and the reason his imagination works unclothed in social particulars is that he lived where social particulars were few and unvaried, in the "simple, democratic, thinly-composed society" of the pre-Civil War New England village (353). James's hypothesis of a causal relation between underdeveloped and democratically organized societies and abstract literary forms has been perpetuated by critics like T. S. Eliot and Lionel Trilling and has only recently begun to lose authority as a truism about American literature. What James's followers have not retained is the concretely historical dimension of his interpretation. "At that time," "fifty years ago, greatly more than now" (342), he keeps repeating: his focus is not on America or democracy as such but on the specific phase of cultural development America had attained in the 1830s and 1840s, in effect a post-colonial phase in which it had cut itself off from a foreign cultural center without having yet evolved maturely developed cultural institutions of its own. His value lies in his attempts to imagine what difference this different stage of cultural development would have made in the workings of an aesthetically inclined sensibility. When Hawthorne goes to Europe late in life and, on the evidence of his notebooks, remains "an outsider, a stranger," "to the end a mere spectator (something less even than an observer)" (433), James understands his failures of participation and assimilation in terms not of personal rigidity but of historical situation; Hawthorne lived at a time when national cultures were more insulated from one another than they have since become, and thus when individual consciousness was less habituated to cultural pluralism: "an American of equal value with Hawthorne, an American of equal genius, imagination, and, as our forefathers said, sensibility, would at present inevitably accommodate himself more easily to the idiosyncrasies of foreign lands. An American as cultivated as Hawthorne, is now almost inevitably more cultivated, and, as a matter of course, more Europeanised in advance, more cosmopolitan." (442) Similarly, James tries to understand the intrinsic qualities of Hawthorne's art in terms of the social organization of aesthetic activity in America "in the year 1830": one of the finest passages in the book is the one where James tries to imagine what it was like to try to be a writer at a time when authorship had not yet become fully institutionalized as a career or profession, when "the literary man . . . lacked the comfort and inspiration of belonging to a class." (342)

James's *Hawthorne* is one of the most brilliant attempts to be found in nineteenth-century literary criticism to reconstruct an author's cultural context and to determine what that context permitted and denied as artistic developments. But it does not lessen the book's power as an exercise of historical imagination to note that every move James makes to place Hawthorne historically functions simultaneously at another level, as part of an effort to put his predecessor at a disadvantage. In practice, by locating Hawthorne at a less highly evolved cultural moment James relegates him to a conspicuously inferior, an almost unbelievably primitive evolutionary epoch. The earlier world he evokes has relatively few features of America in the 1830s, but all of the features of a pastoral Arcadia. It is rustic, natural, nature itself there seeming "fresh and innocent, as if it knew as yet but few of the secrets of the world." (327) Human life in it is "homely, simple, frugal" (332), diversified with only the simplest pastimes. (In James's hands both Transcendentalism and the New England custom of sharing books with neighbors turn into quaint forms of entertainment characteristic of an unsophisticated age; by a cunning sleight-of-hand he manages to make Hawthorne's college education appear to have consisted largely of blueberry picking). The men of Hawthorne's time are a vanished race, "American[s] of the earlier and simpler type" (425), basking in the unreflective optimism that, according to James, prevailed in America until the Civil war produced "a more critical person," on who "has eaten of the tree of knowledge." (428) Hawthorne gets pastoralized in this volume; and this by an author who leaves no doubt that the state of innocence, for all its simple charms, is essentially a state of restriction, a state of impoverishment—specifically, impoverishment of aesthetic consciousness. James himself comes across as almost preposterously worldly in *Hawthorne*. His modish tone is caught perfectly in his definition of original sin—"this baleful substantive, with its attendant adjective" (326)—as the doctrine "that we are really not by any means so good as a well-regulated society requires us to appear" (396), or in his remark that the Abolitionists "were as unfashionable as they were indiscreet—which is saying much." (427) Through his elaborate feats of stylistic self-display he makes it clear that he, for one, is of a much later and more complicated type than Hawthorne, as fully a man of the world as Hawthorne was little one. The difference cannot help counting in his favor in a volume that takes it as axiomatic that art can only grow where social complexity proliferates, where the differentiation of cultural forms fuels a various knowledge of life.

The distinction James draws between the experience of pre- and postwar Americans abroad, illuminating as it may be as a historical generalization, functions in a similar way to put Hawthorne in an inferior position. Hawthorne remained an outsider to European society, Hawthorne remained inexpert in European culture (James positively gloats over the signs of Hawthorne's aesthetic incompetence: his revulsion from nudity in statuary, his attention to the picture frames rather than the canvases of the Old Masters, and so on): according to James, the richer spectacle of Europe forced Hawthorne not out of but deeper into "the provincial point of view." (431) He himself, however, is obviously on the inside; one of the purposes of his style in *Hawthorne* is to dramatize his cosmopolitanism, his firm grasp of and easy movement among the distinctive outlooks of the great Western cultures. The invidiousness of the distinction between his cosmopolitanism and Hawthorne's provincialism comes clear when we realize that in *Hawthorne* James equates knowledge of Europe with knowledge *tout court.* His is the point of view of "the initiated mind" (372); Hawthorne, by contrast, "lacks the final initiation into the manners and nature of a people of whom it may most be said, among all the people of the earth, that to know them is to make discoveries." (433)

James's ultimate cruelty to Hawthorne, which it is the tendency of the whole volume to enforce, is to make him out as, simply, uninitiated—lacking in mature knowledge of mature human experience. He did not just live at an earlier period; he lived at the time of immaturity, when "a large juvenility [was] stamped upon the face of things." (327) No wonder his writing is merely charming: he has no knowledge of life with which to back up his artistic efforts. James confers on Hawthorne all of the disadvantages of his own state during his season of apprenticeship. By means of his critical appreciation he executes an exact reversal of their earlier roles, making Hawthorne not older and wiser than himself but younger and less humanly expert—"so fresh and unsophisticated that we find ourselves thinking of [him] as a young man," although, sad to say, his is really only "the simplicity of inexperience, not that of youth." (430)

Hawthorne is the work of a recently emerged author bent on putting the tutors of his youth behind him. James's historiography cordons Hawthorne off in an epoch that is now extinct, bearing no discernible relation to James's own. He offers absolutely no indication that Hawthorne has survived as a cultural or literary presence, no indication that later authors have—or even *could*—derive anything from Hawthorne's writing. If the James of 1875 makes Hawthorne an ancestor whose estate he lays claim to, the James of 1879 denies that Hawthorne is anybody's ancestor. For his part, he remembers Hawthorne not as an artistic parent but only as an aged figure in need of charitable attentions—"poor Hawthorne," as he is termed in James's menacingly caressing epithet.

As far as James is concerned, his relation with Hawthorne is over and done with. But to a student of the history of this relation, few developments are so interesting as what happens next. Just after James turns away from Hawthorne with such apparent finality, Hawthorne reenters his fiction with unprecedented force. *The Portrait of a Lady,* written in 1880–81, reveals that during his 1878–79 re-reading of Hawthorne some part of James was recognizing and assimilating what his critical perception blocked out. The James of *Hawthorne* insists that Hawthorne had a serene and sunny mind, undisturbed by the moral reality of evil, but the author of *The Portrait of a Lady* knows better. In the figure of Gilbert Osmond, particularly in Osmond's relation to his daughter Pansy, James reimagines a specifically Hawthornesque mode of villainy, in which a stronger spirit converts a weaker one into the passive object of its tyrannical will, cold-bloodedly violating its sacred autonomy. Similarly, having repeated that it would be a mistake to think of Hawthorne as a tragic author, James re-creates a specifically Hawthornesque form of tragedy in *The Portrait of a Lady*. Like Hester Prynne, Isabel Archer, determined to view the world as a place of bright and free expansion, finds herself condemned to restriction and frustration not by external circumstances but by the nature of her expansive desire itself. She returns from England to Rome at the end of her book as Hester returned from Europe to Boston in hers, freely choosing to subject herself to the limitations she has temporarily escaped, because she recognizes them as more humanly authentic—the scene of a "more real life"—than desires fulfilled.

In *The Portrait of a Lady,* the work James regarded as inaugurating the stage of full-fledged mastery in his career,[23] Hawthorne is not left behind, but rather incorporated into the deepest levels of his imagination. This novel brings to a climax the long process by which James has learned to re-express more and more of the resonances of Hawthorne's voice, and thereby to release to expression a voice of his own. At the end of his beginning Hawthorne has become for James what he remains for the rest of his career: an intimate possession, part of the basic equipment of his artistic consciousness. In the thirty years after 1881 James sometimes moves away from Hawthorne, but never for long. He keeps finding his own directions anticipated and clarified in Hawthorne, returning to him again and again as a resource whose usefulness to his writing is never exhausted, whose relevance to his thought is never at an end.

Chapter Eight

JAMES, REALISM, AND
THE POLITICS OF STYLE

For the inner life of man, its essential traits and essential conflicts can be truly portrayed only in organic connection with social and historical factors.
LUKÀCS, *Studies in European Realism*

"If you knew more about me you'd understand what has led me to turn my attention to the great social questions. . . . I'm convinced that we're living in a fool's paradise, and that the ground's heaving under our feet."
"It's not the ground, my dear; it's you who are turning somersaults."
JAMES, *The Princess Casamassima*

THE NOVELS that James wrote between 1881 and 1886—*The Bostonians* and *The Princess Casamassima*—are linked by a set of emphases that, while not identically managed, are equally marked in both books. These novels insist on their relation to the world outside them. Their fictional spaces—charted, in both cases, by elaborate pedestrian tours—carefully mirror those of real cities, Boston and London; their fictional societies, they underline in a hundred ways, reproduce the forms and relations of actual social groupings, with the reductive clarity of a scale model. The vigorous gesture outward toward contemporary reality that determines these books' choice of world also governs the way they render their world. These novels are addicted to what James calls redundancy of touch. Their representation is always dense with detail, hyperresolved—registering the world in the fulness (fulness even to excess) of its circumstantial particularity. And the urge to render the full form of the contemporary that motivates this highly particularizing style informs as well their making of plot. James labors in these novels under the will to make his fiction's actions typical, in the high realist sense of that word.[1] In choosing a cast politicized around the issue of sex roles and gender identifications in *The Bostonians,* then of class inversion and revolutionary action in *The Princess,* James is striving for more than topicality of social theme. He aims to find the forms of personality and relationship in the present world that will most fully exhibit the strains that modern social dislocations are putting on individual lives. By plotting the interactions of such figures in a fiction he can then claim to be charting real modern history, disclosing how collective human reality is being transformed in his time.

Writing novels (in the phrase of his 1883 notebook) "very national, very typical . . . very characteristic of our social conditions"[2] is a new ambition for James in the 1880s. The compositional initiatives that group *The Bostonians* with *The Princess Casamassima* are in no sense extensions of his earlier writing. They are the work, exactly, of an author who is putting his earlier accomplishments behind him, and setting himself tasks he knows have been out of his line. In this sense James's public novels of the 1880s stage an authorial drama of self-renovation along with their political plots. Behind the new style of representation these books are rendered in we can read a powerful and sustained *act* of stylistic choice: an author willing a new way of writing to be his work, then holding up his newly appointed manner through the whole performance of two long works. And this act of stylistic rectification clearly aims to remake James's authorial self. The way to make oneself another kind of author, the author of these books knows, is to write another kind of book. In giving a new answer to the questions what and how he shall write, James is attempting to reanswer the question who he is as a writer, who his writing shall establish him to be.

What James is trying to turn himself into in the 1880s is not at all hard to determine. The style of work he attempts to convert to is, this once in James's career, easily identified outside of his practice. The thrusts I mention in *The Bostonians* and *The Princess*—toward emphasized contemporaneity of material, thick registering of the realm of social accidents, the typifying conception of character and plot—are all well-marked features of nineteenth-century literary realism, central components of what Peter Demetz, with proper regard both for the separability of its elements and their tendency to manifest themselves together, calls the realist syndrome.[3] And they would have been known as such in James's time. James comes late enough in the nineteenth century for the constituents of the realist syndrome, originated as so many separate innovations in the work of many separate authors, to have become gathered together, integrated in both idea and practice into a recognizable transpersonal *style*.

Realism comes to James already consolidated as a literary project. And it comes consolidated on terms that would seem amply to explain its attraction for him. Much more than any other widely distributed fictional form in the nineteenth century, realism succeeded in erecting a dense mythology around itself, powerfully establishing its literary superiority and its right to prevail. To list the schemes of value that realism promoted itself as aligned with is to list every major construct of nineteenth-century ideology. By 1880 it had long since established itself as the socially inclusive form of fiction, hence as the literary equivalent to political democracy (as in the Goncourts' preface to *Germinie Lacerteux*); as the fiction of human brotherliness and fellow feeling, hence as the literary agent of liberalized, secularized Christianity (as in George Eliot's interchapter in *Adam Bede*); as the fiction undistorted by narrative intrusion, hence as the literary equivalent to scientific objectivity (as in Zola's "Le roman experimental"); and so on.⁴ Powerfully legitimated in ideological terms, it is an essential fact of realism's status in the nineteenth century that it also seemed legitimated directly in the world. In a century of accelerated and often violent social transformation, realism appeared uniquely the literature *of* social transformation. With its new techniques of verisimilitude and its central emphasis on contemporaneity and social dynamism, it looked to deal with reality immediately, and in its most critical dimensions. And to deal with it in such a way as to open its crises to understanding: since the realist's claim, from Balzac on, is that he does not merely mirror the contemporary, but actively reveals the forces that are producing the present world, and pushing that present toward a different future.

These features of literary realism's late-nineteenth-century status are the basis for the authority this style exerted when it was imported into America in the 1880s. Howells, who converted to realism somewhat before James, and Hamlin Garland, who converted somewhat after him, embrace it with all its attendant doctrines, and so show how strongly realism's then-well-consolidated legitimating mythology could validate this style for writers in their position. Their cases show as well realism's perennial ability to recruit new power to itself from its coincidence with sociohistorical developments. The 1880s—decade of rapid urbanization and industrialization, of labor consolidation and labor strife, of the bomb in Haymarket Square and the specter of anarchism, of agrarian impoverishment and the Populist revolt—is the time when the social transformations produced by capitalist development were most glaringly visible in nineteenth-century America. Imported at this social moment, literary realism seemed to speak with special power *to* this moment: so that Garland could embrace realism as the literary form of Populist political action; so that Howells could preach realism, after the Haymarket Anarchist trial, as the only adequate (and at that not *quite* adequate) literary response to the social crisis of his time.

Since he turns toward the same style at the same moment, we might expect James to be moved toward realism by the same sorts of causes that moved his contemporaries. In fact this is not the case: the explanations that do so much to account for his fellow-writers' self-transformations signally fail to account for James's. Fully conscious of realism's self-naturalizing arguments, James is remarkable for the extent to which he abstains from putting forth such arguments himself, and for the uninterest—really it is more like disdain—with which he regards such arguments in others. James made a highly publicized visit to associate himself with the incumbents of the French realist tradition in Paris in 1884; but although he wrote, at this time, that "there is nothing more interesting to me now than the effort and experiment of this little group,"⁵ it was never their ideas about their work that he found impressive: the naturalist doctrines, as doctrines, always strike James as the stupid part of an impressive effort. When, in an 1886 essay on Howells, James must bring himself to speak of the "definite and downright convictions" of Howells's realist polemics, he writes as if such convictions are almost intrinsically ludicrous ("he thinks scarcely anything too paltry to be interesting, that the small and vulgar have been terribly neglected")[6]—as if they could only detract from, never add to, the achieved power of an artistic effort.

Little impressed by realism's official rationales, James could also scarcely be said to come to realism out of any strong engagement with the social dramas of his moment. The argument is sometimes made that James, like Howells or Garland, underwent a growth of political consciousness under pressure of the events of the 1880s, a growth that his political novels then reflect. But such an argument gives James involvements he does little to claim. To the extent that we can establish an actively political awareness for James outside his novels, it is highly occasional—geared to isolated public events—and almost invariably spectatorial. ("If I had nothing else to do I think I should run over to Ireland. . . . I should like to see a country in a state of revolution," James writes in one letter, as if revolution were a kind of exotic touristic spectacle. The continuation, in any case, makes clear that he has brought up this topic only as part of the talk of the town: he goes straight on to talk about London's winter weather.)[7] A handful of James letters from 1885 and 1886 do display a more concrete sense of the sources of current social conflict and of James's stake in such conflict. But such letters read, arguably, more like outtakes from the novels James is writing than like these novels' "real" historical source; it is notable that James shows no further interest in their social subjects after these fictional experiments are done.

Such considerations bring us up against what I take to be the central anomaly of James's realist episode. In transforming his work as he does in the 1880s, James adopts what was no doubt the most strongly legitimated literary style of his time. But he adopts it, paradoxically, without regard for its customary legitimations—in spite of, not because of, its usual grounds for support. This is not to say that James sees realism simply as a style among others. When he adopts it, it is because he too finds it more compelling than other available styles, including that of his own early work. But the reasons why James finds it compelling are very much of his own construing: products of the peculiar logic by which Jamesian authorship in general is structured.

What makes literary realism impressive to James in the 1880s? To the extent that we can reconstruct an answer, it has much more to do with realism's literary history than with its claims to extraliterary truth. When James engages a component of the realist style, he always does so with a strong sense of *whose* style it has been before. "The compendious, descriptive, pictorial touch," in James's usage, is synonymous with *"à la Daudet"*:[8] he registers it as a form of representation, but simultaneously and equally as the work of *that* writer. James's visit to the haunts of the naturalists in 1884 shows the same tendency to think of realism in its late-century evolutions interchangeably as a kind of writing and as a group of figures. The strong writers of my time, James declared by making this visit, are those writing modern realism—a message that also suggests the converse: realism is the masters' style because the living masters write it. *The Princess Casamassima,* the book James intended as the centerpiece of his realist phase, is the most variously and visibly derivative of all of his novels, with its *arriviste* straight out of Balzac, its grotesques and hyperconnected city straight out of Dickens, its researched institution (Millbank Prison) and its heavy interior decoration straight out of Zola, and its aristocrat-bastard sensitive political hero straight out of Turgenev. The realist tradition does not contain another novel so strongly allusive as *The Princess Casamassima.* Its allusiveness tells us on what terms James takes realist fiction on: he knows its forms as from the hands of the masters, as bearing their mark upon them.

One of the distinctive features of James's encounter with realism—the consequence, in this phase of his career, of his organization of a canonical literary sphere of reference around the novelist's work—is that he apprehends it centrally as a *literary* phenomenon. Rather than thinking that realist representation somehow escapes from the literary realm to embrace life directly, James always regards it as a *literary* operation: a potential literature possesses, a power literature can exert. Similarly, its origin, for him, is not outside literature but *in* its *literary history.* Realism exists for James as something evolved by the work of certain writers; as its power for him is the power their authorial strength has given it.

Its status as the masters' form of work, I am suggesting, is what makes realism a privileged style for James. And his reason for turning toward this style in the early 1880s is also not remote from his most strictly literary concerns. The deepest pressure James knows in the time just after *The Portrait of a Lady* is the need to establish himself on new grounds; more particularly, to establish himself on terms that will give proof of full maturity finally achieved. This pressure comes from many directions. James's parents both died in 1882, requiring him (as his haste to eliminate the Junior after his name indicates)[9] to reassert himself as free from childhood dependencies. His fortieth birthday approached in April, 1883—like his thirtieth, a source of intensified developmental self-consciousness, and of an anxious will to confirm his movement forward. What makes this period typical of James is the way these biographical exigencies, coming together by coincidence and quite remote from his literary labors, nevertheless get translated into and reexperienced in terms of his writing life. James's most revealing writing of this time is this notebook entry, from November 1882:

> If I can only *concentrate* myself: this is the great lesson of life. I have hours of unspeakable reaction against my smallness of production; my wretched habits of work—or of un-work; my levity, my vagueness of mind, my perpetual failure to focus my attention, to absorb myself, to look things in the face, to invent, to produce, in a word. I shall be 40 years old in April next: it's a horrible fact! I believe however that I have learned how to work and that it is in moments of forced idleness, almost

alone, that these melancholy reflections seize me. When I am really at work I'm happy, I feel strong, I see many opportunities ahead. It is the only thing that makes life endurable. I must make some great efforts during the next few years, however, if I wish not to have been on the whole a failure. I shall have been a failure unless I do something *great!*[10]

This passage is one of the great expressions of James's addiction to work, and his internalization of an economy geared to total productivity. To be at work, it suggests, is the only way to feel fully alive; and whether one will have lived successfully, in its curious time-scheme, remains always contingent on what one will have gone *on* to produce. The passage is characteristic too in the way it orchestrates the demands of work into the patterns of a career. Work, in it, is what one must *keep* performing. And its expectations are not static: its requirements are scheduled to rise over time, so that to move forward through it one must keep mounting to new levels of performance. The Jamesian literary career, this passage well shows, has its own structure of inner requirements. But it also shows how that structure, without losing its autonomy, takes into itself the pressures of James's extraliterary life. With the sudden eruption "I shall be 40 years old" a biographical anxiety surfaces alongside the more strictly literary anxiety of production, amplifying, clearly, James's felt need to "make some great efforts during the next few years." At the same time, as it absorbs such extraliterary demands, the structure of career also makes the work-life the place where such demands can be resolved. The need, approaching forty, to have moved into a fully productive maturity fuels James's authorial need to have attained, in literary terms, a major phase. But by this process doing the *work* of that phase—*writing* something *great*—becomes the means by which he can satisfy that other need, establish the fact of his proper personal growth.

The exigencies of literary career serve peculiarly strongly as motives for realism in James's case. Much more than any extraliterary source, it is James's sense of his place in his career that makes him so urgently desire to do a new *form* of work in the early 1880s. (His notebook projection of *The Bostonians*—the entry in which he pledges himself to write books "very characteristic of our social conditions"—is dated April 8, 1883, or seven days before his ominous birthday, suggesting how closely the new ambition there expressed is tied to James's more general desire to have redefined his work in advance of a deadline in his developmental schedule.)[11] And the needs generated by his career position explain why, in attempting such a self-conversion, he should cast his work in *this* direction. Realism carries the weight for James in the early 1880s of the masters' work, the literary expression of fully developed power. Faced with the need to undertake a form of work that he can think of as *great,* James turns to realism as the available form of greatness: as the style equipped, through its literary descent, to signify *major* work; and so to establish, when he shall have mastered it, that he is now major himself.

If I am right about the motives for realism in James, they help explain a matter even more obscure: namely, what James means by this style, or how he intends it. From the point of view of his completed oeuvre, with its famous and striking later developments, the kind of work represented by *The Bostonians* and *The Princess Casamassima* seems most unJamesian: an aberration of manner, a kind of detour off the high Jamesian way.* But seen from within James's movement forward through his career, these books have a completely different status. James plans them to *be* his major phase; theirs is to *be* the high Jamesian style, at the moment when he projects them. James may not believe in realism in the terms that its more orthodox votarists do, but his way of engaging it has its own gravity and its own depth of commitment. For in mid-career James invests this style with the fund of his ambition. He entrusts this style to establish his maturity and power. In the strictest sense he puts himself at stake in his realist experiments: his "great efforts" in this form are what will confirm him as *"great,"* or else make him "shall have been a failure."

As what I have said will have suggested, as he adopts this new style and invests it with this new ambition James also constructs a new tradition for himself, and a new place for himself *in* tradition. Embracing the realist project on James's terms entails drawing in a new literary past—the line of the continental realists, from Balzac through Turgenev to Daudet and Zola—around his labors, as defining the work he is now attempting. (I note in passing that, since he associates it so heavily with such antecedents, the style James appoints to establish his maturity actually renews and intensifies his dependence on masters.) But one of the curious facts about James's reconstitution of his tradition in the early 1880s is that while it gives him a new line of forebears, it does not remove Hawthorne from his ancestry—if anything, it reinforces his centrality. Visibly and intentionally in *The Bostonians,* then unexpectedly but no less powerfully in *The Princess Casamassima,* Hawthorne returns as the dominant organizing presence in James's new social fictions. In James again as in Howells, America's old romancer turns out to be continually implicated in the new work of American realism; and he plays in James's realism something like the double role he played in Howells's. He appears there, rather surprisingly, as helper and guide—James, like Howells, producing what he thinks of as realistic in these novels by following Hawthorne's moves. But he is by no means only an acquiescent resource. In James's practice—as in Howells; as in every nineteenth-century author's encounter with this form (only the problems vary)—realism proves an unexpectedly tricky phenomenon. Massively coherent seen from afar, when practiced it proves to be rife with internal conflicts; imposing in its conviction of its rightness, when embraced it shows itself based on contradictory intentions and

---

* Late James, of course, helps promote this belittling of his realist phase, excluding *The Bostonians* from the Jamesian canon in the New York Edition, and reinterpreting *The Princess Casamassima* (in his preface in that edition) in such a way as to make it really a center-of-consciousness novel, just like his usual work.

dubious claims. And in James's practice it is Hawthorne who helps bring realism's latent problems into focus. Engaged to show the way into a new form of authorship, Hawthorne takes on the power here again of that authorship's principle of self-questioning. In doing so he also helps James to the discovery that is the real yield of his realist experiments: the discovery that realism is after all not his style.

No James work makes a more sustained or detailed allusion to Hawthorne than *The Bostonians* does; and a consideration of this book might begin by asking why James has Hawthorne so much on his mind in it. What the last two chapters have suggested about Hawthorne's place in James's idea of his work gives a partial answer. Since he looks to Hawthorne as something like the founder of his authorship, it is not surprising that James should go back to this origin here, as he plots a new line for his work. It might be added that Hawthorne, never really *past* anyway in nineteenth-century literary culture, was even more present than usual at this book's moment. The year James plotted and contracted for *The Bostonians*—1883—was the year Houghton Mifflin brought out the Riverside Edition of Hawthorne's Complete Works, an event that called forth, in the journals James was to publish his new novels in, a flood of reconsideration of Hawthorne's art. (*The Bostonians* was literally surrounded by the memory of Hawthorne in the pages of *Century Magazine*.)[12] Hawthorne would have been strongly present too in the more strictly literary portions of James's publishing setting. In going from *The Undiscovered Country* to *A Modern Instance*, Howells had just preceded James in the double move he would make in *The Bostonians,* into self-conscious literary realism and into the *Century*'s larger circulation. Always more important to James than Jamesians will allow, Howells's work here would have shown James how a studied revival of Hawthorne might help him accommodate himself to both his new style and his new place of literary production.

But it must be said too that there is something about James's new project itself that draws Hawthorne especially near to him. Commissioning himself to write about "the most salient and peculiar point in our social life," and determining that it lies in "the situation of women, the decline of the sentiment of sex, the agitation on their behalf,"[13] when James now looks back at Hawthorne he finds this ground already covered there. Another Hawthorne—Hawthorne the political novelist—gets brought to light for the first time here, by James's change in his authorial position. More, James finds in Hawthorne a stance toward the subject of social agitation that nearly prefigures his own. Hawthorne, known to both himself and his readers for his deep detachment from contemporary social causes, was nevertheless regularly driven, in revulsion from his detachment, to try to join the excited interest in social programs that he found around him. But one of Hawthorne's most distinctive marks, in both his life and his work, is that his attempts to thrust himself inside the burning social dramas of his time always have the effect of exploding them—of making them seem afflicted with intense unreality.[14] James, who feels impelled to write about political aspirations in the 1880s without much participating in those aspirations, is always bringing himself, by his effort to treat them seriously, to a deeper sense of their delusoriness*; so that the terms on which he takes up political fiction put Hawthorne in new symmetry with his thought. As he ascends to the role of fictive historian of modern social dislocation, James finds his subject already treated in Hawthorne, from an attitude much like his own. If he models his work more closely on Hawthorne now, it is to the end of learning how to express the nature of political action, from the source whose account of this subject he finds most definitive.

Not surprisingly, *The Blithedale Romance* now becomes the central Hawthorne text for James. *The Bostonians,* a novel in which every effort to enlist another in a cause masks a move to enlist that other in the service of one's desires, concisely reenacts what James takes to be the lesson of *Blithedale:* "the unconscious way in which the search for the common good may cover a hundred interested impulses and personal motives."[15] What James specifically lifts out of *Blithedale* is Hawthorne's way of representing the operation of abstract ideas in dramatic action. His prototype here is the fourteenth chapter of *The Blithedale Romance,* the scene in which Hawthorne's characters gather at the rock in the forest from which Apostle Eliot preached to the Indians in order to preach their own latter-day social gospels to one another. Hawthorne lends each speaker full use of his declamatory powers, such that each ideological position is forcefully presented. But he also conducts the scene in such a way that the formulation and opposition of public platforms never becomes separated from other dimensions of the action. Zenobia here vigorously denounces the social tyranny that denies women the right to full public expression and vows "to lift up my voice on behalf of woman's wider liberty." But though her feminist polemic is powerfully argued, Miles Coverdale does not respond to her argument as an argument. Instead he insists on reading back behind

---

* I say this because James's work with the political as a subject culminates in passages like this one late in *The Princess Cassamassima,* as summary and heartfelt a statement of his emerging views as I know. (Its subject is Anastasius Vetch, the music-hall musician radical who, like several other characters, simply repudiates politics in the middle of the novel, as if it were too tiresome an act to keep up.)

> The idea of great changes, however, took its place among the dreams of his youth; for what was any possible change in the relations of men and women but a new combination of the same elements? If the elements could be made different the thing would be worth thinking of; but it was not only impossible to introduce any new ones—no means had yet been discovered for getting rid of the old. The figures on the chessboard were still the passions and jealousies and superstitions and stupidities of man, and their position with regard to each other at any given moment could be of interest only to the grim, invisible fates who played the game—who sat, through the ages, bow-backed over the table.

The resonances with the direly ironic conclusion of Hawthorne's "Earth's Holocaust"—with its similar belief that the forms of human desire and suffering are permanent, not products of transitory social arrangements, and that the hope for making changes in elemental human reality is therefore delusory—are striking.

her social views to the personal exigencies their stridency expresses, the "inward trouble" in her "individual affections" that has made her take up "the general quarrel of woman against man."[16] Hollingsworth does respond to Zenobia at the level of her social assertions, brutally mocking her feminism and making a crude countercase for masculine supremacy and feminine dependency. But his ideas operate within the sphere of abstract social thought no more than Zenobia's do. As the scene unfolds, his speech brings about not a persuasion but a seduction: when he is finished Zenobia ceases to argue, and, when the others turn away, she declares her love for him by pressing his hand to her bosom.

Speech is made powerful, in "Eliot's Pulpit," not by the truth or falsity of its contentions but rather by the emotional and sexual energy that is invested in it. Zenobia is a powerful orator because the vexed energies of what Hawthorne calls her "womanhood" are now being expressed in the form of speech. Hollingsworth is an even more powerful orator because an even more potent and concentrated masculinity is channeled into his oratory. ("What a voice he has! And what a man he is!," [21] Zenobia comments, as if the two were interchangeable.) What public speaking produces in its audience, then, is not so much enlightenment as attraction. Zenobia is converted into that loving and dependent thing Hollingsworth says woman rightly is not because she sees the truth of his position but because she feels the force of his masculine presence, enacted in his ideological language.

Many scenes in *The Bostonians* bear the marks of James's fascination with the "Eliot's Pulpit" chapter of *The Blithedale Romance*. What he takes over from it is a dramatic technique that shows political ideas as operating not just in their own sphere, but also as moves in the personal and sexual exchange between those who speak them and those who hear them. His characters like Coverdale before them can decipher the emotional messages encoded in others' political pronouncements—as Basil Ransom can tell from the hysterical aggressiveness of Olive Chancellor's feminist rhetoric at the Burrages' that she feels neglected by Verena, or as Verena can guess, from the bitterness with which Basil attacks "the institutions of her country and the tendencies of the age," that "probably something had gone wrong in his life—he had had some misfortune that colored his whole view of the world." (335–36)[17] And his characters like Zenobia before them are aroused by the covert emotional content of others' political declarations. In *The Bostonians* as in *Blithedale* sexual presence gets channeled into and communicated through the speaking voice, so that here as there oratory's effect is always the creation of desire—as Verena's first speech at Miss Birdseye's leaves Olive with "a red spot in each of the cheeks" (67); or as Verena's grand performance in New York makes Basil aware that by listening "he was falling in love with her" (275); or as Basil's own lapse into oratory in Central Park makes Verena, for the first time in her life, blush. In James's fiction as in Hawthorne's political sentiment is always seen as emerging from a prior "trouble" in the "individual affections," then as acting back on the affections to produce new states of desire and need. The business of the political novelist, as Hawthorne pioneers it in *The Blithedale Romance* and as James recreates it in *The Bostonians,* is then to uncover the play of passion taking place through and under the play of public ideas, and more specifically to bare the mechanisms by which the energies of sexuality, voice, and political conviction transform themselves into one another.

One of the Hawthornesque ironies revived in *The Bostonians* is the sense that every exchange of ideas on the roles of the sexes in society is at the same time an exchange between the sexualities of the parties to the debate. Another is the sense that every exchange of ideas about the proper distribution of power in society also effects a redistribution of power between its speakers. For James's most obvious debt to Hawthorne in this novel is to his way of representing the nature and action of power. The author of *The Bostonians* has clearly noticed those parts of Hawthorne's work that treat characters as if they were fields of force—zones of charged energies that repel or attract one another, and that interpenetrate one another in such a way that the force of the weaker field gets captured by and reorganized on the lines of the stronger. The *locus classicus* for this sort of representation in Hawthorne is Holgrave's tale "Alice Pyncheon" in *The House of the Seven Gables,* in which Matthew Maule and the haughty Alice engage in what is simultaneously a mesmeric contest and an erotic power struggle. When Maule undertakes to mesmerize Alice, she knows that an alien power is attempting to penetrate the boundaries of her field—"that some sinister or evil potency was now striving to pass her barriers"—but she assents to the contest because

> this fair girl deemed herself conscious of a power—combined of beauty,
> high, unsullied purity, and the preservative force of womanhood—that
> could make her sphere impenetrable, unless betrayed by treachery within.[18]

But her "womanhood" has already shown itself responsive to Maule's conspicuous masculine potency (she has "glowed with approval" at the sight of Maule, whose breeches are suggestively "open at the knees, and with a long pocket for his rule, the end of which protruded" [201]); so that her force cannot ward him off, but treacherously invites him inside her barriers. She joins the fight of "woman's might against man's might" (203) only to find herself overcome by a superior force: "She is mine!" Maule exults, "Mine, by the right of the strongest spirit!" (206) Hereafter she becomes "Maule's slave," her "maiden soul" enthralled to "a power, that she had little dreamed of." (208)

In his *Hawthorne* James comments disparagingly on Hawthorne's weakness for "spheres" and "sympathies." But he is obviously impressed by the form of psychological representation that Hawthorne creates in an episode like this, and in *The Bostonians* he imitates its terms and processes quite carefully. Character in *The Bostonians* is elaborately decked out with costume, manner, and contextual situation; but whenever its ultimate concerns are engaged, character acts simply as power—a force enmeshing others in "the fine web of [its] authority." (170) Similarly, James is seldom more skillful as a novelist of manners than he is in *The Bostonians,* but in all of their decisive confrontations his characters interact not as a manner with a manner but as a power with a power. "What a power—what a power, Miss Tarrant!" (81), says Olive, overcome by Verena's first speech; but when Verena calls on her the next day Olive subjects her to an even stronger "force of will," such that Verena "felt that she was seized, and she gave herself up" (79); a surrender that persists until Basil casts his "spell" over her in Central Park, putting her (in language that clearly echoes Matthew Maule's victory cry) to "the struggle of yielding to a will which she felt to be stronger even than Olive's." (337)

In *The Blithedale Romance* Hawthorne works the vision of "Alice Pyncheon" into a full-scale plot. This plot is where James follows Hawthorne most closely in *The Bostonians,* and also where he revises him most interestingly. The plot Hawthorne projects and James recreates has at its center an "obscurely inspired maiden" (54), a girl whose very weakness of will makes her something like a power vacuum, inviting the strong wills of others to flow out into her domain such that she becomes a living register of the intrusive potencies of others. In both versions a stronger spirit takes possession of this "maiden soul," and maintains his hold by turning her into a public spectacle—Westervelt controls Priscilla by controlling the form of her self-presentation, constraining her to appear as the Veiled Lady; Olive keeps Verena her exclusive property by constraining her into the role of female orator, such that she is allowed to appeal not to other individuals but only to "communities." (133) In *Blithedale* control of Priscilla is renewed and exchanged in complicated ways, until, in the final public exhibition recorded in the chapter "The Village Hall," she is released from her bondage. Called forth by Hollingsworth, who has taken the stage along with her manager Westervelt, Priscilla throws off her enslaving veil, breaks loose from the spell of Westervelt's power, flees to Hollingsworth's embrace, and (so we are told) "was safe forever." (203)

This is the point at which James diverges from Hawthorne's plot. The last scene of *The Bostonians* is, and by a hundred touches announces itself to be, a reprise of "The Village Hall" in *Blithedale.* James too makes his climax a scene of exploitative public display (he transfers Hawthorne's vaguely localized audience into the Boston Music Hall) from which the heroine is, at the last moment, rescued, by a hero bent on "wresting her from the mighty multitude." (441) But James rewrites the scene in such a way as decisively to change the meaning of its outcome. His revisions begin with the role of the maiden. Such intense possessive passions as this woman evokes could not, James reasons, be caused by her absence of vitality, but only by her excess of it; so he makes Verena gay, vibrant, and girlishly attractive, not, like Priscilla, anemic and droopy. He also reasons that the submissiveness of this heroine to the wills of others could not result merely from her absence of desires, but must itself embody a form of desire; so Priscilla's passivity is converted, in Verena, into a positive will to submission: "it was in her nature," James writes, "to like being overborne." (337) As a result of these changes, James's version of the final scene is much more of a liberation for its heroine. Much more convincingly than Priscilla, in getting carried off by the male rescuer Verena gets what she likes: after all, she likes Basil, and like the self Basil would have her be; "Ah, now I am glad!" (464), she says at the end, and she is, even if gladness is not her only emotion. Because Verena loves Basil, even loves being overborne by him, her final surrender to her rescuer is another thing Priscilla's is not: a positive and willing act. "Come," Hollingsworth says to Priscilla, and she obeys; but Verena opens her door to Basil—comes out, in other words, to be claimed by his desire.

James's revisions of the role of the rescuer are, if anything, even more interesting. Something is clearly wrong with the notion of Hollingsworth leading Priscilla off to spiritual safety. (*Blithedale* is obviously embarrassed by this scene: it renders it as briefly as possible, and hurries away as soon as Priscilla has been pronounced "safe.") Hollingsworth makes an unlikely redeemer because he has been previously seen only as an exploiter, arousing others' love to the end of putting them at the service of his political purposes. Further, if the murky plot of *Blithedale* gives him any motive for turning his attention to Priscilla, it is because he now plans to obtain through her the funds that previously belonged to Zenobia— hardly a motive for disinterested behavior. The language describing Hollingsworth's conduct in "The Village Hall" suggests not the freeing of another from enchantment but the subjection of another to a yet more potent form of enchantment. He brings

the whole power of his great, stern, yet tender soul, into his glance.
"Come," said he, waving his hand towards her. "You are safe!" (203)

What James does in *The Bostonians* is to recover these effaced suggestions of Hollingsworth's motive, and then reconsider his act of liberation in their light. Basil's wish to rescue Verena, James underlines, is not untinged by an element of coercion (he "wrenches" her from Olive "by muscular force" [463]), and not unmixed with a desire for domination (the sight of Verena's submission "flamed before him and challenged all his manhood"; "you are mine," "she's mine, . . . and if she's mine, she's all mine," [455, 457] he repeats, in words surely meant to remind us of Maule's "Mine! mine, by the right of the strongest spirit!") When he leads Verena offstage, then, he is not leading her out of the sphere of enthralling power, as Hawthorne would have us believe Hollingsworth is doing; he is submitting her to the force of a power stronger than his rival's—the power, exactly, of his love.

Not that Ransom thereby becomes a malign enchanter, or an imperialist in the region of souls—a Westervelt, or a Matthew Maule. The point is that he subjects Verena to his power because he loves her; or rather the point is that his love and his urge to domination are simultaneous, are even identical. Here it becomes clear that what James is bent on rectifying in *The Bostonians* is not a faultily motivated narrative sequence in *The Blithedale Romance* but a central feature in Hawthorne's psychology of love. Hawthorne's brilliance, as James sees it, lies in his understanding of the inseparability of love, sexuality, and the will to power—his understanding that to come within the loving presence of another is to come within the field of an energy that would incorporate us within itself, and align us with the lines of its desires. But then Hawthorne negates his own insight by treating love tinged with power as if it were demonic, and writing as if the only "true" love were a love that had renounced its elements of power—as Holgrave, the model groom in Hawthorne, attains "the rare and high quality of reverence for another's individuality" by renouncing his "opportunity of acquiring empire over the human spirit."[19] The polarization of love into an evil, power-tainted and a pure, power-free form is what causes the narrative distortions in "The Village Hall." To make Priscilla the female half of a true love match, *Blithedale*'s narrative must here erase her previously suggested will to submission and make her merely passive; as to make Hollingsworth into the male half of such a union it must hastily cleanse him of his previous possessive designs.

All of James's revisionary energies in *The Bostonians* are put to the task of resuscitating Hawthorne's vision of the linkage of power and love, and then freeing that vision from the (to James) false dichotomy in which Hawthorne shackles it. In his version of Hawthorne's tale, the woman in love both courts her lover's domination and is freed, through his domination, to discover her own authentic love for him. In his version of Hawthorne's tale the man in love is tenderly considerate of the "individuality" of his beloved, but he is also, exactly *through* his acts of consideration, bent on fitting her to the shape of his desires. Their love contains in it energies of domination and submission not because it is perverted, but because it is love. *That* is what "true" love is, James declares: a form of generosity that is also a form of selfishness, a form of distinterestedness that is never without an element of interestedness.

James's final word to Hawthorne is that love cannot be imaged either as a liberation or as an enslavement, but only as a liberation that also enslaves and an enslavement that also liberates. In *The Blithedale Romance* to cast a veil over someone is knowingly to deliver that person into bondage; antithetically, to lead someone out of the coercive sphere of spectacle is to deliver that person to freedom. In a move that both affirms his imaginative indebtedness to Hawthorne and declares his freedom to remake him, James signals the identity of love's enthrallments and love's rescues by making these two gestures continuous at his novels' close. On the last page of *The Bostonians* Basil leads Verena away from the hooting mob waiting to hear her perform at the Boston Music Hall; but as they depart he throws a cloak over her, pulling its hood up "over her head, to conceal her face and her identity." (464)

❀   ❀   ❀

This revision in Hawthorne's reading of love is one of the most brilliant ever performed on Hawthorne. It is one of the few, in the long history of such revisions, to convince us that it does not change Hawthorne's sense, but actually makes the sense Hawthorne is trying but refusing to make. But this is only one of the corrections James intends in *The Bostonians,* and it is not the chief of them. What he really offers to repair is less *Blithedale*'s representation of love than its representational style as such.

It needs to be remembered here that James's image of Hawthorne in the late 1870s and early 1880s—the most intensely competitive phase of their relation—is as an author intriguing in his fantasies but deficient in method. Hawthornesque romance, for James at this stage of his career, is at best an immature or imperfectly developed form of realism.[20] In *Hawthorne* he disallows romance's claim to be a genre in its own right, with its own legitimate but nonrealistic procedures. He thus reads "the very slight embroidery of outward manners"[21] in Hawthorne's fiction not as the result of a deliberated act of abstraction or stylization but always as the sign of a lack—yet more evidence of that "something cold and light and thin, something belonging to the imagination alone"[22] that indicates Hawthorne's lack of exposure to social life in its richer forms. James never subscribes to the realist movement's doctrines as doctrines, but his critical writing in the 1880s shows increasing admiration for the realists' methods and aims. Part of realism's growing prestige for him is as the style of initiated intelligence: it is the style, James implies in his fullest statement on it (in his 1883 essay on Daudet), generated by and expressive of the most advanced developments in contemporary social reality:

> It is scarcely too much to say that (especially in the Parisian race), modern manners, modern nerves, modern wealth, and modern improvements, have engendered a new sense, a sense not easily named nor classified, but recognizable in all the most characteristic productions of contemporary art. It is partly physical, partly moral, and the shortest way to describe it is to say that it is a more analytic consideration of appearances. It is known by its tendency to resolve its discoveries into pictorial form. It sees the connection between feelings and external conditions, and it expresses such relations as they have not been expressed hitherto. It deserves to win victories, because it has opened its eyes well to the fact that the magic of the arts of representation lies in their appeal to the associations awakened by things. It traces these associations into the most unlighted corners of our being, into the most devious paths of experience. The appearance of things is constantly more complicated as the world grows older, and it needs a more and more patient art, a closer notation, to divide it into its parts.[23]

Methodological superiority is one more advantage James can claim in his ongoing struggle with Hawthorne, and during his realist phase it is the tactical weapon he relies on most heavily. By affirming the value of realism's "closer notation," he can construe Hawthorne's fiction as, in effect, unachieved—suggestive in idea, but imperfect in its realization. All of Hawthorne's work, to this way of thinking, becomes eligible for fuller realization; and by bringing the realist style to Hawthorne's conceits James can pose as something like Hawthorne's perfecter, an artist rescuing bright ideas from primitive hands and conferring upon them the benefit of an advanced technique.

The Blithedale Romance is an obvious target for James's refurbishings. It has, for James, the fascination of the intermittently realistic. He describes it in *Hawthorne* as "a mixture of elements," an "alternation" of elements drawn from "the vulgar, many-coloured world of actuality" with others drawn "from the crepuscular realm of the writer's own reveries."[24] Every reader of *Blithedale* knows how it slips back and forth between an urbanely realistic and a rather hoakily magical form of action; how it renders certain elements with a very high resolution of detail, but then blurs out their surrounding context—describing for several pages the back view of a single apartment house, in a city that is not only never seen but never even named; or turning up every facet of Hollingsworth's reformist obsession, but giving no clue who Hollingsworth is when he is not at Blithedale, and from what social circumstances his obsession has proceeded. As James recognizes, "the human background is left vague" in *The Blithedale Romance*. It is vague, as James now reads Hawthorne, not because Hawthorne chose to shroud his action in obscurity, but simply because Hawthorne does not know how to make it definite: because he lacks the extensive, particularized knowledge of the social field available to those who have been "drawn within the circle of social accidents."[25]

Every blurred element in *Blithedale* becomes an element James can show off his superior initiation by correcting, so his goal in *The Bostonians* is to refashion *Blithedale* in such a way as to leave nothing vague. His phrase "solidity of specification" does not begin to describe the degree of circumstantial particularity this strategy leads him to produce in *The Bostonians:* this novel suffers from something like specification-compulsion. *Blithedale's* physical and social geography is, as I noted, largely unimagined. As in traditional romance, the scenes of its action are visualized, but the relative location of these scenes and the routes between them are left undetermined. By contrast, *The Bostonians* is emphatically localized. James renders the actual places where his novel is set in abundant, even excessive detail—the Cambridge Basil and Verena stroll through has brick-paved streets lined with detached houses displaying their house numbers in large silver figures, the streets having in them the half-frozen puddles of the spring thaw; Marmion (Marion, Massachusetts) has weathered shingle-style houses, scrubby vegetation, and (since it is August when the book visits) "tall, bright goldenrod at the bottom of the bare stone dykes." (356) In some of its dimensions character in *Blithedale* is as unimagined as place. Miles Coverdale's method of "insulat[ing]" the subjects of his inquiry "from many of their true relations"[26] means that others are all seen in isolation from the circumstances of their ordinary existence in this novel. By contrast, characters in *The Bostonians* are elaborately furnished with what James calls "accessories" and "material conditions" (16, 177)—with places of origin, decorated homes, sets of acquaintances, financial positions, and ideological affiliates, all of them specified in precise detail.

James's idea is that when the "human background" get filled in, the action of a novel like *Blithedale* does not merely grow more concrete; it gets more concretely understood. Its characters and conflicts get known in relation to the determinate situations in social reality from which they arise, and in which they act themselves out. But to James it might be replied that, in fact, the extravaganza of specification in *The Bostonians* does not change the understanding of character quite as much as one might expect. Unlike Hawthorne's Priscilla, James's Verena has a concretely apprehended point of origin. James touches and retouches his description of her home in Monadnock Place, her parents and their prior family life, her social life as a Harvard townie, and so on. But the salient fact about Verena is that her social situation has not marked her.

> She had cooked and washed and swept and stitched; she had worked harder than any of Miss Chancellor's servants. These things had left no trace on her person or her mind; everything fresh and fair renewed itself in her with extraordinary facility, everything ugly and tiresome evaporated as soon as it touched her. (176–77)

Olive thinks it proof of the "genius" of Verena that she seems to derive "straight from the divine generosity, much more than from [her] ugly and stupid progenitors" (117), but this is in large measure the case with all of the novel's people. Olive herself is allied by a hundred traits with Boston's cultured class: she displays books on little brackets in her dressing room; she exchanges visits with other well-bred spinsters who carry each other little bouquets or giftbooks; she has (how James piles it on!) "a crackling hearth, where she threw in pine-cones and made them snap, an imported tea-service, a Chickering piano, and the *Deutsche Rundschau*." (184) But Olive does not seem in any important way given *by* her social background. None of these details shed light on the source of her obsessions; and Olive quivering, panting, and clutching at Verena behaves not like someone raised in Boston but like someone possessed by a passion. James tries to make out that Basil's hunger for victory and success are products of his participation in the South's defeat in the Civil War, but the South is no more concretely imagined in *The Bostonians* than the city was in *Blithedale* (actually it is much less so); and in any case, when he resolves to win Verena, his motive does not seem to be regionally or culturally conditioned—he is governed by exactly the same kind of will to possession that also governs Olive.

This is to say that elaborately as *The Bostonians* specifies the circumstantial settings of its characters, those settings do not operate in any essential way as the origin of character or motive. Much as James fills in the "human background" of *The Bostonians,* he still maintains it *as* a background: as a scene that characters stand off from, rather than as the medium in which and through which their lives are given.[27] What James does not change from *The Blithedale Romance* makes the change he does effect in the direction of increased realism a change of stylistic surface only: in its depths *The Bostonians* unfolds as a battle of possessive and submissive wills, much as *Blithedale* did. And since it fails to operate except *as* surface—since the physical and social world it concretizes fails to become the ground of motivation—the realism of *The Bostonians,* however brilliant it is as an act of stylistic notation, becomes, in the novel's own terms, somewhat extraneous: an ornate marginal decoration around the action's text. James adds in those "odd figures" he missed in *Blithedale,* but in such a way that they remain odd figures—local curiosities, not participants in the novel's plot. He fills in the scenery he found lacking in Hawthorne, but in such a way that it remains scenery—a backdrop the characters pass in front of, not the physical dimension of their life. He renders the "bundle of antecedents"[28] that Hawthorne's characters did not have, but in such a way that they remain bundled up—confined to discrete passages of information, standing outside the flow of action. For once William James's description of one of his brother's novels is just. Catching both the laborious excess of the realist effort in *The Bostonians* and its failure quite to fuse with the story, he writes:

> Really the *datum* seems to me to belong rather to the region of fancy, but the treatment to that of the most elaborate realism. One can easily imagine the story cut out and made into a bright, short, sparkling thing of a hundred pages, which would have been an absolute success. [It would have been, of course, *The Blithedale Romance*.] But you have worked it up by dint of descriptions and psychologic commentaries into nearly 500[29]—

The method that had looked, in advance, like a means to triumph proves instead, when implemented, to be a source of problems. James himself feels, upon completing *The Bostonians,* that its "elaborate realism" has produced a work "too diffuse and insistent—far too describing and explaining and expatiating."[30]

But if writing *The Bostonians* discloses problems of this sort, James is not yet ready to abandon the realist effort: if anything he intensifies it in his next book. *The Princess Casamassima* is the one of his novels governed by what James thinks of as the Balzacian urge: the urge to master contemporary life in all its social variety and physical particularity, and to reconstruct it, without a sacrifice of aspects, within a fictional text. For once the principle of social inclusiveness governs James's fictional construction; in *The Princess* he risks structural looseness and bagginess in order to go after yet one more representative social type, or in order to get in yet one more representative milieu. And for once an author more noted for his abstractions is lovingly, even lingeringly specific in his rendering of the palpable world. *The Princess* possesses a descriptive amplitude unknown even to *The Bostonians:* " 'The Princess Casamassima,' so frankly panoramic and processional," James aptly calls it.[31]

In keeping with the amplitude James aims at here, *The Princess Casamassima* renders the material and social situation of character with even greater specificity than *The Bostonians.* Interiors in *The Bostonians* are furnished; interiors in *The Princess* are practically inventoried—registered item by item, with minute specification of their pattern, texture, and degree of wear. The characters in *The Bostonians* have a certain number of relatives and associates; those in *The Princess* are elaborately affiliated—equipped with a full complement of parents, godparents, childhood friends, former neighbors, fellow workers, and fellow travellers, each of whose relations, both to the central characters and to one another, are intricately traced.

Such increases of density suggest that one way James strives to remedy the problems of *The Bostonians* is simply by prosecuting the strategy of circumstantial specification yet more vigorously. But the other, more important change he seeks to make is in the way circumstance is related to self. Information about Verena's parents becomes finally inessential in *The Bostonians* because Verena does not turn out to derive her nature from her "dirty progenitors." This is the assumption James labors to reverse in *The Princess.* In this book he makes who and what one's parents were the first fact of one's being. Unlike Verena, who apparently forgets her family as soon as she leaves it, Hyacinth Robinson's mind is haunted by the presences of his actual and possible parents, and imagining these figures—in the book's words "reconstruct[ing] his antecedents" (127)[32]—is something like a full-time job for him. James underlines that how he understands himself as parented also governs his acts in contexts apparently unrelated to the familial one. To have Florentine Vivier for one's mother is to be allied by birth with the revolutionary proletariat; it is to know in the intimate terms of family history how the lower classes have been victimized by the upper; and it is therefore to be given common cause with "the struggles and the sufferings of the millions whose life flowed in the same current as his." (121) To have Lord Frederick Purvis for one's possible father, however, is to feel simultaneously allied with the privileged classes; but to be disclaimed by one's noble kin is also to know, again in intimately personal terms, how the privileged erect the barrier between themselves and those they exclude from privilege. As *The Princess Casamassima* plots it, to know oneself as someone's child is a form of political consciousness: it is not only to know one's station, but also to experience the general social process by which differences of station are established. (Let Hyacinth know who his mother is, Mr. Vetch urges Pinnie as the book opens: "Let him know . . . the state of the account between society and himself." [43]) And family feeling shapes political action as well as political consciousness. Both strains of his ancestry contribute to Hyacinth's desire to strike a blow at an unjust social order. And in the end both strains work to make him withhold his terrorist act—

to kill the Duke would be, Hyacinth feels, to kill his father over again, and thus too to slander his mother by reproducing her crime in the public eye.

What I find most interesting about James's account of Hyacinth Robinson's politics are not the particular conversions he charts between familial and political sentiment but rather the general motivational model he thereby implements—a model quite different from that of any of his earlier books, including *The Bostonians*. The case of Hyacinth suggests that the way one is placed in the structure of family and, through one's family, of class determines the cast of one's mental life, and specifically the stance one takes toward social institutions. Hyacinth is the most complicated example of a character thus determined, but James enforces the same principle throughout *The Princess Casamassima*. To understand Paul Muniment's highly mentalized brand of working-class radicalism, Rosy Muniment tells Hyacinth, you would have to have "known my father and mother" (108)—whose qualities as parents and creatures of their class she then describes at length. Lady Aurora's eagerness to put aside the privileges of her station and share in the life of the poor is similarly understood as the result of her experience of a definite family and social situation: an unattractive daughter of an aristocratic family with too many daughters and too few dowries, she is condemned to the life of an overbred spinster, with "nothing to do but to go out with three or four others in mackintoshes" (176), unless she breaks with her class position and finds a more vital life elsewhere.

The new kind of determinative power that James assigns to social situation in *The Princess Casamassima* makes a major difference in the status of political ideas in his fiction. When characters in *The Bostonians* talk in general social terms they always sound more or less mad. Political rhetoric can be equally overheated in *The Princess*, but here social beliefs never seem merely like queer birds that have come to roost in the characters' heads. This is because in *The Princess* social beliefs are represented as they are not in *The Bostonians:* not as the products of vapours, but as abstractions that derive from and express a person's daily actual experience of the social order. Not coincidentally, the shift in motivation that gives political ideas the appearance of a real social base in *The Princess* also helps mitigate the problem of *The Bostonians'* unintegrated surface realism. One's circumstances, one's upbringing, the particulars of one's living quarters, the details of one's working life—in *The Princess Casamassima*'s notation these are the external realities through which the inner reality of character is given. As a result they do not stand off in the background, as in *The Bostonians,* but participate in and redirect the flow of the novel's action.

James's panoramic ambitions and his will to show character as given through its concrete social setting lead him to turn to other models than Hawthorne in *The Princess Casamassima*. But Hawthorne's influence, so absent as to seem refused in the novel's first half, resurfaces as the book goes on. The return of his influence is first felt in a contained form, in the characterization of the Princess. Princess Casamassima, the Christina Light of *Roderick Hudson,* is one of only two or three instances in James's whole oeuvre of a character revived from another work. When she first appears here, her role is almost solely that of striking Presence: she exudes the glamour of a self-conscious star in the otherwise shabby theater of revolution. But when James comes to plot a more active involvement for her in revolutionary politics, he clearly begins to remember how Hawthorne wrote the part of the imperious, high-spirited woman experimenting at radical living. For the more she appears in *The Princess,* the more the Princess comes to resemble Hawthorne's Zenobia.

What these heroines have in common is first off their natural theatricality. Both of them perform themselves before others: they are likened to actresses a hundred times. Their gift for projecting themselves into roles is what enables them to leave their situations of "costly self-indulgence and splendid ease"[33] and to take on the parts, in Zenobia's case, of a country maiden in Blithedale's Arcadia, and in Christina's of a "small bourgeoise" (359) in deepest Paddington. At the same time, because they enter into these parts as into theatrical roles, the new social identities they assume never cease to be pretences, are never free from an element of play acting. The Princess, like Zenobia, parades her renunciation of social advantage by dressing in ostentatious simplicity; but the expensive gloves she continues to wear, like the silk kerchief and exotic corsage that accompany Zenobia's rural frock, make clear that she is wearing a costume, which she can put off when she chooses. The Princess stages the spectacle of a lower middle-class tea, but she continues to serve with her fried fish and muffins, as Zenobia did with the rustic fare she offered the Blithedalers, "such tea as not many of the world's working people . . . will find in their cups tonight"[34]—again announcing that the rigors of her lower-class life are clever and amusing simulations, not the products of necessity.

In *The Princess Casamassima* James follows Hawthorne in emphasizing the inevitable self-deception and self-indulgence involved in a willed descent of social status. But he also follows him in finding this form of insincerity deeply moving. No one in either *Blithedale* or *The Princess Casamassima* longs with more genuine ardor for a new social order than Zenobia and the Princess. No one more longs for the political changes that would let them live authentic lives, in place of the decadent ones that are their lot in the existing order. But it is their plight that even as they revolt against that order they continue to derive from it, both temperamentally and financially. It is then a mark of their bad faith, but also of their poignant predicament, that the gestures through which they would destroy their tie to worldly society actually underline their continuing participation in the worldliness they depise—as the Princess's expressions of revolutionary daring all display her modish sophistication: "I want to know *à quoi m'en tenir.* Are we on the eve of great changes or are we not?" (156); "And do you think that *il y va* of my neck?" (427); or as even suicide, for

Zenobia, is tainted with posturing affectation: "Zenobia, I have often thought, was not quite simple in her death. She had seen pictures, I suppose, of drowned persons, in lithe and graceful attitudes. And she deemed it well and decorous to die as so many village-maidens have, wronged in their first-love." (236)

The Princess's descent from Zenobia shows what I mean in saying that James knows elements of his own work by means of Hawthorne's aid. And, very strikingly, once James assimilates the Princess to the model of Zenobia, the plot in which she figures begins to move in *Blithedale*'s steps. At a certain point Paul Muniment, the scientist of revolution in *The Princess Casamassima*, begins to perform the part of Hollingsworth: the charismatic reformer who inspires deep affection in others, and who uses this affection to make them work toward his political ends, without responding to it at the level of love. When the Princess meets Paul she is stirred by his masculinity (he has "eyes which seemed to project their glance further and drive it harder than any she had seen" [384]), and she tries to capture his love by offering her fortune to his cause. But in using her fortune as a kind of erotic bait the Princess, like Zenobia, falls prey to a design even more ulterior than her own. Muniment, like Hollingsworth, accepts her funds for his cause without reciprocating the love they represent. When the woman in this plot finally loses control of her fortune—as Zenobia does when Old Moodie diverts her inheritance to Priscilla; as the Princess does (no less implausibly) when the Prince cuts off her allowance—she finds herself simply ditched. Muniment delivers onstage the blow that Hollingsworth delivered between chapters in *The Blithedale Romance:*

> "I've no intention whatever of saying anything harsh or offensive to you, but since you challenge me perhaps it's well that I should let you know how inevitably I *do* consider that in giving your money—or rather your husband's—to our business you gave the most valuable thing you had to contribute." (500)

The recreation of *Blithedale*'s plot within *The Princess Casamassima* is stunning proof of how deeply engrained Hawthorne is in James's fictional imagination. Long after he has outgrown the phase of conscious artistic dependency, and in dealing with a subject (European terrorist movements) to which Hawthorne's relevance is not at all obvious, here again James turns to Hawthorne to give his own work an action. But for our purposes what needs to be underlined is that when James resuscitates *Blithedale*'s plot in the latter half of *The Princess Casamassima*, he also resuscitates the vision of the political that that plot expresses. James borrows from Hawhorne, thus, the biographical information that his heroine has been driven to political activism by an unhappy marriage. Coverdale surmises that when Zenobia found that "the real womanhood within her has no corresponding part in [Westervelt]," "there had ensued the character of eccentricity and defiance, which distinguished the more public portion of her life." (103) The Princess tells Hyancinth that the misery of marriage to a European aristocrat has caused "her rebellion against the selfishness, the corruption, the iniquity, the cruelty, the imbecility of the people who all over Europe had the upper hand. . . . She had been humiliated, outraged, tortured: she considered that she too was one of the numerous class who could be put on a tolerable footing only by a revolution." (202) Clearly, to repeat this sort of detail is also to recreate a Hawthornesque sense of political motivation. James here revives *Blithe-dale*'s notion (as he had in *The Bostonians*) that political engagement has its origin in an "inward trouble," in a prior frustration in the emotional sphere, and that the passion for social change thus involves a displacement of energies thwarted at the emotional level. Along with this notion of the origin of political passions, James also revives a Hawthornesque sense of political action's real end. He suggests increasingly, as the novel continues, that in their work for social change his characters are seeking in "the more public portion of their life" for substitute forms of the gratification they have been denied in the private. The Princess, like Zenobia and Olive Chancellor, has so diverted the energies of sexuality into her public program that her invitations to political partnership are indistinguishable from invitations to sex. "What in the world is it I'm trying to do," she pleads with the bashful Hyacinth, "but by every clever trick I can think of fill up the inconvenient gulf that yawns between my position and yours?" (270) Like them, the pleasures she seeks through political action and association are the ones normally derived from love affairs.

> "Is that what you go in for—keen emotion?"
> "Surely, Mr. Muniment. Don't you?"
> "God forbid! I hope to have as little of any sort as possible."
> "Of course one doesn't want any vague rodomontade, one wants to do something. But it would be hard if one couldn't have a little pleasure by the way." (425)

Taken together with *The Bostonians, The Princess Casamassima* permits us to say that whenever James returns to Hawthorne in his political fiction, it is with the effect of committing himself to a certain kind of political vision: a vision that sees the struggle for public social change as growing out of private emotional distress and as disguising the pursuit of private emotional goals. This vision governs *The Bostonians* from the start. But the interest of *The Princess Casamassima* is that it also reasserts itself there, after having been initially rejected. The new sense of things in *The Princess* that I began this section by describing, according to which social belief grows out of concrete experience of the social order, is a reversal of the attitude James associates with Hawthorne. But that new sense prevails, really, only in the novel's first half. Lady Aurora, whose wish to "come out of her class" (416) was earlier related to her family and class experience, is later seen as motivated simply by love for Paul. Hyacinth, who took his terrorist vow in Book Two in response to the miserable spectacle of a city filled with the unemployed, turns his violence against himself in Book Five not because he now accepts such conditions, but primarily because he has discovered that his friends are going out with his friends—because, like Zenobia, others do not claim the love he offers them. What began as a story of people pressed by their social situations to seek for social change becomes, in others words, a love story; and the political becomes not a sphere of experience with dramas of its own but a colorful setting in which a love plot of seduction, exploitation, betrayal, and rejection can play itself out.[35]

In reverting to a model that locates the essential determinants of public action in the private emotional sector James comes to see things quite differently from the contemporaries he had wished to draw near to when this phase of his career began. In early 1884 he had proclaimed modern French realism "the only kind of work, to-day, that I respect,"[36] but the turn he takes in *The Princess Casamassima* leads him away from that kind of work. The divergence is clear if we compare this novel with a book like *Germinal,* which was published in the year *The Princess* was begun. In *Germinal* Zola clearly recognizes that displaced sexual passions help fuel the miners' mob attack on the mines. (The mob's castration of the proprietor of the company store and their public display of his severed member leave no doubt on that score.) But in Zola's novel the presence of such energies does not therefore imply that the miners' quarrel with the mine owners is caused by disturbances in their love lives. The mob action is precipitated by the strike; the strike, by the institution of new regulations on the timbering of the mine shafts; the new regulations, by the owners' wish to cut wages and coal production. However unhappy Monsieur Hennebeau is in his marriage, the owners' wish to cut wages and production is not caused by marital misery, but by the fact that chronic overproduction has brought on a depression throughout the French economy. The riot's cause, this is to say, lies not in the emotional state of its participants but in their objective social situation, the state of the French economy. This is the sort of causation that James might envision in the early chapters of *The Princess,* but that ceases to interest him in the later ones. Zola also recognizes the secret personal motives hidden under political efforts—he recognizes, for instance, how Étienne Lantier's vanity makes him aspire to a position of leadership in the strike. But in *Germinal* the fact that political action incidentally serves private needs does not deprive it of public consequence. Although the strike is crushed, Zola's ending implies that it has sown the seed of more successful action to come. We do not see those effects, but Zola protects the potentiality of his characters' actions to produce real change in the objective social realm. This is, again, the sort of notion that James considers but then rejects in *The Princess Casamassima.* Hyacinth's final acts hurt no one but himself.

I have noted that James's reversion to the sense that all political stories are really love stories in disguise is related to his return to Hawthorne as a literary model. But the vision James expresses through his Hawthorn-esque plots is, in fact, even more politically attenuated than Hawthorne's. In *The Scarlet Letter* and *The Blithedale Romance,* after all, female re-formers are not *just* unhappy women. Far more than James does with Olive Chancellor or the Princess, Hawthorne understands Hester's and Zenobia's unhappiness as sourced in the way their sex's position is given at their social and historical moment. So too Hawthorne's activists, like James's, finally refuse political action; but in Hawthorne, the significance of an individual's refusal of action is still always measured in social terms. When Hester, recognizing the interestedness of her motives, disqualifies herself for the office of revolutionary sexual prophetess at the end of *The Scarlet Letter,* she still knows (and her book knows too) that the need to establish the relation of men and women on a surer ground of mutual happiness is as pressing as ever, and that it still requires someone's action, if not hers. By contrast, when Verena chooses privacy and Basil over Olive and the movement at the end of *The Bostonians,* the potential cost or contribution of her decision to the general sexual welfare is simply not considered. At the end of *The Blithedale Romance* all of the characters know better than to think that their actions could implement their political intentions, but the book still registers their withdrawals of will and sym-pathy from the public sphere as bringing a general loss of power—as en-tailing the decline, seen in Hollingsworth, of public spirit into an unhealthy domesticity; the decline, seen in Coverdale, of artistic will into a self-defeating aestheticism; the decline, seen in Priscilla's triumph over Zeno-bia, of a full-bodied eroticism into a wanly etherealized form of love. By contrast, what Hyacinth Robinson's withdrawal from politics portends for humanity at large (the failure of the terrorist movement? the exclusion from the revolution of humaner spirits?) remains, in *The Princess Casa-massima,* simply unimagined. However James may amplify him in other respects, James always thins down Hawthorne's sense of the public, his-torical dimension of human experience. Slightly adapted, T. S. Eliot's aphorism describes their difference well: Hawthorne has a sense of the political, but James has a sense of a sense.

If, having tried the alternative, James reverts to seeing the search for the common good almost exclusively as a cover for interested impulses and personal motives, he is welcome to his view. But it must be noted that his choice of political outlook also bears on his choice of style. Nineteenth-century realism is, James is right, a system of literary representation. And in thinking of it as such, rather than as an unmediated record of reality, James avoids the misunderstanding of realism's inescapably *literary* na-ture that plagues so many practitioners of this form. But by engaging this style in its literary aspects—in separation from the social cares and com-mitments that usually attend it—James averts one set of problems only to raise another. For if realism is first and last a form of literary representa-tion, it is the nature of this representation to express certain social under-standings. With its "more analytic consideration of appearances" nineteenth-century realism "sees," as James rightly says in his essay on Daudet, "the connection between feelings and external conditions." Its reason for rendering physical and social environment in such massive detail is that it understands this environment as the medium in which character moves, as the ground from which the inner life is given. To believe that the play of human passion is prior to the particularized social context in which it appears, as James comes to in *The Princess Casamassima,* is to believe that reality is not as the realists represent it. Practicing their style in the absence of their convictions can only produce two outcomes: a conversion of realism's recorded "external conditions" into an inactive externality, as in James's "correction" of *Blithedale* in *The Bostonians;* or a connecting of self and circumstance that, as his reversion to Hawthorne in *The Princess* shows, he can only feign to believe.

I started this chapter by saying that James invests his will to literary greatness in the realist project. What he learns from pursuing this project is that he has made a bad investment. He approaches these works with high hopes of what they will make him be: "I am just beginning a shortish novel . . . which is to mark a new era in my career, and usher in a series of works of superior value to any I have yet produced," he writes as he begins *The Bostonians.* When they are completed, he speaks of them as "the *Bostonians* and the *Princess,* from which I expected so much and derived so little."[37] His disappointment was no doubt, as is often said, based on the miserableness of their public reception: *The Bostonians* and *The Princess Casamassima* are the novels that definitively lost James the larger form of the literary reading public of his time. But I do not believe that his disappointment can have been wholly due to external causes—since what James discovers, in the writing of these novels, is that he cannot practice this sort of work on its terms, and that it will not work on his. Projected as the novels of his major phase, these books leave James still in search of a way to attain that status. But writing them has made this difference in the search: that his writing now needs to adjust to a new public basis; and that, in looking for the fit form for his work, he no longer believes, as he had told Julian Hawthorne in 1879:

> Your father was the greatest imaginative writer we had, and yet, I feel that his principle was wrong. . . . Imagination is out of place; only the strictest realism can be right.[38]

LATE JAMES
The Lost Art of the Late Style

No READER is likely to forget the great scene recorded in the fourteenth chapter of *The Golden Bowl,* at the opening of Part Third. The occasion is a diplomatic reception, a "great official party" (191),[1] but this aspect of the scene is rendered as a mere swirl or blur—a "glitter of star and clink of sword" (192)—of undeveloped detail. This dimension of the scene remains an unfocussed background because the foreground is so strongly held by Charlotte Stant, a figure *in* the scene who, by her way of engaging it, *makes* a scene of another order. Charlotte appears here for the first time in her new role as Mrs. Adam Verver, to face our intense curiosity about what a union so strangely motivated on both sides will have turned into. As she pauses, halfway up the party's monumental staircase, it is as if she grows aware of her audience's interest in her marriage, and sees how her physical position here could say what her marriage has made her: taken to wife by a husband who fails to give himself to the role of husband, intimately joined with a man who prefers the earlier intimacies of father and daughter, she is, as at this moment, left alone by her marriage, "exposed . . . to the public . . . in her unaccompanied state." (192) With this recognition of its expressive possibilities, Charlotte acts her solitary pause in a way that radically alters its mode of signification. She performs this casual and subsignificant act with a degree of deliberation that lifts it out of the flow of ordinary gesture and gives it the eerie stasis and heightened visual relevance of an iconic tableau. *Held* with such intensity of intention, her pose becomes a throbbing statement of everything that is wrong with the structure of her marriage, everything open to danger— "exposed"—in the position it puts her in; as her next act—taking Prince Amerigo's arm as he ascends the stair—becomes a statement of the consolations she will feel herself driven or entitled to, by her marriage's failure to "take."

It needs to be added that Charlotte's gesture on the staircase, raised to this almost hideous degree of expressive intensity, is performed toward an audience. Her moves complete themselves when Fanny Assingham, watching down below, receives her sent signal of her marriage's failure and its contemplated consequence: reads her display of her solitariness, followed by her taking the Prince's arm, to mean "So you're staying on together without her?" (195) But this decoding, though begun in an "attentive arrest" (195), is not instantaneous: Charlotte's and the Prince's moves are so fraught with intended sense that Fanny has to store the scene in the "crystal flask of her innermost attention," then return "chemically to analyse it" in the "sung laboratory of her afterthought." (208) The interrogation she subjects their moves to in the next chapter, where she fixes them with her attention and prods them to release their possible further messages, is in this sense strictly required by the way Charlotte and the Prince act. This inquisition, with its ardent commitment to interpretation and further interpretation, is the complementary process by which presented images overstored with expressive intention can have their meanings developed, brought forth in the full array of their latent possibility.

Charlotte's silent moment on the stair is a great example of a scene produced in Henry James's late style. I feature it here because it also stands, more or less consciously, as an emblem of that style's mode of operation. The style James develops in the late 1890s, then perfects in the series of great works culminating in *The Golden Bowl* (1904), takes as its medium a thoroughly conventional social world. This social world is caught, if anything, in the most formal of its aspects (seen here in the ceremony of the reception, and in the small formality of the offered arm). Even there it is rendered in the slightest, apparently least significant, of its signs (a pause, an accepted arm), rather than in its larger gestures. But the ingredients that remain in an expressive medium so tightly reduced and restricted are presented with such heightened deliberation that they come to seem, like Charlotte's small move on the stair, monstrously charged with possible sense. The world of James's late fiction is a world of violently maximized disproportions: a world where human action and expression appear reduced to their most trivial guises, but where the resultant trifles, without ceasing to function at the level of minor social accidents, nevertheless become fraught with exorbitant meaning, seem to have the extremest of existential possibilities uncannily lodged within them.[2] This is a world where the sight of a wife sitting dressed for dinner at her own home carries the dire further message that marital treachery has been detected; where "the horror of finding evil seated, all at its ease" (459) is encountered not in "some bad-faced stranger" of a criminal housebreaker but in a foursome at a civil game of bridge; where the most banal remark about summer weather—Charlotte's "It's too close indoors"—gets "uttered . . . with an expressive weight that verged upon solemnity" (463), and so seems to speak of the strain involved in human intimacy as such. The double action of reduction and heightening that gives these novels their familiarly overwrought texture also makes them require of us, as Charlotte's sign does of Fanny, a peculiar kind of reading. The late Jamesian style is a style designed to yield nothing to casual perusal. It begins to communicate only when it effects an attentive arrest: a disruption of ordinary habits through which reading gets slowed down, then shifted to a more active mode. We become a fit audience for this style when, Fanny-like, we start to *work* at it: to bear down on its obscurities, to pull its possible implications out of it through renewed acts of surmise.

The style that opens itself to our inspection in Charlotte's great scene embodies a new way of writing for James in his late career. His earlier work shows nothing like the violent disproportions it produces; as every reader knows, this powerful expressive deformation is the mark by which we know James's late work *as* late. Less obviously but just as critically, the advent of this altered way of writing within his work signals James's movement toward an altered conception *of* his work. Near the time of his late novels, and in close conjunction with them, James begins to put forward a characteristically late vision of the novel's nature and function. We read it here, for instance, in the preface to *The Wings of the Dove:*

> The enjoyment of a work of art, the acceptance of an irresistible illusion, constituting, to my sense, our highest experience of "luxury," the luxury is not greatest, by my consequent measure, when the work asks for as little attention as possible. It is greatest, it is delightfully, divinely great, when we feel the surface, like the thick ice of the skater's pond, bear without cracking the strongest pressure we throw on it.

Or here, in the Preface to *The Golden Bowl:*

> The ideally handsome way is for [the writer] to multiply in any given connection all the possible sources of entertainment . . . [to make the reader] feel immediately the effect of such a condition at every turn of our adventure and every point of the representative surface. . . . The essential property of such a form as that is to give out its finest and most numerous secrets, and to give them out most gratefully, under the closest pressure—which is of course the pressure of the attention articulately *sounded.*[3]

Such statements express in abstracted form the theory of fiction already immanent in James's late style. The consciously intensified production of meaning that we feel in Charlotte's gesture and throughout James's late prose gets generalized, in pronouncements like these, into an aesthetic of total significance: an equation of the novel's fully realized form with an expression so wrought as to have meaning packed into its "every point." And here as within James's writing this ideal of textual production carries with it a corresponding prescription of how the novel should be consumed. The reader's right use of the novel, as James posits it here, is not to "get into" it but throw a maximal pressure against it. Only by subjecting it to the full force of our interpretive powers, he implies, can we read out of the well-made novel the store of "secrets" so densely packed within it.

This notion of the novel's nature and function is not only new to James in his late career. It is substantially new as well in the history of prose fiction. The novel, most elastic and compliant of literary forms, has been produced on a hundred theories and put to a hundred uses in its pre-Jamesian life. In this book's examples alone we have seen the novel redeployed as an act of prophecy, as a high-cultural art object, as a recorder and builder of communal reality-systems, as a plotter of social history; and we have not touched on other ambitions and self-understandings that are even more standard to the nineteenth-century novel—the theory of the novel as pleasurable entertainment, as enabler of emotional participation and trainer of sympathy, as instrument of social criticism, and so on. But with late James the novel defines itself, and really for the first time, as an object of critical attention—as a work whose *end* is to tighten our concentration, then provide us with enriched occasions for interpretive activity. This Jamesian innovation—more wrenching than we can feel, who read all novels (at least in public) as if this were the only end they could have—is the more significant because the literary conceptions that are new in it take on a more general life, soon after. In James's idea of the fully signified text—the text so perfectly deliberated that meaning can be endlessly produced in it—we read an early form of an idea that becomes widespread, even normative, with the coming of modernism. Similarly, James's invention of the ideally hyperattentive and text-*pressuring* reader adumbrates a figure who takes on substantial reality just after his writing—first in the corps of patient scrutinizers recruited and trained by the great modernist texts, then in the legion of "close readers" produced when the New Criticism took hold of the institutions of public instruction. (Such readers in significant measure learned to *be* close readers by reading and writing on James.)

What James's late novels embody, this suggests, is a transformation not just in the style of the novel but in the novel's whole way of defining and asserting itself—a transformation the more important because it reflects, as it helped produce, a more general transformation both in the novel's inward textual nature and in its public life and use, early in this century. Recognizing that this larger change is implicit in it, we might turn back again to James's change of style, to ask of his case where this new kind of writing came from.

Some of the occasions for James's late style are well known. Theodora Bosanquet, his devoted typist, linked the thickening of James's style to his conversion to dictation as a method of composition in the 1890s—suggesting a more general correlation, it may be, between the newer, denser forms of modern literary writing and modern technologies of verbal production.[4] James's writing grew notably more difficult after he lost a more general readership in the late 1880s and early 1890s, making him a striking early case of Frederic Jameson's larger contention about the roots of modernist opacity: "Style is always an individual and problematic solution to the dilemma of the absence of a public."[5] But if James's writing changed in response to such external circumstances, in his case such changes also proceed quite directly from the changed sense of authorial position that came with his late career. We have seen how strongly the will to write is allied, in James, with the will to have and perform a career. In his idea to be an author is to commit oneself to a program of continuous achievement, and to the performance of a whole series of set labors—tasks that he always feels *must* be complied with, since they compose, when performed together, the ideally *realized* form of authorship itself. In this context it can be noted that—as it had before to James's beginning, then to his attainment of majority—James's self-elaborated and powerfully self-directing plot of authorial career gives new salience to the close of the writing life. With its highly articulated plan of sequences and stages, this plot brings the late phase to definition as a chronologically distinct period of artistic labor. It also makes the late phase have its own appropriate projects and face its own peculiar challenges and risks.

The nature of these projects and challenges is most fully revealed in a tale James published in 1893, "The Middle Years." This tale is a major entry in the Jamesian literature of transition anxiety. As "The Madonna of the Future" marked his authorial debut by fantasizing an artist's failure to begin, and as *Roderick Hudson* marked his arrival at the hurdle of self-continuation by envisioning an artist's failure to go past his great beginning, "The Middle Years" signals James's contemplated movement beyond his mid-career by imagining the plight of a writer doomed to reach only his work's middle life. The writer Dencombe, dying in the knowledge that his work is "unfinished," has a vision of what might have rescued him from this anguishing state:

> Dencombe soaring again a little on the weak wings of convalescence and still haunted by that happy notion of an organised rescue, found another strain of eloquence to plead the cause of a certain splendid "last manner," the very citadel, as it would prove, of his reputation, the stronghold into which his real treasure would be gathered. While his listener gave up the morning and the great still sea appeared to wait, he had a wonderful explanatory hour. Even for himself he was inspired as he told of what his treasure would consist—the precious metals he would dig from the mine, the jewels rare, strings of pearls, he would hang between the columns of his temple.[6]

This is an important passage because it suggests how much, in James's thinking, the close of career is associated with the achievement of a special "manner." (The *Spätstyl* is another self-organizing category James imports from the fine arts.) More, it suggests how much such a manner carries the meaning for James of that which *makes* a career *be achieved*. The late manner, in this tale's powerful conceit, is what redeems work from an unfinished state: it gives a life's work a fit conclusion or finish, and so makes it retroactively integrated, closed, and complete. Even more poignantly, the late manner appears here as that which protects or shields from dreadful openness. A splendid late manner is a "citadel," a "stronghold," in essence a protective enclosure. To have achieved this manner is (in fantasy at least) to be securely defended. To have failed of it is to leave oneself permanently vulnerable, at the mercy of the unrealizing powers of time.

"The Middle Years" was written some years before James began producing his own late manner, but it shows very clearly the terms on which he came to that new style. It makes clear that in James's case the late style, so far from being merely the way one happened to write late on, knows itself in advance as a style, and as a style with a certain place in the chronology of a career. "The Middle Years" also shows that the Jamesian late style has as one of its most deeply informing motives the aim of *being* a late style—and so of winning his work the achievedness a late style is uniquely empowered to accomplish. James's late style is a style large with strain, a style that suggests outsized energies being brought to bear on more humbly scaled materials. The energies that contort this writing might be identified on one level as the energies of James's fierce will to completion—his will to give his life-work, through a yet more intense expense of effort, the character of a completed thing. (Seen in this sense the labor of style in James's late novels is of a piece with the labor of selection, revision, and prefacing that made the New York Edition of James's work— another act designed to give his writing the retroactive character of a completed *oeuvre*.) Read in this tale's light, the late style, like James's self-editing, indeed like all of his acts of self-making, has the look finally of a struggle against natural time itself: an effort, through the act of work, to realize oneself in a willed form, and so escape the "desolation"[7] time makes of everything insufficiently *made*.

The late style of Henry James derives both its idea of itself and its peculiar urgency, I am arguing, from the Jamesian structure of authorial career. But I would claim that that changed style also embodies, and no less centrally, a response to James's changed sense of literature's public situation. James's last novels are largely purged of direct references to the contemporary social world. This fact, coupled with the (partly self-propagated) mythology of late James as the Master, supremely indifferent at last to all claims but his art's, has conspired to make his late work seem unconnected to and untouched by an external social situation. But if we read these novels together with James's other contemporaneous writings, the picture changes. For the essays James wrote alongside these novels—particularly "The Question of Opportunities" (1898) and "The Future of the Novel" (1899), but also "Émile Zola" (1903), the letter to the Hawthorne centenary (1904), and "The Lesson of Balzac" (1905)—show an author obsessed with the state of letters in the present world: interested in nothing so much as the modern expansion of reading publics; the new forms of production that have arisen to feed a newly literate public's appetites; and the question what will become of literature as traditionally understood in the new world of "literature for the million, or rather for the fast-arriving billion."[8]

James's usual response to these developments is expressed in concentrated form in a 1902 letter to Howells:

> Of course, in our conditions, doing anything decent is pure disinterested, unsupported, unrewarded heroism; but that's in the day's work. The *faculty of attention* has utterly vanished from the general anglo-saxon mind, extinguished at its source by the big blatant *Bayardère* of Journalism, of the newspaper and the *picture* (above all) magazine; who keeps screaming "Look at *me, I* am the thing, and I only, the thing that will keep you in relation with me *all the time* without your having to attend *one minute* of the time."[9]

The immediate occasion of this letter is the publication of *The Wings of the Dove,* a novel that (like *The Golden Bowl* after it) failed to be accepted for magazine serialization and came forth (in James's words) "unnotedly to lose itself" in "a world of periodicals and editors, of roaring 'successes' in fine."[10] The larger cultural case James builds from his own failed reception has, accordingly, the taste of sour grapes. We can also recognize in it a perennial prejudice of James's caste: thirty years before this letter Charles Eliot Norton was already blaming the upstart popular press for causing America to "los[e] the capacity of thought";[11] we have seen the same sentiment surface in Howells's *A Modern Instance* (1882), which regards the new journalism of Bartley Hubbard as portending little less than the death of responsible selfhood. But if it originates in such sources, this anti-media barrage has an unusual concreteness of historical reference. James is registering here the sudden and simultaneous emergence of the host of new mass-media forms that marked the turn of the century in both England and America—forms like the cheap illustrated magazines with unprecedentedly large circulations that sprang up in the 1890s, *Ladies Home Journal, McClure's, Munsey's,* and the like; or the new forms of popular journalism pioneered at this time by Joseph Pulitzer and William Randolph Hearst in America, and Alfred Harmsworth (later Lord Northcliffe) in England; or (James finds this especially odious) the cheap new picture-journal, heavy on illustration and light on text, made possible by advances in economical photographic reproduction. (England's most successful picture-journal, Harmsworth's *Daily Mirror,* found its format and built its audience in 1903–1904, or during the composition of *The Golden Bowl.*) Such organs made a conscious editorial policy of reducing textual length and difficulty, and even advertised the light demand they made on readers as a selling point. ("The Busy Man's Daily Journal" was the slogan of Harmsworth's hugely successful *Daily Mail.*) Accordingly, when James weighs the significance of such organs, he reads them not just as adding to the sum of reading matter but as portending a larger change in the nature of printed expression, and even more gravely in the reading habits such expression subtends. As it becomes stronger and shriller—"look at *me, I* am the thing"—what James takes to be a peculiarly modern kind of media stimulus asks the viewer to do less and less work in receiving it, finally to do nothing but be passively filled with images that come unsought. So it is that he can hold the new journalism and its offshoots responsible for the death of the faculty of attention, extinguished by being rendered unnecessary to the act of perception.[12]

As this letter and many similar expressions show, late James writes in a situation that he sees as defined by two related facts: the birth of aggressive new instruments of mass culture ("now illiteracy has an enormous literary organization,"[13] William James said of the same developments); and the decay or even active sapping of older habits of reading and seeing. But we need to look past the new media themselves if we want to see why they so preoccupy James. What needs to be remembered here is that the insurgent magazines, newspapers, and picture-journals of the turn of the century did not merely add new items to the array of existing cultural institutions: they caused a redistribution of power among all such institutions. To say that such organs built new reading publics is really to say that they took on the power of organizing culture for such publics; and such power as they took to themselves they took away from other agencies. In particular, they took it from the older, in retrospect more serious and intellectual organs of general culture of the 1870s and 1880s—monthlies like *The Atlantic, Harper's,* and *The Century* (their somewhat parallel English numbers are *Cornhill* and *Macmillan's*). Such magazines survive through the 1890s, but they rather abruptly lose their power to monopolize the world of reading and writing at this time. Responding to the encroachment of the newer media on their old terrain, they either retreat into self-conscious conservatism and cultural marginality or else start aping popular features of their popular rivals. (Frank Luther Mott, the historian of American magazines and newspapers, assures us that the old-guard literary magazines that now refused to serialize James novels became "resplendent with color plates after the turn of the century."[14]) And at the same time that they felt such pressure from the popular side, these older institutions also faced a threat to their other flank. The decade of the vigorous expansion of popular magazines and newspapers, the 1890s are also the time when another new kind of publishing institution and cultural agency first appeared (*The Yellow Book* and its publisher Bodley Head is the chief English example, *The Chap-Book* and the firm of Stone and Kimball the chief American[15]): an institution grouping around itself not the old-style hypothetical audience of all respectable citizens but a frankly elite class of readers with specially educated tastes, and producing for them not "good" writing defined in the older, more generally civic-minded way but writing "good" in a freer, more purely literary sense of the word—writing like that of the fin-de-siècle decadents and the Continental *symbolistes* whom these organs brought to public life.

What is going on in the 1890s, all of this suggests, is something far more sweeping than the rise of the mass magazine or the rise of the new journalism. Those developments are by-products of a larger transformation: a breakdown and reformation of literature's whole system of cultural structures. Earlier in this book I traced a reorganization of the literary sphere in mid-nineteenth-century America: showed how a weakly differentiated literary field got split into popular and literary zones in the late 1840s and early 1850s, then how that separated literary sphere, strongly institutionalized by 1860, maintained itself as a cultural reality for the three decades that followed. What happens in the 1890s is that the literary order instituted in the 1850s loses its cultural force. The agencies that sustained it survive, but in a condition so weakened that they can no longer even pretend to represent a unified, national literary culture, as they could through the 1880s. Part of their old territory gets taken over by new forms of popular literature—forms that link the popular, in this incarnation, with the stylistic and social agendas of the new mass media.[16] Another part of their territory gets broken off as a new kind of literary preserve: the anti-popular or avant-garde writing space that Melville could not find in the 1850s begins to be established in the 1890s, guarded and supported by institutions of its own. As with that earlier one, this reorganization of literature's public sphere produces not just new external positions for literature to appear in, but, along with them, new forms and conceptions of literature itself. The new mass media of the 1890s provide the place where a new kind of authorship, historical successor to that of James's and Howells's generation, can get organized—the authorship founded in the world of journalism and taking its idea of literature largely from journalistic practice that we find in such beginning authors of the 1890s as Dreiser, Crane, and Upton Sinclair.[17] Similarly, the birth of the little magazine, the literary specialty-house, and the specially educated audience they recruited lays the institutional ground from which another kind of authorship can emerge later on: the college-educated, cosmopolitan, securely minoritarian, and intensely *literary* authorship we associate with early modernism.[18]

James's late career has this much in common with Hawthorne's: that he wrote in the midst of a massive reworking of writing's cultural categories. As it had been for Hawthorne, the effect of these developments for James was partly to open up new havens for his work. An *Atlantic,* then an *Atlantic-Macmillan's* author through the 1880s, James was eagerly adopted by the new avant-garde publishers of the 1890s. Stone and Kimball, American publishers of Verlaine, Ibsen, and a Beardsley-illustrated edition of Poe, also published James's *What Maisie Knew* and *In The Cage;* Henry Harland solicited stories from James when he first conceived of *The Yellow Book,* and gave them pride of place in the first two issues. In fact James was the only author from his generation to be taken up into the proto-modernist literary order of the 1890s, the order which in its mature form would build him (as the mid-nineteenth-century order had built Hawthorne) his first fully canonical position.[19] But if they gave him such openings, James's deeper sense of these developments is not as an opportunity but as a threat to his base. The young writers of the 1890s could simply accept the new literary world and set to work in it. But a writer of James's age had to see that new order as destroying an old one—as eroding the system of understandings and relations that his authorship had been established in and that gave his work's internal self-conception external confirmation and support. In the figure of "The Middle Years," James experiences the literary reorganization of the 1890s as an assault on his work's citadel (the big *Bayardère* of journalism represents for him everything that has breached its securing structures), and this threat has two immediate consequences. It makes him, for the first time, intensely conscious of literature's public organization as a historical phenomenon. (We read this awareness in his late essays.) And it challenges him to put his work itself on new ground.

This reestablishment of his work's public position is what his conversion to the late style performs. By remaking its verbal and representational form, James changes his novel's nature and function as a medium, makes it we might say a conscious counter to the media he feels besieged by. Through this change of style he changes who his work is for—limits its audience from readers of high-average literary aptitude to the more restrictive form of an anti-mass readerly elite. Quite as crucially, through this change he changes what his novel offers to do for its public. Positioning itself against a media-induced sapping of the faculty of attention, the late Jamesian novel now consciously undertakes to intensify attention, to require for its reading "the closest pressure . . . of attention articulately sounded" and to repay such attention with the "luxury" of "its finest and most numerous secrets."

James's drama of career makes him urgently want a splendid style, productive of senses as rich as jewels, for his late work. His sense of the modern situation of literacy makes him want to write in a way that will heighten and strengthen attention as much as the new newspapers and picture-journals seem to be lowering and vitiating it. But neither of these exigencies can provide the late style with its particular expressive form. For that James must look into literature's own resources, as embodied in earlier writing, and in this process Hawthorne becomes newly important to James. Hawthorne is at least as deeply implicated in James's late work as he was in his beginner's pieces or his realist experiments. The supersignified style James formulates for his late works is clearly derived from Hawthornesque precedents. And curiously, but very strikingly, Hawthorne's presence in that style seems to be part of what makes it, in James's terms, adequately *late*. For the more splendidly late a James work is in manner, and the more decisively it is associated with the completion of his work, the more it displays Hawthorne as its manner's source.

Coming after the long history of indebtedness I have already traced, this late development might seem anything but surprising. But it is important to insist that there is nothing natural or inevitable about James's late return to Hawthorne. James as I read him begins as and long continues to be a highly derivative author: his very structure of authorship, I have tried to show, commits him to literary derivativeness as a kind of first principle. But late James is not derivative in anything like the same fashion. His late work notably ceases to bear the marks of its masters. (One thing the late manner does for James is to make his manner more assertively *his*.) To the extent that his late novels do revive and revise earlier works, those works tend to be James's own; to be in late career, James's case suggests, is to have oneself as one's chief tradition.

Not only is James now in a state of reduced dependency: in his late career Hawthorne also ceases to surround him with anything like the same power. Literary institutions, this book has been arguing, work in part by *making* literary pasts. They institute a particular formation of literature by making some segment of previous writing be the significant past—a past that, reinternalized by the readers and writers who inhabit that institution, helps naturalize and validate its definition of what literature is. Here I might anticipate the story of my next chapter to say that when the institutional setting of literature was remade at the end of the nineteenth century, the literary past got remade in the process. Other formations of authors and texts were erected as models at this time; conversely the older past— the one figured in the nineteenth century's literary canon—rapidly lost its authority, as the structures that supported it lost theirs. When this happened, Hawthorne, for so long after his death still an intensely *living* author, largely vanished for the field of living writing. The figure of incandescent power for readers of the 1860s and 1870s is more usually seen, by the late 1890s, as a kind of fossilized relic of a defunct official culture. The inevitable precursor in those earlier decades, by the end of the century Hawthorne has become an author it would take an effort to revive.

Such an effort—not a continuing reception but really a new *invention* of Hawthorne as a source of tradition—is what James performs in his late return to Hawthorne. And this act is in turn not separate from the larger drama of his late career. Faced with the need to make his writing new—to find a manner suited to completing a life's work, and to clinching a new cultural function and place for his work—James at the close of his career reaches back into his oldest literary past, a past becoming newly *past* in the world around him. Working from a different context from the one in which he knew Hawthorne before, James is able here to invent a substantially new version of his old mentor's art and power. This new-found or new-made Hawthorne then helps him find how to meet the requirements of his own new position: how to write a close to his career, and how to adapt his work to the modern situation of literary expression.

James's late relation to Hawthorne can be said to begin with an essay he wrote in 1897. For an introduction to the Hawthorne selections in a multivolume compendium of world literature, James wrote a brilliant short essay, a piece that is all the more interesting because it embodies a change of heart. This change of heart is registered in the following long paragraph (I give it in full because it is little known):

These things—the experiments in the shorter fiction—had sounded, with their rare felicity, from the very first the note that was to be Hawthorne's distinguishing mark,—that feeling for the latent romance of New England, which in summary form is the most final name to be given, I think, to his inspiration. This element, which is what at its best his genius most expresses, was far from obvious,—it had to be looked for; and Hawthorne found it, as he wandered and mused, in the secret play of the Puritan faith: the secret, I say particularly, because the direct and ostensible, face to face with common tasks and small conditions (as I may call them without prejudice to their general grimness), arrived at forms of which the tender imagination could make little. It could make a great deal, on the other hand, of the spiritual contortions, the darkened outlook, of the ingrained sense of sin, of evil, and of responsibility. There had been other complications in the history of the community surrounding him,—savages from behind, soldiers from before, a cruel climate from every quarter and a pecuniary remittance from none. But the great complication was the pressing moral anxiety, the restless individual conscience. These things were developed at the cost of so many others, that there were almost no others left to help them to make a picture for the artist. The artist's imagination had to deck out the subject, to work it up, as we nowadays say; and Hawthorne's was,—on intensely chastened lines, indeed,—equal to the task. In that manner it came into exercise from the first, through the necessity of taking for granted, on the part of the society about him, a life of the spirit more complex than anything that met the mere eye of sense. It was a question of looking behind and beneath for the suggestive idea, the artistic motive; the effect of all of which was an invaluable training for the faculty that evokes and enhances. This ingenuity grew alert and irrepressible as it manoeuvred for the back view and turned up the under side of common aspects,—the laws secretly broken, the impulses secretly felt, the hidden passions, the double lives, the dark corners, the closed rooms, the skeletons in the cupboard and at the feast. It made, in short, and cherished, for fancy's sake, a mystery and a glamour where there were otherwise none very ready to its hand; so that it ended by living in a world of things symbolic and allegoric, a presentation of objects casting, in every case, far behind them a shadow more curious and amusing than the apparent figure. Any figure therefore easily became with him an emblem, any story a parable, any appearance a cover: things with which his concern is—gently, indulgently, skillfully, with the lightest hand in the world—to pivot them round and show the odd little stamp or sign that gives them their value for the collector.[20]

Any reader familiar with his 1879 *Hawthorne* will feel at once how James revises his earlier estimations here. His earlier reading of Hawthorne is based on what might be called a theory of symmetrical deficiencies. In its account Hawthorne lived in a new and underdeveloped nation, a nation in which social reality was still only very simply elaborated. But he did not miss the resulting loss of social texture because he himself was averse to social contact—infinitely fonder of being absent than of being present, in James's elaborate locution. Hawthorne's own withdrawn imaginings have much the same quality as his social surrounding: both can

be described by words like "cold," "light," and "thin."[21] And his characteristic literary mode is this double deficiency's inevitable yield—stylized
forms like symbolism and allegory being the abstractions the imagination
is condemned to produce when it cannot clothe itself in richly experienced
social particularity.

In the 1897 essay, by contrast, the same reading of Hawthorne's cultural situation is used to explain not why Hawthorne's art is thin but why
his art takes nonrealistic forms. Here again James makes Hawthorne's
situation out to have been grimly impoverished: a world at best of "common tasks and small conditions." But now he sees Hawthorne as having
resisted such external deprivation—resisted it, precisely, through his art.
In face of a world poor in imaginative opportunities, Hawthorne posited
(James is unclear whether he really divined this or merely asserted its
existence to make things more interesting) a richer, more complicated life
hidden "behind and beneath" the poverty of presented appearances. The
art that would register a really rich reality, once this assumption had been
made, would have to refuse realistic representation, with its rendering of
what meets the "mere eye of sense." Rather it would have to aim to break
through such appearances, or to treat them as *signs of* that hidden "life
of the spirit" it was their intention to conceal. By such a procedure "any
figure . . . became with him an emblem, any story a parable, any appearance a cover."

This essay, in my opinion far more than James's more famous book,
deserves to stand with the great nineteenth-century readings of Hawthorne.
Like Melville's "Hawthorne and his Mosses" and unlike James's 1879
Hawthorne, this essay locates Hawthorne's art on a serious social and
moral ground. James gives full weight here to Hawthorne's fathoming of
the Protestant legacy of "moral anxiety," aestheticized in his 1879 account
as his favorite "pigment" merely. Similarly, he grasps the real logic of
Hawthorne's imaginative mode. He understands Hawthorne's art as a
move made against a surface: "manouevring under" and "pivoting around"
are James's new equivalents for Melville's figures of Hawthornesque plum-
meting and mask-tearing. And he beautifully describes how that art produces a latent dimension of further significance around the face of "common
aspects": his "casting . . . a shadow more curious and more amusing
than the apparent figure" reinvents Melville's conceit of "the infinite obscure of [Hawthorne's] background." James attains to a new understanding of Hawthorne in this essay; but what makes the essay noteworthy is
that in doing so he also attains to a more general sense of representational possibilities. For in this paragraph the stylizations that had been
the signs of Hawthorne's deficiencies of mind and world get reconsidered,
even legitimated. James sees Hawthorne's as an art that is radically fabri-
cated—an art that vigorously "deck[s] out" and "work[s] up" its subjects.
He sees it also as radically distortionary—an art of odd heightenings, producing shadows of sense out of all proportion to the objects that cast them.
But so far from regarding them as mere whims or toys, he now considers

these expressive acts to exercise their own mimetic power: to make visible, within and around the apparent forms of common experience, an over-drama or "life of the spirit" that goes on behind surface life; a deep reality not visible to us except *through* the unnatural representations that art itself constructs.

We might even say that it is in this essay, and through the new encounter with Hawthorne that it stages, that James comes to a positive understanding of what Angus Fletcher calls the theory of a symbolic mode. This understanding is not part of James's critical consciousness earlier on: it appears for the first time in the late Hawthorne essay and receives its most cogent Jamesian statement within that essay.[22] If we have doubts that Hawthorne and a new appreciation of "things symbolic and allegoric" are so mutually entailed as this, James's fiction dispels them. For when he himself embraces the kind of form he describes in this essay, he practices it in a way that underlines its Hawthornesque descent.

The work I have in mind in saying this is "The Beast in the Jungle." The masterpiece of the late form of James's short fiction, this story strongly identifies its own formal possibilities with Hawthorne's work. "The Beast in the Jungle" is one of the most beautifully realized of all James's stories, sustaining its conceit with perfectly controlled intensity from sentence to sentence and page to page. Nevertheless, the chief fact about "The Beast in the Jungle" is that its carefully drawn-out whole permits, even invites, reduction to a single sentence. The tale is still complete in so reduced a summary as this: "A man thinks something special will happen to him. The special thing is nothing; it has been happening as he waits." Reduced to this starkness, it is, uncannily, as if Hawthorne had become the real author of "The Beast in the Jungle." Not only does this conceit have extremely close precedents in Hawthorne. It represents a *kind* of idea we know as Hawthornesque—a skeleton plot that is perfectly, even freakishly, arbitrary in its conception, but that in its very freakishness seems imbued with fatality, seems to portend the working of some large but enigmatic law. The story's conceit finds its doubles in ones like these, from Hawthorne's notebooks:

> Two persons to be expecting some occurrence, and watching for the two principal actors in it, and to find that the occurrence is even then passing, and that they themselves are the two actors.

> A young man and girl meet together, each in search of a person to be known by some particular sign. They watch and wait a great while for that person to pass. At last some casual circumstance discloses that each is the one that the other was waiting for.

> To have a life-long desire for a certain object, which shall appear to be the one thing essential to happiness. At last that object is attained, but proves to be merely incidental to a more important affair; and that affair is the greatest evil fortune that can occur.

> The search of an investigator for the Unpardonable Sin;—he at last finds

it in his own heart and practice.[23] (As realized in "Ethan Brand" this might also be rendered: "A man thinks he can find the Unpardonable Sin. The Unpardonable Sin is to have searched for it; he performed it the whole time he was searching.)

The idea of "The Beast in the Jungle" is, strange to say, more nearly hit on in Hawthorne's notebooks than it is in James's. And when he sets to work on this idea, James weaves the resulting story out of Hawthorne strand by strand. The particular form of his hero's felt mission—"the sense of being kept for something rare and strange, possibly prodigious and terrible, that was sooner or later to happen to you, that you had in your bones the foreboding and conviction of" (359)[24]—has its antecedent in Hawthorne's "The Threefold Destiny," a tale that can be summarized: "A man believes an extraordinary life is promised him. He finds that promise fulfilled when ordinary life turns out to be extraordinary." But as a man with a mission James's John Marcher descends more generally from the whole race of Hawthorne's daimonized heroes. James finds late in the day what other writers are usually struck by first in Hawthorne: the figure of a hero who has a fate descend on him out of the blue, a fate that has no origin or explanation, but that perfectly masters him as it descends on him, compelling him to rigidly unswerving performance of its obscure imperatives. In "The Beast in the Jungle" as, for instance, in "Wakefield" (whose hero's program is secretly to live one block away from his home) or "The Minister's Black Veil" (whose hero's mission is to wear a black veil over his face) there is no prehistory for the hero's obsession. His obsession descends when the story begins, indeed makes the story able to begin. Here as in Hawthorne, as his obsession claims him, it immediately alters his place in the world of relation. Marcher goes through all the motions of life as a bibliophile bachelor and minor bureaucrat while he waits for his new life to break out. In doing so, he converts his life in the everyday social world into pure simulation. Like Roderick Elliston in "The Bosom Serpent," he makes his real life be his obsession's "life within a life"; his other life continues, but it is perfectly drained of real content. More specifically, his daimonization removes him from the world of intimate passion and married love. The fact that he is appointed to have a great adventure puts it "out of the question" for Marcher to take a wife: "his conviction, his apprehension, his obsession, in short, was not a condition he could invite a woman to share. . . . A man of feeling didn't cause himself to be accompanied by a lady on a tiger-hunt." (365) In this he of course resembles Wakefield, whose program of absentee husbandhood opens "a gap in his matrimonial felicity";[25] and even more closely Reverend Hooper, whose veil functions among other things to make marriage to his prospective bride impossible. (The Elizabeth of "The Minister's Black Veil" is one of many Hawthornesque prototypes for James's May Bartram, the all-loving woman unclaimed by the obsessed hero who embodies everything his refusal to be "a man like another" (375) has cost him at the level of common experience.)

Absenting himself from the full relation of love, Marcher like many of his Hawthornesque fellows tries to reclaim that relation in a limited or contained form. Marcher wants May as a friend, if not as a wife, and even goes so far as to allow *her* a share in a friendship otherwise all at the service of his obsession: "He would [he tells himself] thoroughly establish the heads under which her affairs, her requirements, her peculiarities—he went so far as to give them the latitude of that name—would come into their intercourse." (365) To Marcher a comforting proof of his unselfishness, this scheduled thoughtfulness strikes the reader more as a neurotic regulation of the possibilities of intercourse. In any case his move resembles nothing so much as Hawthorne's Prefaces, which seek us out as readers, impelled by the need for "some true relation" to a "friend," only to assure us as soon as they find us that we will be "not the closest friend" and that his openness to us will be only very partial: "the inmost Me [I keep] behind its veil."[26] Even more effectively, Marcher both claims and contains a relation with May by proposing to her to "watch with me." (362) Having assumed a spectatorial distance from his own life, he lets May into his life on the condition that she assume that distance as well. The resulting spectatorship *à deux* perfects a perversion pioneered by Wakefield, who best likes to *have* his married life by stepping out of it and invisibly *watching* it.

James's contribution to the study of such delimiting of relatedness is to show it as proceeding from a certain form of consciousness. What he dramatizes in Marcher—it is one of his great inventions—is the working of a mind literally incontinent: a mind incapable of holding others *in* mind. At the tale's opening, Marcher vaguely recognizes May, but he cannot place the "beginning" this meeting might be the "sequel" to, from which he concludes "that any contact between them in the past would have had no importance." (352) But he finds himself regretting that there had not been more between them in the past, since their present relation "would have been so much better if the other, in the far distance, in the foreign land, hadn't been so stupidly meagre." (355) In fact we learn that his earlier meeting with May had been the one occasion in his entire life when he had shared the secret of his special fate with another. The failure, we learn, has not been the past's failure to hold more, but Marcher's to hold onto that past. His is revealed as an actively unretentive mind: a mind that goes out to others, shares vivid experiences with them, but then voids the record of these transactions. (His mental erase-mechanism makes those "gaps" [353] Wakefield had to leave home to enjoy.) Then since it does not incorporate those moments into itself as its experience, this mind has no mental residue to found or sustain new experiences in the present. Marcher embodies a negative version of the Wordsworthian spot of time. *His* past is the history of his failures to participate, and so to store the mind with a fund of remembered strength. Accordingly, the past that comes back to enrich participation in the Wordsworthian present can only come back to impoverish it in his. His is that self-negation James elsewhere eloquently calls "the wasting of life"[27]—a term suggesting of squandering or the failure to have and exploit life, but also more actively of devastation: the laying waste of that which is life.

James's dramatization of this self-voiding act of mind is a powerful and original discovery. Certainly it has no precedent in Hawthorne. But exactly through this achievement James brings his work to another proximity with Hawthorne's. For the hero as waster of life—the hero of what James calls "negative adventure"—embodies a revival of another Hawthornesque figure, the figure Hawthorne too christens the "negative."[28] In his self-neutralization Marcher vividly recalls Hawthorne's representation, in "The Old Apple Dealer," of a wholly anesthetized or armored personality: a personality constituted by its perfect failure to respond to the life that goes on around it and by its stance as a nonconductor in the field of experiential force. Marcher looks back even more directly (who but James knows these stories?) to Hawthorne's other chief tale of life without affect, "The Christmas Banquet." At a banquet offered annually to the most miserable of sufferers, only the prosperous and quite unravaged Gervayse Hastings appears every year. This is a mystery until we learn that his is the most miserable of sufferings: to be unable to suffer, and so to be unable to experience life in its *life*. The conceit of "The Beast in the Jungle" is of course that the worst human fate would be *not* to suffer; and in seeing this conceit's descent we can see that what James really revives from Hawthorne is not the daimonized hero only but the vision of the existential predicament that hero (in one of his forms) embodies. The James of "The Beast in the Jungle" (he shares the title with the Melville of "Bartleby the Scrivener") is the discoverer of Hawthorne's imagination of nonentity. He revives and clarifies the state both he and Hawthorne call being *"outside* of [one's] life":[29] the restriction of sympathy by which experience gets located across the limits of one's participation, and the self given otherwise than through the sum of its participations. Or we might say that he revives Hawthorne's vision of radical inexperience: the deprivation we enter not from a lack of opportunities, but from our constitutional incapacity to appropriate life as experience by living ourselves fully into it.

Loaded with this weight, Marcher has the resonance of a representative man. He figures—by bringing forward a figure from the Hawthornesque past—a state of being that we think of as peculiarly modern: a state defined by imprisoning self-absorption, the forfeiture of the power of agency, and the sense of living in exile from reality. More specifically, he figures the condition the modern mass media are said to induce: a condition of stunted powers of empathy, passivity, a spectatorial stance toward one's own life, and isolation "from one another, from [oneself], and from experience."[30] (Marcher's invitation to "watch with me" sounds like nothing so much as an invitation to a life together before the television—a big *bayardère* of a medium James was spared the knowledge of.)

Marcher is equally resonant inside James's oeuvre, where he figures with almost apocalyptic concentration the central forms of a moral world. James like Hawthorne is in an important sense a moralist, and like Hawthorne's his ethic is largely a species of vitalism, having as its chief good intense participation in what Lambert Strether calls "life" and Hawthorne (not much more precisely) "the deep, warm secret—the life within the life—which, whether manifested in joy or sorrow, is what gives substance to a world of shadows."[31] Marcher, like Gervayse Hastings and his other Hawthornesque predecessors, functions as a caution against the complementary evil of egotistical coldness and self-enclosure; but their message is more complicated than that. For living all one can, so far from being the normal state of living things in James or Hawthorne, is what they have more usually managed not to do—and this for reasons that go deeper than personal failure. Isabel Archer does not want to "separate" herself "from life. From the usual chances and dangers, from what most people know and suffer."[32] But the very need to will life into one's life, like the need to exhort such engagement, bespeaks a prior state *of* separation as an experiential origin, the separation we see still maintained in James and Hawthorne's characteristic observer-figures. And James and Hawthorne know better than any other authors how the hunger for fullness and immediacy that is bred by this separation covertly works to renew it. James and Hawthorne have as the deepest bond between them their sense of literature's essential vicariousness. Both of them know the need imaginative creation appeals to as the need (in Miles Coverdale's words) "to live in other lives": the need to remedy a felt life-deficiency not by living one's own life more fully but by appropriating life in simulated or surrogate forms. (Here is James's final explanation for "man's general appetite for *picture*":

> If we are pushed a step farther backward, and asked why the representation should be required when the object represented is mostly so accessible, the answer to that appears to be that man combines with his eternal desire for more experience an infinite cunning as to getting his experience as cheaply as possible. He will steal it whenever he can. He likes to live the life of others, yet is well aware of the points at which it may too intolerably resemble his own. The vivid fable, more than anything else, gives him this satisfaction on easy terms, gives him knowledge abundant yet vicarious.)[33]

In the perennial human appetite for fiction James and Hawthorne read what they take to be an elemental human fact, the fact that human consciousness is in a constitutive way *dis*engaged from immediacy, and sustains itself by struggling *against* such immediacy. Their vision of the unnatural naturalness of human disengagement is what gives figures like Marcher or Gervayse Hastings or Wakefield their power. Cautionary emblems against the monstrosity of human separation, they also image its inevitable human reality: show a "chill" as or more fully human than the "warm life" it makes us think we crave.

James recovers a kind of hero from Hawthorne. Through that figure he re-expresses a Hawthornesque ethical sense. But it is just as crucial that in "The Beast in the Jungle" James recovers a Hawthornesque mode of figural expression. In Hawthorne, daimonization as a form of character is inextricably linked to symbolic allegory as a form of expression. As their obsessions descend on them, Hawthorne's heroes typically exit into allegory: they give up the individuating complexities of a whole human self to take on the expressive flatness of emblematic signs. James works out the logic of this linkage, for in writing "The Beast in the Jungle" he uncovers not just the methods of Hawthorne's hypermimetic mode, but also their deep bond to the daimonized hero's negative life.

The mimetic form of "The Beast in the Jungle" bears a sharp resemblance to the "presentation of objects" James described in Hawthorne's work in his essay of 1897. This tale's is a world of powerful simplifications. Its operative aspects have been harshly reduced: the populous world to one couple, the fullness of talk to one topic, the largeness of space to one room. But these remaining items are concentrated on so intensely that a penumbra of heavy portent comes to loom around their apparent smallness—as conversation in this tale seems to have the largest possibilities for human salvation and loss attendant on its banalities of phrase; or as May's room, without ceasing to show the minor elegances of tasteful spinsterly lodgings, comes to seem also the place of the sphynx, the place where men either know themselves in an ultimate way or else meet the doom of those who fail so to know.

But the penumbra of heightened significance is not a constant of the tale's style. It gathers intensity from page to page as Marcher waits out his life—and gathers it, in the tale's weird logic, *because* he waits. Every moment that Marcher devotes to watching for his life is a moment in which he forfeits anew his chance to have his life. And by an occult process that James renders highly persuasive, the life Marcher forfeits by this refusal to live it lodges outside of him as a meaning he has failed to know. (So James says of May in his notebooks: *"She is his Dead Self: he is alive in her and dead in himself."*)[34] The Weatherend scene of the tale's beginning, accordingly, does not strain much beyond a familiar world of country houses and country-house parties. But by the third chapter Marcher's still quite casual words have begun to reverberate, re-sounded by May in a way that freights them with senses he fails to realize:

> "You help me to pass for a man like another. So if I *am,* as I understand you, you're not compromised. Is that it?"
> She had another of her hesitations, but she spoke clearly enough. "That's it. It's all that concerns me—to help you to pass for a man like another." (375)

A chapter later, through a further forfeiture of power, May herself becomes a figure of almost supernatural intensity, straining toward Marcher with the uncanny force not just of her love but of his own life desperately offering him a last chance to claim it, then expiring (I know no more appalling moment in James) of his failure to *make* it his life. At the end even this extraordinary heightening gives way to something like pure hallucination. Marcher's world reduces itself first to the name on May's grave, a name that throbs for him like the name of his fate, a fate written outside of him because he has failed to know it inside his life; then to the face of another mourner, heightened in hideous expressionism to a "raw glare of grief" (400) as it absorbs the whole violent charge of Marcher's unexperienced feelings.

So intensified as it is here, the apparent figures of Marcher's world cease to have any particularity of reference. They become instead stark embodiments of ultimate mysteries, or of experience pressed toward the purity of ultimate states. Within this landscape of pure icon, Marcher himself can be identified in his final stark emblematic significance. By following his peculiar deviation through to its end, a character like Wakefield presents himself at last as a representative man, an image of a fact of our condition caught in the clarity of a limiting case. Hawthorne concludes the tale:

> Amid the seeming confusion of our mysterious world, individuals are so nicely adjusted to a system, and systems to one another, and to a whole, that, by stepping aside for a moment, a man exposes himself to a fearful risk of losing his place forever. Like Wakefield, he may become, as it were, the Outcast of the Universe.[35]

The end of Marcher's adventure, every bit as quirky as Wakefield's, is to read himself (like Wakefield) as an ultimate emblem of a general existential possibility:

> He had seen *outside* of his life, not learned it within, the way a woman was mourned when she had been loved for herself. . . . The fate he had been marked for he met with a vengeance—he had emptied the cup to the lees; he had been the man of his time, *the* man, to whom nothing on earth was to have happened. (400–401)

In Marcher's case, as regularly in Hawthorne, the disengagement that produces negativeness as a state of being also produces the means for expressing it *as* a state of being. The same abstraction that shows itself socially as a withdrawal from intimacy and relatedness is also the source, at the level of expression, of those abstract iconic or emblematic signs by which extreme experiential conditions can come to be represented. I say iconic or emblematic; but the real name for the kind of story James writes here is parable. "The Beast in the Jungle," for all its technical sophistication, exhibits the primitive features of the parabolic form. It is a simple, almost oversimple story; a story that is pure *story*—the narrative conceit of a storyteller, quite unconcerned to disguise its fabulousness with realistic decoration; but that unaccountably manages to embody, in the very lines of its story, something that feels like a truth of our condition, a truth never before so clear to us as it becomes through this simple story's telling. (How well did we know what unmerited love was before we heard the *story* of The Prodigal Son? How well did we know the look of nonexistence before we read the *tales* of The Outcast of the Universe, or of The Man To Whom Nothing Happened?) Parable is a form that locates the capacity to express human life in its largest significations directly within the act of narrative invention. In this sense parable represents an extreme case of the authority fiction can claim, as a means to human knowledge. This augmented power, surely, is what qualifies parable to be a self-transcendingly final form for James's short fiction; but he cannot have that power without reinventing for himself the parabolic form. The re-*creation* of parable as an expressive possibility is James's real achievement in "The Beast in the Jungle." To which it can be added that James repossesses this form as he repossesses fictional possibilities in general: by retracing their lineaments in Hawthorne's work.

"The Beast in the Jungle" represents a great knowing of Hawthorne. Reviving and gathering together a disparate set of Hawthorne texts, this tale forges a striking account of what Hawthorne's essential work is, and of what its power consists of. And this act of knowing is inseparable from James's own late self-extension: in "The Beast in the Jungle" James seizes new forms for his work quite directly by reading those forms out of Hawthorne. The double learning process this tale records is the more interesting because it extends on beyond the writing of this tale. The novels James goes on to write realize further forms of the hypermimetic possibilities grasped in "The Beast," continuing to know those forms by way of Hawthorne's writings. *The Golden Bowl* is the culmination of this process. James's ultimate late novel, the book he could call "the most *done* of my productions," the book he found so "composed and constructed and completed"[36] that after it his work could be *done, The Golden Bowl* represents James's turn, at last, toward what he had always regarded as the greatest of Hawthorne's novels, *The Scarlet Letter,* and his vigorous reinvention, as his own last form, of its form of symbolic romance.

The relation of books like *The Scarlet Letter* and *The Golden Bowl* has lent credence to the modern notion, popularized by Richard Chase and others, that American fiction's central tradition is a tradition of romance. Properly qualified, this notion has much to recommend it; but we must not take it to mean that romance has been perpetually alive in America, a product always available to authors in the supermarket of literature. One of the defining peculiarities of romance as a genre (sophisticated romance, at least—in its popular form romance is always thriving) is that it is always being lost as a serious category. Romance has built into it the liability to look, in many lights (the later nineteenth century's is one of them), mechanical, formula-ridden, artificial, juvenile; like parable it has perpetually needed to be reinvented to become accessible as a form. And this is true in a more particular way of Hawthornesque romance. For though Hawthorne labelled his work romances, it has never been clear what exactly their romanticism consists of. It has little to do with any established definitions of the form. Except in *The House of the Seven Gables,* Hawthornesque romance makes no use of the stock plots Ben Jonson called romance's mouldy tales, and Northrop Frye romance's *mythos*. With the same exception it can scarcely be said to serve romance's familiar aim, to remake the world in the image of our desire. Hawthorne's fiction is indisputably romance, but what romance then *is* is (as they say in "The Beast in the Jungle") the wonder *of* the wonder. Like sophisticated romance in general its Hawthornesque variant has had no further life except as it has been remade, invented anew by later readers and writers.

Such a reconstruction of Hawthornesque romance—an act that both revives the form and establishes, retroactively, what the form consisted of—is what James performs in *The Golden Bowl*. In the whole cast of its expression *The Golden Bowl* embodies a kind of gloss on what Hawthorne means when he defines romance, in the Preface to *The House of The Seven Gables,* as the genre that presents 'truth under circumstances . . . of the writer's own choosing and creation." (1) Romance's kind of nonrealism or counterrealism has something to do, as James reinvents it, with the abrogation of the laws of natural possibility. With its merchant of astonishing memory who comes forward in fateful hour to expose the golden bowl's ominous prehistory, *The Golden Bowl* makes its own detour into what Hawthorne calls the Marvellous. This device is only one element in a conscious primitivism that James is the first author to understand and revive in Hawthorne. His angelical representation of Maggie Verver, for instance—she who can "bear anything," "for love . . . for love . . . for love" (379)—works the same way as Hawthorne's diabolical representation of Roger Chillingworth, to write the clash of transpersonal Good and Evil of melodrama or morality play into a work otherwise striking for its extremely unprimitive sophistication.

Supernatural forces are within its range. But where James really shows romance to deviate from verisimilitude is less in its marvellous content than in its representational form. As James creates it in *The Golden Bowl* and retroactively reveals it in *The Scarlet Letter,* romance is a genre that announces itself in every feature as a radically stylized product. The obtrusions of style and its makings is felt throughout these works' prose: *The Golden Bowl* extends to really baroque thickness *The Scarlet Letter*'s heavily figured verbal style, the style that makes both books unfold less like an advancing line of action than like an expanding field of significant connection. It is evident too in their structure; with its dancelike pairings and re-pairings of couples, *The Golden Bowl* makes its own equivalents for the obtrusive symmetries (for instance) of *The Scarlet Letter*'s scaffold scenes, those patternings that tell us, each time we notice one, that this is not nature but a formal world—a world produced and ruled by design. Indeed the making power of style is written into every represented act in these books. With its catechistical rites and stilted freezes, *The Golden Bowl* does the same violence to natural conversation that *The Scarlet Letter* does with its ahistorical archaisms and operatic exchanges: this is language, these books say, but language used in a way *we* have invented.

Gesture, similarly, is always denaturalized in these books, given the anti-natural formality of ceremonious conduct. (Charlotte's behavior on the stair might be compared here to Hester's conscious symbolism of gesture as she removes her letter, in the forest scene.) This is *not* "real life," they say: it is life as art can make it, presented quite literally "under circumstances . . . of the writer's own choosing and creation."

What James recovers in *The Golden Bowl,* I am trying to suggest, is not just Hawthornesque romance's stylistic mannerisms, but its stylistic insistence on itself as something radically constructed—something wholly artificial, in the sense of being wholly artificed; a perfect fabrication, in the sense that a maker's act has fashioned it all. James's romance like Hawthorne's gives us a world on the condition that we recognize it not as the familiar one repeated but as one produced *through* its representational act—what James calls elsewhere "a world of different values and relations, a blest world in which we know nothing except by style."[37] But their work is distinguished from other equally artificial productions by the fact that the heightened display of artifice in it goes along with a parallel heightening of the force of passion or "life" that artifice is asked to bear. Intimate and erotic passion has the customary status, in James as in Hawthorne, of a pleasure at second hand. The love-ideal of their most typical characters is to get someone else to fall in love, so that they can watch and speculate—a scenario perfected in *The Blithedale Romance,* then compulsively repeated in *Roderick Hudson, The Aspern Papers, The Sacred Fount,* and *The Ambassadors,* to name no more. Part of what gives *The Scarlet Letter* and *The Golden Bowl* their status as major self-extensions for their authors is that the passionate dramas they elsewhere prefer to displace are claimed for the foreground here, and seized in their most primary forms. They realize such passion on similar terms. In both cases love tends innately toward adultery, a relation that as these books show it puts a licit and illicit form of love (Hester's affair with Dimmesdale and her marriage with Chillingworth, the Prince and Charlotte's covert liaison and their marriages to the Ververs) in strong opposition but also in taut symmetry with one another. In both, the illicit form of love also has the peculiar status of having come *before.* These books begin when a love outside marriage has been enflamed, then subjected to a social arrangement (Amerigo's contract of marriage with Maggie, Hester's exposure and punishment) designed to check and supersede it. But this arrangement, so far from curtailing that love, only drives it out of sight. (That love *is* what is "behind and beneath" in these novels, as it *is* in large sense their active past.) Holding that love back, Hester will not tell her lover's name, and the Prince and Charlotte will not tell Maggie of their own prior union: love survives, in other words, on conditions that link it inextricably with concealment and deceit. So kept back, it also takes on the hideous fascination of something that might at any moment break back out—a fact that explains why daily life has the menaced air of perpetually immanent crisis, inside both novels.

In his 1879 *Hawthorne* James chided Hawthorne for his cold and highly wrought rendering of a warm, natural love story in *The Scarlet Letter*.[38] We might surmise that in *The Golden Bowl* James has set himself the penance of repeating and justifying everything he had dispraised in Hawthorne. For he recreates in this book exactly that incongruous union of intense formal workedness and passionate matter that he had described in Hawthorne's novel. These two forces conjoin most intensely in the feature the James of 1879 had found most distasteful, but that he now replicates most exactly: *The Scarlet Letter*'s dominant symbol.

The Scarlet Letter properly begins when adultery is placed under the sign of adultery. The scarlet letter A that Hester wears begins its life as an instrument of civil punishment—one of those visible markings that Foucault finds characteristic of pre-modern punishment, where punishment takes the form of publicly inscribing the power of the state on the body of the offender.[39] From this origin the letter already suggests a conjunction of love and transgression, of private desire and public law. But Hester famously complicates this message by fantastically embroidering the badge she accepts. Subjecting the sign of her condition to her own labor, Hester makes the scarlet letter into something simultaneously objective and created, a socially completed designation that is indistinguishably the work of her expressive power. Gorgeously elaborating the stiff form she receives, she makes the badge of her legal and moral status also an aesthetic object: an object imaging the oneness, in her, of aesthetic and erotic energies. But in her letter this self-proclaimed fecundity, generative at once of aesthetic beauties and human children, expresses its identity at the same time *with* transgression; takes the sign of its transgressiveness, the original A, as the untransfigured ground of its elaborations.

The letter thus wrought is a great example of that "presentation of objects" James had observed in Hawthorne in 1897, by which "apparent figures" become charged with large, even exorbitant signification. But in this instance, much more than in the tales James looked back to in "The Beast in the Jungle," this monstrously overloaded sign reads less like an emblem of some truth or condition, however large, than like the focal point for a whole field of sense. Everything it is possible to mean in *The Scarlet Letter* is simultaneously present in its title symbol. And what the letter really is is a sign of such meanings' possible simultaneity: the sign of the possible coexistence, even convertibility, of such apparently opposite terms as public and private, law and desire, beauty and criminality, pride and shame, created and received, sacred and polluted, and so on.

When James sets himself to working out the logic of Hawthorne's symbolic art in *The Golden Bowl,* he determines it to involve an act of powerful distortion. His bowl, like Hawthorne's letter, is the product of a warping that makes one object in a field of objects come forward to gigantic prominence. He determines it to involve an almost magical intensification of the life of things. His bowl too is a quasi-occult agency, materializing and announcing itself (like Hawthorne's letter in the midnight sky) by its own animistic powers. But above all James understands Hawthorne's symbolic art to involve this overproduction and con-fusion of sense. "My Golden Bowl" (it resists the lesser life of the lowercase) appears in the novel in connection with shopping for a present. A rare *morceau,* of aesthetic value quite apart from its use value,[40] the bowl focuses the whole issue of collecting in the novel, all of the problems it shows to be produced by the human will to appropriate "good things" for its possession. But it just as strongly images a human will to generosity, a will to *give* something to others (the golden bowl is first and last a contemplated *gift*) that raises problems of its own. The chief giving the bowl figures is that of erotic passion: the bowl only comes forth when Charlotte and the Prince (on the eve of his marriage) have renewed their old meetings in Rome, then slipped into the language of their old intimacy to discuss on what terms their love might be renewed. But as it figures the generosity of such passion as Charlotte's, it also figures that generosity's inextricable link to deceitfulness and treachery; if the bowl images her love for the Prince, what Charlotte contemplates, in considering it as a wedding present for Maggie, is her own willingness to make her friend a present of a husband who is, unknown to Maggie, her own old and possibly future lover. As the bowl mirrors these particularities of Charlotte's and Maggie's and the Prince's relations it also links them, symbolically, to larger truths of relationship in general. The golden bowl is made of crystal—not perfect crystal but a piece joined at a fault-line, along which it is liable to crack if placed under violent pressure—but its surface is so artfully gilded that its fault or joining utterly fails to show. As such the bowl is an emblem for the possibility of human union itself, that artful making in which two persons lose their distinctness and come together as one. But if so, it also stands for the crack that never ceases to be latent in union. It images the lurking difference that union's oneness can cover over, but not eliminate; even the violence that may be implicit in union, in its never-reduced potential for disintegration. Yet while it shows union's ground in separation and concealed difference, the perfectly surfaced bowl never ceases to be impressive in its own right. It stands in the novel for the actual flawedness of every presented relationship, but also for each of their possible beauty; for their real imperfection, but also for their possible perfectedness; for the difference that underlines union always, but no less for the possibility that the different could be *made* one, by the workings of a now "lost art." (105)

What James reconstitutes through this weaving of contrary senses onto an object in his text is not just a Hawthornesque form of figuration (though the art of forging a symbol in Hawthorne's manner is itself not at all obvious). What he really reconstructs is the form and force of signification that symbol embodied in Hawthorne's work. In *The Golden Bowl* James both learns *from* Hawthorne and shows that *in* Hawthorne symbol arises through an enforced collapsing of multiple ethical distinctions upon a single textual point. In his bowl, as in Hawthorne's letter, all of the generalized moral possibilities that any actual relationship realizes itself amidst—here fidelity and treachery, generosity and acquisitiveness, obligation and desire, union and disintegration—get activated and brought to urgent expression, not in their familiar forms as separate things but as coterminous possibilities, opposed faces of a single form. So produced, these symbols open up within their texts a place of pure potential: a place where experience is no longer sorted out into categories of opposition, but where all of its possible meanings are simultaneously co-present, in a state of unreduced possibility.

To say this is to say that in reinventing the Hawthornesque symbol James also finds his way back to something more elemental about Hawthornesque romance: its sense of the radical interinvolvement of the ethical forms ordinary thinking makes distinct (Hawthorne calls this the "mesh of good and evil," and James "the close connexion of bliss and bale, of the things that help with the things that hurt");[41] and its sense that its own peculiar power is that of dissolving factitious boundaries and *representing* reality in its undistinguished state. (Romance's action, as "The Custom House" figures it, is to erase lines like that between the Actual and the Imaginary, to reveal such apparent opposites as commingling and reciprocally generated.) The strong sense of significant possibility of which the symbol is a kind of home base in these novels also leads these books to plot deeply similar actions. I have no wish to collapse *The Golden Bowl* into *The Scarlet Letter*. But I know of no post-Hawthornian novel that so catches *The Scarlet Letter*'s essential movement, in the middle phases of its plot.

I noted before that *The Scarlet Letter* and *The Golden Bowl* begin by showing a (in narrative terms) prehistoric love affair being contained in a structure designed to rechannel its energies. But the logic of these books is such that, so far from supplanting it, these structures work exactly to regenerate that love. Placed outside the communal circle by the town's sentence, Hester is thereby freed to move outside the Puritans' mental horizon. In this way her punishment itself breeds the (to her punishers) greater crime of free thinking: thinking whose real fruit is the renewal of love she proposes to Dimmesdale in the forest. *The Golden Bowl*'s marriages—first of the Prince to Maggie, then of Charlotte to Maggie's father—have as part of their aim the reclaiming of the lovers' love for marriage. But the Ververs fail to engage their spouses through marriage, preferring the relation of their own old intimacy; so that the unions designed to re-pair them in fact throw the Prince and Charlotte back together.

Adultery or illicit passion takes on the quality, by this logic, of that which *recurs*. *The Golden Bowl* knows in its Part Third the renewal of love *The Scarlet Letter* showed in the forest scene, a moment made thrilling by the prospect of gratification it throws open but also fearsome by its nature as a recurrence of the proscribed. Even more impressively, when adultery renews itself in these books it finds itself in a condition of dreadful indeterminacy. The extreme figuration of *The Scarlet Letter*'s style makes Hester's out to be an adventure novel—she wanders, we are told, "without a clew in the dark labyrinth of mind; now turned aside by an insurmountable precipice; now starting back from a deep chasm" (166); and the specific terrain her adventure is staged on is the one *The Scarlet Letter* calls "moral wilderness." (183) Placed outside the bounds of the Puritan community, Hester is also placed where the Puritans' codes cease to structure her thought. In addition, her crime itself puts her, by mid-novel, in a situation without precedent in the tables of orthodox morality: the laws that condemn her have no light to shed on the question of what right action is when, having promised one's husband not to reveal his identity, one learns that he has subjected the undetected partner of one's adulterous love to near-fatal psychological torture. The whole form of Hester's experience forces her, as she faces this question, into an uncharted ethical *terra incognita,* a place where known imperatives lose their authority and essential questions come open again. On such a ground the ethical world both can and must be newly constructed—the act Hester performs when she backs off of it the meaning that has been assigned to her love, then gives it a new moral valency that is radically her creation: "what we did had a consecration of its own." (195)

With their hired cabs, butlers, and well-appointed tea-things, the seventeenth and eighteenth chapters of *The Golden Bowl* are a world away from Hester's New England forest. But the moral situation James projects here is that of Hawthorne's moral wilderness exactly. The lonely Charlotte, seeking out the lonely Prince, finds herself too in the moral exotic of the "unprecedented" (220); their situation as former lovers who have married a father and a daughter only to be thrown back on each other by their spouses' persisting intimacies rivals Hester's in the originality of its presented difficulties. Here too the "heaven" is "without stars" (220): to appeal from their plight to the normal proprieties of marriage is to appeal to the very system that has placed them where they are. When adulterous passion resurfaces here, it does so in an atmosphere thick with possibilities for fidelity and treachery, gratification and obligation, but where there is no code to sort out these possibilities or securely to attach them to any action. This predicament again both permits and requires an act of courage: the act, in full awareness both of one's desires and of all the duties to oneself and others that one might possess, of venturing into an ethical indeterminacy in order to forge both a way for one's love and a meaning for one's conduct; the act, in the absence of external authority or support, of improvising a definition of right and wrong, in full knowledge of other ways those values might be determined and of the peril one runs in forging them one's own way.

This moment of ethical openness and of seized opportunity and responsibility is a thrilling one for the characters in these novels. But what we really mean by saying that is that this moment is thrilling for the reader. For where is this *terra incognita* located? Not in the Massachusetts woods surely, still less in London's Portland Place. It exists inside these texts; it is a space they open up by the manner of their writing, by the textual processes that both multiply the ethical issues at stake within them and render such issues insecurely determinable. We are the ones who enter into this openness, by participating as readers in a certain kind of text. It is we who find ourselves framing risky inversions of ordinary value, as we involve our attention in these books' written form.

Here, I think, we come closer to seeing what romance really is, as Hawthorne pioneers it and as James reinvents it. Romance is a literary form that aims not to be like reality—by which we mean in part, not to organize meaning as it is coded in the systems of understanding we call the real. Instead romance aims to produce its own, frankly literary world: not the one we know already but a new one, the yield of the work's own representational act. But this wrought world is not wholly separate from our familiar one. For its difference is that it gives us our same experience in another form: renders in the fullness of its potential sense what reality always realizes in constricting terms. Returning us to a primal state of un-differentiated possibility, this genre allows us to participate in the making of moral signification—in the heady and risky act of giving such possibility determinate shape. I said before that James and Hawthorne were moral artists; this is what their moral art consists of, at least in its romance form. Instead of designating a moral world it restages the act through which any and every moral world was first established—that primal *definition* or reduction of possibility by which meaning is brought to an actual form.

In *The Scarlet Letter* as in *The Golden Bowl* romance's whole tendency is toward the recovery of this large constructive freedom. In the extremity of the forest scene Hester asserts herself as an unconditioned agent and proclaims that reality itself is hers to choose and create: "The past is gone! . . . With this symbol, I undo it all, and make it as it had never been." (202) Charlotte echoes the radicalism of Hester's new makings—"It's sacred" (237), she too says of adultery's new covenant—as she echoes the boldness of her assertions of self: "I risk the cracks." (269) But these characters' constructivism—an assertion within the books that resonates with their own assertively constructed literary forms, and that mirrors the en-riched constructions of sense they enable for us as readers—gets contained, in a further phase of romance. And the way they manage this containment shows Jamesian and Hawthornesque romance beginning to diverge.

"With this symbol, I undo it all," Hester says as she lifts off the badge of love's transgression. But the joyously rehumanized freedom she thereby recovers lasts one moment only. Part of what restricts it is that the same passionate creativity that Hester asserts here has already brought forth, in a past that is *not* gone, a daughter. As her love announces its power to undo the scarlet letter, another product and object of that same love says: "Come thou and take it up!"; then, when Hester has resumed her stigma, speaks the grimly tender: "Now thou art my mother indeed!" (210–11) To love in this book is to be restricted by one's love. In any case, as the book dramatizes it, the real effect of the energy Hester reasserts in the forest is not to liberate but to precipitate its own containment. Her gospel of power and possibility does indeed vitalize Dimmesdale—but it vitalizes him first to the compulsive perversities recorded in "The Minister in a Maze," then to the inspired orthodoxies of his election sermon (so convertible are the energies of the righteous and the unholy in *The Scarlet Letter*), then to his public claiming of the judgment made on him by the Law. Hester's asserted power of choosing and creation instigates a series of transformations that always spell that power's undoing—in recognition of which romance relocates itself, in the novel's last chapter, in the category of the consciously counterfactual. Hester offers her vision of a redeemed society founded on a new relation of men and women at last as a kind of supreme fiction: something it assists our humanity to believe in, but that we know is not the case, outside the sphere of our imaginings, hopes, and desires.

Having followed Hester into the adventures of moral wilderness, Charlotte too finds her projects negated. But in this case her power is contained by no reality but the greater power of a rival creator. That rival, Maggie Verver, might be said to play out the same schematic role that Phoebe did in *The House of the Seven Gables,* or that Hilda did in *The Marble Faun.* The Una or light lady of this romance, she is innocent not relatively or among other traits, but constitutionally: she "wasn't born to know evil" (80); hers is "the state of our primitive parents before the Fall." (253) But the extremely unHawthornesque conceit James unfolds in Book Second of *The Golden Bowl* (we remember how Hilda repelled this possibility) is the conceit that the light lady could be initiated into knowledge of "the harsh, bewildering brush, the daily chilling breath" of "Evil—with a very big E." (284)

In *The Golden Bowl*'s version of the Fall, knowledge begins with the creation of a lack. Maggie first becomes accessible to the revelations that await her when, after years of marriage to the Prince, she suddenly "misses him" (286). Knowledge begins here with a surplus of desire, a wanting that opens up a gap that knowledge then can fill. As a result of the fact that she misses the Prince during his stay at Matcham, Maggie strays, without conscious intention, into a new way of behaving. In a "small breach with custom" (310), a "small variation and mild manoeuvre" (305), she positions herself at her home, not her father's, to receive him, and puts on a showy new dress, so that the Prince will "get the impression of her rather pointedly, or at least all impatiently and independently, awaiting him" (305) when he returns. This is to say that Maggie immediately shifts, through this new excess of desire, into the mode of behavior we have known as Charlotte's: the mode of conscious impression management, of the calculated construction and presentation of appearances. And as soon as Maggie herself begins to construct conscious presentations, she also learns to see that others' behavior may be similarly calculated. Producing the little spectacle of the waiting wife "with an infinite sense of intention" (305) (if with no knowledge of *what* she intends by it), Maggie can watch the Prince be struck by her little show and read the momentary uncertainty it affects him with. When he then resumes the studious inexpressiveness of his ordinary manners she can read through his simulation, know that this "blankness" (it sounds for all the world like "The Whiteness of the Whale") "might, should she choose to insist on it, have a meaning." (310)

Beginning from this moment, Maggie moves by inexorable stages toward full knowledge of the duplicitousness of the Prince and Charlotte's performances as perfect spouses. But Maggie comes *to* knowledge, this moment shows, by herself engaging in the fabrication of appearance. And in her adventure deepening knowledge brings along with it deepening expertise at and commitment to pretence. In this sense Maggie represents a possibility that Hawthorne finds, throughout his work, unimaginable. She is so to speak a Hilda who, so far from purging herself of dark knowledge vicariously acquired, accepts and even revels in that initiation. Or she is a Phoebe who seizes and augments Holgrave's powers of countercreation, instead of requiring him—for love—to give them up.

Maggie embodies the unHawthornesque possibility that loving innocence, without incurring the guilt or treachery or adultery, could venture into their experiential territory, and there appropriate for itself those energies of willing and making that have heretofore been the prerogatives of the fallen. What she achieves with her new-found power Hawthorne would find even more unimaginable. Refusing to announce her true suspicions, Maggie makes it impossible for anyone else to allude to the two marriages' betrayal—a straying into truth that as this book sees it would cause those marriages to collapse irreparably into so many hideous human fragments. As she enlists others in the collective pretence of happy marriage, she also manages to convert that at first *mere* pretence into a substantial reality. By acting the part of the wife who selfishly adores her husband, Maggie manages to make her father agree to separate from her, and so frees them both from that overinvolvement of parent and child that has made their marriages into empty forms. By acquiring the experiential expertise demonstrated in her colossal pretence Maggie also manages to make herself interesting to the Prince—more interesting than Charlotte, whom the Prince finds, next to the overachiever his wife has become, just "stupid" (533). By holding up the form of her marriage to the Prince, in other words, Maggie generates the reality of that marriage: weans both partners from their earlier attachments and makes them turn to one another for their completion. And while Charlotte and Adam remain opaque to us in Maggie's half of the book, the possibility is at least indicated that Maggie's counterrealism might have a similarly transforming effect on their union. Keeping up the known deceit that she wants to keep her father from Charlotte, Maggie enables and requires Charlotte to produce a corresponding act. (James writes that Maggie's act "fairly produce[s] in her the sense of highly choosing" [509]). Charlotte uses the freedom from literal truth that such pretence affords her to improvise the performance of a devoted wife who has yearned to take her husband back to America, only to be thwarted by his possessive daughter. What would before have been a simply false account of her motives reads, in this great scene in the thirty-ninth chapter, instead like Charlotte's experimental consideration of a part she might take up. (To believe that she is simply compelled into banishment at the novel's end is to disbelieve in Charlotte's continuing aptitude for "making her life." [534]) And as Charlotte masters the part she rehearses here, she and Adam become in new measure the couple they have only technically been before. The last chapter sees them "conjoined in it, conjoined . . . as Maggie had absolutely never yet seen them." (539)

Hester ends *The Scarlet Letter* where she began, under the sign of her letter. At her book's end she knows and accepts, as a reality more final than any alternative she can fashion, the inseparability of desire from transgression, creativity from restriction, that her letter always figured. But because of the form of power James invents for her, Maggie can write the opposite ending for *The Golden Bowl*. Through an art unknown to Hester she can make the hideous contraries co-present in the golden bowl separate out. She can purge the book's unions of the flaws of prior attachment they incorporated within them. She can break union's bond to treacherous concealment. Accordingly, she can make real what Hester only dreams of: she actually founds the relation of men and women on a surer ground of mutual happiness, before our eyes. To the Hawthorne whose romance imaged the radical human power to "make it as it had never been" only to hedge that power with renewed restrictions, James makes Fanny Assingham's rebuke to Maggie: "Where's your faith?" (419) His own work knows restriction and imperfection but simply refuses to allow them to be final forms. With Maggie it refuses to let things be the painful ruin of what they merely *are* because it believes they also *are* what they could be made *into,* through the force of a generous imaginative act.

In *The Golden Bowl* James follows the premises of Hawthornesque romance to a much more romantic conclusion than Hawthorne ever reached. He drives Hawthorne's form back to its oldest generic assertions—makes romance again the genre of reclamation and redemption and of the omnipotence of creative power. Or we might say that he drives romance out of its Hawthornesque line and back into the countertradition of the American High Romantics. The power James images in Maggie shares its credo not with Hawthorne but with Whitman on poetical imagination: "It is that something in the soul which says, Rage on, Whirl on, I tread master here and everywhere"; or with Dickinson on the redeemed land: "To Him of adequate desire / No further 'tis, than Here—"; or with Stevens on poetical making (this describes Maggie's power exactly):

> She was the single artificer of the world
> In which she sang. And when she sang, the sea,
> Whatever self it had, became the self
> That was her song, for she was the maker.[42]

While we have been describing it as a difference between two books, it is hard not to feel that the different romanticisms of *The Scarlet Letter* and *The Golden Bowl* reflect larger differences in the spirit Hawthorne and James bring to their late work. With its abrupt drop in published production and its swelling masses of uncompleteable projects, Hawthorne's career ends in virtual ruin. Hawthorne writes the sorry history of his own self-conclusion in a late letter to James T. Fields:

> I hardly know what to say to the public about this abortive Romance [the discontinued *Dolliver Romance*], though I know pretty well what the case will be. I shall never finish it. . . . I cannot finish it unless a great change comes over me; and if I make too great an effort to do so, it will be my death; not that I should care much for that, if I could fight the battle through and win it, thus ending a life of much smoulder and scanty fire in a blaze of glory. But I should smother myself in mud of my own making.[43]

At the end of his career writing has become the asphyxiating and self-befouling product of a hideous incontinence for Hawthorne. And since he cannot write the hypothetical last work that could bring his oeuvre to retroactive completion, his whole work is condemned to stand radically unachieved, exposed as an affair of much smoulder but scanty fire. James's late phase is the perfect reverse of Hawthorne's. Always a productive writer, James is more boomingly productive than ever—in his own words "bursting, late in the day though it be, with violent and lately too much repressed creative (again!) intention[44]—in his last phase. Through this productivity he makes, in his own eyes, the blaze of glory he too thinks a writing life should end with. And through this achievement he finds his way toward a final celebration of writing that late Hawthorne can no longer even begin to entertain, a celebration of art as the work that produces value from unworked life's mere stuff:

> life has no direct sense whatever for the subject and is capable, luckily for us, of nothing but splendid waste. Hence the opportunity for the sublime economy of art, which rescues, which saves, and hoards and "banks," investing and reinvesting these fruits of toil in wondrous useful "works" and thus making up for us, desperate spendthrifts that we all naturally are, the most princely of incomes.

a celebration too of literature as the great school, *the* institution that enables us full knowledge of ourselves and our world:

> [works of art] are capable of saying more things to man about himself than any other "works" whatever are capable of doing—and it's only by thus saying as much to him as possible, by saying, as nearly as we can, all there is, and in as many ways and on as many sides, and with a vividness of presentation that "art," and art alone, is an adequate mistress of, that we enable him to pick and choose and compare and know, enable him to arrive at any sort of synthesis that isn't, through all its superficialities and vacancies, a base and illusive humbug.[45]

Why is it that James can reach a terminus so different from Hawthorne's? Surely it is not because external conditions were more favorable to him. It is because, as *The Golden Bowl* shows, James's creativity does not know the obstacles Hawthorne is always putting before it—does not know them because it believes in its power to overcome them. In an earlier chapter I linked Hawthorne's lapsing productivity to his sense that his work is taking on a separate existence, objectifying itself in a way that makes it ever harder for him to stand toward it as its maker. No doubt James's work—like every human work—took on as unwilled an objective life as Hawthorne's did, after it was completed. James's difference is that, in the egregiousness of his self-affirmation, he simply denies to himself that his work is anything but his to make. In rewriting his early books for the New York edition, late James refuses to allow that any of his works could ever have escaped from him, insists that after whatever lapse of time he can always become their writer yet again by a renewed assertion of his artistic will.[46] Part of the reason Hawthorne's works became strangers to him, I have argued, is that they were taken over by new literary-cultural institutions that organized their public life on their own new terms. The history we glimpsed at the start of this chapter hints that this was also true for James. Claimed first by the avant-garde literary circles of the late 1890s, then by the emerging modernism of the 'teens and 'twenties, then by the academic New Criticism of the 'forties and 'fifties, James's writings took on institutional lives quite as alien to their initial intentions as any work of Hawthorne's did. If these developments did not daunt James, it is because, in the outrageousness of his fantasized power, James is always persuaded that he can *create* his work's publicly instituted forms. In selecting the works to include in his Collected Edition, James himself undertook to determine the canonical form of the Jamesian oeuvre. In sending out lists of the order in which his books should be read (alternative lists for ordinary and advanced readers yet),[47] James curricularized himself, claimed for himself the power to organize his work as an object of instruction. In telling (for instance) the Duchess of Sutherland to "read five pages a day" of *The Ambassadors*—"be even as deliberate as that," "keep along with it step by step."[48]—James himself undertook to propagate the close reading he felt his work should receive—as if (again more like Whitman than Hawthorne) he thought he could control how his work was consumed, not only how it was produced.

Extravagant as James's personal fictions of creative power are, the array of books he wrote out of such persuasions shows the real difference it can make to work with a self-affirming rather than a self-obstructing will. Standing his collected writings up against Hawthorne's, James is fully entitled to say, as Spencer Brydon does in the face of his *alter ego,* that *his* is "the achieved, the enjoyed, the triumphant life."[49] Indeed it is part of James's special interest, as a figure in the school of Hawthorne, that he should so conspicuously outdo the master at his work, while remaining so tightly focussed *on* his work.

But to call James's work (as we must) more fully achieved than Hawthorne's is not quite the same thing as saying that Hawthorne is transcended in it. The comparison *The Golden Bowl* invites with *The Scarlet Letter,* after all, does not work wholly in James's favor. If we actually place the novels alongside one another, we immediately notice how densely historical *The Scarlet Letter* is, how firmly its moral situation is rooted in the legal structure of a particular historical community. By contrast, the moral order of *The Golden Bowl* simply has no external ground—as the bowl itself is an artifice without known origin, not, like the scarlet letter, a historically specific social production. Before such a comparison we might wonder whether James is not able to show human creativity triumphing over past history in part because he has reduced history to a form imagination can triumph over—deprived it, in other words, of its objective social dimension. Seen next to *The Golden Bowl The Scarlet Letter* is also striking for its extremely concrete imagining of family life. The product and object of Hester's love, Pearl also embodies the obligations that love entails, images love's creation in the family of a form that fulfills and restricts it at the same time. Unlike Pearl, Maggie's child the Principino is always well offstage in *The Golden Bowl,* his care wholly delegated to the equally unseen Miss Bogle. But by eliminating the child from the family James also considerably simplifies his family drama. "Where's your faith?," James says to Hawthorne, as he shows the family happily reconstituted by the human power of fiction making. But Hawthorne might reply that James can show the family reclaimed by imagination because he has first imagined certain troublesome features out of existence—simplified it to its most reclaimable elements.

James's romance, such a comparison suggests, "transcends" the limits romance runs up against in Hawthorne by eliminating terms from the human problems it sets itself. And such a conclusion is in some sense immanent in the book: for part of *The Golden Bowl*'s own history in the world is that readers who have been deeply impressed by it have still found it wanting (as early James did *The Scarlet Letter*) in a certain elemental human reality. ("What was your idea in suspending the four principal characters in 'The Golden Bowl' in the void? . . . Why have you stripped them of all the *human fringes* we necessarily trail after us through life?," an otherwise-admiring Edith Wharton wrote James, leaving him to reply: "My dear—I didn't know I had!")[50] Another part of its history is that Maggie's romantic triumph, achieved to all appearances to the book's perfect satisfaction, has left readers less than satisfied. Do the Ververs ever properly recognize their own complicity in producing the betrayal of their marriages? If not, how maritally expert do they ever truly become? To what extent do Maggie and her father overcome their commodification of others into beautfiul objects they might acquire? To the extent that they do not, what is one to think of a happy ending founded on the notion of the spouse as "human furniture" (541)? The Prince is made "restless" (29) at the start of *The Golden Bowl* by the one-sidedness of his marriage, by the Ververs' possession of a bounty that makes reciprocity impossible. But if the final form of his happy marriage is his wife's whole creation, does this not really intensify the problem of asymmetrical generosity—while also suggesting that the book has somehow lost sight of this issue? In any case, is there not something antithetical to the very idea of mutuality in the vision of marriage as a single artificer's august creation? However we feel such questions should be answered, it is a fact of literary history that they have regularly come up for readers of *The Golden Bowl*,[51] and come up not because the book raises them but because it so conspicuously fails to raise them. As such they form as real a part as any of the consciousness this book produces—a consciousness, curiously, of what it excludes from the question, in resolving itself as it does.

All of which is to say that if James goes beyond Hawthorne in his late writing, he does not do so without paying a price. And, in showing this, his case brings us near a deep truth about Hawthorne's tradition. Hawthorne has a tradition because other writers see him to have grasped radical potentials of their own work. But he also has a tradition because his own work seems so unfinished: because he seems only very partially to have realized the potentials he senses, in the writing of his work. Taking their bearings from his fiction, other writers undertake to produce the powerful forms they see only half-achieved in him. In this way Hawthorne sponsors some of Anglo-American fiction's most extreme experiments: who else can claim as his progeny such feats of assertion as *Moby-Dick,* where fiction strives toward the condition of pure prophecy, or *The Golden Bowl,* where it grazes the limit of pure romance? But this tutor of extremists is himself no extremist. And when others go past where he left off, they show, however extraordinary their achievements, the reasons for his moderation. Hawthorne always seems to have stopped short out of simple limitation (James's theory of Hawthorne is that he is just unambitious or weak in artistic will)[52] until his ways are extended. Then those extensions reveal him to have checked his assertions of fiction's power in recognition of some countervailing reality—a reality that his extenders have not grasped so well as he, and that thus becomes a measure of their own incompletion. Hawthorne needs his followers to exhibit the full forms of literary potentiality he entertained. But he needs them too to reveal the logic of his self-limitations. As such they show what Borges means when he says, *a propos* of Hawthorne and his heirs: "A great writer creates his precursors. He creates and somehow justifies them."[53]

~ Chapter Ten ~

THE MODERNIZATION OF TRADITION

AT ONE POINT in *Moby-Dick* Melville asks: "Does the Whale's Magnitude Diminish?—Will He Perish?" His brave answer is that such reductions are unthinkable; but from a later point in environmental history we know that his confidence was misplaced. If we vary the question to ask whether the literary giants diminish, the ready answer would be like Melville's: that these figures are in a different class from punier creatures; a class exempt from the ravages of time. But for authors no more than for whales can the imposing stature possessed at one moment guarantee that they will survive in that form to another.

Hawthorne well illustrates the vicissitudes of the literary immortals' life in time. His history after his own century is the history of just such an unforeseen diminution. And his loss of power, I would insist, is as much part of the history of his literary-cultural life as were his rise to and perpetuation in power. Studies of tradition tend to concentrate on places where tradition is strongly continued. But we do not know the whole form of a tradition's life until we know too where it ceases to inspire such extensions. The lapsing of this authority, especially visible in Hawthorne's case, has a larger instructiveness there as well. Like his rise, Hawthorne's decline was intimately connected to a broader action of canon-construction in America. His decay presents a historical locus in which to study the questions raised by canonical degradation in general: by what process canons get dislodged or drained of force; what happens to the work such canons had included when it loses this system's cultural backing; and what the effects are for possible followers when authors get displaced from traditional positions of influence.

The forces responsible for the impairment of Hawthorne early in this century need to be traced outside the literary sphere into the whole drama of generational politics played out in America in the 'teens and 'twenties. We can mark off nineteenth-century generations with reasonable accuracy, for the convenience of historical narration. But no nineteenth-century generation has the sharp definition as a generation that the one that came of age between 1915 and 1922 had, both for itself and its adversaries. (Malcolm Cowley's autobiography of this generation, *Exile's Return,* moves with perfect ease from a personal "I" to a generational "we." Willa Cather was born not long before Cowley, but long enough that his "we" is her "they": *Not Under Forty,* her 1936 reminiscence is defensively titled, in the presumption that *her* experience and feelings will not be available to anyone born after 1896.) The reason for this differentiation is that the young cohort that succeeded in making itself seem representative of its age group around 1920 was bound together not alone *by* age but by a distinctive generational culture: not just by actual common experiences but by a common *form* for experience, an integrated set of life-organizing practices and beliefs that intensely allied them with one another and intensely distinguished them from denizens of an older ethos. The culture this generation identified itself with is best known to us through the self-consciously young or modern styles of the post-World War I period: those racier or jazzier self-expressions that flaunt themselves in the 'twenties, making older forms of conduct look painfully restrained and inhibited by contrast. But this culture asserted itself not alone through such new cultural practices but also by raising culture itself as an issue: by articulating the fact that received or prevailing American culture was not an inevitable reality but an enforced construction, one of many possible forms in which this culture might be selected and maintained.[1]

The true measure of the success of the nineteenth-century institutionalizers of a national high culture is that when the insurgents of the 'teens undertook this kind of criticism, it was still the culture erected in the eighteen-fifties and 'sixties that they found themselves up against. Literature, as we saw (for instance) in the educational reforms of Horace Scudder, was given an especially central place in the formation and transmission of this national high culture. And an unforeseen consequence of this positioning is that when the whole institution came in for concerted opposition, its literary manifestation—the nineteenth century's American canon—was the stronghold singled out for attack. Van Wyck Brooks's *America's Coming-Of-Age* (1915), the influential first instance of the kind of criticism I am describing, argues that American culture has been organized through a separation of the spheres of ideality and practicality impoverishing to both sides. His attack, we should notice, is not on some universal cultural "establishment" but on a historically specific establishment *of* culture: on that militant segregation and stratification of cultural zones that produced a separate high culture in the 1850s and thereafter. And the way Brooks brings this larger cultural model up for criticism is by focussing on what he calls "Our Poets." America's (by Brooks's new reckoning) wan, slen-

derly achieved canonical authors become his prime exhibits of the dereal-
ization this scheme forced on all creators by making them work in isolation from practical American life. And the same authors become his proof
of the unreality a culture so organized has for its recipients. The authors
Americans revere do not keep them, Brooks says, from pursuing material-
istic values in practice—and this because in America *culture* is maintained
as something separate from the world of practical pursuits. The canonical
authors, exemplary victims of American cultural stratification, become in
this way exempla of a legacy that victimizes its receivers: figures of a culture that fails to inform its culture, a culture that fails really to *acculturate*
the men and women who need it to live by.[2]

Brooks's book and the sequels it inspired—works like Waldo Frank's
Our America (1919), Lewis Mumford's *The Golden Day* (1926), and
Brooks's own important later essays—form the first movement of conscious
canon-revisionism in American literary history. Clearly for this movement
(as for later ones), the stakes involved in literary renovation are much
more than literary. Brooks and his cohort attack the traditional canon as
the symbolic locus of a whole organization of experience they find alien
and depleting; they reconstruct the canon in the faith that they can thereby
help construct a collective mental world that will realize their experience instead of ignoring or denying it. This project really of lived-*world*-
remaking—not just a shift in taste, or a war against the fathers narrowly
conceived—is what is being acted out in the canon-bashing that becomes a
kind of organized youth-entertainment around 1920: that ritual defacing
in which Longfellow was said to be to poetry "what the barrel-organ is to
music," not just "a very small poet" but one who "did not partake of the
poetic character at all"; Holmes, "hopelessly faded"; Lowell, "greedy for
pudding and praise"; Emerson, "pale and shredded," and (this is T. S.
Eliot) "already an encumbrance."[3]

Hawthorne came to his late-nineteenth-century prominence through the
construction of the nineteenth century's American canon. Hawthorne was
disseminated in the dissemination of that period's official culture. So it is
not surprising that, while he escaped the grosser abuse reserved for Longfellow, he too suffered discredit in the attack on those structures. Randolph
Bourne's 1919 "History of a Literary Radical" shares Brooks's glowing
sense that an authentic culture is now available to be created. His essay,
like Brooks's, seems suddenly able to see the organization of what has
heretofore passed for culture; to Brooks's critique of its separation and
isolation of levels Bourne adds a powerful exposure of American high culture's authoritarianism, its use of art to enforce the thought that value objectively exists and that to be cultured is to learn to accept such unchallenge-
able designations. And in Bourne's piece, Hawthorne embodies traditional
culture *par excellence*. The form in which high culture was daily present to
the young radical Bourne describes, Hawthorne is also the emblem of that
culture's lack of presence to the *mind:*

The classics were stiffly enshrined behind glass doors that were very hard to open—at least Hawthorne and Irving and Thackeray were there, and Tennyson's and Scott's poems—but nobody ever discussed them or looked at them. Miro's busy elders were taken up with the weekly *Outlook* and *Independent* and *Christian Work,* and felt they were doing much for Miro when they provided him and his sister with *St. Nicholas* and *The Youth's Companion.* It was only that Miro saw the black books looking at him accusingly from the case, and a rudimentary conscience, slipping easily over from calvinism to culture, forced him solemnly to grapple with *The Scarlet Letter* or *Marmion.* All he remembers is that the writers of these books he browsed among used a great many words and made a great fuss over shadowy offenses and conflicts and passions that did not even stimulate his imagination with sufficient force to cause him to ask his elders what it was all about.[4]

Oh heavy change! The same standard-author set of Hawthorne that was a revelation to the young Hamlin Garland has become, in Bourne's latter day, simply so much musty furniture. *The Scarlet Letter,* the book that gave the child Henry James glimmerings of fascinating subjects tabooed by adults, piques this modern child's curiosity so little that he does not even care to ask adults to explain it. What we are seeing here is what happens to once-great writing at the moment of its loss of force. As Hawthorne's case shows, when literary work is alive its life is a palpable experience. It is felt as compelling the imagination, as Hawthorne made Howells feel possessed and overpowered. It plays into deep desires and fears: "Hawthorne appalls—entices," Emily Dickinson once said. It connects, as a reading experience, with experience in the fullest sense; when the political scandals of the Grant regime made Horace Scudder think Hawthorne the author for his time, secret sin in the real historical world brought Hawthorne's thematics to *life* for Scudder, and this revived author gave him the terms in which to read the meaning of his age. When an author goes dead on his readers, it is life in this sense that he loses—as, in Bourne's account, Hawthorne exerts no force, moves no interest, connects with nothing outside his closed case. More specifically, when canonical authors fade, they do not just lose centrality but retain a centrality now revealed as factitious. Bourne's Hawthorne, grown inert as an imaginative presence, is thereby exposed as a cultural contrivance: something *produced* in a certain cultural *form* (the collected-works format devised by Fields and Scudder); something *maintained* in a certain cultural *position* (in the honorifically separate sphere emblematized by the glassed-in shelf); something whose value is institutionally enforced *for* it (as in the "dead rituals"[5] of Bourne's professors), no longer felt living *in* it.

It was Hawthorne's peculiar fortune to be made into an embodiment of the classic as the nineteenth century conceived of the classic. As Bourne's and similar contemporary comments show, his corresponding fate was to come to seem to embody the "classic" in an oppressive, merely official sense of the word, when that conception lost its currency. But an intriguing fact about Hawthorne's devitalization is that it was not only experienced by that older culture's opponents. Justice Oliver Wendell Holmes, son of a canonical author and companion of James and Howells as young insurgents of the 1860s, is hardly the kind of person Bourne or Brooks meant by "we." But Holmes shows that the old guard too could feel the life passing into work the young generation revived—and passing out of the works it shelved as *passé.* In a 1921 letter he writes: "Did I mention *Moby-Dick,* by Herman Melville? . . . It shook me up a good deal. It's wonderful already that a book published in 1851 doesn't seem thin, now. Hawthorne did when last I read *The Scarlet Letter.*"[6] And this lapse of life appears to have been felt not just by the expected adherents of the older literary culture but by its creators and enforcers—and not just after the cultural revolution of the 'teens, but well before that revolution began.

William Crary Brownell gives a revealing example here. Brownell was the chief editorial advisor at Charles Scribners' Sons from the 1890s on, and so controlled access to America's leading "serious" literary publisher at the turn of the century. (Brownell was Edith Wharton's editor at Scribners', and helped bring Henry James to Scribners' in the form of the New York Edition.) From this base Brownell accrued a massive critical authority, which he put at the service of a conservatively classical literary vision. His *Victorian Prose Masters* (1901), in Arnoldian or Hilda-like fashion, makes Victorian writing an affair of masters—masters six in number, as in Scudder's American canon. (In another classicizing use of his culturally vested authority he also rejected *America's Coming-Of-Age* for Scribners' in 1915 on the grounds of its canonical irreverence.)[7] To the insurgent generation of the 'teens, Brownell was the personification of the entrenched culture they opposed. So it is significant that in 1909, in a six-author sequel *American Prose Masters,* Brownell gave Hawthorne a trashing unequalled by any of his later detractors. The still-powerful Hawthorne chapter of Brownell's book is a scathing assault on Hawthorne's lack of artistic will, limited artistic range, and incuriousness about human experience at large. And this piece registers Hawthorne's current *life* in exactly the same way Bourne does, ten years before him. Brownell's Hawthorne is mostly a tedious official treasure, an honored past that forms no part of its honorers' present experience, a writer enforced on our attention not by his intrinsic power but by the cultural institutions that find him to their taste:

> His writings satisfy academic standards and appeal to the conservatism of culture. And their style, clear, chaste, and correct, is of the preservative order. They form a large constituent portion of our classics—our somewhat slender shelf of truly classic production. As such they are read—more precisely, have been read—by everybody. Up to the present time at least that have been universally part of the "required reading," so to speak, of youth and the recollection of eld—a recollection always roseate if afforded half a chance, and in Hawthorne's case, one suspects, enjoying practical immunity from the readjustments and rectification of later rereading.[8]

Brownells' interring, we know, was received with joy by at least some of his 1909 readers. Edith Wharton wrote of her pleasure in seeing "the egregious Nathaniel expire without shedding of blood."[9] But this episode's real interest lies in what it reveals about canonical reformation in general. Revisionist histories—Van Wyck Brooks's among them—have the trick of making their struggle seem to have been fought against the concerted opposition of a massively defended establishment. But this historical episode suggests that canons do not become available for a new group's remaking until they have already lost their compelling reality for a strategic portion of their original supporters; and that the work of dismantling is originally performed not by insurgents fighting against the entrenched but by unrecognized cooperation between elements of both sides.[10]

In any case, the erosion of cultural authority that had these effects on Hawthorne's public status and on the experience of readers of his now-dimmed work had immediate consequences for the way he entered others' writing. The revival and recreation of Hawthorne in late James might seem to argue that Hawthorne's tradition was still going strong after the turn of the century. But James's late play with Hawthorne is really a Jamesian idiosyncrasy: if we look at other writing of this time, we would scarcely conclude that the love of Hawthorne (in James's phrase) knew no lapse. Harold Frederic's 1896 bestseller *The Damnation of Theron Ware* might seem to dispute this point. With its scaffold scene, forest scene, cold scientific experimenter, and ministerial midnight vigil, this book makes as sustained an allusion to Hawthorne as any work in Hawthorne's line. Frederic, in my judgment, writes the best *ersatz* Hawthorne of any American writer, and he makes one of the cleverest uses of a Hawthorne text: *Theron Ware* invokes *The Scarlet Letter* not just as a past model but as a textual incarnation of the past itself, against which the liberalizations and trivializations of its own later day can be continually measured. But no one who had gauged Hawthorne's weight for Melville or James could fail to note the difference with Frederic. Hawthorne informs Frederic's novel, but that is the least of what he did for the authors who felt his full power: he informed *their* idea of their vocation, challenged and helped extend their idea of what it meant to be an author at all. Wittily revived in Frederic's work, Hawthorne does not structure Frederic's *idea* of his work. And it might already be a mark of Frederic's increased distance that he can treat Hawthorne, for the first time in my acquaintance, humorously—without the earnestness or reverence (or competitiveness) that had been Hawthorne's usual due.

The Damnation of Theron Ware is, anyway, an exception or sport even inside the Frederic canon; other books give a better index to Hawthorne's life at this time. *The Red Badge of Courage* (1895) has, in its ninth chapter, one of those sudden intensifications of literariness that make Stephen Crane's such a *conscious* form of writing, and this time Hawthorne is its palpable referent. Asked to see his wound by the anonymous tattered soldier, Henry Fleming, who has fled the battle not for a hurt but for loss of nerve,

> now felt that his shame could be viewed. He was continually casting side-long glances to see if the men were contemplating the letters of guilt he felt burned into his brow.[11]

In its connection of guilt first with visibility, then with a letter that pub-lishes secret shame, this passage embodies a strong memory of Hawthorne. But to weigh Hawthorne's tradition-making powers in this instance we also need to measure this allusion's limits; we need to note, for instance, that what Crane remembers is the single most obvious thing in Hawthorne, the title image of his most famous novel, and in any case that Hawthorne's presence to Crane is strictly momentary, not sustained or deeply informing. From the Pennsylvania edition of the first unedited text of *Sister Carrie* (1900) we now know that when Carrie first entered the stage-world, Drei-ser had thought of Hawthorne. A later-excised passage reads:

> The life of the world behind the curtain is a fascinating thing to every outsider with theatrical leanings, as we well know. It would require the pen of a Hawthorne and the spirit of the "Twice-Told Tales" to do justice to that mingled atmosphere of life and mummery which pervades the chambers of the children of the stage. The flare of the gas jets, the open trunks suggestive of travel and display, the scattered contents of the make-up box—rouge, pearl-powder, whiting, burnt cork, India ink, pencils for the eyelids, wigs for the head, scissors, looking glasses, drapery—in short all the nameless paraphernalia of disguise have a remarkable atmo-sphere of their own. They breathe of the other half of life in which we have no part, of doors that are closed, and mysteries that may never be revealed.[12]

Dreiser in truly traditional fashion goes back to Hawthorne and carries him forward into a new circumstance, we could say of this passage. But to study the passage as an allusion is to see at once its perfect vagueness: Dreiser's reference is not even to an obvious work but just to "Hawthorne" in general, as characterized in his most clichéd public reputation. And here the text's activation of Hawthorne is so purely of the moment and on the surface that cutting it, as Dreiser later did, makes no difference whatever.

The naturalist writers of the 1890s have read Hawthorne, but he has very largely receded from them as writers. He is no longer a distinct or forceful presence in their consciousness as authors. He no longer helps shape the terms in which they *think* their work or envision the writer's role. And if we look forward another generation, this loss of influence becomes even more pronounced. Hemingway or Dos Passos can be scanned in vain for evidence of their interest in Hawthorne. They may or may not have read him, but as writers they do not know him: he forms no part of their operative literary consciousness.

Such nonconductors of Hawthorne's influence take us a stage beyond the one this chapter began by examining. Van Wyck Brooks and Randolph

Bourne remember the likes of Hawthorne, if only to defame them; Hemingway and Dos Passos have let them slip their mind. Brooks and Bourne say that America's venerables do not connect with living thought and action; these writers make that severance simply be the case. What they exemplify, of course, is the state authors move into when their decertification is complete. The canon-reformers of the early twentieth century rightly argued that a canon suppresses other possible pasts by instituting an official past. When they revived systematically forgotten authors they rightly claimed that they were recovering not just lost reading-matter, but lost *experience* the present could know itself through and practice on. But canon-revision destroys as it creates; and the form of its destruction is to consign old pasts to the same oblivion it rescues new ones from. The canon that first included Hawthorne could survive canon-bashing, but not the indifference and inattention that succeeded it. When they became ignored, its authors finally truly *passed;* they became not a past the present lives forward from but a past passed out of mind.

"Great men die twice," Valéry says, "once as men and once as great." What I have been chronicling here is Hawthorne's second death; and, obviously, once Hawthorne dies this second way, the story this book has been telling ceases to be instructive. The history of American literature can be revealingly told in terms of the transmission of Hawthorne because when Hawthorne has been strongly present to other authors—as he was to Melville, as he was (for cultural reasons) to James's and Howells's generation—they have regularly conceived of their work in his light. When Hawthorne ceases to be present to later authors, he ceases to reveal how authorship itself has been constructed. Continuing my story past this point would require the description of other organizations of the writer's position than the ones I have charted, and of other amassed pasts through which writers have learned (and learned to modify) their roles.

But the story is not entirely over: for the great fact of Hawthorne's modern history is that although he did dim with the twilight of the nineteenth century's canon, that was not the end of him. In this century's new creation of the American literary past, writers denied place in the old canon were given heroes' welcomes. (Whitman is the author really celebrated by the insurgents of the 'teens.)[13] But even at the start of this process Hawthorne was not quite dismissed. As he polishes off Longfellow and Bryant, Brooks declares that "Thoreau, Emerson, Poe and Hawthorne are possessions forever"—though his point is that "not one of them, not all of them, have had the power to move the soul of America from the accumulation of dollars." T. S. Eliot, exemplary asserter of a new model of literary tradition, and himself so soon accepted as a new chief of tradition, writes in an 1918 essay that the traditional New England authors "all can, and perhaps ought to be made to look very foolish," but he makes Hawthorne a sole, if heavily qualified, exception. Hawthorne "has permanence, the permanence of art," Eliot declares; in the impoverished American situation "Hawthorne, more tentacular and inquisitive, sucked every actual germ of nourishment out of his granite soil." ("But the soil was mostly granite,"[14] Eliot feels compelled to add.)

Spared relegation to full oblivion at the start, as the reconstruction of American literature continued Hawthorne was increasingly new-found as the kind of author moderns preferred. H. L. Mencken's 1924 essay "The American Tradition"—a really vituperative attack on the traditional canon as a racist political tool, and on "Dr. William Crary Brownell, *de l'Académie Américaine*" as the doyen of "the native, white, Protestant *Gelehrten*"—displays the typical move by which Hawthorne gets reclaimed as an exemplum of a new culture's stances and values. Mencken writes:

> Go through the list of genuinely first-rate men: Poe, Hawthorne, Whitman, Mark Twain. One and all they stood outside the so-called tradition of their time; one and all, they remained outside the tradition that pedants try so vainly to impose upon a literature in active being today.[15]

Through such polemics the fact that Hawthorne was once the centerpiece of the old tradition gets so to speak erased, and Hawthorne made over as one of us: an outsider to nineteenth-century official culture, a noble resister of its incorporating powers. ("Puritanism" being the mark of America's traditional culture for him, Mencken modernizes Hawthorne most powerfully by making him a great anti-Puritan: "Hawthorne's onslaught upon the Puritan ethic was the most formidable and effective ever delivered, save only Emerson's.") D. H. Lawrence's *Studies in Classic American Literature* is marked as a work of the early 1920s by its sense that American literature is in need of redefinition and by its confidence that it knows at last what America's real classics are. Lawrence is a much more powerful literary critic than Mencken, but he too delivers an authentic American literature by finding an incipient modernity—the explosion and re-formation of the Victorian cultural ethos—in certain now-ancient American writings. In this process Hawthorne becomes important again, the exemplary *American* author in this new sense:

> Surely it is especially true of American art, that it is all essentially moral. Hawthorne, Poe, Longfellow, Emerson, Melville: it is the moral issue which engages them. They all feel uneasy about the old morality. Sensuously, passionally, they all attack the old morality. But they know nothing better, mentally. Therefore they give tight mental allegiance to a morality which all their passion goes to destroy. Hence the duplicity which is the fatal flaw in them: most fatal in the most perfect American work of art, *The Scarlet Letter*. Tight mental allegiance given to a morality which the passional self repudiates.[16]

Through such reinventions Hawthorne, now a substantially new author, won a new centrality in American literature—a centrality that was then translated into a powerful cultural fact in this revisionism's sequel. If the history of the cultural organization of literature's place that I have attempted for the later nineteenth century were extended into the twentieth, one of the central mysteries it would need to piece out is how the revised American literary past, originated by critics who were all self-consciously nonacademic, and asserted in opposition to the past maintained by the academy (Mencken's WASP *Gelehrten,* Frank's cadaver-guard of professors), was assimilated into the American educational establishment, then validated and disseminated by that establishment in its much more assertive twentieth-century phase.

Critics like Brooks thought the Yankee professoriate were the perpetrators of the stale literary culture that malnourished modern youth.[17] We have seen that professors were in fact latecomers to the work of maintaining the nineteenth century's American canon. *Our* century is when classic American literature found its chief home in the academy—and it found its home there in the new form the anti-academic critics had invented for it. (The appropriation began early on: a 1926 poll of "thousands" of high school and college teachers shows them rating Poe, Hawthorne, and Twain America's greatest authors only two years after Mencken berated them for ignoring those authors.)[18] As the reformulated American literature was incorporated back into the schools, Hawthorne regained the same place in institutionalized cultural transmission he had had of old. Charles Francis Richardson called Hawthorne "the Only" in his pioneering academic literary history in 1887; a UNESCO survey found American professors ranking Hawthorne at the top of the list of great American authors in 1949. (Now his companions are Poe, Melville, James, Twain, Emerson, Thoreau, and Whitman—one generation's insurgency become another's orthodoxy.)[19] The New Critical pedagogy popularized by Cleanth Brooks and Robert Penn Warren, arguably the most major reassertion of literary study's role in mental training since Scudder's reforms of the 1880s, built Hawthorne almost as deeply *into* that pedagogy: "The Birthmark" is the sixth story printed in their immensely influential *Understanding Fiction* (1943), and the story where "successful" techniques of close reading are first fully explained. F. O. Matthiessen's *American Renaissance* (1941), treating the new authors of the 1920s to the joint dignities of old-fashioned national literary history and new-fangled arts of close reading, did more than any other book to set the American canon as it would be taught in American universities after World War II, when they began to teach more of American literature to a greater share of the American population. In this book Hawthorne (with Melville—reunited at last!) becomes the centerpiece for the close analysis of American works, and the place where crucial organizing categories—symbolism and tragedy, in particular—are developed.

For these reasons, the story of Hawthorne in modernity is not, finally, the story of how the past passes, but really of how the past renews itself through time. What Hawthorne shows about this process, we might say, is that when a past carries over from one cultural formation to another, it does so by exceeding the transitory meanings that have been made for it; there still seemed to be something *to* Hawthorne (as there did not, say, to Holmes) when the first cultural representation of him was stripped away.

But his lesson could more accurately be said to be that pasts endure not by transcending local cultural organizations but through their continuing adaptation *within* such organizations. Hawthorne, carried over, still survived in the new culture of the early twentieth century because the figures of that altered world took a new kind of interest in him, literally *made* him (as Mencken and Lawrence did) an expression of its new interests. And he survived because after being so remade, he was adopted into a new age's institutions of cultural conservation and transmission.

This reincorporation yields what I take to be Hawthorne's profoundest lesson for the history of canons in general. Pasts can indeed be repossessed, the early twentieth-century American case shows. Nothing is more exciting in this cultural episode than the tangible proof it offers that traditions can be reclaimed from institutional possession and made plastic again to their inheritors' wishes and needs. But that does not keep new-made pasts from objectifying themselves in turn—as the freshly invented personal canon of Lewis Mumford in the 1920s became the objective truth of our past for Matthiessen in 1940,[20] then the official line for students schooled in Matthiessen later on. This episode shows too that canons can be reopened. Having lifted an oppressively tight exclusion-system off of itself, American literary criticism in the 'teens and early 'twenties is alive to wide new worlds of expression: witness John Macy's *The Spirit of American Literature* (1913), with its uncanonical enthusiasms for William James, James Whitcomb Riley, and Mary Wilkins Freeman, as well as such still-beginning writers as Wharton and Dreiser and such yet-unrevived ones as Melville.[21] But as the new-found authors of this time got put in their academically transmitted form, they contracted into a formation almost as exclusive as the nineteenth century's—suggesting that though canons can be pried open they are much less easily *kept* open, when they enter on their institutional lives.

The grim conclusion to be drawn from this history is that every fresh finding of the past, to the extent that it succeeds in asserting itself, moves toward a future of renewed authoritarianism and renewed closure. This fact is historically well established; but the other half of this paradox is that it is *as* a past gets instituted anew that it becomes available again as a general resource. Hawthorne's modern history can be told with heavy irony as a release from cultural compulsoriness into the same compulsoriness again. But it is striking that as Hawthorne has been returned to the organized past, he has again become (in Brooks's word) usable to later workers.

A distinguished list could be drawn up of modern writers who have renewed old interests in Hawthorne. (Since the South earlier this century assumed the position of Hawthorne's New England as economic backwater and former center of historical drama, the figures are commonly Southerners.) It would include Robert Penn Warren, whose sense of human disability has led him to deepening identification with Hawthorne's moral vision; also Eudora Welty, who has been known to read Hawthorne's "The Birthmark" (Brooks and Warren's story) in her public appearances; also

Flannery O'Connor, whose crucial artistic statement "Some Aspects of the Grotesque in Southern Literature" defends her deformations of ordinary reality by reviving the conception (academically mediated this time) of Hawthornesque romance.[22] And it would include, as the greatest modern exploiter of Hawthorne's reconstructed legacy, Faulkner, whose use of Hawthorne I will look at to conclude.

Faulkner is known as one of literature's great brooders on the burden of the past. But we do not sufficiently recognize that Faulkner's sense of the *literary* past is, at least at first, curiously shallow. Faulkner's early poems are encumbered with remembered sources, but those sources go back little further than the *fin de siècle:* to Wilde, Verlaine, Mallarmé, and so on. (I for one believe Faulkner when he says that he did not know the title of his first book—*The Marble Faun*—had been used before: writers like Hawthorne are, at this point, before Faulkner's time.)[23] If we look ahead to the work where Faulkner emerges fully as Faulkner, his operative tradition grows if anything even more foreshortened. *The Sound and The Fury* like all mature Faulkner is aggressive in its literary virtuosity, but the games it plays so briskly are clearly learned from Joyce and Eliot. The masters that set as worthy projects to wrench narrative continuities, to new-order the representation of consciousness, and to sketch overarching mythic structures around fragmented contemporary experience are Faulkner's virtual contemporaries; this book's tradition is the tradition of the new.

In a sense *The Sound and The Fury* shows the novel's usual way to generic renovation. Faulkner gives a modern instance of the novel's regular habit of renewing itself by taking the contemporary as its inspiration—as Melville took his lead from his contemporary Hawthorne; as the American realists, the modernists of the 1880s, took their lead from modern Russia and France. But this book also shows the more specific consequences of the early twentieth century's "modern" organization of the literary past. In *Exile's Return* Malcolm Cowley lists the *symbolistes* and *fin-de-siècle* decadents as the preferred reading of his cohort in their youth, and Joyce and Eliot (along with Proust, Pound, and Valéry) as the acknowledged masters of their early manhood. This is Faulkner's working past exactly: so idiosyncratic in one sense, his early writing is perfectly standard in the past it looks toward to define the writer's tasks.

In a recently recovered 1933 essay Faulkner describes *The Sound and The Fury* as having produced a kind of literary apocalypse for him. He describes the act of writing this book as having touched off a recognition of the nature of literary writing, a recognition in which he also discovers both the masters of literature's past and what they embody *as* literature:

> when I finished The Sound and The Fury I discovered that there is actually something to which the shabby term Art not only can, but must, be applied. I discovered then that I had gone through all that I had ever read, from Henry James to Henty to newspaper murders, without making any distinction or digesting any of it, as a moth or a goat might. After The Sound and The Fury and without heeding to open another book and

in a series of delayed repercussions like summer thunder, I discovered the Flauberts and Dostoievskys and Conrads whose books I had read ten years ago. With The Sound and The Fury I learned to read and quit reading, since I have read nothing since.[24]

Faulkner, always untrustworthy on the subject of his work-life, is more than usually misleading when he addresses questions of influence. But there is reason to credit the outline, if not the detail, of this statement: for Faulkner's writing visibly re-traditions itself, draws in a past of quite different weight and shape, in this book's wake.

Light in August (1932) is where this augmentation of literary memory becomes evident. Michael Millgate has noted how behind its modernist wrenchings and obfuscations *Light in August* resembles the multiple-plot, highly manipulated novels of Dickens and Hardy.[25] Many readers have noticed this book's debt, in its racial fable, to the Twain of *Pudd'nhead Wilson*. As I read them such likenesses involve not just literary resemblances but a literary *act* on Faulkner's part: the act of seizing a remoter and more extended past as a guide for his work. In this seizure Faulkner reaches out to Hawthorne especially forcefully. For the book *Light in August* remembers more strongly than any other is *The House of the Seven Gables*.

The first thing that makes one suspect the revived influence of Hawthorne is the abrupt return of daimonization as the normal state of selfhood in this book. The masculine (and masculinized) characters of *Light in August* all live in a Hawthornesque state of recoil from their natural, embodied, generative condition, a recoil that makes them compose rigidly antinatural personal programs as an alternative form of selfhood. (Identity is so committed to inflexibility in *Light in August* that its characters invariably move in straight lines, even in flight from rigidification. So other *to* themselves are the programs they have *as* themselves that they too, like Chillingworth or Reverend Hooper or Ahab, experience their courses both as willed *by* and as necessities imposed *on* them: *"Something is going to happen to me. I am going to do something,"*[26] is this syndrome's motto in Joe Christmas.) Hightower, the character in whom Faulkner first focuses this state of rigidification, specifically relives the disability Hawthorne imaged in Clifford Pyncheon. Self-removed from but then stuck outside of truly lived experience, Hightower is a reimagining of Clifford's condition of immobility and stagnation, and like Clifford spends his novel dreading and desiring re-immersion in an abstracted Life that now seems to be located wholly outside his life. (Hightower like Clifford is a sitter at the window.)

These resemblances are already striking. But where *Light in August* shows the full extent of its Hawthornesque origin is in Faulkner's linkage of such immobility to problems of personal and family time. Hightower is devitalized by his self-withdrawal, certainly: "I am not in life" (284), he keeps telling Byron Bunch. But he is also devitalized by his overinvestment in his family past. His life like the House of the Seven Gables is "overfilled with the dead man's presence." He is so attached to the image of his grandfather that he will not allow his grandfather's time to *pass*—with the consequence that he forfeits *to* that figure's time the strength that could be his own. Hepzibah Pyncheon, also afflicted with "consciousness of long descent," becomes thereby a "time-stricken virgin": her excessive conservation of the past shuts her out of the domain of generation. The Pyncheon family chickens, perpetuating the whole "accumulation" of their "ancestry" instead of letting past time pass, lose, thereby, the force to be full ancestors themselves: "diminutive eggs"[27] are all they can now produce. Hightower, heir to the same sense of time, is also heir to its consequences. For what Faulkner shows him achieving, through the over-maintenance of ancestral memories, is the murder of his own reproductive power:

> as though the seed which his grandfather had transmitted to him had been on the horse too that night and had been killed too and time had stopped there and then for the seed and nothing had happened in time since, not even him. (59)

What Faulkner spins out of this recovered topos is a Hawthornesque fable first of bad perpetuation, then of time renewed. Hightower was at the heart of Faulkner's first working conception of *Light in August*. Faulkner's manuscript suggests that the Burden family chronicle and the history of Joe Christmas came to him later, as he wrote.[28] These stories—both great Faulknerian inventions—are much less tightly bound to Hawthornesque prototypes than Hightower, but they expand on the *sense* of time Faulkner had seized in that figure. Joe Christmas, who replays with Joanna Burden the affronts of maternal nurture and paternal authority first played out with Mr. and Mrs. McEachern; and the Burden family, who run away again every generation only to marry again, father a dark child again, and return home again; extend out into Southern racial history the kind of pattern Hepzibah had decried in Jaffrey Pyncheon: "You are but doing over again, in another shape, what your ancestor before you did."[29] When this course reaches its violent crisis, Faulkner follows Hawthorne in showing time purged of the past's overpresence not by a release from compulsive repetition but first by its controlled and conscious intensification. Holgrave lifts the curse in *The House of the Seven Gables* by returning to the cyclical moment where victimized Maules revictimize the Pyncheons, then replaying that scene in a reversed way. Hightower similarly is delivered from his immobility by returning and doing otherwise the past scenes that have fixed his world in place: by redelivering the baby he had earlier delivered dead. (The rhetoric of this revival, in *Light in August* as in *The House of the Seven Gables,* is the regeneration rhetoric of full-scale romance: "Poor, barren woman. To have not lived only a week longer, until luck returned to this place. Until luck and life returned to these barren and ruined acres." [385])

Light in August represents a great knowing of Hawthorne. Discovered in so many other forms by his earlier recipients, Hawthorne awaits Faulkner, really, to find him as plotter of the past's transmissions. But if Hawthorne gets realized in a new way in this transaction, so, much more crucially, does Faulkner. The fiction of remembering; the way later experience retains, even hoards, the memory of earlier experience; the psychic tolls in freedom and fresh life exacted by this preservation; *family* history, understood as involving fatal connections between the present day and the remote, forgotten past—these are Faulkner's great subjects, the matters he establishes his literary self through his mastery of. But they *become* Faulkner's in a much more fully possessed way in *Light in August.* (*Flags in the Dust* had charted generational repetitions without quite knowing what to make of them; *The Sound and The Fury,* a one-generational family chronicle, does not yet know what Hawthorne called "a connection with the long past.")[30] And if he possesses these subjects through the writing of *Light in August,* he does so in significant part by grasping their earlier literary treatment: by reaching further back into the past of writing and reading there how history could be fictively projected. Representative of the creative receiver of tradition in general, Faulkner around 1930 is able to access, in Hawthorne, the past kept in instituted life in his time. (In *Absalom, Absalom!* he appropriates not just Hawthorne but those of his heirs featured in the modern canon: Melville and James.)[31] Through his vigorous *work* he is able (in Malraux's word) to conquer that inheritance: to make it part of his consciousness, the consciousness he works from as a writer. And this act's yield is both the past revived—here, Hawthorne known in the fullness of his intelligence—and the extension of present power: the fuller realization of himself as a writer the Faulkner of *Light in August* achieves.

Does Hawthorne's magnitude diminish? Will he perish? American literature's great survivor, Hawthorne did not perish in the cultural reorganization early in this century. He survived in the official past of new institutions—but survived too, as Faulkner shows, as a source of living tradition: a past a later present can find its way in. Whether he will survive the next reorganization of American literary culture is not so certain. I sometimes suspect that his place will be considerably reduced, in the new version of the collective past we are clearly moving toward. But the final lesson of his history is that the fate that awaits any past cannot be known in advance. Pasts great to the past have passed into forgetfulness, and Hawthorne might not recover so fully should he die a third time. But pasts, even apparently exhausted ones, have also taken on new life. What Hawthorne will need is what every potential past needs in order to survive—for the living present to continue to make it the image of its living concerns and needs.

NOTES

Chapter One

1. On modern political tradition formation, see, for instance, Eric Hobsbawm and Terence Ranger, eds., *The Invention of Tradition* (Cambridge: Cambridge University Press, 1983). For a powerfully sustained meditation on the Renaissance recreation of the classical past and its artistic consequences, see Thomas M. Greene, *The Light in Troy: Imitation and Discovery in Renaissance Poetry* (New Haven: Yale University Press, 1982).

2. Van Wyck Brooks, "On Creating a Usable Past," reprinted in *Critics of Culture,* ed. Alan Trachtenberg (New York: John Wiley & Sons, 1976), p. 168. Brooks's critique of the professoriate is brilliant, but he seems unaware that the academic custody of American literature was quite new at his time, a late offshoot, as I suggest below in Chapter Three, of a cultural organization centered largely outside the university.

3. The concurrent rise of the new American literature and of academic professionalism in the early twentieth century is treated from different angles in Richard Ruland, *The Rediscovery of American Literature* (Cambridge, Mass.: Harvard University Press, 1967), and Paul Lauter, "Race and Gender in the Shaping of the American Literary Canon: A Case Study from the Twenties," *Feminist Studies* 9 (Fall 1983), 435–63. On the rise of specialized expertise and of the university as its seat, see especially Alexandra Oleson and John Voss, eds., *The Organization of Knowledge in Modern America, 1860–1920* (Baltimore: Johns Hopkins University Press, 1979); and for a case study, Thomas L. Haskell, *The Emergence of Professional Social Science: The American Social Science Association and the Nineteenth-Century Crisis of Authority* (Urbana: University of Illinois Press, 1977), pp. 144–210.

4. Edward Shils, *Tradition* (Chicago: University of Chicago Press, 1981), p. 35.

5. Elaine Showalter, *A Literature of Their Own: British Women Novelists from Bronte to Lessing* (Princeton: Princeton University Press, 1977), p. 10.

6. Brooks, "Usable Past," p. 171; Lauter, "Race and Gender in the Shaping of the American Literary Canon."

7. Brooks, "Usable Past," pp. 170, 169.

8. John Tomsich, *A Genteel Endeavor: American Culture and Politics in the Gilded Age* (Stanford: Stanford University Press, 1971), p. 22. As this example and

217

many others suggest, American authors have typically been more hampered by the thinness of their available tradition than by its weight; as later chapters will reveal, the greatest of them have uniformly tried to increase the weight of the past upon them by constructing more formidable models of tradition. In Harold Bloom's famous term, American authors have had to try to augment the anxiety of influence they suffer, as if in recognition of Bloom's maxim: "poetic strength comes only from a triumphant wrestling with the greatest of the dead." *A Map of Misreading* (New York: Oxford University Press, 1975), p. 9.

9. See More's appropriately titled "Hawthorne: Looking Before and After," *Shelburne Essays,* Second Series (New York: G. P. Putnam's Sons, 1905), pp. 173–87.

10. D. H. Lawrence, *Studies in Classic American Literature* (1923; rpt. New York: Viking Press, 1964), p. 2; see also pp. 83, 99, and 101. Lawrence's move has its own tradition, and has been repeatedly invoked to rescue a dark and deceptive Hawthorne from the embrace of cultural orthodoxy. Melville, the inventor of this move, uses it this way in his 1850 "Hawthorne and His Mosses"; more recently, Frederick Crews uses it to rescue Hawthorne from the neo-Christian New Critical line that dominated Hawthorne studies in the 1950s and early 1960s: see *The Sins of the Fathers: Hawthorne's Psychological Themes* (New York: Oxford University Press, 1966), pp. 3–8.

11. Cowley reflects on this essay and its role in the institutionalization of Hemingway and American Studies in his essay "Hemingway's Wound—And Its Consequences for Amercan Literature," *Georgia Review* 38 (1984), 223–39.

12. Rebecca Harding Davis, *Bits of Gossip* (London: Archibald, Constable, 1904), pp. 30–31 (Davis adds that this was "the first cheap book I ever saw"); James, *Hawthorne* (1879), in *Literary Criticism: Essays on Literature, American Writers, English Writers,* ed. Leon Edel (New York: Library of America, 1984), p. 402; Garland, *A Son of the Middle Border* (New York: Macmillan, 1917), p. 219.

13. See W. C. Brownell, *American Prose Masters* (New York: Charles Scribner's Sons, 1909), especially pp. 63–65, and William Dean Howells, *My Literary Passions* (New York: Harper and Bros., 1895), pp. 139–40.

14. Laurence Bedwell Holland, *The Expense of Vision: Essays on the Craft of Henry James* (Princeton: Princeton University Press, 1964), p. 21.

15. Sally Fitzgerald, ed., *The Habit of Being: Letters of Flannery O'Connor* (New York: Farrar, Straus, and Giroux, 1979), p. 457.

16. A work that develops this argument rather differently but gives a comparable importance to the institutional ground of literature's social life is Peter Bürger's *The Theory of the Avant-Garde,* trans. Michael Shaw (Minneapolis: University of Minnesota Press, 1984). As Bürger also recognizes, the history of the changing forms of literature's institutional life has only begun to be written. Case studies on the history of American authors' social roles that I have found helpful include Robert Ferguson's "Literary Vocation in the Early Republic: The Example of Charles Brockden Brown," *Modern Philology* 78 (1980), 139–52; Christopher P. Wilson's *The Labor of Words: Literary Professionalism in the Progressive Era* (Athens: University of Georgia Press, 1985); Mary Kelley, *Private Woman, Public Stage: Literary Domesticity in Nineteenth-Century America* (New York: Oxford University Press, 1984); and, above all, William Charvat's *The Profession of Authorship in America, 1800–1870* (Columbus: Ohio State University Press, 1968).

17. See Nina Baym, *Woman's Fiction* (Ithaca: Cornell University Press, 1978), pp. 11–50, and any example of the genre. (My list is drawn up with Susan Warner's *The Wide, Wide World* in mind.) Baym's lists of other works her novelists wrote makes clear that fiction was not, for them, so much a differentiated literary form

as part of a larger complex of writing forms that also included religious writings and advice for the home.

18. See *Mosses From an Old Manse,* Centenary Edition volume 10, p. 34, where Hawthorne criticizes his imaginative forms and vows "I have done enough in this kind"; and his 1851 comment (cited in the Introduction to *The House of the Seven Gables,* Centenary Edition volume 2, p. xvi) that *The House of the Seven Gables* was a kind of book "more proper and natural for me to write, than 'The Scarlet Letter.' "

   Throughout this book, quotations from Hawthorne's writing come from The Centenary Edition of the Works of Nathaniel Hawthorne (Columbus, Ohio: Ohio State University Press, 1962–   ). Volume number is indicated in a note in the first citation from each volume.

19. Cited from a letter of February 1864 in James T. Fields, *Hawthorne* (Boston: James R. Osgood and Co., 1876), p. 117.

20. Cited in Jay Leyda, ed., *The Melville Log: A Documentary Life of Herman Melville, With a New Supplementary Chapter* (New York: Gordian Press, 1969), p. 926.

21. William Dean Howells, *Literary Friends and Acquaintance,* ed. David F. Hiatt and Edwin H. Cady (Bloomington: Indiana University Press, 1968), p. 64.

22. The aging Melville purportedly told Julian Hawthorne that "Hawthorne had all his life concealed some great secret, which would, were it known, explain all the mysteries of his career." *Melville Log,* p. 782.

23. Merrell R. Davis and William H. Gilman, eds., *The Letters of Herman Melville* (New Haven: Yale University Press, 1960), p. 125.

24. Harriet Beecher Stowe, "How Shall I Learn to Write?," *Hearth and Home* 1 (Jan. 16, 1869), pp. 56–57. (This is one of four essays run in sequential weekly installments.) Since we have now lost the tradition of Hawthorne the author of the everyday, it is perhaps worth noting that the works Rebecca Harding Davis found so impressive were "Little Annie's Ramble," "A Rill From the Town Pump," and "Sunday at Home." She writes of them: "In these papers the commonplace folk and things which I saw every day took on a sudden mystery and charm, and, for the first time, I found that they, too, belonged to the magic world of knights and pilgrims and fiends." *Bits of Gossip,* p. 30.

25. See O'Connor's Introduction to *A Memoir of Mary Ann,* collected in *Mystery and Manners,* ed. Sally and Robert Fitzgerald (New York: Farrar, Straus, and Giroux, 1969), pp. 213–28.

26. Howells, *My Literary Passions,* p. 140.

Chapter Two

1. *Melville Log,* p. 924; *Clarel,* ed. Walter E. Bezanson (New York: Hendricks House, 1960), pp. 91 and 94–95. Consideration of Melville's encounter with Hawthorne has the status almost of a *topos* in American literary criticism. For a useful survey of earlier discussions, see James C. Wilson, "The Hawthorne-Melville Relationship: An Annotated Bibliography," *American Transcendental Quarterly,* 45–46 (1980), 5–79. Among the discussions Wilson reviews, two deserve special mention for their success, despite the overstatement both indulge in, at bringing forth features of the dynamics of this exchange. They are Edwin Haviland Miller's *Melville* (New York: George Braziller, 1975), a biography that makes Melville's relation with Hawthorne virtually the sole determinant of his mental life, and Sidney Moss's "Hawthorne and Melville: An Inquiry into Their Art and the Mystery of their Friendship," *Literary Monographs,* 7 (1975), 45–84, the fullest consideration of this relation's meaning from the Hawthorne side. Perhaps the best short treatment of this relation is Walter Bezanson's dis-

cussion of Vine in his Introduction to the Hendricks House edition of *Clarel,* pp. xc–xcix.

2. *Letters of Herman Melville,* p. 119. For the remainder of this chapter this volume will be abbreviated *LHM* in the notes.

3. *LHM,* p. 121.

4. On the advent of the cult of domesticity and its stimulus to reading, see Nancy F. Cott, *The Bonds of Womanhood: "Woman's Sphere" in New England, 1780–1835* (New Haven: Yale University Press, 1977) and Ann Douglas, *The Feminization of American Culture* (New York: Knopf, 1977), especially pp. 3–13 and 44–79. Charvat's historical researches were collected by Matthew J. Bruccoli in the volume *The Profession of Authorship in America.*

5. See Douglas, *Feminization,* pp. 227–40, and the whole of Kelley's *Private Woman, Public Stage.*

6. Myra Jehlen's important essay "Archimedes and the Paradox of Feminist Criticism," *Signs* 6 (Summer 1981), 575–601, takes the Melville/literary domestics dichotomy as a test case in its call for a comparatist and historical study of men's and women's authorship. The phrases cited come from p. 593.

7. *Melville Log,* pp. 925 and 926.

8. See *LHM,* p. 130.

9. *LHM,* pp. 46, 39, and 66.

10. *LHM,* p. 70.

11. From an 1863 note by Whitman on Emerson, printed in Edmund Wilson, ed., *The Shock of Recognition* (New York: Farrar, Straus, and Cudahy, 1955, 2nd ed.), p. 272.

12. *LHM,* p. 102. Duyckinck's importance for Melville is that he urged literary non-derivativeness as a patriotic duty, while also giving Melville access to his library (and deep personal knowledge) of older writing. On Duyckinck's literary nationalism, see Perry Miller, *The Raven and the Whale* (New York: Harcourt Brace, 1956). For a specimen of the depth and seriousness of his learning, see Donald and Kathleen Malone Yannella's edition of his 1847 diary in *Studies in the American Renaissance,* ed. Joel Myerson (Boston: Twayne, 1978), pp. 207–58, where we see Duyckinck (for instance) reading Machiavelli, indexing Walton's *Compleat Angler,* and planning a study of Sidney's *Arcadia.*

13. *LHM,* p. 86.

14. *Mardi,* pp. 1213, 1023, 1254, 1256; *LHM,* p. 71. (Since it embodies the only complete edition of the authoritative text of Melville's prose, the three-volume Library of America edition [New York, 1982–84] is the source of my quotations from Melville's novels. *Mardi* is printed with *Typee* and *Omoo* in the first of these volumes, to which these page numbers refer.)

15. *LHM,* p. 85; *Mardi,* p. 1262.

16. *LHM,* pp. 78–79 and 77.

17. *LHM,* p. 86.

18. *LHM,* pp. 86, 71, 85, 86.

19. *Mardi,* p. 1214. On Melville's theory of writing as thought-generating or mind-producing activity, see my *"Mardi:* Creating the Creative," in *New Perspectives on Herman Melville,* ed. Faith Pullin (Edinburgh: Edinburgh University Press, 1978), pp. 29–53.

20. Charvat makes this point about American literary culture in *Profession of Authorship,* p. 211. (His chapter "Melville," pp. 204–61, is an important discussion of Melville's interaction with a culturally unstratified audience.) On the nonsegregation, in the 1840s, of cultural levels that became segregated later on, see especially Lawrence W. Levine's "William Shakespeare and the American People: A Study in Cultural Transformation," *American Historical Review* 80 (1984), 34–66. As I argue in the next chapter, Evert Duyckinck, Melville's men-

tor at the *Mardi* phase of his career, was an important agent in early (and still quite unsuccessful) movements to institutionalize a high artistic culture in America. Melville's Duyckinck connection thus provides the real social basis for his imaginative assertion of a "high" counter-public—when Melville spoke of *Mardi* reaching "those for whom it is intended," the Duyckincks are the actual readers he had in mind.

21. LHM, p. 86.
22. *Mardi*, p. 1262.
23. *LHM*, pp. 91–92.
24. Page numbers refer to the text of "Hawthorne and His Mosses" printed in the third volume of the Library of America edition of Melville's complete prose.
25. Duyckinck's 1845 essay on Hawthorne for the *Democratic Review*—an essay that prefigures a number of other turns and phrases from "Hawthorne and His Mosses" as well—is reprinted in J. Donald Crowley's valuable *Hawthorne: The Critical Heritage* (London: Routledge and Kegan Paul, 1970), pp. 96–100. (Duyckinck, one of Hawthorne's two or three most influential critics before 1850, was Melville's houseguest when Melville met Hawthorne and wrote this essay.) For the source of the Carlyle echoes—first noted by Luther S. Mansfield and Howard P. Vincent in their notes to the Hendricks House edition of *Moby-Dick* (1952)—see *On Heroes, Hero-Worship, and the Heroic in History* (Lincoln: University of Nebraska Press, 1966), pp. 42–68. Two recent essays helpful for describing Melville's use of reading as a means to thought are Robert Milder's "Nemo Contra Deum . . . : Melville and Goethe's 'Demonic,'" in *Ruined Eden of the Present*, ed. G. R. Thompson and Virgil L. Lokke (West Lafayette, Ind.: Purdue University Press, 1981), pp. 205–44, and James McIntosh's "Melville's Use and Abuse of Goethe: The Weaver-Gods in *Faust* and *Moby-Dick*," *Amerikastudien* 25 (1980), 158–73.
26. *LHM*, p. 121; *Melville Log*, pp. 926, 419, and 528–29.
27. *LHM*, p. 133.
28. *LHM*, pp. 124–25.
29. *LHM*, pp. 127–29.
30. Frank Lloyd Wright, *An Autobiography* (New York: Horizon Press, 1977, rev. ed.), p. 27; *Paradise Lost*, XI:701–704.
31. *LHM*, pp. 108–109; *Melville Log*, p. 385. Robert Milder usefully surveys the evidence about *Moby-Dick's* composition and the theories of composition this evidence has invited in "The Composition of *Moby-Dick:* A Review and a Prospect," *Emerson Society Quarterly* 23 (1977), 203–16.
32. I say this in view of the very mixed review Duyckinck wrote for the *Literary World* in November 1851. This review is reprinted in the Norton Critical Edition of *Moby-Dick*, ed. Harrison Hayford and Hershel Parker (New York, 1967), pp. 613–16.
33. *LHM*, pp. 133 and 143–44.
34. *LHM*, p. 142.
35. Newton Arvin, *Herman Melville* (New York: William Sloane Associates, 1950), p. 138; Sidney Moss, "Hawthorne and Melville," p. 62; Hyatt H. Waggoner, *The Presence of Hawthorne* (Baton Rouge: Louisiana State University Press, 1979), p. 137. For another important assessment, see Leon Howard, *Herman Melville: A Biography* (Berkeley and Los Angeles: University of California Press, 1967), pp. 168–69.
36. *Melville Log*, p. 410.
37. References to *Moby-Dick*, taken from the Library of America volume that also includes *Redburn* and *White-Jacket*, are followed by page numbers in parentheses.
38. Angus Fletcher, *Allegory: The Theory of a Symbolic Mode* (Ithaca: Cornell University Press, 1964), pp. 25–69 and 279–303.

39. William Godwin, *Caleb Williams* (New York: Holt, Rinehart, and Winston, 1960), p. 124; Mary Shelley, *Frankenstein* (New York: New American Library, 1965), p. 47.

40. *Mosses From an Old Manse,* p. 39. "The Birthmark" is one of the most heavily marked tales in Melville's copy of *Mosses.* For the record of Melville's marks and annotations see Walker Cowan, "Melville's Marginalia: Hawthorne," *Studies in the American Renaissance* (1978), 279–302.

41. *Twice-Told Tales,* Centenary Edition volume 9, p. 49; *Mosses,* pp. 277–78.

42. The place to begin the study of the heroic sources of Ahab is in Mansfield and Vincent's notes to the Hendricks House edition of *Moby-Dick,* especially pp. 637–52; see also Howard, *Herman Melville,* pp. 169–73. Charles Olson describes the Shakespearean origins of Ahab in *Call Me Ishmael* (San Francisco: City Lights, 1947), pp. 35–73; on Ahab and Goethe, see Milder, "Nemo Contra Deum"; on Ahab and Carlyle, see Jonathan Arac, *Commissioned Spirits: The Shaping of Social Motion in Dickens, Carlyle, Melville, and Hawthorne* (New Brunswick: Rutgers University Press, 1979), pp. 139–63.

43. See Carlyle, *Heroes and Hero-Worship,* pp. 45–46.

44. Page numbers refer to *Pierre* as printed in the third Library of America volume of Melville's complete prose.

45. Other sources, much more incoherently amalgamated than the sources for Ahab are in *Moby-Dick,* include Romeo and Hamlet; the Romantic tradition of inspiration through a female muse or damsel with a dulcimer; and especially, I think, Emerson, who states the principle of being Pierre acts out in "Self-Reliance": "O father, O mother, O wife, O brother, O friend, I have lived with you after appearances hitherto. Henceforward I am the Truth's;" "when good is near you, when you have life in yourself, it is not by any known or accustomed way; . . . the way, the thought, the good, shall be wholly strange and new."

46. On prophetical authorship in the American Renaissance, see Roy Harvey Pearce's Introduction to the 1860 edition of *Leaves of Grass* (Ithaca: Cornell University Press, 1961), pp. xv–xviii; Stanley Cavell, *The Senses of Walden* (New York: Viking Press, 1974), pp. 14–20; Lawrence Buell, *Literary Transcendentalism* (Ithaca: Cornell University Press, 1973), pp. 30–45; and Buell, "Literature and Scripture in New England Between the Revolution and the Civil War," *Notre Dame English Journal* 15 (Spring 1983), 1–28. Buell's essay, pp. 17–18, anticipates my sense of the instability of prophecy as a literary program. Of course the prophetical program of authorship, so seriously enacted by American authors, is also a strong element in the English Protestant poetic tradition. For considerations of this program's pre-American life see, among many other sources, William Kerrigan, *The Prophetic Milton* (Charlottesville: University Press of Virginia, 1974); Geoffrey Hartman, "The Poetics of Prophecy," in *High Romantic Argument,* ed. Lawrence Lipking (Ithaca: Cornell University Press, 1981), pp. 15–40; and John Guillory, *Poetic Authority: Spenser, Milton, and Literary History* (New York: Columbia University Press, 1983).

47. *The Education of Henry Adams* (New York: Modern Library, 1931), pp. 25–26. I do not know of a comprehensive treatment of the antislavery movement's crucial dependence on the prophetic as a personality type and rhetorical stance.

48. *The Blithedale Romance,* Centenary Edition volume 3, p. 56; "Chiefly About War Matters," *Miscellanies: Biographical and Other Sketches and Letters by Nathaniel Hawthorne* (Boston: Houghton Mifflin, 1903), pp. 397–98.

49. *The House of the Seven Gables,* p. 140.

50. *The Scarlet Letter,* Centenary Edition volume 1, p. 195.

51. *The Scarlet Letter,* p. 164.

52. For an important connection of Hawthorne with "repose," see Poe's 1847 review of Hawthorne, *Edgar Allen Poe: Essays and Reviews* (New York: Library of America, 1984), p. 579. Melville had used this word for Hawthorne in "Haw-

thorne and His Mosses," p. 1156. *Clarel*, p. 256; Preface to *The Snow Image*, Centenary Edition volume 11, p. 4.

53. Stephen E. Whicher, ed., *Selections from Ralph Waldo Emerson* (Boston: Houghton Mifflin Riverside Edition, 1957), p. 403.

54. For evidence of such embarrassment, see Melville's letters to Hawthorne of 1? June and 29 June 1851, *LHM* pp. 126–32, where Melville's venting of his prophetical voice keeps pivoting him into an abased consciousness of himself as "conceited and garrulous" and of his talk as "my old foible—preaching." The anxiety and self-criticism Hawthorne's reserve inspired in Melville were no doubt reasons why their close friendship dissolved after 1851; but the larger truth is that their relation, literary as well as personal, was worn out by the energies it had unleashed.

55. *LMH*, p. 155. The "Agatha" letters appear on pp. 153–63 of this volume.

56. *Twice-Told Tales*, p. 140.

57. Not that his presence disappears. In *The Presence of Hawthorne*, pp. 131–43, Hyatt Waggoner has convincingly argued that Hawthorne is pervasive in *The Piazza Tales* ("The Bell Tower" is certainly the most straightforwardly Hawthornesque tale Melville ever wrote); he is present again in the Vine sections of *Clarel;* and it would be possible to argue that *Billy Budd* is an amplified version of the sort of allegorical parable Melville found in Hawthorne's tales.

Chapter Three

1. *Letters of Herman Melville*, p. 143.

2. *Letters of Herman Melville*, p. 152.

3. Howells, *My Literary Passions*, p. 139.

4. Henry James, *Notes of a Son and Brother*, collected in *Henry James: Autobiography*, ed. F. W. Dupee (New York: Criterion Books, 1956), p. 478. This passage is discussed more fully in Chapter Seven.

5. Garland, *Son of the Middle Border*, p. 219.

6. *Henry James: Autobiography*, p. 478.

7. In view of the crucial and direct lines of descent from her work to Freeman's and Jewett's, then through Jewett's to Cather's, it might be argued that Harriet Beecher Stowe is the originator of the nineteenth century's chief countertradition. The workings of this tradition deserve fuller study; but it might be mentioned here that the authors in this line were also always special admirers of Hawthorne, beginning with Stowe herself.

8. For example, Richard Watson Gilder grouped Hawthorne with the newly discovered Turgenev in the 1870s, as models of an art that shows instead of telling. Arlin Turner, *George W. Cable* (Durham, N.C.: Duke University Press, 1956), pp. 70–71. Howells coupled him with George Eliot as models for a "finer art" of inconclusive analytical fiction in the early 1880; see Edwin H. Cady, ed., *Howells as Critic* (London: Routledge & Kegan Paul, 1973), pp. 70–71.

9. Duyckinck's comment appeared in the *Literary World* of 30 March, 1850; Whipple's in *Graham's Magazine*, May 1851; Griswold's in the *International Magazine*, also May 1851. They are all reprinted in Crowley, *Heritage*, pp. 157, 199, and 208. On the history of Hawthorne's reputation see, along with Crowley, Bertha Faust, *Hawthorne's Contemporaneous Reputation* (Philadelphia, 1939); Edwin H. Cady, " 'The Wizard Hand': Hawthorne, 1864–1900," *Hawthorne Centenary Essays*, ed. Roy Harvey Pearce (Columbus: Ohio State University Press, 1964), pp. 317–34; and Jay B. Hubbell, *Who Are the Major American Writers?* (Durham, N.C.: Duke University Press, 1972), pp. 39–42. The most recent treatment of this subject, Jane Tompkins's, resembles mine in its emphasis on institutional factors; though I implicitly dispute her historiog-

raphy throughout this chapter, I should acknowledge the importance of her work, which I heard delivered as a talk in 1981, to my later thinking. See "Masterpiece Theater: The Politics of Hawthorne's Literary Reputation," *Sensational Designs: The Cultural Work of American Fiction, 1790–1860* (New York: Oxford University Press, 1985), pp. 3–37.

10. It is noticeable that even mild dissent from these views covers itself by affirming their truth. J. W. de Forest, in his essay "The Great American Novel" (*The Nation,* 6 [January 9, 1868], pp. 27–29), disclaims Hawthorne's relevance to later writing, but still pays tribute to him as "the greatest of American imaginations." At the far end of this period, W. C. Brownell shows clear boredom and irritation with Hawthorne the official classic, but cannot avoid reiterating the fact of his greatness. See *American Prose Masters,* pp. 63–65.

11. On voting for the Hall of Fame, see Neil Harris, *The Land of Contrasts, 1880–1901* (New York: George Braziller, 1970), pp. 304–12, and Hubbell, *Major American Writers,* pp. 94–97. Hubbell also gives the results of *The Critic*'s poll, p. 88. On the new statuary of the Library of Congress, see Rita Gollin, *Portraits of Nathaniel Hawthorne: An Iconography* (Dekalb: Northern Illinois University Press, 1983), pp. 111–12.

12. "Letter to the Hon. Robert S. Rantoul: The Hawthorne Centenary" (1904), in *Literary Criticism: American Writers,* pp. 472–73. This letter, James's major statement on the issue of the classic, also shows to perfection his usual stand toward Hawthorne: that he is undeniably great, but that institutional circumstances have also helped inflate his stature. For an intriguing recent consideration of the "better machinery" that effected James's own classicization, see Alfred Habeggar, *Gender, Fantasy, and Realism in American Literature* (New York: Columbia University Press, 1982), pp. 289–302.

13. See Crowley, *Heritage,* p. 4. Crowley's introduction to this volume is the best brief discussion I know of Hawthorne's publication history.

14. My principal source on Duyckinck, for lack of a more recent one, is Perry Miller's *The Raven and the Whale.* Miller alludes to Duyckinck's role on the *Democratic Review* on pp. 109–10 and 130.

15. Julian Hawthorne printed this letter in his *Hawthorne and His Wife* (Boston: J. R. Osgood and Co., 1884), 1:285. On the political coordinates of 1840s literary history, see Miller, *The Raven and the Whale,* and Michael Paul Rogin, *Subversive Genealogy: The Politics and Art of Herman Melville* (New York: Alfred A. Knopf, 1983).

16. W. S. Tryon, *Parnassus Corner: A Life of James T. Fields* (Boston: Houghton Mifflin, 1963), p. 179. My discussion of Fields is indebted throughout the Tryon's illuminating account of his work as a promoter-publisher.

17. Fields's practices are discussed in fascinating detail in Tryon, *Parnassus Corner,* pp. 178–204. See also Charvat, *Profession of Authorship,* pp. 168–89.

18. Cited in Tryon, p. 199.

19. See Tryon, pp. 181–82.

20. On the changing fiction market of the 1850s, see Henry Nash Smith, "The Scribbling Women and the Cosmic Success Story," *Critical Inquiry,* 1 (1974), 47–70, and *Democracy and the Novel* (New York: Oxford University Press, 1978), especially pp. 3–15. Fields's case reinforces Smith's hints that what is taking place in fiction at this time is not only an expansion of the popular market, but also a new differentiation of the market into separate popular and literary or highbrow categories. (When Cooper was "our national novelist," we might remember in this regard, he was both a popular and a literary success—or, more accurately, the two had not begun to be sharply distinguished.) It is not sufficiently remembered that American fiction from 1850 on is all written within (and against) a new differentiation of literature into the high and the popular, a differentiation that, on the evidence of Donald David Stone's *Novelists in a*

Changing World: Meredith, James and the Transformation of English Fiction in the 1880s (Cambridge, Mass.: Harvard University Press, 1972), took place considerably earlier in America than it did in England, at least in the realm of prose fiction.

21. Howells reminisces of Ticknor and Fields: "Their imprint was a warrant of quality to the reader, and of immortality to the author, so that if I could have had a book issued by them at that day I should now be in the full enjoyment of an undying fame." *Literary Friends and Acquaintance*, p. 16.

22. I have this anecdote from Forrest Wilson's *Crusader in Crinoline: The Life of Harriet Beecher Stowe* (Philadelphia: J. B. Lippincott, 1941), pp. 508–509. Stowe herself might be thought of as the author who crashed Fields's system. Ticknor and Fields became her publisher too, but only after she changed her European travel plans so as to ride home on the same ship with Fields in 1860, having, as she told Mrs. Fields, "some particular *business* to arrange with your husband" (Tryon, *Parnassus Corner*, p. 247). After Fields's Hawthorne gift, Stowe took to giving away white leatherbound sets of her own works as wedding presents—again appropriating Fields's newly fashioned literary discriminations for her own promotion.

23. For evidence of the impression Fields could make on new arrivals to the literary world, see Howells's recollection of his first visit to the Ticknor and Fields office and to Fields's Charles Street house, in *Literary Friends and Acquaintance*, pp. 33–41.

24. There is no full history of the American literary canon as such. Jay Hubbell's *Who Are the Major American Writers?*, a compendium of rankings of great writers from the early nineteenth century to the present, is the best source available on who has been recognized as canonical, how widely, and for how long. Paul Lauter's "Race and Gender in the Shaping of the American Literary Canon," cited in Chapter One, attempts to plot the institutional processes that produced the new canon of the early twentieth century; Richard Ohmann's "The Shaping of a Canon: U.S. Fiction, 1960–1975," *Critical Inquiry*, 10 (1983), 199–223, gives a similar account of more recent developments.

25. On the articulation of a separate American high culture in the nineteenth century, see, among many other sources, Henry Nash Smith, *Popular Culture and Industrialism, 1865–1900* (New York: New York University Press, 1967), pp. 379–464; Neil Harris, *The Artist in American Society: The Formative Years, 1790–1860* (New York: George Braziller, 1966); Alan Trachtenberg, *The Incorporation of America: Culture and Society in the Gilded Age* (New York: Hill and Wang, 1982), pp. 140–81; and Lewis A. Erenberg, *Steppin' Out: New York Nightlife and the Transformation of American Culture, 1890–1930* (1981; rpt. Chicago: University of Chicago Press, 1984), pp. 5–29.

26. The establishment of literary writing as a well-defined and well-supported profession in America is the theme of Charvat's *The Profession of Authorship in America*. I would only add to Charvat's account that the establishment of what he calls professional authorship was also the result of a new differentiation of writers into a higher and a lower status grade, which was itself the result of a reinstitutionalization of writing into separate literary and popular categories.

27. Fields cites this letter in his reminiscence *Hawthorne*, p. 98.

28. See Fields, *Hawthorne*, pp. 16–22.

29. "I find that my facility for labor increases with the demand for it," Hawthorne wrote Horatio Bridge in 1851. Cited in Bridge, *Personal Recollections of Nathaniel Hawthorne* (New York: Harper and Bros., 1893), p. 127.

30. Tryon cites Griswold's letter in *Parnassus Corner*, p. 189. He discusses the Fields–Whipple connection on pp. 29–30, 43–44, and 191–92.

31. The *National Magazine* essay, an important source for later biographical myths about Hawthorne, is reprinted in part in Crowley, *Heritage*, pp. 286–91. Stod-

dard reveals his source for the piece, and remembers his introduction by Fields to Hawthorne, in "Nathaniel Hawthorne," *Harper's Monthly*, 45 (October 1872), 683–96. On Stoddard's collusion in Fields's promotional efforts, see Tryon, *Parnassus Corner*, pp. 196–99. His role in the directorate of culture in the later nineteenth century is discussed in Tomsich, *Genteel Endeavor*, pp. 1–26.

32. On the setting and reception of Stedman's ode, see *Life and Letters of Edmund Clarence Stedman*, ed. Laura Stedman and George M. Gould (New York: Moffat, Yard, and Co., 1910), 2:286–93. For the centenary celebration, see *The Proceedings in Commemoration of the One Hundreth Anniversary of the Birth of Nathaniel Hawthorne* (Salem, Mass.: The Essex Institute, 1904). (It is a revealing indicator of the shift of literary authority in the twentieth century that when the centenary of Hawthorne's death was celebrated, sixty-four years after the centenary of his birth, the participants were all—with the ornamental exception of Robert Lowell—academic critics. See Roy Harvey Pearce, *Hawthorne Centenary Essays*.)

33. See Ellen B. Ballou, *The Building of the House: Houghton Mifflin's Formative Years* (Boston: Houghton Mifflin, 1970), pp. 216–23, for the business side of this story. Henry Nash Smith reconstructs Twain's side of it in *Mark Twain: The Development of a Writer* (1962; rpt. New York: Atheneum, 1972), pp. 92–112.

34. See Ballou, *The Building of the House*, pp. 303–27, for the relevant publishing history. On the furnishing of the home with libraries of standard authors, see above all Howells's *The Rise of Silas Lapham* (1885), and also the spate of new guidebooks in the 1880s designed to help the uncertain negotiate this cultural hurdle—books like David Pryde's *Highways of Literature, or What to Read and How to Read* (New York: Funk and Wagnalls, 1883), or Charles Francis Richardson's *The Choice of Books* (New York: American Book Exchange, 1881). (Richardson quotes Henry Ward Beecher with approval: "books are not made for furniture, but there is nothing else that so beautifully furnishes a house.")

35. On Scudder and the Riverside Literature Series, see Ballou, *The Building of the House*, especially pp. 103–26, 156–61, and 328–39. The pedagogical and education-administration background to Scudder's efforts is discussed in Dee Garrison, *Apostles of Culture: The Public Librarian and American Society, 1876–1920* (New York: Free Press, 1979), pp. 51–60, and David Tyack, *The One Best System: A History of American Urban Education* (Cambridge, Mass.: Harvard University Press, 1974), pp. 30–77.

36. Horace Scudder, "American Classics in School," *Atlantic Monthly*, 60 (July 1887), 85–91. See also Scudder's "Nursery Classics in School," *Atlantic*, 59 (June 1887), 800–803, and "Literature in the Public Schools," *Atlantic*, 62 (August 1888), 223–30. The social anxieties unleashed by the Haymarket anarchist trial are well described in John G. Sproat, *"The Best Men": Liberal Reformers in the Gilded Age* (New York: Oxford University Press, 1968).

37. On the late-nineteenth century promotion of culture and the cultural-political agendas that lay behind this campaign, see Garrison, *Apostles of Culture*, especially pp. 36–66; Tyack, *One Best System*, pp. 68–77; Tomsich, *Genteel Endeavor;* and Trachtenberg, *Incorporation of America*, pp. 140–81. The vision of culture and its institutions as sources of social stability, clear enough in Scudder, is even more overt elsewhere. Tyack cites an educator writing in 1882: "If we were to define the public school as an instrument for disintegrating mobs, we would indicate one of its most important purposes" (p. 74). Garrison finds this statement in the *Library Journal* of 1877: "Every book that the public library circulates helps to make . . . railroad rioters impossible" (p. 43). The Arnoldian notion of literature as a source of social and moral stability in a democratic world has New England roots that go back to the earliest proponents of the

value of secular letters. See Lewis P. Simpson, *The Man of Letters in New England and the South: Essays on the History of the Literary Vocation in America* (Baton Rouge: Louisiana State University Press, 1973), pp. 3–31 and 56–58.

38. Ballou, *The Building of the House*, p. 337; Hubbell, *Major American Writers*, p. 22.

39. For the rather different story of the educational institutionalization of French classical literature, see Anne-Marie Thiesse and Hélène Mathieu, "Déclin de l'age classique et naissance des classiques," *Littérature*, 43 (May 1981), 89–108.

40. Brander Mathews, *An Introduction to American Literature* (New York: American Book Co., 1896), p. 123.

41. Mary E. Burt, *Literary Landmarks, A Guide to Good Reading for Young People, and Teachers' Assistants* (Boston: Houghton Mifflin, 1889), pp. 29–30. Burt's book also includes a full curricular plan for a classic grade-school literary education.

42. Crowley, *Heritage*, p. 32.

43. The rise of the situation in which " 'literature' is effectively what we teach in departments of English; or conversely, what we teach in departments of English is literature" (p. 58) is a theme of Leslie Fiedler's *What Was Literature?: Class Culture and Mass Society* (New York: Simon and Schuster, 1982). One of Fiedler's most telling points is that the academicization of American literature in the twentieth century proceeded by delegitimating the popular portion of the previous canon and constructing a new canon that was thoroughly nonpopular (hence the final arrival of such writers without audiences as Melville, Dickinson, and Thoreau).

44. See the entry on Richardson in the *Dictionary of American Biography*, 15:564, which also reveals that he wrote a novel in the manner of Hawthorne.

45. My thinking here is indebted to Raymond Williams's historicization of the concept of literature in *Marxism and Literature* (New York and London: Oxford University Press, 1977), pp. 45–54.

46. Burt, for instance, recommends having children make lists of the literary bibles and draw mountain-charts of literary history, showing who are the tall peaks. The Houghton Mifflin schooltext *Masterpieces of American Literature* (Boston, 1891), identified as "suitable for use in the most advanced class of grammar schools," promises that its selections are "fitted to develop a sense of what real literature is"—so that, circular fashion, students read those works that are distinguished as literature in order to learn to distinguish those works that are literature. (This reasoning receives its classic nineteenth-century formulation in Matthew Arnold, especially in "The Study of Poetry.")

47. I allude to Rufus Griswold's *The Poets and Poetry of America* (1842) and *The Prose Writers of America* (1847), Evert and George Duyckinck's two-volume *Cyclopedia of American Literature* (1855), and Charles D. Cleveland's *Compendium of American Literature* (1859).

48. Charles Francis Richardson, *American Literature, 1607–1885* (New York: G. P. Putnam's Sons, 1887–89), 2:388.

49. Barrett Wendell, *The Literary History of America* (New York: Charles Scribner's Sons, 1900), p. 425.

50. Henry James, in *English Hours* (Boston and New York: Houghton Mifflin, 1905), glorifies "English speech" as the "medium of Shakespeare and Milton, of Hawthorne and Emerson" (p. 14) as if the two pairs were of identical cultural weight. This is a far cry from Melville's "Hawthorne and His Mosses" (1850), where the coupling of Hawthorne and Shakespeare is still risky and tendentious.

51. *Henry James: Autobiography*, p. 480.

52. Garland, *Son of the Middle Border*, p. 220.

53. *Literary Friends and Acquaintance,* p. 7.
54. *Henry James: Autobiography,* p. 475.
55. See Turner, *George W. Cable,* pp. 70–71, and also Herbert F. Smith, *Richard Watson Gilder* (New York: Twayne, 1970), pp. 68–69, which cites Gilder writing Cable: "I do not object to . . . philanthropy . . . but its expression must—in a work of art—take an artistic form. You and I do not object to the morality and spiritual teaching of Hawthorne, and to the patriotism and philanthropy of Tourguenieff . . . because the form is always artistic."
56. Henry Nash Smith emphasizes Twain's resistance to a high cultural definition of literature throughout *Mark Twain: The Development of a Writer;* Twain specifically connects this aversion to his aversion to Hawthorne in a letter to Howells: "I can't stand George Eliot, & Hawthorne & those people; I see what they're at, a hundred years before they get to it, & they just time me to death. And as for [Henry James's] *The Bostonians,* I would rather be damned to John Bunyan's heaven than read that." Twain to Howells, 21 July 1885, in *Mark Twain-Howells Letters,* ed. Henry Nash Smith and William M. Gibson (Cambridge, Mass.: Harvard University Press, 1960), 2:534. But as Smith, Justin Kaplan, and James M. Cox have all shown, Twain is completely ambivalent about the values of high culture—the other half of his ambivalence surfacing in his perfectly orthodox statement, in the privacy of his notebook, that "Nobody writes a finer & purer English than Motley Howells, Hawthorne & Holmes." *Mark Twain's Notebooks and Journals,* ed. Frederick Anderson, Lin Salamo, and Bernard L. Stein (Berkeley and Los Angeles: University of California Press, 1975), 2:348.
57. This logic is clearly suggested in the central chapters "Enter a Friend" and "A Visit to the West" in *A Son of the Middle Border,* where Garland reveals that his earliest literary pieces were attempts to write like Hawthorne, and that he turned to the West in search of a subject the old New England authors had not exhausted. The fiercely anti-canonical posturing in *Crumbling Idols,* of course, only demonstrates the continuing hold the canonical and institutional form of literature always had on Garland—a hold evident in the resurfacing, in the lead story in *Main-Travelled Roads,* of the forest scene from *The Scarlet Letter,* or in the fact that Garland attended a 1913 book fair disguised as Hawthorne.
58. Harriet Beecher Stowe, "How Shall I Learn to Write?," p. 56.

Chapter Four

1. "Alphonse Daudet" (1883), in Henry James, *Literary Criticism: French Writers, Other European Writers, The Prefaces to the New York Edition,* ed. Leon Edel (New York: Library of America, 1984), p. 223.
2. But the necessity here is partly self-inflicted. Trollope's case shows that civil service employment could be made compatible with egregious literary productivity by an author who really wanted to do both kinds of work.
3. *The American Claimant Manuscripts,* Centenary Edition volume 12, p. 115. The Historical Commentary to this and to volume 13, *The Elixir of Life Manuscripts,* are indispensable companions to the study of Hawthorne's unfinished works.
4. *American Claimant,* p. 286.
5. *The Marble Faun,* Centenary Edition volume 4, p. 8. On the composition of *The Marble Faun* see the Introduction to this volume, pp. xix–xxvii.
6. Cited in Crowley, *Heritage,* p. 327.
7. Fields, *Hawthorne,* p. 115. Hawthorne's late letters to Fields show his sense of failed self-completion and of his late writing as a self-befouling and suffocating labor: "I cannot finish it," he writes of the abandoned *Dolliver Romance,* "unless a great change comes over me; and if I make too great an effort to do so, it will be my death; not that I should care much for that, if I could fight the battle through and win it, thus ending a life of much smoulder and scanty fire in a

blaze of glory. But I should smother myself in mud of my own making." Fields, *Hawthorne,* p. 117.

8. On Hawthorne's decline and its causes, see especially Edward H. Davidson, *Hawthorne's Last Phase* (New Haven: Yale University Press, 1949), pp. 1–12 and 142–57. Hawthorne and the Civil War is most usefully discussed in Daniel Aaron's *The Unwritten War: American Writers and the Civil War* (New York: Oxford University Press, 1973), pp. 41–55; Hawthorne connects the war with the abolition of romance in the preface to *Our Old Home,* and memorably in the opening paragraph of "Chiefly About War Matters." On Hawthorne's deterioration of mental and bodily power, see Fields's moving account of his last years in his *Hawthorne;* Davidson, cited above; and Arlin Turner, *Nathaniel Hawthorne* (New York: Oxford University Press, 1980), pp. 375–94. The phrase "broken-down author" comes from Fields, *Hawthorne,* p. 115.

9. Rebecca Harding Davis gives a striking instance of the newly sharpened distinction of literary levels. Her first writings were welcomed into the *Atlantic,* but, unable to get the *Atlantic* to take enough of or pay enough for her work to support her fully, she also wrote anonymous potboilers for the self-defined "entertainment" magazine *Peterson's.* Tillie Olsen's afterword to Davis's *Life in the Iron Mills* (New York: Feminist Press, 1972) makes clear that Davis found this split-level authorial identity distressing, and her eventual fall out of the literary and into the popular category degrading. Hawthorne himself began, about 1860, to define his works in terms of separate and opposed categories of high and low literature: "My own opinion," he writes Fields, "is, that I am not really a popular writer. . . . Possibly I may (or may not) deserve something better than popularity; but looking at all my productions, and especially this latter one [*The Marble Faun*], with a cold or critical eye, I can see that they do not make their appeal to the popular mind." Fields, *Hawthorne,* p. 77. On the extension of the hegemony of the nineteenth-century American canon, see Hubbell, *Major American Writers,* pp. 17–28, as well as Howells and Davis, as cited in notes 13 and 16 below; Howells was from Ohio, Davis from Virginia (the eventual West Virginia).

10. Turner discusses Hawthorne and his lionization in his biography, especially pp. 289–300. On Hawthorne and autographs, see Turner, p. 385.

11. See Gollin, *Portraits of Nathaniel Hawthorne,* pp. 52–111.

12. On Hawthorne's undercover authorship of portions of this essay and its later importance in establishing biographical myths, see Crowley, *Heritage,* pp. 28 and 286.

13. *Literary Friends and Acquaintance,* p. 16.

14. *Ibid.,* p. 51.

15. Rebecca Harding Davis, *Bits of Gossip,* p. 47. My attention was drawn to this book by Henry Nash Smith's *Popular Culture and Industrialism,* which cites Davis's reminiscence of Concord in part.

16. See Davis, *Bits of Gossip,* pp. 55 and 33–35.

17. See F. O. Matthiessen, *The James Family* (New York: Alfred A. Knopf, 1947), pp. 479–80 for a long and droll excerpt from James's letter.

18. Norton and the sacralization of high art are discussed in Tomsich, *Genteel Endeavor,* pp. 51–59, 182–83, and 189; and more generally in Kermit Vanderbilt, *Charles Eliot Norton: Apostle of Culture in a Democracy* (Cambridge, Mass.: Harvard University Press, 1959). Lewis Simpson charts the relation of the Bostonian sacralization of letters to the decline of ecclesiastical authority in *The Man of Letters in New England and the South,* pp. 3–31. James describes his "consecration" in Norton's library at Shady Hill in *Henry James: Autobiography,* p. 477.

19. *Literary Friends and Acquaintance,* pp. 32, 26, 48, 59.

20. *Ibid.,* p. 14; Holland's remarkable letter—which reminds us that all of the canoni-

cal American authors except Hawthorne lived well on through the nineteenth century, growing to look as venerable as they were made to appear—is cited by Henry Nash Smith in *Popular Culture and Industrialism,* p. 390.

21. Joel Porte comments on Hilda as "apostle of light and uplifting popular culture" in a reading of *The Marble Faun* I have always found useful, in *The Romance in America* (Middletown, Conn.: Wesleyan University Press, 1969), p. 143.

22. See for instance Nancy F. Cott, "Passionlessness: An Interpretation of Victorian Sexual Ideology, 1790–1850," in Nancy F. Cott and Elizabeth H. Pleck, eds., *A Heritage of Her Own* (New York: Simon and Schuster, 1979), pp. 162–81.

23. This trait links up with what Nina Baym has called "reverence for the authoritarian," which she sees as a central concern in *The Marble Faun. The Shape of Hawthorne's Career* (Ithaca: Cornell University Press, 1976), p. 229.

24. *The Scarlet Letter,* p. 102.

25. Baym correctly notes, of the nineteenth-century reception of *The Marble Faun:* "the public approached the work as Hilda did the paintings of the Renaissance, selecting here and there a detail and rhapsodizing over its beauty, delicacy, and spirituality," so that "if it was successful it succeeded with people who were largely unaware of what Hawthorne had been doing." *Shape of Hawthorne's Career,* pp. 249–50. (I might say here that Baym's reading of this novel is the best that I know.) G. P. Lathrop, Hawthorne's son-in-law and the author of the first critical book on him, is only the most overt practitioner of what might be called the late-nineteenth-century Hildaization of Hawthorne: "By virtue of his mental integrity and absolute moral purity," Lathrop writes for instance, "[Hawthorne] was able to handle unhurt all disintegrated and sinful forms of character; and when souls in trouble . . . wrote to him for counsel, they recognized the healing touch of one whose pitying immaculateness could make them well." Crowley, *Heritage,* p. 506.

26. Fields, *Hawthorne,* p. 87.

27. Cited in the Historical Commentary to *The American Claimant Manuscripts,* p. 501.

28. Turner, *Nathaniel Hawthorne,* p. 392.

Chapter Five

1. Jay Hubbell verifies Howells's contemporaneous status in his survey of late-nineteenth-century readers' polls in *Major American Writers:* Howells regularly figures as the most highly admired contemporary author. Howells stood as the personification of letters, similarly, to younger writers of his time, from Henry Blake Fuller and Hamlin Garland to Crane and Dreiser. (Even Gertrude Atherton, later to become one of Howells's great revilers, put a picture of Howells over her desk, when she began writing; see *The War of the Critics Over William Dean Howells,* ed. Edwin H. Cady and David L. Frazier [Evanston: Row, Peterson and Co., 1962], pp. 100–101.) For the generation immediately following him, Howells was a much more influential precursor than Twain or James—but later writers located his power less (as in Hawthorne's case) in his works themselves than in the figure he presented, as a public example of the life of letters.

2. Hawthorne's definition of romance is elaborated in all of his prefaces, most crucially in the preface to *The House of the Seven Gables.* For Howells's critique of romance, see especially the "Editor's Study" columns in *Harper's Monthly,* 72 (May 1886), 972–73, and 74 (April 1887), 824–26. (These are conveniently reprinted in *Howells as Critic,* pp. 81–83 and 97–103.)

3. Howells, *Literary Friends and Acquaintance,* p. 51.

4. See especially *Literary Friends and Acquaintance,* pp. 51–60.

5. *Ibid.,* pp. 14–15.

6. *Ibid.,* pp. 14, 37, and 26.
7. *Ibid.* pp. 15–16.
8. For examples of this thinking, see Mildred Howells, ed., *Life in Letters of William Dean Howells,* 2 vols. (New York: Doubleday, 1928), 1: 23 and 57, and William Dean Howells, *Years of My Youth,* ed. David J. Nordloh (Bloomington: Indiana University Press, 1975), p. 179.
9. Howells to James T. Fields, 19 August 1865, in *Life in Letters,* 1: 96.
10. Lionel Trilling, "William Dean Howells and the Roots of Modern Taste," *The Opposing Self* (New York: Viking Press, 1959), p. 79. Trilling's essay is a masterful example of the kind of institutional exercise that has kept Howells a marginal or sub-canonical writer in the twentieth century, arguing as it does the reasons why "we" "cannot" find Howells deeply important nowadays.
11. Howells's addiction to salary is, as he later recognized in *Hazard,* really an addiction to economic security; in an 1873 letter he explains to his father that editing while he writes is the only way he can be *"sure of enough"* (my italics). When Howells quit the *Atlantic,* he arranged for his publisher to pay him his royalties in the form of a weekly salary; the salary offered was no doubt his inducement for taking on the "Editor's Study" for *Harper's Monthly* (in 1886) after he had sworn off such editorial labors; and when, to his amazement, he signed on as editor of *Cosmopolitan* in 1891, he again explained to his father: "I suppose that the lifelong habit of being on a salary had something to do with it." See W. D. Howells, *Selected Letters,* ed. George Arms, Christoph K. Lohmann et al., 6 vols. (Boston: Twayne Publishers, 1979–83), 2:20, 2:275, and 3:329.
12. Howells reminisces about his offers of positions at Harvard, Yale, and Johns Hopkins in *Years of My Youth,* pp. 96–97; see also his fascinating correspondence with Gilman on the Hopkins professorship, *Selected Letters,* 3:44–49. On the developments in the social position of the university that lay behind these offers, see Burton Bledstein, *The Culture of Professionalism: The Middle Class and the Development of Higher Education in America* (New York: W. W. Norton, 1976) and Wallace Douglas, "Rhetoric for the Meritocracy," in Richard Ohmann, *English in America* (New York: Oxford University Press, 1976), pp. 97–132.
13. See *Literary Friends and Acquaintance,* p. 117, where Howells describes the relation of the New England classical authors to the *Atlantic* in this way: "They had set it in authority over American literature, and it was not for me to put myself in authority over them." Note the implication that the authority of the original founders was not to be inherited by the *Atlantic*'s later managers, but always relocated, by those managers themselves, back in the founders' hands.
14. See *Literary Friends and Acquaintance,* p. 134: "[I wished] to signalize our accession to control of the magazine by a stroke that should tell most in the public eye, and we thought of asking Dr. Holmes to do something again in the manner of the Autocrat and the Professor at the Breakfast Table." On the *Atlantic* dinners as public displays of literary continuity, see Howells's letter of dismay at the "absence of some of the older contributors" from the 1875 dinner (*Selected Letters,* 2:85).
15. On these relations, see, in addition to *Literary Friends and Acquaintance,* Kenneth Lynn's *William Dean Howells: An American Life* (New York: Harcourt Brace Jovanovich, 1971), and Lewis P. Simpson's chapter "The Treason of William Dean Howells" in *The Man of Letters in New England and the South.* Simpson brilliantly traces the conflict between Howells's eventual revolt from and continuing loyalty to the literary order these figures represented.
16. Howells, "Recollections of an *Atlantic* Editorship," *Atlantic,* 100 (November 1907), 605.
17. Trilling, *Opposing Self,* p. 89.

18. This is one of the striking differences between Howells's reminiscences of his Columbus and his Boston years, in *Years of My Youth* and *Literary Friends and Acquaintance,* respectively.

19. "Recollections of an *Atlantic* Editorship," p. 602.

20. *Atlantic,* 40 (December 1877), 753; *Atlantic,* 45 (February 1880), 282–85.

21. I say this in recognition that James's early international theme formula was first developed in Howells's novels, especially *A Chance Acquaintance* and *A Foregone Conclusion.*

22. See, for instance, George E. Woodberry, "The Fortunes of Literature under the American Republic," *Fortnightly Review,* 35 (May 1881), 607: "Irving, it is true, had imitators, who came to nothing; but our fiction does not seem to be different because Hawthorne lived, no poet has caught the music of Longfellow, no thinker carries forward the conclusions of Emerson. These men have left no lineage."

23. Henry James to W. D. Howells, 7 April 1879, in *Henry James Letters,* ed. Leon Edel, 4 vols. (Cambridge, Mass.: Harvard University Press, 1974–84), 2:226–27.

24. Howells to Charles Dudley Warner, 4 September 1875, *Selected Letters,* 2:103.

25. Howells to Charles Dudley Warner, 1 April 1877, *ibid.,* 2:160. As this letter makes clear, Howells's adherence to the short novel also represents a turning away from the long and complicatedly plotted Victorian novel, a form that becomes outdated, in American literary writers' eyes, at this moment.

26. See Howells's reference to this novel as "a longer story than I've written before," *Selected Letters,* 2:239; and W. C. Brownell's hostile review of Howells's perceived turn toward the "serious and 'important'" in this novel, *Nation,* 31 (July 1880), 49–51. Public scrutiny of the emerging marks of Howells's belated artistic puberty is evident in Thomas Wentworth Higginson's review of *The Lady of the Aroostook* (1879): "He has now . . . allowed himself a bolder sweep of arm, a more generous handling of full-sized humanity; and with this work begins, we may fain believe, the maturity of his genius." Cited in *Selected Letters,* 2:238.

27. Howells, *The Undiscovered Country* (Boston: Houghton Mifflin, 1880). Quotations from this novel are followed by page numbers in parentheses. Robert Emmet Long has noticed and briefly described the resemblances of *The Undiscovered Country* to *The Blithedale Romance* in "Transformations: *The Blithedale Romance* to Howells and James," *American Literature,* 47 (January 1976), 552–71. There is also a rather different reading of this relation in my "Hawthorne Among the Realists: The Case of Howells," *American Realism: New Essays,* ed. Eric J. Sundquist (Baltimore: Johns Hopkins University Press, 1982), pp. 25–41.

28. Robert Emmet Long plausibly suggests, in the essay cited above, that Howells's *Undiscovered Country* brought this phase of Hawthorne's work to the attention of Henry James, who reworks it again in *The Bostonians.*

29. *Selected Letters,* 2:275.

30. *Ibid.,* 2:274. As I mentioned earlier, Howells did not become nakedly exposed to the workings of the market when he made this move; his publisher James R. Osgood continued to pay him his earnings in the form of a weekly salary. It might be noted here that in transferring his place of serial publication from the *Atlantic* to the *Century Magazine* in 1881, Howells was significantly broadening his work's social reach—the *Century's* subscription crossed the 200,000 mark in the 1880s, while the *Atlantic's* had fallen below 15,000 under Howells's editorship. (When it was serialized in *Century,* the Indiana editors of Howells's works estimate, *The Rise of Silas Lapham* was read by a million readers.) In this sense *Century* represents a major expansion, in the 1880s, of the cultural base that the *Atlantic* had earlier achieved for literary writing. See Frank Luther Mott, *A History of American Magazines,* 5 vols. (Cambridge, Mass.: Harvard University Press, 1930–68), 2:505–506 and 3:475.

31. Howells to James R. Osgood, 18 February 1881, *Selected Letters,* 2:277.

32. We can recognize in Howells's analysis the persistence of the assumptions of the

nineteenth-century ideology of domesticity, according to which "character" is formed through the disciplining agency of the family, and the family has as its social mission the forming of strong character. The best account that I know of this ideological structure is in David Brion Davis, ed., *Antebellum American Culture* (Lexington, Mass.: D. C. Heath, 1979), pp. 1–34; see also Cott, *The Bonds of Womanhood*, pp. 84–97. Alfred Habeggar's *Realism, Gender, and Fantasy in American Literature* shares my sense of the connection between the rise of American realism and the decay of American domesticity (at least as an ideological form).

33. Howells uses this phrase in *My Literary Passions*, p. 170. I should add that the form of psychological representation I am describing derives equally visibly (as some contemporary readers noted) from George Eliot's *Romola*. Howells lists Hawthorne and Eliot as joint models for the "finer art" of fiction that he claimed, just after completing *A Modern Instance*, to see developing in his day: a fiction that, unlike the Victorian novel it succeeded and transcended, placed dramatic interest not in plot but in the analysis of motive. Howells, "Henry James, Jr.," reprinted in *Howells as Critic*, pp. 59–72.

34. I quote from the Riverside edition of *A Modern Instance*, ed. William M. Gibson (Boston: Houghton Mifflin, 1957). Quotations are followed by page numbers in parentheses.

35. Not that the difference between the novel's halves is total: Henry Nash Smith has noted the presence of overdetermined moral structures even in the early chapters of *A Modern Instance* in his important essay "William Dean Howells: The Theology of Realism" in *Democracy and the Novel*, pp. 75–103. But, as Smith notes, these structure are recessive through most of the novel, then heavily dominant in its last ten chapters.

36. For a historian's account of the social situation Howells is engaging in this novel, see T. J. Jackson Lears, *No Place of Grace: Antimodernism and the Transformation of American Culture, 1880–1920* (New York: Pantheon, 1981), especially pp. 10–18 and 32–48. Lears's cultural description is at many points so close to Howells's as to seem like a defictionalization of *A Modern Instance*.

37. On Howells's collapse, see *Life in Letters*, 1:303–307. Edwin H. Cady establishes that Howells's collapse took place near the end of Chapter 31 of *A Modern Instance* in *The Road to Realism* (Syracuse, N.Y.: Syracuse University Press, 1956), p. 210. I am aware that Cady, bolstered by new evidence that Howells suffered from cystitis in the winter of 1881–82, has recently recanted the theory of Howells's breakdown (see the appendix to the Penguin edition of *A Modern Instance*, 1984, pp. 457–59). But the evidence of the letters Mildred Howells reprinted surely suggests a more widespread malady; and the changes of imagination within *A Modern Instance* surely suggest a crisis more than urinary in nature.

38. See Lynn, *Howells*, pp. 237 and 253–54. Kermit Vanderbilt links Howells's collapse to his distress at the fatalistic logic that governs the breakdown of the Hubbards' marriage, and notes Howells's revival in the novel's final phase of a rhetoric of responsibility and free moral agency. *The Achievement of William Dean Howells* (Princeton: Princeton University Press, 1968), especially pp. 80–82.

39. I have in mind especially Richard Ohmann, "Where Did Mass Culture Come From? The Case of the Magazines," *Berkshire Review*, 16 (1981), 85–101, and Christopher P. Wilson, "The Rhetoric of Consumption: Mass-Market Magazines and the Demise of the Gentle Reader, 1880–1920," in *The Culture of Consumption*, ed. Richard W. Fox and T. J. Jackson Lears (New York: Pantheon, 1983), pp. 39–64. Howells's tie to the reformulation of the magazine as cultural object and cultural power in the 1880s and 1890s is direct: *Century*, besides publishing *A Modern Instance* and *The Rise of Silas Lapham*, also pioneered the newly close

relations of magazines to advertisers in the 1880s; when Edward Bok, who learned about magazine advertising on the staff of *Scribner's, Century's* prede- cessor, took over the *Ladies Home Journal,* one of the first of the new mass- circulation, consumer-oriented, magazines, he quickly bought rights from Howells for two not-yet-written works. See *The Americanization of Edward Bok* (New York: Charles Scribner's Sons, 1921), pp. 191 and 202. The coming of the new mass media—and especially of the mass media as successors to older in- stitutions of public consciousness-formation—might be said to be a secret theme of *A Modern Instance:* Bartley's work—the public form through which he ex- presses his moral condition—is as writer and editor of a newer, cheaper, and more popular grade of newspaper, a newspaper, as Ohmann and Wilson would have us expect, newly sensitive to its obligation to the work of advertising.

40. "Editor's Study," *Harper's Monthly,* 74 (April 1887), 825.

41. Trachtenberg, *Incorporation of America,* p. 185.

42. Howells had diagnosed exactly this process at work in the literature of his New England forebears. He reads their "intense ethicism" as a compensatory device, a response to the guilt that they feel for having broken faith with the certainties of an earlier cultural moment: "they or their fathers had broken away from orthodoxy in the great schism at the beginning of the century, but, as if their heterodoxy were conscience-stricken, they still helplessly pointed the moral in all they did." *Literary Friends and Acquaintance,* p. 101.

43. *My Literary Passions,* p. 140. Hawthorne's influence on Howells, I might add here, does not end with *A Modern Instance.* While it is not visibly present in the major novels of the 1880s, it appears strongly in some of Howells's later stories, such as "The Shadow of a Dream" and "A Difficult Case." For discussion of this later phase of relation, see John W. Crowley's essays "Howells's Minister in a Maze: 'A Difficult Case,'" *Colby Library Quarterly,* 13 (1977), 278–83, and "Howells and the Sins of the Fathers: *The Son of Royal Langbrith,*" *Old Northwest,* 7 (Summer 1981), 79–94.

Chapter Six

1. See F. O. Matthiessen, *American Renaissance* (New York: Oxford University Press, 1941), pp. 292–304 and 351–68; T. S. Eliot, "The Hawthorne Aspect," *The Little Review,* 5 (August 1918), 47–53; Howells, "Henry James, Jr.," re- printed in Cady, ed., *Howells as Critic,* p. 70; and William James to Henry James, 19 January 1870, in Elizabeth Hardwick, ed., *Selected Letters of William James* (New York: Farrar, Straus, and Cudahy, 1961), p. 85. Since any work on Hawthorne and James is inevitably indebted to the critical tradition on this subject, I should mention here as well the other important modern discussions: Marius Bewley, *The Complex Fate* (London: Chatto and Windus, 1952); Peter Buitenhuis, "Henry James on Hawthorne," *New England Quarterly,* 32 (1959), 207–25; R. W. B. Lewis, "Hawthorne and James: The Matter of the Heart," *Trials of the Word* (New Haven: Yale University Press, 1965), pp. 77–96; Richard Poirier, *A World Elsewhere* (New York: Oxford University Press, 1966), pp. 93–143; and Robert Emmet Long, *The Great Succession: Henry James and the Legacy of Hawthorne* (Pittsburgh: University of Pittsburgh Press, 1979). John Carlos Rowe's "What the Thunder Said: James's *Hawthorne* and the American Anxiety of Influence," *Henry James Review,* 4 (Winter 1983), 81–119, is a valuable review of the history of the consideration of the James–Hawthorne relation, and of the larger literary issues this relation has been used to focus.

2. F. O. Matthiessen and Kenneth B. Murdock, eds., *The Notebooks of Henry James* (New York: Oxford University Press, 1947), pp. 71–72.

3. See Howells, "Henry James, Jr.," in *Howells as Critic,* p. 65 and Ballou, *The Building of the House,* pp. 446–48.

4. Richard Watson Gilder's letters to James on the *Century*'s audience's response to *The Bostonians*—correspondence that made James later say that "the late R. W. Gilder, of that periodical, wrote me at the time that they had never published anything that appeared so little to interest their readers"—is published in an appendix to Alfred Habegger's recent edition of that novel (Indianapolis: Bobbs-Merrill, 1976), pp. 436–43. On James's break with Macmillan, see Leon Edel, *Henry James: The Middle Years* (Philadelphia and New York: J. B. Lippincott, 1962), pp. 263–65. James's contributions to *The Atlantic*—of which I have named only a handful—can be identified in *The Atlantic Index* and *The Atlantic Index Supplement*, published in 1889 and 1903.

5. See Edel, *Henry James: The Untried Years* (Philadelphia and New York: J. B. Lippincott, 1953), pp. 246–47 and 273–76.

6. See Vanderbilt, *Charles Eliot Norton*, p. 81.

7. These reviews are collected in *Notes and Reviews by Henry James* (Cambridge, Mass.: Dunster House Bookshop, 1921); see pp. 16–32 and 108–16 for two egregious examples.

8. *Henry James Letters*, 1:264 and 262. (This collection is hereafter cited as *HJL*.)

9. *HJL* 1:84, 253, and 351.

10. My point here applies in other contexts as well. Jean-Christophe Agnew, for instance, has recently traced the relation of the Jamesian cult of appreciation and appropriation to the rise of modern consumerism in the late nineteenth century in a brilliant and persuasive way. But it could be added to Agnew's account that James reelaborates the figures of consumption as he is informed by them—such that acquisition becomes, in the first three of four pages of *The Golden Bowl* alone, fused with ingestion, with ransom and redemption, in short, with a dense and continuously expanding field of figurative signification, as the Jamesian text unfolds. See "The Consuming Vision of Henry James," in Fox and Lears, eds., *The Culture of Consumption*, pp. 65–100.

11. James, "The Question of Opportunities" (1898), *Literary Criticism: American Writers*, p. 651; *The Princess Casamassima* (New York: Harper and Row, 1959), p. 334.

12. James, "The Lesson of Balzac" (1903), *Literary Criticism: French Writers*, p. 133; Arnold, "The Study of Poetry," in Lionel Trilling, ed., *The Portable Matthew Arnold* (New York: Viking Press, 1949), p. 304. Charles Eliot Norton's form of culture worship—the form most immediately accessible to the young James—is described in Vanderbilt, *Charles Eliot Norton*.

13. *HJL* 1:262.

14. For discussions of these developments see Bledstein, *Culture of Professionalism*, especially pp. 80–128 and 159–202; Haskell, *Emergence of the Professional Social Sciences;* Garrison, *Apostles of Culture;* Frank M. Turner, "The Victorian Conflict Between Science and Religion: A Professional Dimension," in John Merriman, ed., *Consciousness and Class Experience in Nineteenth Century Europe* (New York: Holmes and Meier, 1979), pp. 219–44; and John Higham, "The Matrix of Specialization," in Oleson and Voss, eds., *Organization of Knowledge in Modern America*, pp 3–18. Among older sociological writings on the profession as social form these pieces are especially instructive in connection with the Jamesian transformation of the writer's vocation: Talcott Parsons, "The Professions and Social Structure," *Essays in Sociological Theory*, rev. ed. (New York: Free Press, 1964), pp. 34–49; Parsons, "Professions," in *International Encyclopedia of the Social Sciences* (New York: Macmillan and Free Press, 1968), 12:536–47; and William J. Goode, "Encroachment, Charlatanism, and the Emerging Profession: Psychology, Sociology, and Medicine," *American Sociology Review*, 25 (1960), 902–14. The novel that best shows James's concern with professions (as well as his commitment to professional specialization) is *The Tragic Muse*.

15. *HJL* 1:253.
16. That the American advocates of high culture in the late nineteenth century divorced culture from creation and used the idea for covert political ends is the theme of all recent discussions of this phenomenon. See, for instance, Tomsich, *Genteel Endeavor,* and Trachtenberg, *Incorporation of America,* Chapter 5.
17. *HJL* 2:193–94. (This letter, to William James, is of 1878.)
18. James, "Honoré de Balzac" (1875), *Literary Criticism: French Writers,* p. 45. The myth of James, partly self-created, partly the work of his admirers, always stresses his unqualified and undiversified investment in his vocation. See, for instance, the memoirs of his devoted typist Theodora Bosanquet: "Many men whose prime business is the art of writing find rest and refreshment in other occupations. They marry and they keep dogs, they play golf or bridge, they study Sanskrit or collect postage stamps. Except for a period of ownership of a dachshund, Henry James did none of these things. He lived a life consecrated to the service of a jealous, insatiable, and supremely rewarding goddess, and all his activities had essential reference to that service." *Henry James at Work* (London: Hogarth Press, 1924), p. 22.
19. James, *Notebooks,* p. 187.
20. See Bledstein, *Culture of Professionalism,* pp. 171–73. The phases of the Jamesian career model are discussed in detail in the chapters that follow.
21. *Literary Criticism: English Writers,* p. 958.
22. For a recent discussion of this enduring consensus see Janice Carlisle, *The Sense of an Audience: Dickens, Thackeray, and George Eliot at Mid-Century* (Athens: University of Georgia Press, 1981), pp. 1–63.
23. Cited in Edel, *Untried Years,* p. 211.
24. James, "The Art of Fiction" (1884), *Literary Criticism: Essays on Literature,* p. 62.
25. See Joseph Kerman, "A Few Canonical Variations," *Critical Inquiry,* 10 (1983), 107–26, and particularly 110–11.
26. R. P. Blackmur has given the best discussion of what he calls "the privation of [James's] relation to the whole body of literature." See *Studies in Henry James,* ed. Veronica A. Makowsky (New York: New Directions, 1983), pp. 100–103.
27. On the earlier history of the idea of mastery, and of its transportation from the artisanal realm into architecture and sculpture, then later into painting, see Walter Cahn, *Masterpieces: Chapters on the History of an Idea* (Princeton: Princeton University Press, 1979).
28. "The Lesson of Balzac," p. 119.
29. Harry Levin, *The Gates of Horn* (New York: Oxford University Press, 1966), p. 16.
30. To give one more example of what I know is a controversial point: in *"The Princess Casamassima:* Realism and the Fantasy of Surveillance," reprinted in Sundquist, ed., *American Realism,* pp. 95–118, Mark Seltzer puts forward a fascinating case for the relation of James's observer fictions to the increasing presence and power of social surveillance in the late nineteenth century. But if that is their social occasion, their origins are nevertheless also more immediately literary: James's fictions of surveillance, from *Roderick Hudson* through "The Aspern Papers" to *The Sacred Fount,* derive quite visibly from Hawthorne's "Rappaccini's Daughter" and *The Blithedale Romance.*
31. Harold Bloom gives the classic account of this structure of influence in post-Renaissance English poetry in *The Anxiety of Influence* and *A Map of Misreading.* Lawrence Lipking details an invention similar to James's—Sir Joshua Reynolds's elaboration of a memorial history for painting as a way of upgrading this art's public status—in *The Ordering of the Arts in Eighteenth-Century England* (Princeton: Princeton University Press, 1970), pp. 169–97.
32. "The Lesson of Balzac," pp. 122, 120.

33. *Henry James: Autobiography,* pp. 478, 475, and 480.
34. "The Lesson of Balzac," p. 120.
35. *Ibid.,* p. 139.

Chapter Seven

1. *Henry James: Autobiography,* pp. 475–78.
2. *Ibid.,* p. 480.
3. *Notebooks of Henry James,* p. 36. The notebook entry is for December 26, 1881.
4. James, "The Middle Years," *The Complete Tales of Henry James,* ed. Leon Edel, 12 vols. (Philadelphia and New York: J. B. Lippincott, 1962–64), 9:67.
5. James, "Honoré de Balzac," p. 33.
6. "The Middle Years," *Complete Tales,* 9:57. Subsequent quotations from James's tales in this chapter are taken from the same edition and are followed by volume and page numbers in parentheses.
7. *HJL* 1:325 and 385. (Both letters are of 1873.)
8. *HJL* 2:193–94.
9. James's idea of apprenticeship perfectly exemplifies the function served, according to Edward Said, by artistic careers in general: "The career permits one to see a sequence of intelligible development, not simply of accumulation. In marshalling his energies to shape his artistic life, the writer accepts the passage of time on his own terms: time is transvalued into a sequence of personal achievements connected by a dynamic of their own." *Beginnings: Intention and Method* (Baltimore: Johns Hopkins University Press, 1975), p. 235. Said's entire discussion of the artistic career in the early modern period, pp. 224–75, is illuminating with reference to James, the most career-conscious of American authors.
10. Cornelia Pulsifer Kelley identified these sources in *The Early Development of Henry James* (Urbana: University of Illinois Studies in Language and Literature, 1930). Her book is the place to begin the study of James's models and his use of models in his early writing. To be fully understood, James's apprenticeship to Hawthorne has to be considered as part of his apprenticeship to older writers in general. On his early reworkings of Balzac, see, in addition to Kelley, Percy G. Adams, "Young Henry James and the Lesson of the Master Balzac," *Revue de Littérature Comparée,* 35 (1961), 458–67; Maurita Willett, "Henry James's Indebtedness to Balzac," *Revue de Littérature Comparée,* 41 (1967), 204–27; and Philip Grover, *Henry James and the French Novel: A Study in Inspiration* (New York: Barnes and Noble, 1973). On his relation to Turgenev, see Dale E. Peterson, *The Clement Vision: Poetic Realism in Turgenev and James* (Port Washington, N.Y.: Kennikat Press, 1975)—the best of the existing studies of James and his influences. While it does not deal specifically with influence, William Veeder's *Henry James—The Lessons of the Master* (Chicago: University of Chicago Press, 1975) provides another view of James's learning process.
11. Kelley, the first critic to spot James's use of Hawthorne in his 1868 tales (although she sees it only in "The Romance of Certain Old Clothes"), attributes James's turn to Hawthorne to Howells's editorial advice. *Early Development,* pp. 78–82. The most extensive description of Hawthorne's presence in early James—marred, however, by its failure to distinguish between specific borrowings and very general resemblances, and by its lack of an idea of how James is using Hawthorne—is in Robert Emmet Long's pair of essays "Henry James's Apprenticeship—The Hawthorne Aspect" and "James's *Roderick Hudson:* The End of Apprenticeship—Hawthorne and Turgenev," *American Literature,* 48 (1976), 194–216 and 312–26. See also Peter Buitenhuis, *The Grasping Imagination: The American Writings of Henry James* (Toronto: University of Toronto Press, 1970), pp. 38–44.
12. Hawthorne, "The Prophetic Pictures," *Twice-Told Tales,* p. 175.

13. Peter Buitenhuis, "Henry James on Hawthorne," *New England Quarterly,* 32 (1959), 209–10. Hawthorne, *Our Old Home,* Centenary Edition volume 5, p. 23.
14. Bewley, *Complex Fate,* pp. 34–36.
15. *The American Claimant Manuscripts,* p. 56.
16. Leon Edel, *Henry James: The Conquest of London* (Philadelphia and New York: J. B. Lippincott, 1962), p. 104.
17. *Roderick Hudson,* pp. 191, 243, 223. (I take my citations from *Roderick Hudson*—hereafter marked with page numbers in the text—from the Library of America volume *Novels 1871–1880,* ed. William T. Stafford [New York: 1983], which preserves the text of the first revised edition.) Roderick Hudson is the mouthpiece for James's most vocal expressions of the anxiety of influence. For instance:

    "I don't want to look at any more of other people's works, for a month—not even at Nature's own. I want to look at Roderick Hudson's. The result of it all is that I'm not afraid. I can but try, as well as the rest of them! The fellow who did that gazing goddess yonder only made an experiment. The other day, when I was looking at Michael Angelo's Moses, I was seized with a kind of defiance—a reaction against all this mere passive enjoyment of grandeur. It was a rousing great success, certainly, that rose there before me, but somehow it was not an inscrutable mystery, and it seemed to me, not perhaps that I should some day do as well, but that at least I *might!"* (223)

    Or again:

    "We stand like a race with shrunken muscles, staring helplessly at the weights our forefathers easily lifted. But I don't hesitate to proclaim it—I mean to lift them again! I mean to go in for big things; that's my notion of my art." (243)
18. *HJL,* 1:357.
19. *Ibid.,* 1:436. On the ages of novelists, see "Honoré de Balzac," p. 33.
20. See, for example, Julian Hawthorne's statement that James told him "again and again": "I don't want to do it; I'm not competent; and yet, if I don't, some Englishman will do it worse. . . . Your father was the greatest imaginative writer we had, and yet, I feel that his principle was wrong." *The Memoirs of Julian Hawthorne,* ed. Edith Garrigues Hawthorne (New York: Macmillan, 1938), p. 127.
21. As Edwin H. Cady makes clear, Lathrop's book consolidated the official position of the Genteel Tradition on Hawthorne. See " 'The Wizard Hand,' " pp. 325–26. James writes in a footnote in *Hawthorne* that while he has depended on it for biographical information, Lathrop's "work is not pitched in the key which many another writer would have chosen, and his tone is not to my sense the truly critical one." (322) The depth of his irritation at Lathrop is evident in his aggressively witty revisions of Lathrop's judgments. Lathrop quotes approvingly a comment that Hawthorne's mother was "a minute observer of religious festivals," of "feasts, fasts, new moons, and Sabbaths," which provokes from James: "Of feasts the poor lady in her Puritanic home can have had but a very limited number to celebrate; but of new-moons she may be supposed to have enjoyed the usual, and of Sabbaths even more than the usual, proportion." (327) Or again:

    We are told by Mr. Lathrop that there existed in Salem, during the early part of Hawthorne's life, "a strong circle of wealthy families," which "maintained rigorously the distinctions of class," and whose "entertainments were splendid, their manners magnificent." This is a rather pictorial way of saying that there were a number of people in the place—the commercial and professional aristocracy, as it were—who lived in high comfort and respectability, and who, in their small provincial way, doubtless had pretentions to be exclusive. Into this delectable company Mr. Lathrop intimates that his hero was free to penetrate. (353)
22. Quotations from James's *Hawthorne* (1879) are taken from the Library of

America volume *Literary Criticism: American Writers* and are followed by page numbers in parentheses.

23. James said of *Portrait*: "It is from that I myself shall pretend to date." Cited in Edel, *Conquest of London*, p. 402.

Chapter Eight

1. On the realist conception of typicality see especially Georg Lukàcs, *Studies in European Realism* (New York: Grosset and Dunlap, 1964), pp. 1–20 and 65–84. Peter Demetz helpfully discusses this notion's history in *Marx, Engels, and the Poets* (Chicago: University of Chicago Press, 1969), pp. 128–38 and 208–14.
2. *Notebooks*, p. 47.
3. Demetz, "Zur Definition des Realismus," *Literature und Kritik*, 2 (1967), 333–45. The classic account of nineteenth-century realism (in addition to Lukàcs's *Studies*) is Erich Auerbach's *Mimesis*, especially Chapters 18 and 19.
4. A thick sampling of nineteenth-century justifications is reprinted in George J. Becker, ed., *Documents of Literary Realism* (Princeton: Princeton University Press, 1963).
5. *HJL* 3:28. Leon Edel reconstructs the story of this visit in *Henry James: The Middle Years* (Philadelphia and New York: J. B. Lippincott, 1962), pp. 95–106. Lyall Powers has argued, in *Henry James and the Naturalist Movement* (Lansing: Michigan State University Press, 1971), that James came to believe in the doctrines of French naturalism in the mid-1880s; this seems to me to get wrong the terms on which he entertained those doctrines, which I take to be allusively and experimentally.
6. James, "William Dean Howells" (1886), *Literary Criticism: American Writers*, p. 502.
7. *HJL* 2:332–34. Compare this letter, which refers to the assassination of Alexander III (by a bolder version of Hyacinth Robinson) but only to turn a graceful compliment: "you must feel *splattered*, like all the world, with the blood of the poor Russian Czar! Aren't you glad you're not an Empress? But you are." *HJL* 2:353. The best considerations that I know of James's politics are Matthiessen's in *The James Family*, pp. 646–51; Edel's, in *The Conquest of London*, pp. 164–66, and *The Middle Years*, pp. 167–71; and Irving Howe's, in *Politics and the Novel* (1957; rpt. New York: Avon, 1970), pp. 143–59. Mark Seltzer's *"The Princess Casamassima:* Realism and the Fantasy of Surveillance," cited in Chapter Six, makes a countercase to the usual argument for James's detachment, arguing that spectatorship *is* politics in James, a reflection of a historically specific arrangement of power.
8. James, "William Dean Howells," p. 506.
9. See Edel, *The Untried Years*, p. 57, and *The Middle Years*, p. 69. Edel well describes James's situation at this time and the steps by which he sought to establish his life on new grounds in *The Middle Years*, pp. 33–106.
10. *Notebooks*, pp. 44–45.
11. James's placing of the yet-unstarted *Bostonians* is part of a frantic effort, in the month of his fortieth birthday, to create a show of increased productivity: a week after this birthday he wrote to Macmillan to arrange a new edition of his stories, and again to J. R. Osgood to propose new collections of his critical essays and travel sketches; two weeks later he wrote Osgood again, suggesting the printing of his dramatic adaptation of "Daisy Miller" as a new volume. See *HJL* 2:410–16.
12. *The Atlantic Monthly*, future home of *The Princess Casamassima*, and *Century Magazine*, future home of *The Bostonians*, were saturated with Hawthorne articles in the early 1880s, put out by the managers of the Hawthorne property, Julian Hawthorne and George Parsons Lathrop. *The Atlantic* ran an essay by

Lathrop and serialized the posthumous *The Ancestral Footstep* in 1883, the year *The Bostonians* was contracted for; *Century* ran five major essays on Hawthorne and used two Hawthorne portraits as frontispieces between 1883 and early 1887.

13. *Notebooks*, p. 47.
14. Hawthorne's politics are considered more fully in my "Hawthorne and the Fate of Politics," *Essays in Literature*, 11 (Spring 1984), 95–103.
15. James, "Nathaniel Hawthorne," *A Library of the World's Best Literature*, ed. Charles Dudley Warner (New York: The International Society, 1897), 12:7058; also printed in *Literary Criticism: American Writers*, p. 464. James's reconsideration of *Blithedale* in *The Bostonians* is given important earlier treatments in Bewley, *The Complex Fate*, pp. 11–30; R. W. B. Lewis, "Hawthorne and James: The Matter of the Heart," *Trials of the Word*, pp. 77–96; and Robert Emmet Long, "The Society and the Masks: *The Blithedale Romance* and *The Bostonians*," *NCF*, 19 (1964), 105–22.
16. *The Blithedale Romance*, pp. 120–21.
17. Quotations from *The Bostonians* are taken from the Modern Library edition (New York: Random House, 1966), and followed by page numbers in parentheses.
18. *The House of the Seven Gables*, p. 203.
19. *The House of the Seven Gables*, p. 212.
20. James's reference to Hawthornesque romance as "puerile" and as belonging "to the fairy-tale period of taste" (*Hawthorne*, pp. 407 and 454) assimilate the opposition of realism and romance to the general pattern of opposition of the mature and the immature, the initiated and the undeveloped, through which James seeks to get the better of Hawthorne in this book. But it is only fair to add that at this stage of his career—as the 1884 "The Art of Fiction" makes clear—the distinction between these two modes never seems persuasive to James.
21. This phrase appears in Hawthorne's preface to "Rappaccini's Daughter," *Mosses From an Old Manse*, p. 92.
22. *Hawthorne*, p. 339.
23. "Alphonse Daudet," pp. 229–30.
24. *Hawthorne*, p. 419.
25. *Ibid.*, pp. 385 and 370. It might be noted as a measure of the persuasive power of James's case against Hawthorne that the critic who opened discussion of *The Bostonians* as a revision of *Blithedale*, Marius Bewley, simply took James's line: that *The Bostonians* is *Blithedale* reconceived on the basis of an adequately funded social consciousness.
26. *The Blithedale Romance*, p. 69.
27. Compare James's curious remark, in the middle of a long description of Basil Ransom's lodgings, "I mention it not on account of any particular influence it may have had on the life and thought of Basil Ransom, but for old acquaintance sake and that of local color: besides which, a figure is nothing without a setting." (190) David Howard comments on this passage and on the removal of character from ground in *"The Bostonians," The Air of Reality: New Essays on Henry James*, ed. John Goode (London: Methuen, 1972), pp. 63–65.
28. James, "Honoré de Balzac," p. 53.
29. Cited in Matthiessen, *The James Family*, pp. 328–29.
30. *HJL* 3:121.
31. The phrase occurs in James's Preface to *The Tragic Muse*, *The Art of the Novel*, ed. R. P. Blackmur (New York: Charles Scribner's Sons, 1934), p. 90.
32. Quotations from *The Princess Casamassima*, in the edition cited in Chapter Six, are followed by page numbers in parentheses in the remainder of this chapter.
33. *The Blithedale Romance*, p. 164.
34. *The Blithedale Romance*, p. 24.
35. This change of direction in *The Princess* has been noticed by J. A. Ward in *The*

Search for Form: Studies in the Structure of James's Fiction (Chapel Hill: University of North Carolina Press, 1967), pp. 123–24. The effects on *The Princess* of the sacrifice of an objective political dimension are considered in important essays by Irving Howe and John Goode: "Henry James: The Political Vocation," in *Politics and the Novel*, pp. 143–59, and "The Art of Fiction: Walter Besant and Henry James," in *Tradition and Toleration in Nineteenth Century Fiction*, ed. David Howard, John Lucas, and John Goode (London: Routledge and Kegan Paul, 1966), pp. 243–75.

36. *HJL* 3:28.
37. *HJL* 3:21 and 209.
38. *Memoirs of Julian Hawthorne*, p. 127.

Chapter Nine

1. Quotations from *The Golden Bowl* are taken from the Penguin edition (1966), and followed by page numbers in parentheses.
2. My discussion of James's late style recognizes its debt to two great accounts of this subject: Laurence Holland's *The Expense of Vision*, especially pp. 57–90, and Peter Brooks's *The Melodramatic Imagination* (New Haven: Yale University Press, 1976), especially pp. 1–23.
3. *Art of the Novel*, pp. 304–305 and 345–47. Leo Bersani gives a good discussion of the importance and appeal of *surface* in late James in the chapter "The Jamesian Lie" in his *A Future for Astyanax: Character and Desire in Literature* (New York: Little, Brown, 1976), pp. 128–55.
4. *Henry James at Work*, p. 13.
5. Frederic Jameson, "Criticism in History," in *Weapons of Criticism*, ed. Norman Rudich (Palo Alto: Ramparts, 1976), p. 34; in context this is part of a larger analysis of the different historical processes by which the novel's old common language broke down into modernism's host of private styles in England and France in the late nineteenth century. On James's relation to his audience, see Henry Nash Smith, *Democracy and the Novel*, pp. 128–65, and particularly Anne Margolis, *An International Act: Henry James and the Problem of Audience* (diss. Yale 1981).
6. *Complete Tales*, 9:70. In addition to "The Middle Years," James's other extended reflection on the late career is his Introduction to *The Tempest* (1907), reprinted in *Literary Criticism: English Writers*, pp. 1205–20. The late phase as a stage of artistic career is discussed in more general terms in Lawrence Lipking, *The Life of the Poet: Beginning and Ending Poetic Careers* (Chicago: University of Chicago Press, 1981), pp. 65–137, and Edward Said, *Beginnings*, pp. 260–61.
7. I take this word from James's moving conclusion to the Preface to *The Golden Bowl*, which describes how "really 'done' things" circumvent time's power over "our conduct and our life." *Art of the Novel*, pp. 347–48.
8. James, "The Question of Opportunities" (1898), *Literary Criticism: American Writers*, p. 653.
9. *HJL* 4:250.
10. *Art of the Novel*, p. 295. On James's fascination with the bestseller at the turn of the century and his sense of his own work's displacement by that form see *HJL* 4:160–61 and 222–24.
11. Vanderbilt, *Charles Eliot Norton*, p. 150.
12. On the new mass media of the late nineteenth century see, for instance, Frank Luther Mott, *American Journalism* (New York: Macmillan, 1941), pp. 519–45; (on England) Harold Herd, *The Making of Modern Journalism* (London: George Allen & Unwin, 1927); Richard Ohmann, "Where Did Mass Culture Come From?"; and Christopher P. Wilson "The Rhetoric of Consumption," both cited in Chapter Five. The conscious de-literarization of style by such organs is

documented in Wilson, pp. 48–50, and Herd, pp. 56–60. The changes these new media produced strike me as a more plausible historical occasion than the one Allon White assembles in his otherwise interesting attempt to link the newly obscure styles of late-nineteenth-century English fiction to a historical change in the act of reading. Allon White, *The Uses of Obscurity: The Fiction of Early Modernism* (London: Routledge & Kegan Paul, 1981). It might be added that James's notion that the new media with their stronger visual stimuli are eroding the possibility for both literature and thoughtfulness in general is at least as old as Wordsworth's 1800 preface to *Lyrical Ballads*, if not Pope's *Dunciad*.

13. Cited in Matthiessen, *The James Family*, p. 647.
14. Mott, *American Journalism*, p. 502.
15. For the background here see Katherine Lyon Mix, *A Study in Yellow: The Yellow Book and Its Contributors* (Lawrence: University of Kansas Press, 1960), and Sidney Kramer, *A History of Stone & Kimball and Herbert S. Stone & Co.* (Chicago: Norman W. Forgue, 1940).
16. On this linkage see Ohmann, "Where Did Mass Culture Come From?," and Wilson, "The Rhetoric of Consumption."
17. The process by which new publishing institutions with journalism as their model led new authors to form new definitions of authorship for themselves is most fully treated in Wilson, *The Labor of Words*, cited in Chapter One.
18. The connections I suggest here remain to be traced, but I might mention two as examples. Stone and Kimball, Harvard undergraduates in the 1890s, looked for new poets they could publish to the *Harvard Monthly* and the *Harvard Advocate*, associated at this time with Santayana and soon after with T. S. Eliot and Wallace Stevens. Harriet Monroe, founder of the important modernist organ *Poetry*, was a figure in Stone and Kimball's Chicago literary salon in the 1890s, and would have known their *Chap-Book* as a model for the little-magazine format. See Kramer, *Stone & Kimball*, pp. 63–64.
19. The interrelated histories of James's canonization and the modern reinstitutionalization of literature have not yet been fully written. James's discomfort in the new literary order he was drawn into in the 1890s is best described by Margolis, *An International Act*, pp. 131–35 and 158–74.
20. James, "Nathaniel Hawthorne" (1897), *Literary Criticism: American Writers*, pp. 459–60.
21. James, *Hawthorne*, pp. 339 and 351.
22. The only comparably powerful formulation of a symbolist aesthetic in James's writing is in his 1897 essay on Ibsen's *John Gabriel Borkman*, *Literary Criticism: English Writers*, pp. 387–92. On the basis of this piece—exactly contemporaneous with the late Hawthorne essay—we might argue that late-century symbolists like Ibsen helped James to a new appreciation of the symbolic art of Hawthorne. But the resemblance of the Ibsen of this essay to the provincial, culturally impoverished, and representationally schematic Hawthorne James had put forward since 1879 might just as well suggest that James came to appreciate Ibsen by first likening him to Hawthorne.
23. Hawthorne, *American Notebooks*, Centenary Edition volume 8, pp. 29, 153, 238, 251. The best discussion I know of such Hawthornesque conceits is in Borges's essay "Nathaniel Hawthorne," *Other Inquisitions*, tr. Ruth L. C. Simms (New York: Simon and Schuster, 1968), pp. 51–57.
24. Quotations from "The Beast in the Jungle" are taken from *Complete Tales* volume 11, and are followed by page numbers in parentheses.
25. *Twice-Told Tales*, p. 130.
26. *The Scarlet Letter*, p. 4.
27. James, *Notebooks*, p. 183.
28. James, *Art of the Novel*, p. 247; Hawthorne, *American Notebooks*, p. 226, and *Mosses from an Old Manse*, pp. 305 and 439.

29. "Beast in the Jungle," p. 400; Hawthorne describes Gervayse Hastings's type as "on the outside of everything," *Mosses*, p. 305. We might note here that James's final vision of Hawthorne is as such an outsider: "In truth, for many persons his great, his most touching sign will have been his aloofness wherever he is. He is outside of everything and an alien everywhere." "Nathaniel Hawthorne" (1897), p. 467. For a psychoanalytic description of such self-removal, linking it (as James and Hawthorne do) both to the sense of special election and to a self-depleting strategy of protection from relatedness, see R. D. Laing's account of schizophrenia in *The Divided Self* (1960; rpt. Harmondsworth: Pelican Books, 1965). But there is a long tradition of meditation on separation from life in American literature. Here, for instance, is Emerson, in "Experience": "In the death of my son, now more than two years ago, I seem to have lost a beautiful estate,—no more. I cannot get it nearer to me. . . . I grieve that grief can teach me nothing, nor carry me one step into real nature. The Indian who was laid under a curse that the wind should not blow on him, nor water flow to him, nor fire burn him, is a type of us all. The dearest events are summer-rain, and we the Para coats that shed every drop."
30. Ernest van den Haag, "A Dissent from the Consensual Society," in *Culture For the Millions?: Mass Media in Modern Society*, ed. Norman Jacobs (Boston: Beacon, 1959), p. 59. See also Guy Debord, *Society of the Spectacle* (Detroit: Black & Red, 1983).
31. *Mosses*, p. 301.
32. *The Portrait of a Lady* (Boston: Riverside, 1956), p. 118.
33. *The Blithedale Romance*, p. 160; James, "The Future of the Novel" (1899), *Literary Criticism: Essays on Literature*, pp. 102–103. James and Hawthorne's universalized senses of vicariousness might be related to the rise of vicarious experience that Alan Trachtenberg describes as a historical process of the later nineteenth century, in *Incorporation of America*, pp. 122–26. In this regard it is also striking how much James's religion of living all one can resembles the cult of "living each day of [one's] life" through which late-nineteenth-century advertisers began to market "life-enhancing" commodities of all sorts. See Jackson Lears, "From Salvation to Self-Realization: Advertising and the Therapeutic Roots of Consumer Culture, 1880–1930," in *The Culture of Consumption*, pp. 1–38.
34. *Notebooks*, p. 184.
35. *Twice-Told Tales*, p. 140.
36. Cited in Leon Edel, *Henry James: The Master* (Philadelphia: J. B. Lippincott, 1972), p. 219.
37. "Gustave Flaubert" (1902), *Literary Criticism: French Writers*, p. 340.
38. See James, *Hawthorne*, pp. 403–409.
39. Michel Foucault, *Discipline and Punish: The Birth of the Prison*, tr. Alan Sheridan (New York: Vintage, 1979), pp. 3–69.
40. For an illuminating discussion of the opposition of commodity-value and use-value in *The Golden Bowl* see Carolyn Porter, *Seeing and Being: The Plight of the Participant-Observer in Emerson, James, Adams, and Faulkner* (Middletown, Ct.: Wesleyan University Press, 1981), pp. 121–64.
41. *The Scarlet Letter*, p. 64; *Art of the Novel*, p. 143.
42. Whitman, 1855 Preface to *Leaves of Grass;* Dickinson, "Heaven is so far of the Mind"; Stevens, "Ideas of Order at Key West." Late James's participation in the (from his point of view regrettable) excesses of American or Emersonian Romanticism is one of the themes of Quentin Anderson's *The Imperial Self* (New York: Alfred A. Knopf, 1971).
43. Fields, *Hawthorne*, p. 116–17.
44. James to Howells, August 1908, cited in Matthiessen, *The James Family*, p. 515.
45. *Art of the Novel*, p. 120; *HJL* 4:513.

46. James regarded "close revision" as "an indispensable part" of his "plan of an *édition définitive*," and the letter that says so clearly links revision to the reassertion of making power: "I exercise a control, a discrimination, I treat certain portions of my work as unhappy accidents." *HJL* 4:371. For James's sometimes droll explanations of his rights to self-revision, see the Preface to *The Golden Bowl*, *Art of the Novel*, pp. 336–45.
47. See *HJL* 4:683. (James's lists are for the benefit of a "dear young man from Texas," first historical avatar of the *student* of James.)
48. *HJL* 4:302.
49. "The Jolly Corner," *Complete Tales*, 12:225.
50. Edith Wharton, *A Backward Glance* (New York: Appleton-Century, 1934), pp. 190–91.
51. To tell who had found what unsatisfactory would be to recapitulate the whole history of *Golden Bowl* criticism. For a good recent review of this famous ground see Ruth Bernard Yeazell, *Language and Knowledge in the Late Novels of Henry James* (Chicago: University of Chicago Press, 1976), pp. 101–30.
52. See James, *Hawthorne*, p. 345: "The truth is, he cannot have been in any very high degree ambitious; he was not an abundant producer, and there was manifestly a strain of generous indolence in his composition." James goes on in characteristic fashion to measure Hawthorne's productivity and chart it on the line of an artistic life.
53. Borges, *Other Inquisitions*, p. 57.

Chapter Ten

1. The most useful personal account of these cultural changes is still Malcolm Cowley's *Exile's Return: A Literary Odyssey of the 1920s* (New York: Viking Press, 1951, rev. ed.); a more straightforwardly historical work helpful in its emphasis on the collapsing of previously established cultural boundaries at this time is Lewis Erenberg's *Steppin' Out: New York Nightlife and the Transformation of American Culture, 1890–1930*. Alan Trachtenberg has made a useful collection of culture criticism of this time in *Critics of Culture*, cited in Chapter One.
2. See Brooks's *America's Coming-Of-Age*, collected in his *Three Essays on America* (New York: E. P. Dutton and Co., 1934), especially Chapters One (" 'Highbrow' and 'Lowbrow' ") and Two (" 'Our Poets' ").
3. These insults come from Brooks, *America's Coming-Of-Age*, p. 43; Ludwig Lewisohn, *Expression in America* (New York: Harper and Bros., 1932), p. 65; Lewisohn, p. 70; Stuart P. Sherman as cited in Ruland, *Rediscovery of American Literature*, p. 81; Waldo Frank, *Our America* (New York: Boni and Liveright, 1919), p. 205; and T. S. Eliot, "American Literature," *Athenaeum* (April 25, 1919), p. 237. On the modern renovation of classic American literature, see Ruland, *Rediscovery;* Howard Mumford Jones, *The Theory of American Literature* (Ithaca: Cornell University Press, 1948), pp. 118–59; and Hubbell's *Who Are the Major American Writers?,* for assorted evidence on reputational history.
4. Randolph Bourne, "History of a Literary Radical," reprinted in Trachtenberg, *Critics of Culture*, p. 58. Bourne's critique of cultural authoritarianism reads in part: "The old attitude was only speciously democratic. The assumption was that if you pressed your material long enough and winningly enough upon your culturable public, they would acquire it. But the material was something handed down, not grown in the garden of their own appreciations. Under these conditions the critic and appreciator became a mere impersonal register of orthodox opinion. The cultivated person, in conforming his judgments to what was authoritatively taught him, was really a member of a herd—a cultivated herd, it is true, but still a herd." (p. 67)

5. Bourne, "Literary Radical," p. 63. Dickinson's comment appears in *The Letters of Emily Dickinson*, ed. Thomas H. Johnson (3 vols.; Cambridge, Mass.: Belknap Press of the Harvard University Press, 1958), 2:649. My source for this reference to Scudder is Ballou, *Building of the House*, pp. 260–61.

6. Cited in Hubbell, *Who Are the Major American Writers?*, p. 62. For comparable testimony of Hawthorne's decline for his old admirers, see Howells's recollection of shuddering when a young man suggested that *The Scarlet Letter* could not bear re-reading now—and that Hawthorne might just belong to Howells's generational culture, not to the literature of all time (*My Literary Passions*, pp. 139–40); and James's curiously Bourne-like remark, *Autobiography*, p. 478, that Hawthorne had known no lapse for him because he had stored Hawthorne "somewhere on a shelf unvisited by harsh inquiry"—exempted him, in other words, both from later experience and from the full action of critical interrogation.

7. Raymond Nelson, *Van Wyck Brooks: A Writer's Life* (New York: E. P. Dutton, 1981), p. 98.

8. Brownell, *American Prose Masters*, p. 64.

9. Cited in R. W. B. Lewis, *Edith Wharton: A Biography* (New York: Harper and Row, 1975), p. 237.

10. For further and even earlier evidence that the custodians of the official canon were the first to announce its demise, see George E. Woodberry's *America in Literature* (New York: Harper and Brothers, 1903), especially pp. 198–203.

11. Joseph Katz, ed., *The Portable Stephen Crane* (New York: Viking Press, 1969), p. 241.

12. Theodore Dreiser, *Sister Carrie*, ed. Neda M. Westlake et al. (Philadelphia: University of Pennsylvania Press, 1981), p. 176. Dreiser too has left a memoir of his introduction to literature through Hawthorne's writings by his teacher in seventh grade: see *Dawn* (New York: Horace Liveright, 1931), p. 198.

13. To mention a few instances only, Whitman appears as the America-realizing poet in Brooks's *America's Coming-Of-Age*, pp. 77–89, and gets a chapter of his own (as he had in Brooks) in Waldo Frank's *Our America*. In the first issue of *The Seven Arts*, the little magazine of the Brooks-Bourne group, Romain Rolland referred American poets to "your Homer: Walt Whitman," and the editors printed selections from Horace Traubel's *With Walt Whitman in Camden*—thus surrounding American modern writing with Whitman as its attendant past as the editors of the *Atlantic* had surrounded their preferred contemporary writing with the now-rejected canon, fifty years before. On Whitman and *The Seven Arts* see Nelson, *Van Wyck Brooks*, pp. 111–14.

14. Brooks, *America's Coming-Of-Age*, p. 39; T. S. Eliot, "The Hawthorne Aspect," *The Little Review*, 5 (August 1918), 47, and "American Literature," *Athenaeum*, (April 25, 1919), p. 237.

15. H. L. Mencken, *Prejudices: Fourth Series* (New York: Alfred A. Knopf, 1924), pp. 9 and 17.

16. Lawrence, *Studies in Classic American Literature*, p. 171.

17. Brooks's critique of the professoriate is mounted in his 1918 essay "On Creating a Usable Past": see Trachtenberg, *Critics of Culture*, pp. 165–71. What the anti-academicism of this cohort disguises is the fact that they were the first American literary critics to have been college trained (Brooks, Eliot, and Cowley at Barrett Wendell's Harvard, Bourne at Woodberry's Columbia, Frank at Henry Beers's Yale). Their concentration on literature—their working belief that literature is at the center of culture and is where culture at large can be overhauled—shows, we might say, how well they were trained by the professors they later reviled: this is the assertion of their teachers, however they use it against them.

18. See Hubbell, *Who Are The Major American Writers?*, pp. 289–91. On the reincorporation of American literature in the twentieth century, see the final chapter of Ruland, *Rediscovery*, and Paul Lauter, "Race and Gender in the Shaping of

the American Canon: A Case Study From the Twenties," cited in Chapter One.
19. See Hubbell, *Who Are the Major American Writers?*, pp. 300–304.
20. Mumford's not-yet-named American Renaissance is worked out in the central third chapter of *The Golden Day* (New York: Boni and Liveright, 1926); Matthiessen acknowledges Mumford's early importance for him in *American Renaissance*, p. xvii. The curiosity here is that, only fifteen years after Mumford's work, Matthiessen's thinks the new canon is a matter of old consensus, not new construction: "during the century that has ensued," he writes, "the successive generations of common readers, *who make the decisions* [my emphasis], would seem finally to have agreed that the authors of the pre-Civil War era who bulk largest in stature are the five who are my subject" (p. xi). For a consideration of some of the exigencies that inform Matthiessen's canon-creation see Jonathan Arac, "F. O. Matthiessen: Authorizing an American Renaissance," in Walter Benn Michaels and Donald E. Pease, eds., *The American Renaissance Reconsidered* (Baltimore: Johns Hopkins University Press, 1985), pp. 90–112.
21. See John Macy, *The Spirit of American Literature* (New York: Doubleday, Page, 1913), pp. v–viii and 11–17; and, for other evidence of such transcanonical openness, the much-maligned Cambridge History of American Literature, published in 1917–21. Lauter has commented on the opening, then reclosing of the American canon at this time in "Race and Gender," cited above.
22. This essay is printed in the volume *Mystery and Manners,* cited in Chapter One. The mediation of O'Connor's Hawthorne by modern academic literary criticism is established by the letters collected in *The Habit of Being* (New York: Farrar, Straus, Giroux, 1979), pp. 408–11, which show that she knew Hawthorne's theory of romance via Richard Chase's *The American Novel and Its Tradition.*
23. Asked by an aghast friend why he had used Hawthorne's title for his book of poems, Faulkner reportedly replied: "Who's Hawthorne? The title's original with me." Joseph Blotner, *Faulkner: A Biography* (New York: Random House, 1974), p. 379. Study of Faulkner and literary tradition might begin with Richard P. Adams's useful survey "The Apprenticeship of William Faulkner," reprinted in Linda W. Wagner, ed., *William Faulkner: Four Decades of Criticism* (East Lansing: Michigan State University Press, 1973), pp. 7–44; there are also some helpful comments on the relation of Faulkner's early writing to its invoked sources in the early chapters of David Minter's *William Faulkner: His Life and Work* (Baltimore: Johns Hopkins University Press, 1980). The most intriguing treatments I know of Faulkner's use of the pasts and texts of international modernism are by Hugh Kenner: *A Homemade World* (New York: Alfred A. Knopf, 1975), pp. 194–210, and "Faulkner and the Avant-Garde," reprinted in my *William Faulkner: New Perspectives* (Englewood Cliffs, N.J.: Prentice-Hall, 1983), pp. 62–73.
24. This passage comes from the unprinted 1933 Introduction to *The Sound and The Fury* recovered by James B. Meriwether in 1972 and reprinted in my *William Faulkner: New Perspectives,* pp. 20–23. The yarns Faulkner repetitiously spun about his literary forebears—yarns in which he obscures real debts by lumping great authors together in lists—can be sampled in James B. Meriwether and Michael Millgate, eds., *Lion in the Garden: Interviews with William Faulkner* (rpt. Lincoln: University of Nebraska Press, 1980). I know of no place where Faulkner ever spoke of a specific debt to (or even interest in) Hawthorne—his usual line is that "Poe, Hawthorne, Longfellow" (more lists!) could not touch him because they were "primarily European, not American." (*Lion in the Garden,* p. 95.) But the debt, palpable in *Light in August,* is clearly evinced by other sources—the Addie and Whitfield chapters of *As I Lay Dying,* at a slightly earlier moment, and the Jail chapter in *Requiem for a Nun,* to name a later work.

25. Michael Millgate, *The Achievement of William Faulkner* (New York: Random House, 1966), p. 124.
26. Quotations from *Light in August,* taken from the Modern Library College Edition (New York: Random House, n.d.), are followed hereafter by page numbers in parentheses. This passage occurs on p. 97.
27. *The House of the Seven Gables,* pp. 265, 80, 34, 123, 153.
28. On the compositional history of *Light in August* as revealed in its manuscript, see Regina K. Fadiman, *Faulkner's Light in August: A Description and Interpretation of the Revisions* (Charlottesville: The University Press of Virginia, 1975).
29. *The House of the Seven Gables,* p. 237.
30. *The House of the Seven Gables,* p. 6.
31. *Absalom, Absalom!,* less indebted to Hawthorne in detail, nevertheless seizes the idea of *The House of the Seven Gables* not quite grasped in *Light in August:* the plot of the founding of a house, accomplished in both books by a violent assertion of dynastic design that calls up the life it dispossesses as a force disruptive of that family design. Faulkner's new receptiveness to Melville is evident in the Ahabisms of Sutpen (in this book Faulkner switches from Hawthorne's to Melville's more heroic vision of daimonization)—reappropriations, we do not sufficiently recognize, that make Faulkner one of the first authors to *use* the twentieth century's revived Melville. I see Faulkner's debt to James here in his subordination of story to the collaborative act through which story is guessed into being. The long American tradition operative in *Absalom, Absalom!* makes Faulkner the chief case of Malcolm Cowley's claim that when they returned from exile, the literary generation of the 1920s reconnected themselves with an American past they had rejected without really knowing it: see *Exile's Return,* pp. 298–300. But while *Absalom!* is almost unique in the density of the American tradition it draws on, Faulkner does not single out American ancestors here: the Victorian Gothic of *Jane Eyre, Wuthering Heights,* and *Great Expectations* is a presence quite as intense; so—a token of how far Faulkner reaches back at the height of his career—is the Old Testament.

INDEX